ALCOHOL AND HUMAN BEHAVIOR

Theory, Research, and Practice

D1301849

P. Clayton Rivers
University of Nebraska–Lincoln

PRENTICE HALL, Englewood Cliffs, New Jersey 07632

Library of Congress Cataloging-in-Publication Data

Rivers, P. Clayton.
    Alcohol and human behavior : theory, research, and practice / P.
Clayton Rivers.
        p.   cm.
    Includes bibliographical references and index.
    ISBN 0-13-019878-1
    1. Alcoholism.   2. Drinking of alcoholic beverages.   I. Title.
RC565.R525   1994
362.29´2—dc20   93-33821
                                                            CIP

Dedicated to the memory of three of my mentors: W. Gordon Ross and Emily Ann Smith of Berea College, and Janet Rafferty of Southern Illinois University–Carbondale. Their counsel and support are missed.

Executive editor: Peter Janzow
Editorial/production supervision
    and interior design: Patricia V. Amoroso
Cover design: Carol Ceraldi
Project coordinators: Herb Klein and Tricia Kenny

 © 1994 by Prentice-Hall, Inc.
A Paramount Communications Company
Englewood Cliffs, New Jersey 07632

Printed in the United States of America

10   9   8   7   6   5   4   3   2   1

0-13-019878-1

PRENTICE-HALL INTERNATIONAL (UK) LIMITED, *London*
PRENTICE-HALL OF AUSTRALIA PTY. LIMITED, *Sydney*
PRENTICE-HALL CANADA INC., *Toronto*
PRENTICE-HALL HISPANOAMERICANA, S.A., *Mexico*
PRENTICE-HALL INDIA PRIVATE LIMITED, *New Delhi*
PRENTICE-HALL OF JAPAN, INC., *Tokyo*
SIMON & SCHUSTER ASIA PTE. LTD., *Singapore*
EDITORA PRENTICE-HALL DO BRASIL, LTDA., *Rio de Janeiro*

Contents

11 GROUP THERAPY 237

12 ALCOHOLICS ANONYMOUS 265

13 PREVENTION AND INTERVENTION 291

Preface

This book is concerned with the most important substance abuse problem in the United States and many other countries. The central premise is that alcohol use and abuse in this country has a historical base and has its origins in physiological, psychological, and social factors. Because the use of alcohol is complex, it can be viewed as a social issue, a theoretical-conceptual problem, and a disorder that needs intervention, treatment, and prevention; that is, it can be seen as a theoretical, research, and applied concern. This book weaves theory, research, and practice into each chapter so that the reader can readily make connections between these different, but complementary, points of view. To understand the problems in the alcohol area, it is necessary to know how different writers in the field view alcohol. This book surveys the critical issues discussed in the field, pointing out how each issue has been approached from several perspectives. The book also explains how each of these different perspectives has influenced the field's attempts to intervene and deal with the issue of alcohol in this and other western societies.

The book can be broken down into three complementary sections. The first section provides coverage of some general issues in the alcohol field including (1) alcohol the substance and the history of its use; (2) definitions and typologies/models of alcohol use and abuse; (3) the epidemiology of alcohol use; and (4) the effects of alcohol on the body.

The chapter on alcohol the substance and the history of its use explains the types of alcoholic beverages and the way they are brewed or distilled. The history section traces the history of the use of alcoholic beverages in the United States and includes a discussion of the temperance movement, which has had a continuing influence on our attitudes and approaches to alcohol use.

The definitions and typologies chapter presents definitions of alcohol use ranging from safe drinking to alcoholism. The typologies/models that have been used to classify alcohol problems are described along with their potential utility and limitations.

The epidemiology chapter outlines the scope of the alcohol problem in the United States. The abuse of alcoholic beverages by a minority of drinkers leads to widespread social, economic, and medical problems. The abuse of alcohol is especially associated with family problems and has a relatively heavier impact of women, adolescents, the elderly, and certain minority groups.

The chapter on alcohol's effects on the body is self-explanatory. Alcohol's impact on major body systems like the brain and the cardiovascular and the gastrointestinal systems is discussed. The acute and chronic effects of alcohol use are explored in discussions of brain damage and fetal alcohol syndrome.

The book's second section reviews some of the major theories that have guided researchers and clinicians in the field. This section includes physiological-genetic, psychodynamic, social learning, and sociocultural theories.

The genetic theories chapter outlines the possible contributions of inherited predispositions to alcohol use and abuse. Several strategies which have been employed to isolate genetic from environmental factors in alcohol abuse are described. These include family studies, adoption studies, twin studies, and biological markers studies.

The chapter on psychodynamic theories (the first of two chapters on psychological theories) gives an overview of how psychoanalytic theory has conceptualized alcohol problems and modified its therapeutic strategies to deal with the special problems of alcohol abusers. Dependency theory and power theory, theoretical offspring of the psychodynamic approach, are discussed. (The chapter also provides important theoretical background for parts of the chapters on individual, family, and group therapy.)

The second psychological theories chapter, social learning theory, traces the involvement of learning theorists in the alcohol field and explains how learning theory has been translated to applications dealing with alcohol problems. The use of specific learning approaches, including the more recent application of Bandura's social learning theory to treatment and the prevention of relapse, is outlined.

The last theories chapter is on sociocultural perspectives. It illustrates how alcohol use and abuse is mediated by the norms and attitudes that society's socializing agents have toward the beverage. Research has suggested that some ethnic or cultural groups (for example, the Jews) have shared, clearly understood, and prescribed ways of using alcohol and have proscriptions against excessive use. Although the vast majority of Jewish people use alcohol, they have low rates of alcoholism. Others (for example, the Irish) have ambivalent attitudes toward alcohol use and no proscriptions against excessive use. The Irish have comparatively high rates of alcohol abuse. The differences in the ways groups are socialized to use alcohol may have implications for both prevention and treatment.

The third major section covers the important ways workers in the field have tried to intervene in, treat, and prevent alcohol problems. There are chapters on assessment and individual treatment, family therapy, group therapy, Alcoholics Anonymous, and prevention and intervention.

The chapter on assessment and individual therapy covers methods of detecting, diagnosing, and assessing alcohol problems. It also deals with two approaches to individual therapy and counseling with the alcoholic. This chapter (as do all of the "practice" chapters) has multiple examples and also includes conceptual/theoretical approaches.

Family therapy and its differences from group and individual therapy, particularly in terms of conceptual approach, are explored in the alcohol and family chapter. Different family perspectives are described, and multiple examples are presented to illustrate how the concepts can be applied in everyday therapy with the family. The impact of the alcoholic family on children of alcoholics is also detailed in this chapter.

The chapter on group therapy describes the history of group work and details the various types of groups that have been used to treat alcoholics. It presents the major theoretical approaches to group therapy and then illustrates with a clinical example the application of Yalom's interactional model of group therapy to alcohol clients. The research on group therapy with alcoholics is also explored.

Alcoholics Anonymous (AA) is discussed from the standpoint of the group's history, why it seems to be so useful to alcoholics seeking recovery, how professionals have described it, and how members describe it. The tenets of AA are presented. There is a personal statement of an AA member describing how the AA fellowship helps to keep him sober. The research of AA is reviewed as well as some of the major criticisms of the AA approach. The positive contributions of this organization to the sobriety of individuals and its indirect influence on the development of alcohol-treatment systems in this country are discussed.

Prevention is presented in terms of various strategies and techniques that could be employed to reduce the number of new cases (ultimately the only way one can reduce alcohol problems). Levels of prevention, including primary, secondary, and tertiary, are defined. Models of prevention, including the public health model, the sociocultural model, and the distribution of consumption model, are described and evaluated. The review of the effectiveness of prevention in this country is discussed from the viewpoint of several writers in the field.

While no single book on alcohol use and abuse can hope to cover every possible concern, this book is organized to cover the majority of the basic areas needed to understand the important issues in the field. The book does not take a stance that there is a preferred and specific way of viewing alcohol problems. Alcohol use and its associated problems are presented as multidetermined with intervention into these problems requiring multiple perspectives. Finally, and most importantly, this book stresses through case studies and examples that alcohol use and abuse affects real people—our friends, our neighbors, our families, and ourselves.

Because alcohol is the major substance abuse problem in this and other western countries, this book should be of interest to several types of people. First, it can be used as a textbook for those undergraduate students interested in an overview of the alcohol area. Students from psychology, sociology, social work, nursing, health education, and substance abuse should all find this volume useful. It should be especially useful to substance abuse professionals who want an overview of the alcohol field and associated theory and research. Those general readers who want a rigorous presentation of the alcohol area should also find this book helpful.

ACKNOWLEDGMENTS

The writing of this book was made significantly easier and the final product tremendously improved by the assistance of numerous people. At the risk of leaving someone out, I want to thank all the people who assisted me in the many revisions of the manuscript.

Several people reviewed specific chapters and gave me detailed feedback. My colleague and friend, Brian Sarata, read and critiqued the group therapy chapter. Jacque Rhodes also read this and other chapters. Daryl Bohac read the material on Alcoholics Anonymous, and his input improved both the breadth and depth of the chapter. Graduate students Cameron White and AnnElizbeth Card used the manuscript in class and provided me with additional feedback from undergraduate students.

Parts of the book were read by community alcohol professionals. Duke Engel, who was at the time Clinical Director of the Independence Center in Lincoln, read the family therapy chapter. His comments were helpful in making that chapter clearer. Terrence Scott, Nancy Kuhnel, and Robin Donahue of the Lincoln Council on Alcohol and Drugs also read chapters and provided valuable feedback. Four nurses—Deborah Kendall of Christchurch, New Zealand (who was a colleague of mine during my stay in that country); Claudette Wallace, a home care nurse (and also my cousin); my aunt and a retired surgical nurse, Evelyn Borden Smith; and Anna Wood, an industrial nurse—all read parts of the manuscript. Another professional, Caren Hunt of the Independence Center, was helpful in finding most of the pictures used in this text.

The manuscript was used in my advanced graduate seminar on alcohol use and abuse as basic background information about the alcohol field. Graduate students in this seminar offered many comments that helped to improve the quality of the manuscript. The same could be said for the undergraduate students who have used the manuscript as their basic text in a sophomore-level course on psychosocial aspects of alcohol here at the University of Nebraska–Lincoln. Many of these students wrote detailed and helpful reviews, which allowed me to modify constructively many of the chapters that were incomplete, unclear, or redundant.

Undergraduate student assistants helped in major ways with finding library sources, doing paperwork, and checking the manuscript. They located important but hard to find references and did the lion's share of work in arranging interlibrary loans. Brian Billingsley and Leslie Wells did excellent work in carrying out numerous and often frustrating tasks. Kris Ahlstedt read the book and pointed out several necessary corrections, which assisted me in making the book more readable. Jodee Mosher was very helpful in the latter stages of this writing in pointing out areas that were still unclear to an undergraduate reader. A very special thanks goes out to Terry Hadley, now a medical student. During his three years as my undergraduate assistant he was always persevering and frequently creative in finding hard to locate references.

I would like to thank the many alcohol agencies, alcohol professionals, and especially the alcohol clients with whom I have had the opportunity to work, both here and in New Zealand, for all they have taught me about dignity and the human spirit. I can only hope that some of their humility and courage has rubbed off on me.

Psychology department staff members were helpful in typing the manuscript. Claudia Price-Decker and Cathy Oslzly typed some of the earlier dictated chapters. Lorraine James typed parts of the manuscript several times and was especially helpful in making the format of the chapters more consistent.

Like all textbooks, this one was reviewed by several anonymous reviewers. Their comments and suggestions have been incorporated throughout the book. While I do not know who they are, it should be said that the book was improved greatly by their input. It goes without saying, that while all the above contributed in large measure to the book, I take sole responsibility for the final product.

Finally, I would like to thank my family. To my children, Price and Rebecca, many thanks for all the support and love and for enduring so many "hard semesters." My wife, Linda, read, edited, and critiqued all of these chapters. Her work in making this a more readable book was invaluable. However, it has been the loving support and encouragement she has shown over the years and during the writing of this book that made this task so much less difficult.

Introduction to Alcohol and the History of Its Use

_____ *chapter* 1

THREE BROTHERS

This is a brief sketch of the lives of three men who ultimately died of the effects of alcohol abuse. These three midwestern men were brothers reared in the same family with two sisters who did not suffer from alcohol problems. The family was blue-collar, and the children were reared during the depression years. The father was a kindly but somewhat retiring man who left the household duties and much of the child rearing up to his wife. His wife was an aggressive, hardworking individual, often caustic and direct in her interactions both with family members and with outsiders. She was also a person who did not always give consistent messages in terms of feelings either to her family or to other people. Many of her interactions with family members were gruff but often loving.

The family members could be described as argumentative with each other and with visitors. However, while strong opinions were held, there was little physical violence, even during the siblings' younger years. Both males and females engaged in long arguments about mundane things during their childhood and later in life at family gatherings. Losing a point in an argument or, worse, losing the entire argument, was difficult for any family member, with the possible exception of the father. Despite these arguments, there seemed to always be an unstated sense of warmth and love between family members, although these feelings were rarely mentioned.

This was a male-centered family. The men were expected to work outside the home. The women were expected to provide support by running the household, minding the children, and being sure meals were on the table when the husband arrived home for lunch or supper. In brief, it was a stereotypical blue-collar family with perhaps more skills than many of its contemporaries. The father and all of the sons developed skills in the trades of welding and mechanics. They all learned their trades through on-the-job training and later held skilled jobs, despite the fact that none had finished high school. All three brothers were relatively successful and made considerable money throughout their lives. It seemed they fit the picture of typical skilled laborers. However, there is one salient aspect of their lives that has been left out. On their father's side they had an uncle who was an alcohol abuser and a cousin who was alcoholic. (The father of the three brothers did not use alcoholic beverages at all.) These men came from the Bible Belt, where the use of alcohol, even in moderate amounts, was seen as a major moral and religious failing. Thus, the uncle and cousin were viewed as the "black sheep" in the family and were rarely asked to family reunions. When they were invited, it was with trepidation, since the family always feared that the alcohol-abusing relatives would show up drunk.

The two youngest brothers served in the military, but the oldest son was deferred from the military draft because his skills were needed in the war industries during World War II. The two youngest brothers were exposed to heavy drinking as a part of the military experience. All three had some exposure to alcohol in their adolescent years, although the exposure had been limited to an occasional drink.

The early years of establishing a family and career for all three brothers were filled with the usual ups and downs of life. Drinking was not a central concern. The oldest brother did show some mysterious behavior when he went off to a major industrial area to find employment and failed to keep in touch with his family, whom he had left with his and his wife's parents. Illness was the excuse he gave for his strange break in communication. However, some family members later wondered if alcohol had been involved. Aside from this incident, all three brothers were responsible, wage-earning parents and heads of households.

As time went on, the task of being a good father and a good provider seemed to become more overwhelming to each brother. One brother, the second oldest, never fathered children, lost his wife to illness, and turned to alcohol for comfort. He later reduced his drinking and married a woman with several children. The stepchildren's behavior was problematical, and his drinking worsened. He eventually died of alcohol-related liver problems before the age of fifty.

The oldest son managed without drinking for several years; but his employment was frequently marginal, and he and his family often faced difficult economic times. One of the ways he coped was through buying a bottle of whiskey and taking a stiff belt each evening after work. This brother continued to suffer misfortunes in employment and low wages. Finally, a government job provided adequate financial support. Things went well until he was promoted to a supervisory position. The increased responsibility of the position eventually led to heavier drinking and loss of employment. Losing his job eventually led him to leave his family, which resulted in his avoiding family responsibility by living a kind of bum's life in the Deep South. Years later he returned home destitute and in poor health. His sons and daughters had by this time reached adulthood. His sons hired him and provided him with a place to live, but their mother was so alienated from the father that she refused to have him in her home. His drinking continued even though physicians told him alcohol would kill him. He died of massive heart failure in his early sixties.

The youngest son, in some ways, represents the most stable life of the three brothers. He worked in construction for several years and then moved into a long-term employment with an automobile manufacturing company. His family was intact, and he was a reliable wage earner and dedicated father. Despite this, he seemed to need alcohol and he drank consistently when he was away from the workplace. Prior to his sixtieth birthday, he died of cancer of the pancreas, a disease probably related to alcohol use and abuse.

These three brothers illustrate how a history of alcoholism in a family can be played out in several ways by different family members. While alcohol seems to have served all the brothers in managing their daily lives (they thought they could not face life's pressures without it), it was integrated into their lives in different ways and for seemingly different reasons. The oldest brother seemed to use it to deal with the strains of poor economic conditions and increased work responsibility. The middle brother seemed to use it to help deal with an unhappy life and a poor family situation. The youngest brother managed work and family responsibilities well, but had difficulty managing day-to-day life without alcohol. What was it about these brothers that made them use and abuse alcohol? Were the reasons different for each brother? Was their abuse of alcohol happenstance? Was it the family life history from which they came that made them susceptible, or was it genetic, inherited, and thus irreversible in these men? Strangely, the two sisters never had alcohol problems. These three brothers point to the multifaceted nature of alcoholism. It can be seen as being situational, as a function of socialization, or as due to different personality types. Alcohol problems can also be seen as due to genetic components.

In truth, most cases of alcoholism probably have all of these elements (and many more) with different weightings of each of the above variables across several cases of alcohol problems. For that reason, this book attempts to look at alcoholism from a multicausal, multiexpression, and multioutcome perspective. The approach of this book is that if alcohol problems are simplified there is an accompanying risk of gaining limited understanding and limited ways to intervene in and treat the disorder.

In line with the multifactor approach, this book reviews the physical, social, and psychological factors that may contribute to alcohol abuse. This book also looks at several ways to intervene and to treat alcohol problems. The assumption is that multiple treatment approaches are needed because of the disorder's complexity. There are multiple alcoholisms and types of alcohol abuse. Each develops in somewhat different ways. The more that can be learned about different ways of viewing alcohol problems, the more likely it is that the most appropriate intervention and help can be provided to those with alcohol problems.

While all of these concepts are important to understanding alcohol problems, it should never be forgotten that it is people who have alcohol problems, and they, in all their complexity, are really what this book is about. All persons with alcohol problems have people who care about them. Alcoholics are frequently as puzzled as anyone else about their difficulties with alcohol. While the pages ahead are filled with concepts, it is hoped that the concepts to be covered will be useful in understanding this complex problem and the people who must deal with it, whether as family members, spouses, or alcoholics.

TYPES OF ALCOHOLIC BEVERAGES

Alcohol as a beverage has a long history. Before alcohol use and abuse can be placed in its proper perspective, something must be understood about how alcoholic beverages are made, how they developed historically, and how people use them.

Alcoholic beverages can be divided into three basic types: beer, wine, and distilled spirits. Beer is a generic term for all malt beverages produced by the fermentation process. Beer includes the beverages ale, porter, stout, and lager. Porter and stout are varieties of ale. These two beverages, along with ale, are the types of beer most often used in Great Britain. In the United States, lager is the type of beer that is generally consumed. The difference between lager and ale is in the manufacturing process. Ale is fermented at warmer temperatures and lager is fermented at cooler temperatures.

The ingredients of beer include malting barley (the basic material), corn or rice used as an adjunct to modify proteins in beer, and hops. Hops provide aroma, flavor, and the general characteristics of the beverage. Beer made in the United States is about 90 percent water, nearly 5 percent carbohydrates, and about 3½ percent alcohol by weight. While the United States produces more beer than any country in the world, per capita consumption is greater in countries such as Belgium and Luxembourg.

The term "wine" used alone usually refers to grape wine in the United States. When wine is made from another fruit source, the fruit source becomes part of the name, for instance, wine made from blackberries is called "blackberry wine." The juice pressed from ripe grapes contains all the ingredients needed for fermentation: sugar, water, and yeast. If left alone, the fermentation of grapes proceeds on its own. However, in order to have drinkable wine, the action of the yeast must be controlled.

Wines can be described in many ways; however, there are four commonly accepted types. The alcohol content varies according to the type of wine.

1. Natural, still wines are the table wines often used with meals. These wines contain less than 14 percent alcohol and are usually about 12 percent alcohol. Above 14 percent the alcohol concentration kills the yeast and stops the fermentation process.

2. Sparkling wines are those "in which effervescence is created either by bottling before full fermentation takes place so that carbonic acid gas (a natural by-product) is trapped or, with an inferior method, by forcing the same gas into still wines at the time of bottling..." (Keller, McCormick & Efron, 1982, p. 270). These wines have an alcohol content of less that 14 percent (usually 12 percent).

3. Fortified wines, such as sherry, have from 16 to 22 percent alcohol content. Distilled alcohol is added to this type of wine to increase the alcohol content.

4. Aromatic wines, such as vermouth, contain up to 20 percent alcohol. Distilled alcohol is also added to this wine to increase alcohol content.

Distilled spirits all start with a fermented alcohol solution. Any fruit, grain, or other carbohydrate source properly fermented and distilled produces ethyl alcohol (also called ethanol). This fermented, distilled substance is diluted by water and carries the smell of the source material used. Thus whiskey made from rye will carry the flavor of this grain.

There are about five principal types of distilled liquors. In the United States the most popular distilled alcoholic beverage is whiskey, which is distilled from grain mash. In North America, the usual types of whiskeys are rye, bourbon, and Canadian whiskeys. Rye is distilled primarily from rye grain, bourbon is distilled predominantly from corn, and Canadian whiskeys are distilled at higher proof and so have less carry-over of flavoring bodies. There are also "blended whiskeys," which are less expensive and more popular.

The chief ingredient for the distilling of brandy is fermented grape juice. "Wine" from sources like apples or peaches can be used to distill brandy, and then the liquor is called "apple brandy" or "peach brandy." Rum is distilled from fermented molasses or sugar cane or a combination of these. Gin is made from pure ethyl alcohol and then flavored, usually with juniper berry. Perhaps the most simple distilled beverage is vodka, which is a mixture of alcohol and water without flavoring. It thus carries no volatile essences and cannot easily be smelled on the drinker's breath. Vodka can be made from any carbohydrate source and is frequently made from potatoes.

Alcohol content of all alcoholic beverages is designated by the word *proof.* In the early years of distillation, a potential purchaser of alcoholic beverages would mix the distilled beverage with gunpowder. If the gunpowder burned when lit by a match, that was "proof" that the liquor was of an adequate standard. Today proof is twice the alcoholic content of the beverage; for example, an 80 proof whiskey would contain 40 percent alcohol. Proof can go as high as 200 (100 percent alcohol) but this is rare in practice. Above 180 proof (90 percent alcohol), alcoholic beverages absorb moisture from the air and this dilutes the beverage.

THE HISTORY OF ALCOHOLIC BEVERAGES IN THE UNITED STATES

The grapevine reached America before the Europeans. When Leif Ericson first visited the North American continent, he found grapes growing in so luxurious a fashion that he called the area "Vineland" or "Wineland." Twenty-six years after the first voyage of Columbus, Cortez, the Conquistador of Mexico, ordered that vine growing become an industry in the New World. The Jesuit fathers carried colonization and vine growing up the west coast of America into the Mexican peninsula to lower California. Their successors, the Franciscans, advanced into what is now the state of California and planted vines at each new settlement or mission. Their vineyards were the beginnings of the modern California wine industry.

During the era when the American continent was being explored, beer was considered to be an essential provision on board ship for a very practical reason. Fresh water stagnated quickly on a long trip while beer remained relatively stable and palatable. According to a journal of the Mayflower voyage, the dwindling supply of beer was a factor in the Pilgrims' decision to seek harbor ahead of schedule. In fact, the Pilgrims had actually exhausted their own beer and wine supply and were using the ship's crew's supply. The new settlers were put ashore to help reduce the pressure on the crew's supply of beer needed for the return voyage. Brewing was started almost at the same time the Pilgrims made it ashore. Soon after, many tavern owners also manufactured their own supplies in the taverns that sprang up in New World communities (Lender & Martin, 1982). The first commercial brewing in America was undertaken in New Amsterdam in about 1633. The first formal license for brewing was issued by the Massachusetts Bay Colony in 1637 at

Charlestown, Massachusetts. Thus alcoholic beverages have had a long history in the United States.

During the American colonial period, roughly from 1620 to 1775, the ambivalence that has always been a part of the American society's reaction to alcohol was clearly evident. However, it was not a time of problem drinking, despite this ambivalence. In fact, the colonists held the opinion that alcohol was both helpful to health and to spiritual concerns. For one 30-year period, an abstainer had to pay a higher insurance rate than a drinker (Kobler, 1973). However, the colonists had conservative and specific prescriptions for consuming alcohol. They also had severe proscriptions against certain behaviors. There were penalties that became progressively more severe as abuse became more flagrant (Krout, 1925). However, the laws passed were directed toward preventing drunkenness and were clearly not designed to eliminate alcohol, which was considered a gift from God.

The American Puritans had a reputation for excessive devotion to drink. As soon as they had settled, they began importing wines and malts. They drank a lot of hard cider and applejack. As a result, they had many difficulties in the community with the alcohol abuser drinking too much and displaying unacceptable behavior. To combat this, they established many rules and laws which were helpful in reducing the amount of flagrant abuse of alcohol. The laws—in addition to the fact that these were small, cohesive communities that were very religious and quite homogeneous in nature—curtailed alcohol use. These communities also exerted strong social pressure, which tended to limit problems with alcohol abuse. The low incidence of problems in the Puritan community did not always represent a low level of consumption. Colonial society was a heavy user of alcohol (Lender & Martin, 1982; Mitchell, 1946). Alcohol was used according to explicit and well-defined rules and rituals. Farmers might drink hard cider instead of water, but this was consumed around a pattern of work. Children and women were allowed to drink rum or cider at ten o'clock during the day, and farm workers took a four o'clock beer break. Religious and political gatherings were also considered official occasions for consumption. Occasions for drinking included ordination of preachers, court sessions, and town meetings (Earle, 1902; Krout, 1925; Lender & Martin, 1982; Mitchell, 1946; Rublowsky, 1974).

An individual family frequently manufactured enormous quantities of alcohol. Some of these families produced between 500 and 1000 barrels of cider per year for personal use. This was hard cider, which had a heavy alcohol content. These same families also made a large amount of alcohol labeled as wine, although it was fermented from a wide range of materials. These alcoholic beverages were consumed at mealtimes because the colonists were fearful of drinking contaminated water. Given the family setting and their reasons for using alcohol, it is no surprise that men and women consumed alcohol together, not only at mealtimes but at all different types of social occasions. There was also no hesitation about different generations drinking together. Children drank along with adults and would frequently join them at the groaning boards where alcohol was served. Each age group consumed its share of the wine, cider, or rum served there (Zinberg & Fraser, 1985). Babies were delivered while mothers were under the influence of "groaning beer." This was a potent beer brewed sometime during the mother's seventh month of pregnancy and consumed with the usual dietary beer, wine, and cider beginning two months prior to and continuing until six months after the birth of the child (Earle, 1902). Toddlers and children were given a daily ration of two to four small beers, a glass of wine, and a glass of cider. These beverages were considered to be helpful in improving the child's health and ability to withstand the rigors of frontier living.

Zinberg and Fraser (1985) find it surprising that, with alcohol used so extensively, there were not more problem drinkers in the Colonies. They attribute this lack of problematic drinking to the colonial ordinances. For example, in both the Connecticut and Massachusetts Bay colonies, no one was allowed more than a half pint of wine at a time. Drinking was restricted to no more than one half hour at one sitting and drinking was not allowed after 9:00 P.M. In Boston, if a man drank more than what the tavern keeper thought was appropriate, the drinker was not allowed any more alcohol. In addition, the amount a person drank was under constant scrutiny by constables, church deacons, ministers, and other members of the community who believed that keeping alcohol consumption under strict control was important (Earle, 1902).

The notion that the community frowned on drinking was a form of social control (Lender & Martin, 1982; Zinberg & Fraser, 1985). Of course, if people became overtly aggressive, violent, or sexually provocative, the sober or less-intoxicated individuals were more than willing to restrain them. These attitudes, plus the fact that alcohol was so widely used and regulated, indicate that alcohol use was accompanied by a low level of emotionalism. Because alcohol was so closely regulated and its limits of use so clearly defined, it may have been stripped of the excessive emotionalism or rites of passage and personal mastery that accompany alcohol in many settings today. Use was so strictly limited that the capacity to hold one's liquor had a low likelihood of being used to demonstrate one's superiority.

Colonial Boston was described as a safe place with little drunkenness, despite the availability of alcohol. In addition, tavern keepers were seen as equal in importance to ministers in regulating drinking and preserving the public order (Zinberg & Fraser, 1985). This was at a time when alcohol abuse was frequent in England and there was much aggressive behavior associated with the abuse in the mother country.

The patterns of American drinking changed drastically over time. There were changes in drinking patterns before and after the American Revolution. These changes were accompanied by dramatic societal changes brought on by the war. By the beginning of the nineteenth century, excessive drinking and the use of liquor had become a social problem of concern.

Part of the reason for the change in drinking patterns was that the production of distilled beverages was very lucrative when these beverages were exchanged for slaves, British dry goods, gold, and molasses in the West Indian markets. It is ironic that the same area that later became a seabed for the abolition of slavery actually supported the slave trade through the production of rum. African slaves were sold in the West Indies and used as laborers for producing molasses. Molasses was brought to New England and sold to make rum. Rum drinking became so popular that the colonial law books became quickly filled with regulations, punishments, and hypocrisies. A drunkard could be arrested, fined, put in stocks, publicly flogged, denied his right to vote, and could find himself in a criminal gang.

The colonists who had initially refused to barter alcohol with Native Americans began to pour alcohol into the fur-rich tribes. Factories originally established as breweries became distilleries. Whiskey and rum were soon more profitable trade goods than corn and sugar. Whiskey and rum that was sold on the western frontiers brought huge profits to southern colonies and the Caribbean settlement (Zinberg & Fraser, 1985).

Taverns now became business enterprises designed to make money, and a profit mentality replaced what had been a political, moral, and respected occupation. The new breed of liquor entrepreneur increased pressure on legislators to pass laws to protect its interests. These businessmen, along with wealthy distillery owners, exerted a powerful influence on laws regulating alcohol. Looser regulations surrounding alcohol use led to more disruptive behavior, violent acts, and morally unacceptable actions in taverns. The result was that taverns continued to be busy places, but they were no longer morally respected. The public's perception of taverns changed. This change signaled a different attitude toward alcohol use. In post-revolutionary America, the consumption of alcohol was the central function of taverns. Taverns were no longer places for social gatherings and leisurely conversation; they were now places where tremendous amounts of alcohol were consumed. As a result of that consumption, considerable loud and unacceptable social behavior occurred. This change in the function of taverns also occurred in society at large. Alcohol was seen as a necessary item in almost every type of social event. For example, both Presidents Washington and Jefferson spent large amounts of money to purchase alcoholic beverages for their homes.

At this point of increased alcohol consumption, temperance issues began to surface in society. Antidrunkenness ordinances were criticized on the grounds of inadequate enforcement. Throughout the society, more drinking began occurring in taverns and saloons and less at home. As less drinking occurred in the home, the usual family constraints that were placed on drinking were lost. This change in drinking patterns lessened the probability that alcohol would be taken with meals and thus keep the blood-alcohol levels lower for people who were drinking. During this period, food was not promoted in taverns because most profit was made on alcohol (Zinberg & Fraser, 1985).

Three factors significantly affected alcohol use in the nineteenth century. These were the Industrial Revolution, the increase in the number of taverns and saloons, and the temperance movement.

The Industrial Revolution brought changes in America and Europe, which had an effect on alcohol. In both parts of the world, the Industrial Revolution led to more separation of men and women. Farm life had dictated that men and women spend a considerable amount of time together. This closeness was lost when people moved into cities and then went off to work in factories. Women of good repute had no place in saloons and taverns. They were placed in the position of minding the children and upholding moral and cultural norms because they were the ones concerned with protecting children and the home from disruption. Thus men spent time drinking in taverns and women stayed home (Zinberg & Fraser, 1985).

This new drinking pattern, which separated the sexes, brought more ambivalence. It also led to a more negative perception of drinking. The increased consumption of alcohol was due in part to drinking patterns brought home by the Revolutionary War soldiers. For various reasons, soldiers had been given large amounts of alcohol during their field duties. For example, alcohol was given as a food source because it was more portable than food and did not spoil easily. Wholesalers persuaded George Washington that alcohol was necessary to maintain a high level of readiness among the troops.

During the revolutionary years, there was a move toward beverages with a higher alcohol content. Rum replaced cider as a casual alcohol drink in the home. Visitors were expected to drink significant amounts of alcohol with their host. The drunk became an object of humor, which found its way into literature. People could see neighborhood soldiers and the comic alcoholic discussed in the popular press and writings (Zinberg & Fraser, 1985).

Street drinking was tolerated, and day-long drinking bouts in local grog shops were not interrupted by local officials. This intense drinking was frequently accompanied by aggressive behavior. Frontier settlers escaped from the rigors and boredom of the farm by socializing with friends through heavy drinking. The only women allowed in frontier saloons were prostitutes, so saloons became centers for sexual activity. Religious leaders became especially concerned about moral decay and put pressure on legislators to deal with the casual use of alcohol (Furnas, 1965).

The behaviors surrounding alcohol use were not unique to the frontier. They were common in all cities and villages. These conditions favored conviviality and emotional release, which were highly valued. Alcohol use became the central element in social behavior. Holding your liquor became a manly behavior worthy of admiration. Drinking was not limited to the working class. Alcohol was also available at the elite universities such as Harvard and Yale. Taverns and saloons were attached to the university dining halls. In the eighteenth century, mixed or hard spirits had not been allowed in these same schools. University drinking matched that of society in general (Warner, 1970). Sons of the middle and upper classes displayed drinking patterns that resembled those of frontier ruffians rather than those of their protestant forefathers.

Because of the violence and barbarianlike actions of visible drinkers (and the general pattern of destructive alcohol use), the early temperance movement began to see alcohol as an exclusively dangerous and negative substance. It was believed that anyone who began to use alcohol would not be able to control its use (Warner, 1970).

The temperance movement began to bloom near the end of the 1700s. The overview of American history needs to be interrupted at this point to look more closely at the temperance movement. The American protestants of the nineteenth century respected temperance ideals. Protestants were part of an American culture that valued self-control, industriousness, and impulse control. Any lapse was a severe threat to the existing system of respect. Being sober was virtuous and necessary in the nineteenth century protestant-dominated society in which they lived.

Temperance was one way the declining social elite tried to retain social power and leadership. In the first quarter of the nineteenth century, the moral supremacy of the educated was under attack by the artisans, the independent farmers, and those from the frontier. During the 1820s, the temperance movement, and the people who founded it, sought to make Americans into clean, sober, godly, and stable individuals who would reflect the moral leadership of New England federalism. While they could not control the politics of the country, they hoped to control the country's morals.

In the 1830s and 1840s, religious dedication and a sober life became the essence of middle-class respectability. Many people joined the temperance movement as a source of self-help, that is, to reform their own destructive drinking. Abstinence was fast becoming a symbol of middle-class membership, and therefore it was a necessity for anyone ambitious. Abstaining was a way of defining oneself as an industrious, steady worker and a good credit risk—characteristics that were not associated with heavy drinkers. As the central definition of the abstainer became one of industriousness and financial responsibility, the movement lost its association with the New England upper classes and became more democratic (Gusfield, 1983).

The temperance movement began to play a political role in the 1840s. Its members continued to curtail alcohol sales as a way of solving the problems of immigrants and the urban poor. These two groups were at variance with American protestantism, and temperance groups could demonstrate the power and dominance of American protestant morality by using temperance legislation. Temperance was one of the three major movements during the 1840s and 1850s. The other two were the abolition of slavery and nativism, i.e., being born on American shores.

Throughout its history, temperance displayed two types of reform: *assimilative* and *coercive*. In assimilative reform, the reformer was sympathetic to the urban poor and critical of the industrial system that led to poverty. By encouraging the doctrine of abstinence (which had become the public morality after the Civil War), the movement could offer the poor and the immigrants a way of living that included respect and success. Through reform of the drinker, middle-class professionals and businessmen reaffirmed their sense of cultural dominance.

Coercive reform was a more hostile approach. Here the drinker was seen as part of the social system which does not want to change. The coercive reformer viewed the object of reform as someone who rejected the social dominance of the reformer. The coercive reformer turned to law and force to assert the dominance of his culture and social status.

In the last fourth of the nineteenth century, the coercive approach to reform was most clearly seen in the popular swing of the temperance movement. It was a phase which reflected the disgust that rural dwellers felt toward the cities. The rural middle class was beginning to feel it was losing power and becoming less dominant. To shore up this waning self-esteem, its members attempted to inflict their version of morality and respectability on everyone else (Gusfield, 1983).

As Americans became more industrialized, the populace influence in the temperance movement grew stronger. With the development of the anti-saloon league in 1896, the temperance movement began to separate itself from a complex of economic and social reform to move to the cultural struggle between rural society and the developing urban and industrial social system. Coercive reform became the central theme of temperance. The Eighteenth Amendment was the high point of the struggle to assert the public dominance of all middle-class values. The Eighteenth Amendment and its effects on American life will be examined in historical perspective. It was necessary to trace the history of the temperance movement to set the stage for the prohibition period.

Prior to prohibition, excessive drinking in saloons actually led to reforms that helped curb the destructive effects of alcohol. For example, group drinking was distinguished from drunkenness as drunkenness became socially disapproved. The idea that one could drink without drunkenness was reestablished. Also, the saloons began to serve food. The free lunch spread of meat, bread, and boiled vegetables became popular throughout the country. In communities where there was a need, taverns became restaurants, serving food in addition to selling alcohol. Also, women began to accompany men to neighborhood saloons; this trend began in the East, and later spread to the Midwest (Zinberg & Fraser, 1985). Despite these constructive actions, there was still a great deal of societal concern about alcohol use. Drinking was no longer seen as a panacea for those wanting to escape personal anxiety or intolerable social conditions. Alcohol was also no longer viewed as a benefit to medical and nutritional problems.

Along with the change in perception about alcohol's psychological, medical, and nutritional attributes, there was increasing concern about the inappropriate behavior that surrounded drinking. Brawling in taverns dropped dramatically. Social conditions improved for families (partly due to unionization of some industries). There was more opportunity for a happy family life. Alcohol was used less to relieve the drinker from intolerable conditions.

Despite the reduced use of alcohol, the temperance movement continued to grow in strength. The movement became dominated by individuals who saw total abstinence as the only goal. Thus at the very time drinking was decreasing, the movement to eliminate it entirely became more dominant. The attempt became less objective and turned to shrill propaganda (Zinberg & Fraser, 1985).

Before World War I, strong sentiment against alcohol spread throughout the United States. The federal government paid attention to this segment of the population. The Webb-Kenyon Law prohibiting the shipment of alcoholic beverages from "wet" to "dry" states was passed by Congress in 1913. In the same year, a "prohibition amendment" was passed by the House of Representatives; however, it failed to receive the required two-thirds vote in the Senate. In 1917, the year the United States entered World War I, statewide prohibition was approved by ballot in Indiana, New Hampshire, Utah, and New Mexico. The same issue was defeated in Missouri, California, and Minnesota. By the end of 1917, prohibition was in force in twenty-five out of the forty-eight states.

On the federal level, congressional action prohibited the manufacture of whiskey after September 8, 1917. The prohibition amendment became effective January 16, 1920. At this time, 85 percent of all the counties in the United States were already "dry." These dry counties included 63 percent of the country's population. Eventually, all of the forty-eight states except Connecticut and Rhode Island approved the Eighteenth Amendment. Almost exactly 100 years after the beginning of the first temperance activity, America began what has been called the greatest "social experiment" of all times.

The Volstead Act, passed over President Wilson's veto in the fall of 1919, set up the details for the enforcement of prohibition, and defined the terms in the Eighteenth Amendment. For example, an "intoxicating beverage" was defined as any beverage that contained ½ of 1 percent of alcohol by volume. The Volstead Act ran into administration difficulties from the beginning because of the magnitude of the enforcement problems involved.

Drinking alcoholic beverages was an integral part of the way of life of the general American public. The mere passage of a law could not change this custom. In addition, there had been a very long history of limited cooperation between federal, state, and local agencies, so enforcement of the act proved to be extremely difficult, if not impossible. The courts on all three levels of government were quickly overrun with cases involving enforcement of the act. From the beginning, little or no emphasis was placed on education of the public; all efforts were put on underlying enforcement. This was a serious flaw, and extensive bootlegging soon developed for an eagerly waiting clientele. Otherwise law-abiding citizens purchased large quantities of illegal alcohol.

In 1929 President Hoover appointed the Wickersham Commission on Law Enforcement to look into the problem. The commission held widely publicized hearings that indicated the widespread violations of the Volstead Act and the ineffectiveness of enforcement measures. The final report of the commission in 1931 was very critical of existing enforcement measures and indicated that the future success of enforcing the law was quite uncertain. Between 1929 and 1931, opposition to the prohibition amendment increased considerably due in part to the hard work of advocates of repeal. Many highly respected American leaders who had previously supported prohibition were persuaded to support repeal.

In February 1933 the United States Senate and House of Representatives urged adoption of the repeal amendment (Twenty-first Amendment). In less than ten months, the amendment was ratified in the necessary thirty-six states, and the "social experiment" was ended. Prohibition had been in effect from January 1920 to December 1933. It had been the most controversial issue in American politics since slavery.

The Twenty-first Amendment removed the responsibility of regulating the conditions surrounding the manufacture and sale of alcoholic beverages from the hands of the federal government. Within 30 years after repeal, the sale of alcoholic beverages was again legal in all states of the union. By the mid-1960s, over two-thirds of all adult Americans reported that they drank alcoholic beverages. Of the remaining 25 to 30 percent, probably less than half would be considered "antialcohol" in the sense that they had strong feelings in favor of a return to total prohibition. Since the repeal, and especially since World War II, the temperance movement has been mostly linked to small-town, rural values and the defense of a very conservative, economic order.

Presently, all fifty states have laws regarding the purchase of alcoholic beverages by youngsters. Some states also prohibit the serving of alcoholic beverages to youngsters by adults, including their own parents (obviously, this law is rarely enforced). Some states distinguish between distilled spirits and beers and wines; others apply a minimum age uniformly to all three types of alcoholic beverages. There has been a generally disorganized approach to this issue among the states.

When the question of lowering the minimum voting age from 21 to 18 was placed on the ballot of the national election, many states placed the question of minimum age to purchase alcohol on the same ballot. The general argument for an 18-year-old minimum age was that if 18-year-olds were treated as adults by being eligible to enter military service and to vote, then they should be considered adults in other matters.

Since the early 1980s, states have returned to an age of 21 as the legal drinking age. Much of this shift has been due to the federal government's threat to reduce or completely cut highway construction funds if a given state did not raise the legal drinking age to 21 years. In addition, grass roots organizations such as Mothers Against Drunk Driving (MADD) and Students Against Driving Drunk (SADD) have brought pressure on legislative bodies to pass laws that severely punish drinking and driving. These laws and the public education accompanying their passage have made the public more aware of the dangers of drinking and driving. Education, these new DWI (driving while intoxicated) laws, and reduction of the speed limit seem to have led to fewer alcohol-related deaths.

It appears that Americans might be moving into an era of more judicious and conservative use of alcoholic beverages. This movement appears to be tied to the passage of laws, public education, and concerns for alcohol's effects on health. All of these factors have changed attitudes about alcohol use and abuse. Only the passage of time will show whether the present pattern is a temporary reduction in drinking or the beginning of a long-range trend.

Alcohol has become so closely interwoven with life in the United States that two-thirds of the adult population use alcohol to some degree. Given the present socialization patterns in the United States, the prohibition and/or the abolition of alcohol would appear to be very difficult if not impossible. A more appropriate task would seem to be to educate the public regarding more judicious and wise use of alcoholic beverages.

REFERENCES

Earle, A. M. (1902). *Customs and fashions in Old New England*. New York: Charles Scribner & Sons.

Furnas, J. C. (1965). *The life and times of the late Demon Rum*. New York: G. P. Putnam & Sons.

Gusfield, J. R. (1983). Symbolic crusade: Status politics and the American temperance movement. In M. E. Kelleher, B. K. MacMurray, & T. M. Shapiro (Eds.), *Drugs and society: A critical reader* (pp. 30–36). Dubuque, IA: Kendall/Hunt.

Keller, M., McCormick, M. & Efron, V. (1982). *A dictionary of words about alcohol.* New Brunswick, NJ: Rutgers University Center of Alcohol Studies.

Kobler, J. (1973). *Ardent spirits: The rise and fall of prohibition.* New York: G. P. Putnam & Sons.

Krout, J. A. (1925). *The origins of prohibition.* New York: Alfred A. Knopf.

Lender, M. A., & Martin, J. K. (1982). *Drinking in America: A history.* New York: The Free Press.

Mitchell, E. V. (1946).*It's an Old New England custom.* New York: Vanguard Press.

Rublowsky, J. (1974). *The stoned age: A history of drugs in America.* New York: G. P. Putnam & Sons.

Warner, H. S. (1970). Alcohol trends in college life. In G. L. Maddox (Ed.), *The domesticated drug: Drinking among collegians.* (pp. 45–80). New Haven, CT: College and University Press Services.

Zinberg, N. E., & Fraser, K. M. (1985). The role of the social setting in the prevention and treatment of alcoholism. In J. H. Mendelson & N. K. Mello (Eds.), *The diagnosis and treatment of alcoholism* (2nd ed.) (pp. 457–483). New York: McGraw-Hill.

Alcohol Use, Abuse, and Alcoholism: Definitions and Typologies/Models

_____ *chapter 2*

Giving precise definitions of positive use, alcohol abuse, and alcoholism is perhaps one of the most difficult things to do in the alcohol field. This chapter reviews some of the definitions, typologies, and models of alcoholism that currently exist in the field. There are several ways of defining and conceptualizing alcohol use and abuse, and many of these overlap while others seem to differ a great deal from each other. A representative sample of these definitions and conceptualizations will be covered since it is impossible to consider all of them.

It is important to understand how alcohol use and abuse has been defined, because frequently these definitions determine how it is dealt with. Definitions and typologies will be treated separately, but in a real sense, they cannot be clearly separated. Almost all definitions imply a model of alcoholism, and all typology models implicitly or explicitly are based on a definition of what alcohol use and abuse is. However, for discussion purposes, these two factors will be viewed separately. First, definitions will be covered and then the various typologies and models in the alcohol field will be reviewed.

DEFINITIONS OF SAFE OR MODERATE DRINKING

There are many more definitions relating to alcohol abuse than to safe use of the beverage. This is because it is easier to designate destructive use based upon the observer's notions that alcohol is disrupting or damaging someone's life. Destructive use of alcohol can be seen and brings forth reactions from observers. On the other hand, safe use usually does not bring forth reactions. When it does, there are strong disagreements as to what safe use is. Definitions of safe use can range from total abstinence to a level of drinking that does not get drinkers labeled as "having a problem." The difficulty with the former is that it is impractical. The difficulty with the latter is that almost all pathological drinkers were at one time nonabusive drinkers.

Perhaps because defining safe or moderate drinking is arbitrary and ever changing, few people have tried to define safe or moderate drinking. Chafetz (1982) is an exception. He devoted a chapter to the topic. Chafetz— concerned with the issues of ambivalence toward alcohol use in the United States and the conflict, guilt, and confusion associated with alcohol use— tries to give a frame of reference for safe and healthy drinking. While he does not specify a nice, crisp definition of safe or moderate drinking, he does make some suggestions as to how to stay within the limits and avoid dangers.

1. Know the actions and effects of alcohol. Being unaware of what effects alcohol can have on you puts you at risk.

2. Be aware of when, where, and under what circumstances you drink. Alcohol should not be seen as impairing one's performance in an activity. If alcohol will impair performance, then it should not be used. On the other hand, in a relaxed setting such as at a meal with friends, alcohol may be used constructively.

3. The amount of alcohol consumed should not exceed 1.5 ounces of absolute alcohol per day. This translates into three 1-ounce drinks of 100 proof whiskey, four 8-ounce glasses of beer, or a half bottle of table wine. This is Anstie's limit (see Chafetz, 1982, p. 485) and should be considered an *upper limit*, not an average that can be applied to everyone uniformly. For some people, one drop of alcohol is too much. Using these rules of thumb, one day's ration cannot be added to the next. (Obviously, one can see that this cumulative daily average when consumed all at one time on a weekend binge is very destructive. Binge drinking is one of the most destructive things one can undertake.)

4. The manner in which alcohol is consumed is critical. Alcohol should be sipped slowly because of its effects on the body. To help control the rate of absorption in the body, alcohol is best taken with food, particularly proteins and fats.

5. Be aware that what one expects from alcohol is frequently what one gets. This means drinkers should be aware of their expectations about what alcohol will do for them.

6. Alcohol should not be used to deal with loneliness or emotional

upset. Alcohol is no substitute for another person. Fantasy and enthusiasm are better shared with someone. Translation: "Don't drink alone" is a good rule.

7. Alcohol used as an adjunct to socializing and to facilitate relationships is a safe and healthy psychological use of the beverage.

8. Where you drink is important. Drinking in a setting where relaxation is both possible and desirable and that is conducive to safe drinking is important. Being in a mob of people at a crowded bar or in a dark, secluded place is not conducive to safe drinking.

9. Social factors influence drinking. For example, not only your expectations but also those of people around you affect your drinking. A university professor is amazed at the differences university students display in drinking at a beer party and at a professor's home. Students are much rowdier and uninhibited at beer parties (so they report) than they are at a professor's home. The level of rowdiness can often be independent of the amount of alcohol consumed.

10. The previous suggestions indicate that social surroundings and wanting to please people help to set limits on drinking. Individuals usually behave in a socially acceptable fashion because they want affection and respect from others. One person's standards of behavior are transmitted to another. Therefore if someone misuses alcohol, persons close to that person should ask themselves if they contributed to it in some way by not clearly communicating the limits of drinking.

11. One should have an image of alcohol use that excludes drunkenness as acceptable behavior.

12. Use a "test of comfort" with alcohol. One simple test is the response of the drinker to the people who do not drink. If drinkers are more comfortable around people who drink than around those who do not, the drinkers may have some problems with alcohol. If so, drinking could be a risk-laden behavior for those persons. (It should also be pointed out that drinking, even in unsafe ways, may be normative for certain time periods and under certain conditions in individuals' lives. College and military drinking are examples. This "normative drinking" does place people at an increased risk for violent death and alcohol addiction. However, in the great majority of cases, abusive drinking levels subside when these individuals' life situations change and they move into new life roles as professionals, heads of families, etc.)

As noted above, this is not a clean, crisp, and brief definition of safe, moderate drinking. However, it does show the difficulties inherent in defining drinking patterns. Problem drinking and severe alcohol abuse also have a great deal of ambiguity associated with their definitions.

DEFINITION OF PROBLEM DRINKING

Cahalan (1970) is one of the leaders in defining problem drinking. He endorses an uncomplicated definition of problem drinking given by Plaut (1967): "Problem drinking is a *repetitive use of beverage alcohol causing physical, psychological, or social harm to the drinker or others.* This definition stresses interference with function rather than any specific drinking behavior" (pp. 37–38). Cahalan sees this definition as compatible with a more general definition "which indicates any problem connected fairly closely with drinking constitutes a drinking problem" (Knupfer, 1967, p. 974).

Cahalan (1970) proposes that eleven types of specific problems be used in a national analysis of drinking problems. His proposal stems from Jellinek's hypotheses and typologies (covered later) and others, including Plaut's definition of problem drinking quoted earlier. The specific problems proposed by Calahan include

1. frequent intoxication—exceeding what is defined as a moderate level in a combination of frequency and amount per occasion or getting intoxicated fairly often

2. binge drinking—being intoxicated for more than one day at a time

3. symptomatic drinking behavior (symptomatic dependence upon alcohol)—inferred from finding it difficult to stop drinking once started, experiencing blackouts or memory lapses after drinking, sneaking drinks

4. psychological dependence on alcohol

5. problems with current spouse or with relatives due to one's drinking

6. problems with friends or neighbors over one's drinking

7. problems related to work or employment occurring in relation to one's drinking

8. problems with the police, accidents in which someone is hurt, or property damage occurring in relation to one's drinking

9. health problems such that physician advises one to cut down on drinking

10. financial problems connected with one's drinking

11. belligerence or fighting associated with one's drinking (Cahalan, 1970, pp. 26–27)

DEFINITIONS OF ALCOHOLISM

There are several very broad definitions of alcoholism. Pattison and Kaufman (1982) outline some of the definitions in common usage in the alcohol field. These definitions are frequently ambiguous and imprecise. It is sometimes difficult to separate typologies and classifications of alcoholism from the definition of alcoholism. Jellinek's definitions of types of alcoholism will be discussed under typologies and models later. The World Health Organization (1954) defines alcoholics as those excessive drinkers whose dependence upon alcohol has attained such a level that they show a noticeable degree of mental disturbance or an interference with their bodily and mental health, interference with their interpersonal relations and their smooth social and economic function, or the prodromal signs of such developments. Pattison and Kaufman (1982) report on a formulation of alcoholism as a syndrome (a cluster of symptoms that tend to occur together), which is called the alcohol dependence syndrome by the World Health Organization. This formulation includes

1. narrowing of drinking repertoire
2. salience of drink-seeking behavior
3. increased tolerance to alcohol
4. repeated withdrawal symptoms
5. relief-avoidance of withdrawal
6. subjective awareness of compulsion to drink
7. reinstatement of syndrome after abstinence (Pattison & Kaufman, 1982, p. 18)

While this formulation seems to be helpful, there are people who are still socially functional despite alcohol dependence. There are others who exhibit few signs of the syndrome even though they engage in severe abuse of alcohol. The American Psychiatric Association's Diagnostic and Statistical Manual (1980) classifies alcohol intoxication, alcohol withdrawal, and alcohol organic disorders, as well as alcohol abuse and alcohol dependence. Alcohol abuse is defined as pathological use for at least one month which leads to impairment in social or occupational functioning. Alcohol dependence includes the above definition and adds increased tolerance to alcohol or withdrawal problems when alcohol is not available.

The National Council on Alcoholism (NCA) has a definition of alcoholism based on a list of signs and symptoms of alcohol abuse. Pattison and Kaufman (1982) are extremely critical of that list because it fails to deal with early-stage alcohol problems, it is unspecific, and it does not provide a unique diagnosis of alcoholism (for instance, it includes family fights, which may be due to some other factor). They see this system as overemphasizing physical consequences. Also, many of the items do not discriminate between alcoholic and nonalcoholic behavior. Other concerns these writers have with the NCA's definition of alcoholism is that it offers only a binary diagnosis (a person either has alcoholism or does not) and it does not allow for various levels of alcohol involvement. There has been considerable argument in the alcohol field about the usefulness of a binary diagnostic system. More and more people believe alcoholism is caused by multiple problems and can be expressed in multiple ways. There is emerging agreement that there should be some type of continuum on which people's level of involvement in alcohol abuse can be placed. There is also agreement that people change their positions on this continuum over time. Obviously, the binary definition does not allow placement on a continuum; you are simply an alcoholic or you are not. Meyer, Babor, and Mirkin also see limits to the NCA's system; these limits will be discussed later under typologies.

TYPOLOGIES AND MODELS OF ALCOHOLISM

As noted previously, definitions and models are not entirely separate issues. The definition of alcoholism used is based on the model that is employed and vice versa. Much of the material covered in this section is based on a review by Meyer et al. These authors maintain that one reason to consider typologies in the alcohol field is that they might prove helpful in the treatment of alcoholism. If a pattern or set of factors can be found, then patients could be classified for various types of treatment. Large numbers of patients could be classified into subcategories which are presumed to have implications for therapy and for predicting the outcome of treatment. Meyer et al. outline some of the major issues in this area.

In the past decade, there has been an attempt in the alcohol field to develop subtypes of alcohol problems. As noted earlier, the NCA has developed criteria for alcoholism based upon addiction variables, including physiological and clinical variables as well as psychological and behavioral variables. This NCA system was proposed to provide a uniform nomenclature designed to promote early detection of alcoholism. It was not designed to differentiate alcoholic subtypes, which would prove to be diagnostically predictive of treatment needs and patient outcome following treatment.

Using multivariate techniques to establish subgroups of alcoholics is another approach to typologies. Most of the research on multivariate techniques has not used information from a wide range of alcoholics in developing classification systems. To get a truly representative system, it is necessary not only to take measures on a wide range of different types of alcoholics, but also to take multiple measures on each group, hence the name multivariate. The multivariate approach establishes separate classification systems for demographic, psychological, historical, and neuropsychological data. In this area, there has been almost no attempt to examine the relationships between biological, psychological, and sociocultural information or to identify the unique importance of distinct variables. One of the reasons for this failure to examine relationships of different variables is that rating scales are not uniform. Classifications of alcoholics in one treatment center cannot be easily compared with classifications in another center. Standardized measurements and rating scales need to be established that can be used in a wide range of different treatment centers so that classifications of alcoholics can be compared.

Shelly and Goldstein (1976) argue that alcohol typologies should be governed by specific principles of measurement, including the following:

1. The procedures used for making classifications should be objective and clearly defined.

2. The classification rules for deciding the type to which an individual subject belongs should be made explicit.

3. The typology developed should not be merely descriptive but ideally should be related to differential treatment and management plans.

Shelly and Goldstein point out that organic alcoholic conditions fall into relatively clear typologies because the diagnostic procedures, the rules for classification, and the treatment implications are all clear. However, regardless of these positive conditions for classification, follow-up is critical to the validation of any typological system. In many cases there have been no validation studies, which employ carefully designed follow-up studies, of classification schemes. Obviously, without follow-up, it is not possible to establish the utility for treatment of various classification systems.

The importance of diagnosis in clinical work is directly related to how helpful the diagnosis is as an indication of prognosis (outcome), and how the diagnosis relates to the choice of therapies. In various therapeutic areas, the development of valid diagnostic criteria has been an important milestone in clinical research which is directed at understanding the cause of the disorder.

Typological approaches are not new in the alcohol field. Two examples of the typological approach are the work of Jellinek (1952, 1960) and Zucker (1987). Jellinek's system is a classical typological one. He outlines the stages individuals go through in developing alcoholism as well as various alcoholic subtypes. Jellinek developed his system intuitively. Zucker's typology is a recent one and illustrates a different way of approaching alcohol abuse.

JELLINEK'S PHASES

Jellinek presents a detailed description of the phases of alcoholism. Many individuals suggest that Jellinek's description of the alcoholic's progression assumes that all alcoholics follow the same course, and therefore, it ignores readily identifiable differences in alcoholics. Despite this criticism, Jellinek's description is important because it does describe the experiences some alcoholics have, and it also points out some of the areas of behavior that separate social drinkers from persons with alcohol abuse problems. It is important to keep several points in mind as Jellinek's description is considered. First, he intended his descriptions to give an "average" picture. The phases he describes, the sequences, and the symptoms within the phases are, he thinks, characteristic of the great majority of alcohol addicts and represent the average trend. Second, he felt that women do not fit the pattern. Frequently, women develop into full-blown alcoholics much more rapidly than the picture given here. Third, the length of the phases varies with individual differences and environmental factors.

Jellinek asserts that the term *alcoholism* should be reserved for a limited and well-defined area of excessive drinking behavior, specifically, to that drinking behavior where physical or psychological pathology is involved. He distinguishes between alcohol addicts who lose control of their alcohol intake after several years of excessive drinking and nonaddictive drinkers who never lose control.

According to Jellinek, alcohol addicts go through four phases as the disease develops. There are rather specific behaviors within each stage.

1. Prealcoholic Symptomatic Phase.   In the beginning, the use of alcoholic beverages is always socially motivated, but prealcoholics soon experience a rewarding relief in the drinking situation. This relief is more marked either because prealcoholics are more tense or they have not learned to handle their tensions as others do. At first, drinkers think their relief is due to the situation rather than to the drinking, and they seek those situations where incidental drinking will occur. Sooner or later they become aware of the relationship between relief and drinking.

Initially, prealcoholics seek relief only occasionally, but in 6 months to 6 years, their tolerance for tension decreases, and they begin drinking daily. Their drinking does not result in obvious intoxication, but it does involve fairly heavy alcohol intake as compared with the use of alcohol by other individuals in their circle. At this point, their drinking is not conspicuous either to themselves or their associates. This type of drinking may last from several months to 2 years. This prealcoholic phase is divided into two stages, beginning with occasional relief drinking and ending with constant relief drinking.

2. Prodromal Phase.   This phase is marked by the sudden onset of behavior resembling blackouts. Drinkers may have had no more than 50 or 60 grams of absolute alcohol and may show no signs of intoxication. They may carry on reasonable conversations or go through quite elaborate activities, but the next day they will not be able to recall these events. These amnesias are called "alcoholic palimpsests." Such amnesias occur in nonalcoholics occasionally after heavy drinking, but prospective alcoholic addicts experience them frequently after only moderate alcohol intake. These blackouts are followed, or in some cases preceded, by drinking behaviors which indicate for these individuals that beer, wine, and spirits have ceased to be mere beverages and are now drugs that they need. Individuals may, at this point, become aware of the fact that they drink in a manner that is different from others.

The drinking behavior characterizing these individuals now includes surreptitious drinking where they seek ways to get extra drinks without others knowing it. There is such a preoccupation with alcohol that they drink before a party because they fear there may not be enough alcohol at the party. They start gulping drinks and begin to realize that their drinking is not of the ordinary sort. They have guilt feelings about their drinking and so start avoiding any reference to alcohol in their conversations. The behavior described here, along with more frequent blackouts, foreshadows the development of alcohol addiction.

During this phase, alcohol consumption is heavy but not conspicuous because it does not lead to obvious intoxication. The first sign of this phase is drinkers' efforts to hide the fact that they are drinking. Jellinek believes that the only possible alternative for drinkers who have reached this stage is total abstinence. The prodromal phase ends and the crucial phase begins when alcoholics lose control of their drinking behavior.

3. Crucial Phase. Loss of control means that any drinking of alcohol starts a chain reaction, which is felt by drinkers as a physical demand for alcohol. It can take hours or weeks for the full development of this reaction, and it lasts until the drinkers are too drunk or too sick to drink any more. This does not seem to be started by any individual need of the moment but by just a simple social drink. The drinkers have lost the ability to control the quantity they drink once they start, but they can still control whether or not they will drink on any given occasion. Once individuals have reached this stage, they can still go through periods of voluntary abstinence ("on the wagon").

It seems logical to ask why individuals would return to drinking after repeated disastrous experiences with alcohol. The answer, according to Jellinek, is that while drinkers will not admit it, they believe they have lost their "willpower" and that they can and must regain it.

At about the same time that they experience this loss of control, drinkers begin to rationalize their behavior. They begin to produce alcoholic alibis. They find explanations that show that they did not lose control, and produce a series of reasons for becoming intoxicated. In effect, they say to themselves that they could drink normally if these things did not occur. They need these rationalizations for themselves as much as for their families and associates; the rationalizations allow the drinkers to continue drinking.

Despite their rationalizations, the drinkers experience a loss of self-esteem, and they begin to compensate for it with grandiose behavior. They may begin to display extravagant spending and weave elaborate tales to convince themselves that they are not as bad as they have at times thought themselves to be. Rationalizations lead to the thought that the fault does not lie with them but with other people. This results in their progressive withdrawal from their usual social environment. The first sign of this attitude is aggressive behavior. Inevitably, this aggression leads to guilt, and they then experience persistent remorse, which leads to more tension and more drinking. In compliance with social pressures, addicts now go on periods of total abstinence as a means of trying to control their drinking. They believe that their troubles arise because they do not drink the right kind of beverage or in the right way, so they change their pattern of drinking by setting up rules such as not drinking before certain times of the day or drinking only in certain places. The strain of the struggle with drinking increases their hostility toward their environment, and as a result they drop friends and quit jobs. Their isolation becomes more pronounced as their behavior becomes more alcohol-centered. They lose their outside interests, they reinterpret their interpersonal relationships, and they indulge in marked self-pity. These feelings and changes are so intense that these individuals may become involved in geographic escape, moving to a new location in hopes that their present life problems will be solved by the move to a new place, either real or contemplated. Under the impact of these events, a change in family habits occurs. Family members may withdraw from social contacts because of the embarrassment caused by the drinker, or they may begin to establish new things to do outside the home in order to get away from the unpleasantness of the alcoholic's behavior. Such behavior is unreasonably resented by alcohol addicts.

The alcoholics' central concern is alcohol, and this leads them to protect their supply by accumulating a large stock of alcohol and hiding it in the most unlikely places for fear that they will be deprived of the most necessary substance in their lives. They neglect proper nutrition, thereby aggravating the effects of heavy drinking on the body. Often, the first hospitalization for some alcohol-related complaint occurs at this time. By this point the doubt, guilt, and loss of self-esteem have made alcoholics so dependent that they cannot start the day without steadying themselves with alcohol. The beginning of regular morning drinking marks the end of the crucial phase and the beginning of the chronic phase. Throughout the crucial phase there is a battle to avoid losing complete social footing, but progressively, drinkers lose their motivation.

4. Chronic Phase.　　Now, for the first time, alcohol addicts are intoxicated during the daytime—and on a weekday. This phase is the beginning of prolonged intoxication ("benders"), which lasts for several days at a time.

This drinking meets with such unanimous social rejection that it involves a grave social risk. Jellinek feels that only psychopathic personalities or individuals who have undergone a psychopathological process would expose themselves to that risk.

Long drawn-out drinking bouts commonly bring about marked ethical deterioration and impairment of thinking. True alcoholic psychosis may occur in about 10 percent of the cases. The loss of morale is so great that the addicts now drink with persons far below their social level, and they may use technical products such as bay rum or rubbing alcohol.

Alcoholics often lose their tolerance for alcohol at this time. For example, they may require just half the previously required amount of alcohol to bring on a stuporous state. Indefinable fears and tremors become persistent. These symptoms occur sporadically during the crucial phase, but in the chronic phase, they are present as soon as alcohol disappears from the organism. The alcoholics also exhibit psychomotor inhibition. For example, they are unable to wind a watch without having previously ingested alcohol. The need to control these symptoms is tremendous, and drinking takes on an obsessive character. In the end the addicts' rationalizations are so frequently and mercilessly tested against reality that their entire rationalization systems fail and they admit defeat, but they continue to drink excessively because they are unable to see a way out.

JELLINEK'S TYPOLOGIES

In addition to this detailed description of the general course of alcoholism development, Jellinek (1960) developed a typological system, which also includes steps of progression. The following types of alcoholics are identified as fitting into either the physical or psychological categories of problems related to alcohol.

1. Alpha Alcoholism. This type of alcoholic exhibits purely psychological, continual reliance on the effect of alcohol to relieve physical, psychological, or social pain. The drinkers who fall into this typology exceed the norms of society but still retain the ability to control their drinking and abstain. Signs of progression are not evident.

2. Beta Alcoholism. These alcoholics experience physical complications resulting from the excessive use of alcohol (for example, polyneuropathy, gastritis, cirrhosis of the liver) but which occur without physical or psychological dependency upon alcohol.

3. Gamma Alcoholism. These alcoholics acquire increased tissue tolerance to alcohol with adaptive cell metabolism, and they experience withdrawal symptoms, physical dependence (craving), and loss of control. There is a definite progression from psychological to physical dependence. This is the most destructive form of alcoholism since it affects the physical, psychological, and social aspects of individuals. This is the type seen in American alcoholism clinics and Alcoholics Anonymous groups.

4. *Delta Alcoholism.* These alcoholics experience an increase in tissue tolerance with adaptive cell metabolism, withdrawal symptoms, and craving; but rather than loss of control they lack the ability to abstain from drinking. They cannot stop drinking alcoholic beverages, but they have some control over the amount consumed when they do drink.

5. *Epsilon Alcoholism.* These alcoholics engage in periodic heavy consumption. It is the least-known form. Individuals can abstain but have a history of periodic binges during which they display all of the recognizable symptoms of alcoholism.

There are a number of objections to Jellinek's typologies. One criticism is that overt behavioral differences and methods of treatment are not differentiated into a certain number of types. Another point against Jellinek's conceptualizations is that the loss of control on which he relies so heavily is not adequately defined. He also uses the term in a retrospective manner. This seriously questions if the term *loss of control*, as Jellinek uses it, would be useful in working with individuals who are not already beyond that point in their drinking behavior. Another difficulty with Jellinek's typologies is that there is no evidence that alcoholics are biologically dependent on alcohol. Clearly, the disease or illness approach to alcoholism may be an oversimplification of a complex phenomenon. Total acceptance of this approach may lead people to believe in a simple and one-dimensional type of alcoholism and, thus, a need for a simple and one-dimensional cure for the problem.

ZUCKER'S TYPOLOGIES

Zucker (1987) presents a different way of viewing typologies and a different way of using them. His typologies attempt to predict the types of problems individuals may face given certain characteristics. Zucker labels these as etiological typologies. (Etiology is the theory of the course or source of a disease or disorder.) From his perspective, different etiologies imply a different pattern of risk elements both within and across developmental periods. Once these patterns are established, individuals' levels of risk are determined by a simple comparison of the degree to which their own biopsychosocial histories fit the already established developmental risk pattern.

Zucker states that his presentation is a "beginning" effort at charting multiple etiologies. He believes that sufficient evidence exists to warrant the delineation of four typologies. These are (1) antisocial alcoholism; (2) developmentally cumulative alcoholism; (3) developmentally limited alcoholism; and (4) negative affect alcoholism.

1. Antisocial Alcoholism. Zucker says this typology is more frequently studied, and more is known about it, than the other three. He cautions that while, in his thinking, it is the most common type of alcoholism, individuals' histories of alcohol problems and antisocial activities may not be sufficient to establish that this disorder exists. This type of alcoholism is characterized by both early presence of antisocial behavior and early onset of alcohol problems. The severity and persistence of antisocial activity into adulthood and an early preadolescent history of socialization to aggressive acts are critical differentiating factors. This type of alcoholism has been previously described as alcoholism with sociopathy, alcoholism with antisocial personality, and primary sociopathy with secondary diagnosis of alcoholism. While documented in women, it is far more common in men. It is also thought to be more common in lower socioeconomic classes where its display is uncomplicated by social/cultural factors that may inhibit the expression of aggression in other classes. This is the subtype that is being tracked most often in high-risk studies that use offspring of alcoholic parents (for more on these types of high-risk genetic studies, see Chapter 5). There is substantial evidence that developmental experiences of this alcoholic type from early childhood onward are the most pathogenic.

2. Developmentally Cumulative Alcoholism (also called primary alcoholism). This disorder is labeled primary alcoholism because the symptomatic behavior considered to be primary to alcoholism is established (typically by respondents' own self-report accounts) to have occurred prior to the onset of any other psychiatric condition. Secondary alcoholism, for example, is a diagnosis considered to occur after a depressive episode or some other psychiatric disturbance. Frequently, the primary versus secondary distinction in the diagnosis is also presumed evidence for cause so that in a case of depression, depression might be considered the cause of alcoholism if it occurs first, and secondary if it occurs after the alcoholism developed.

Another reason why the term *primary* is used is that the alcoholic process is construed as a primarily biological event or sequence that is triggered by the availability of and pressure to use alcoholic beverages. Once exposure to alcoholic beverages has occurred, this course is seen as a physiologically driven event series. Thus alcoholism as a biological disease entity is considered to be the primary cause in the development of this type of alcoholism.

Zucker notes that the notion that this is a strictly biologically driven disease course is based upon the presumption that the available etiology literature has adequately assured that the possibility of an earlier developmental influence upon alcoholic outcome has been eliminated. That is to say, there is no possibility of a prior developmental contribution to the establishment of the disorder. However, Zucker notes that in most studies the developmental data begin at adolescence.

Zucker uses developmentally cumulative alcoholism as a term to describe this particular type of alcoholism. Developmentally cumulative means or implies that risk is more closely tied to normal, culturally prescribed processes of drinking and problem drinking than to the antisocial alcoholism described in the first type. In this type of alcoholism, over the life course, the addictive process has become sufficiently cumulative so that there is a different trajectory of this drinking pattern than would be the case were it simply regulated by normative developmental trends in the culture.

In this regard, it is a more severe form of alcoholism problem than the third type, developmentally limited alcoholism (discussed later). However, developmentally cumulative alcoholism has a more benign origin and course than antisocial alcoholism has. The occurrence of the developmentally cumulative typology cuts across social class and gender. The probability rate should be lower than type one, and the onset of developmentally cumulative alcoholism should be later in life. It differs from antisocial alcoholism in adulthood in that antisocial involvement is less in this type. The lack of obviously disordered behavioral characteristics in adulthood make it difficult to point precisely to the developmental issues and circumstances that led to the disorder. Nonetheless, based on the lack of antisocial involvement and the lack of gender differences, a more benign set of family experiences in childhood would be expected in this type than would be expected in the type one alcoholics. Recent work that examines this issue strongly substantiates Zucker's hypothesis.

To understand how this disorder develops, the earlier origin of the problem and the cumulation across life's stages must be taken into account. Parent-child interactions are more harsh than for nonalcoholic individuals; the parents' characteristics as models are more deviant. In addition, the individuals have been socialized to a great degree to regard alcohol consumption as a way of coping with stress. Early, erratic socialization of individuals with this type of alcoholism should result in the greater likelihood of peer, career, and marital difficulty during later life stages. When such individuals have difficulties with the transitions in life across several stages, for example, adolescence to young adulthood or middle to late life, a reactive alcohol process may result. When these persons are faced with any situation that they find difficult to handle, they might be expected to use alcohol in reaction to their difficulty coping with those changes.

3. Developmentally Limited Alcoholism   (also called frequent heavy drinking). This type has also been described by Jessor (1985), one of the investigators who has looked at drinking during early adulthood. The type refers to a pattern of drinking involving high consumption levels that peak in early adulthood and result in the highest age rates of alcohol problems throughout the life span. This typology is somewhat more common in men than in women, but it does cut across social classes and it contains individuals who, for the most part, lower their drinking rates by the time they reach their mid-twenties.

Blane (1979) calls this type of drinking "frequent heavy drinking" and defines it as drinking five or more of any alcoholic beverages at least once per week. Frequent heavy drinking is not chronic in the sense of being continuous, nor pervasive in the sense of affecting all spheres of the individual's life. Intake is episodic and occurs within a more or less conventionally ordered lifestyle. More crucial, perhaps, alcohol is not a guiding principle in the lives of frequent heavy drinkers. Drinking episodes are self-limited, circumscribed events that occur independently of other significant life events. While drinking episodes are important at the moment, they recede into the background as other life activities come to the fore. Further, consequences of frequent heavy drinking on physical health stem from acute consequences of alcohol intake, such as hangovers, blackouts, and gastritis. Except for the possibility of a fatal overdose, all of the physical disorders associated with this drinking pattern are temporary and, as far as is known, are not hazardous to an individual's health. In the heavy drinker type of alcohol problems, there are only one or two signs of alcohol abuse. There are multiple signs of alcohol abuse in other types of alcoholics.

What seems to happen is that individuals who fit this type grow out of the disorder. Their development in their mid- and late-twenties appears to be in the direction of greater personality, environment, and behavior conventionality. Drinking frequently drops off following the assumption of new life roles where work and family and new social contacts, other than school, reduce the amount of alcohol consumed.

4. *Negative Affect Alcoholism.* This type was first identified in the psychiatric literature in the mid-1960s and has since been heavily tied to alcoholic symptomatology in women (where it is called affective disorder alcoholism). This type has been linked to a family history of unipolar affective disorder and to the likelihood of higher suicidal risks. Women with affective disorder alcoholism are more likely to have more benign social histories than women without the disorder. After hospitalization, they also recover more quickly and completely.

Zucker (1987) cites a number of empirical studies that appear to begin to provide evidence for his typologies. A study of college student drinking and the follow-up of subjects after leaving college found that drinking for psychological adjustment during college years (to overcome shyness or to aid in forgetting disappointments) was a significant indicator of problem alcohol use among women in midlife. This pattern of use could be interpreted as fitting the relief of negative affect.

Williams (1966, 1968) studied middle-class male college students and found that higher initial levels of anxiety and depression and lower levels of self-esteem were associated with greater alcohol consumption and more signs of problem drinking. Zucker (1987) cites data from a longitudinal study that indicates that the presence of a cluster of developmental events during individuals' high school years is associated with problem drinking in adulthood. Those events include a great deal of depression and an adaptation to that depression, a family history of conflict, and a sour and disagreeable mother.

Zucker states that data in this area are sparse. There is a growing amount of developmental literature on past behavior and child-rearing practices in depressive homes which suggests that there is a linkage between the social deprivation occurring in these type of households, the greater vulnerability to interpersonal stress, and problem use of alcohol in adulthood by children reared in these homes.

This is especially true if one member of the household uses alcohol excessively and thus acts as a model. Zucker's typologies are only a beginning point, but they show how research data and multivariate information can be used to lead to the establishment of typologies that may be both theoretically and practically useful.

OTHER APPROACHES TO TYPOLOGIES

Attempts to establish typologies that are based on empirical information are increasing. In their review, Meyer et al. (1983) note that in the 1960s and 1970s two empirically based procedures were developed.

1. The a priori Comparative Approach.   In this approach, two or more groups of alcoholics are selected according to a priori or previously chosen criteria. The groups are compared on a number of empirical measures that represent relevant variables and constructs. This approach has used dichotomies to classify alcoholics and has often been employed to evaluate the validity of previous "armchair" or intuitively derived approaches. Examples of criteria used in this approach include gender, nationality, psychopathology, drinking pattern, drinking history, personality characteristics, childhood minimal brain dysfunction, urological status, and family history of alcoholism.

The a priori approach has a number of limitations. The variables tested have been very specific so it is difficult to generalize the findings. It has focused almost exclusively on males. There has been a tendency to study female alcoholics only in contrast to male alcoholics. The implication is that

Women alcoholics have been placed into two typologies: those who are primary alcoholics and those who have alcoholism secondary to affective (usually depression) disorder. *(Photograph courtesy of the Independence Center, Lincoln, Nebraska.)*

female alcoholics comprise a separate typology. Several writers (e.g., Schuckit, Pitts, Reich, King, & Winokur, 1969) suggest that there are at least two groups of female alcoholics: a group that has primary alcoholism, i.e., the cardinal features are that they are alcoholic, and a second group with alcoholism that is secondary to an affective disorder—usually depression. Despite the fact that there is some agreement in the literature that the relationship between alcohol problems and affective disorders may be stronger for women than for men, these same subtypes have been proposed for men.

2. The a posteriori Approach.   This second empirical methodology relies on statistical procedures to establish homogeneous groupings of the same type of alcoholics. This is done by measuring a large number of variables and constructs. This approach, like the a priori approach described previously, is empirical. Various observations and measurements can be applied to clinical samples. Statistical techniques are applied to find commonalities between homogeneous subgroups or among sets of variables. Typically, factor analysis is applied to a large data base representing aspects of alcoholism. The findings across a variety of studies indicate that alcoholics differ along several dimensions, each of which may vary in degree of severity. Strictly speaking, factor analytic multidimensional studies are not always typological but rather a means of identifying individual differences among alcoholics in terms of their unique profiles on several dimensions. In order to classify alcoholics into subtypes, cluster analysis or discriminant analysis has been employed. For example, efforts have been made to group alcoholics according to personality traits, clinical syndromes, demography, and rehabilitation needs.

Studies using this procedure have important limitations which may compromise their generalizability and clinical usefulness. One limitation is small sample size; however, even larger studies must be evaluated on the basis of the sample being representative of the population studied.

Comparative studies are especially sensitive to selection bias and failure to control for variables that are seen as extraneous to alcoholism. In general, researchers have failed to provide a rationale for the selection of variables, especially in these multivariate correlational investigations. Because these multivariate studies employ different measures, it is difficult to compare results across studies.

Other limitations in the current state of typology research are related to treatment relevance. Bowman and Jellinek (1941) suggest that a classification system that goes beyond "pigeon holing" to prediction is of greater value. Clearly studies that attempt to subclassify alcoholics must examine the clinical utility, predictive value, and generalizability of empirically derived classification systems. Meyer et al. (1983) report on research that was in progress at the University of Connecticut in the 1980s. They note that the focus of their research is on several issues.

> The typology study is examining the relative predictive utility of psychopathological, genetic, behavioral (including drinking history), and alcohol dependence history (social, neuropsychological, and psychophysiological variables relative to long-term outcome in a population of hospitalized alcoholics). The study is based on the assumption that one can identify subgroups of alcoholic patients which suggest etiological, prognostic, and therapeutic implications. (p. 242)

A more detailed look at how variables may be included in the development of typologies is given in Box 2–1.

EXAMPLES OF THE USE OF TYPOLOGIES

Several examples in the literature show how typologies might be used in the diagnosis and the planning of treatment of alcoholics. For example, Wanberg and Knapp (1970) identify four dimensions that can be used to differentiate alcoholic subtypes in a treatment population. These include (1)

BOX 2–1

Some Examples of the Sources of Typologies

It should be possible to classify alcoholics on the basis of the following:

1. Premorbid characteristics, e.g., presence of alcoholic parents, psychological dependence, alcohol expectancies, gender.
2. Patterns of alcohol use, e.g., binge drinking, drinking in response to stress.
3. Degree of alcohol dependence, age of onset, tolerance level, history of alcohol-related health problems.
4. Pattern of consequences resulting from alcoholism, e.g., blackouts, cirrhosis, problems with interpersonal relationships, financial problems, marital problems, decreased job performance

It would be possible to expand each of the above dimensions of possible classifications of alcoholics. As an example, there are considerable data on premorbid characteristics. Some possible premorbid indicators are:

1. *Personality factors and psychopathology.* For example, the findings by Hoffmann, Loper, and Kammeier (1974) and Jones (1968, 1971) that premorbid personality factors play a role in the development of later alcohol problems is a useful approach. The fact that junior high students who push the limits and take risks have a higher probability of alcohol problems is potentially useful in planning early intervention.
2. *The presence of minimal brain dysfunction in childhood.* There is some evidence that a history of hyperkinetic childhood and minimal brain dysfunction in childhood is associated with alcohol problems later on in life.
3. *Genetic factors.* There is considerable evidence from twin studies, adoption studies, and family history data from alcoholic patients that indicates that at least some alcohol problems may be genetically determined. (See Chapter 5, particularly references to Cloninger [1987] for an example of genetic typologies.)
4. *Family constellation.* By observing alcoholics and their families, it may be found that certain patterns of family interactions are predictive of later alcohol problems.

5. *Demographic and sociocultural factors.* Cross-cultural studies of alcohol use and alcoholism and different rates of alcoholism in ethnic groups suggest that the ways individuals are acculturated to perceive alcohol can have an effect on whether or not they abuse alcohol.

It is not clear that all these factors are related to one type of alcoholism. They may be significant in the etiology of one or more subtypes of alcoholism. Moreover, these factors and their premorbid level of adjustment may suggest a different prognosis in individuals who become alcoholic or may modify their response to treatment (taken in part from Meyer et al., 1983).

general severity (of drinking); (2) tension relief as a reason for drinking; (3) drinking as a means of socialization and/or self-enhancement; and (4) pattern of drinking (periodic versus controlled heavy drinking). While any brief attempt to use these dimensions as treatment guides is likely to be overly simplistic, it may be useful here to point out some possible treatment questions that might be raised regarding individuals scoring high on one of the above categories. (Because in real life, patients frequently have high scores on several of the dimensions noted by Wanberg and Knapp, single-dimension recommendations are used here only as illustrations.) If a patient has a high score on general severity, you might suspect that this person's life is being disrupted by alcoholism. Your interventions with this client might involve more structure to provide stability, inpatient as opposed to outpatient treatment to remove the client from the drinking milieu, and longer time in treatment. You might also attempt to spend more time on social rehabilitation, i.e., teaching him how to handle social interactions without alcohol. you might also see this patient as at high risk for relapse. Therefore, you might want to be sure that a very structured aftercare program is planned, which might include the patient's living in a halfway house for several months.

Those who score high on the tension relief dimension may need to learn ways of dealing with tension that do not involve alcohol. This might include learning progressive relaxation, finding avocations that may be naturally relaxing, recognizing situations that tend to arouse high levels of tension. Equally important is attaching labels to emotions, since this helps to discriminate positive from negative emotions and to identify more subtle emotional and tension-enhancing signals. (It is important to remember here that positive emotions can also cue drinking and need to be monitored by the drinker.) Assertiveness training may also help, since one of the ways one can become tense is in handling conflict and anger.

It is possible to view drinking that is conducted as a way of enhancing social situations and as a method of self-enhancement as being related to issues of self-esteem and to temperament or behavioral patterns that have been found to be ineffective, such as shyness. Certainly, these individuals could profit from the assertiveness training suggested earlier. However, these individuals' problems are located more in the way they view themselves. While not often used in alcohol treatment, some of the "stupid thinking" procedures developed by Ellis (1970) might often be useful here. A more typical procedure in alcohol treatment programs would be to confront the alcoholic's erroneous perceptions via group feedback. Valley Hope, an alcohol treatment program located in several midwestern and southwestern states, employs a group format that puts a person in the "hot seat" after several weeks in the group. The nominated individual passes a can into which each of the other members deposits written negative and positive descriptive characteristics observed in the person. It is interesting that persons in the hot seat are more able to accept and believe the negative comments about them than the many positive things members of the group attribute to them. Exercises like the hot seat help individuals confront some of their erroneous thinking about themselves. However, it is quite difficult to get persons to accept a "new psychological picture" of themselves, and this may be one of the most difficult things to do in alcohol treatment. More specific suggestions for where and how to socialize may also be taught to individuals, including learning to recognize social situations that increase the person's probability for relapse.

Finally, the pattern of drinking, whether periodic or controlled heavy drinking, might be used as a basis for treatment. If periodic drinking is the problem, you might try to find precipitants for drinking such as the stress of relatives visiting or problems in the workplace. You might also want to know more about what happens immediately before the person starts to drink. If it is long-term controlled drinking, then the surrounding environment may be even more important, since occupational roles can both support and maintain heavy drinking. For example, if the drinker is in a profession that requires alcohol use as a part of the job (for example, a salesperson or an entertainer), a career change may be explored. A visiting senior psychologist in New Zealand saw several individuals in treatment who ran pubs and who found it difficult to refuse an offer of a drink from one of their customers. Many of these people decided to change professions following treatment because they were always drinking rather heavily in this job setting.

One should accept this overly simplistic use of the typological system with caution since, in the real world, attempting to establish treatment programs for patients is usually much more complex and a number of factors, like availability of resources and the feasibility of possible changes, must go into the decision about which treatment plan will be followed. Still, the examples given do show that typologies have the potential to add a great deal to treatment decisions and to making judgments about the prognosis of a client.

The preceding is not an exhaustive review of typologies. However, the review does point out the potential utility of this approach to classifying alcohol problems. There are also some inherent dangers. It is easy to drift into the habit of seeing the assignment of a patient to a typology as explaining all that must be known in order to understand and treat that particular patient. There is a danger of ignoring important individual differences that may bear on treatment if typologies are blindly accepted as a way of understanding people and of planning for their care. When that occurs, the treatment is based upon stereotypes of the alcoholic and not on the people being seen for treatment. Thus, while typologies are potentially useful in planning treatment, they can become a negative factor if they are used in place of planning an individualized program for a person in treatment.

REFERENCES

American Psychiatric Association. (1980). *Diagnostic and statistical manual of mental disorders* (3rd ed.) Washington, DC.

Blane, H. T. (1979). Middle-aged alcoholics and young drinkers. In H. T. Blane & M. E. Chafetz (Eds.), *Youth, alcohol and social policy* (pp. 5–38). New York: Plenum Press.

Bowman, K. M., & Jellinek, E. M. (1941). Alcohol addiction and its treatment. *Quarterly Journal of Studies on Alcohol, 2,* 98–175.

Cahalan, D. (1970). *Problem drinkers.* San Francisco: Jossey-Bass.

Chafetz, M. E. (1982). Safe and healthy drinking. In E. M. Pattison & E. Kaufman (Eds.), *Encyclopedic handbook of alcoholism* (pp. 483–489). New York: Gardner Press.

Ellis, A. (1970). *Reason and emotion in psychotherapy.* New York: Lyle Stuart.

Hoffman, H., Loper, R. G., & Kammeier, M. L. (1974). Identifying future alcoholics with MMPI scales. *Quarterly Journal of Studies on Alcohol, 35,* 490–498.

Jellinek, E. M. (1952). Phases of alcohol addiction. *Quarterly Journal of Studies on Alcohol, 13,* 673–684.

Jellinek, E. M. (1960). *The disease concept of alcoholism.* New Haven, CT: Hillhouse Press.

Jessor, R. (1985). Adolescent problem drinking: Psychosocial aspects and developmental outcomes. In L. H. Towle (Ed.), *Proceedings: of the National Institute on Alcohol Abuse and Alcoholism–World Health Organization Collaborating Center Designation Meeting and Alcohol Research Seminar.* (DHHS Publication No. ADM 85–2370 (pp. 104–143). Washington, DC: U.S. Government Printing Office.

Jones, M. C. (1968). Personality correlates and antecedents of drinking patterns in adult males. *Journal of Consulting and Clinical Psychology, 32,* 2–12.

Jones, M. C. (1971). Personality antecedents and correlates of drinking patterns in women. *Journal of Consulting and Clinical Psychology, 36,* 61–69.

Knupfer, G. (1967). The epidemiology of problem drinking. *American Journal of Public Health, 59,* 973–986.

Meyer, R. E., Babor, T. F., & Mirkin, P. M. (1983). Typologies in alcoholism: An overview. *International Journal of the Addictions, 18,* 235–249.

Pattison, E. M., & Kaufman, E. (1982). The alcoholism syndrome: Definitions and models. In E. M. Pattison & E. Kaufman (Eds.), *Encyclopedic handbook of alcoholism* (pp. 3–23). New York: Gardner Press.

Plaut, T. F. (1967). *Alcohol problems: A report to the nation by the Cooperative Commission on the Study of Alcoholism.* New York: Oxford University Press.

Schuckit, M. A., Pitts, F. N., Reich, T., King, L. J., & Winokur, G. (1969). Alcoholism I: Two types of alcoholism in women. *Archives of General Psychiatry, 20,* 301–306.

Shelly, C. H., & Goldstein, G. (1976). An empirically devised typology of hospitalized alcoholics. In D. Goldstein & C. Neuringer (Eds.), *Empirical studies of alcoholism* (pp. 193–229). New York: Ballinger.

Wanberg, K. W., & Knapp, J. (1970). A multidimensional model for the research and treatment of alcoholism. *International Journal of the Addictions, 5,* 69–98.

Williams, A. F. (1966). Social drinking, anxiety, and depression. *Journal of Personality and Social Psychology, 3,* 689–693.

Williams, A. F. (1968). Psychological needs and social drinking among college students. *Quarterly Journal of Studies on Alcohol, 29,* 355–363.

World Health Organization. (1954). Expert Committee on Alcohol, First Report, *World Health Organization Report Series,* No. 84.

Zucker, R. A., (1987). The four alcoholisms: A developmental account of the etiologic process. In P. C. Rivers (Ed.), *Alcohol and addictive behavior: Vol. 34. Nebraska Symposium on Motivation* (pp. 27–83). Lincoln: University of Nebraska Press.

Scope of the Problem

_____ *chapter 3*

Drinking alcoholic beverages is a common behavior in the United States. While drinking patterns vary, the majority of drinkers use alcohol in constructive ways. Some people drink only as a part of religious ritual or to celebrate special occasions. Some people may drink a cocktail when they come home in the evening as a means of relaxing and forgetting about the world of work, while others may have a drink at lunch as a part of their jobs. Still other individuals drink only when they are with other people as part of a social gathering and they find themselves more at ease after having had a drink or two. Most people who drink do not abuse alcohol nor do they become problem drinkers or alcoholics.

However, an estimated 9 to 12 million drinkers in the United States have drinking patterns that are significantly different from the others. These drinkers are the alcohol abusers and alcoholics. Their drinking causes difficulties for themselves and the people around them.

In the United States, there has been a longstanding awareness and fear of problems caused by other drugs such as marijuana, heroin, cocaine, and crack (one of cocaine's most addictive forms). It is only in recent years that the public has become aware of the damage alcohol abuse causes to society. This chapter surveys the epidemiology of alcohol use and abuse in the United States, that is, the incidence (frequency or range of occurrence of a condition) and prevalence (the number of cases of a disease existing in a given area or at a given time). It also discusses the economic, social, and physical impact of alcohol abuse on American society and culture.

Alcoholism is the most widespread drug problem per capita in the United States in terms of physical, social, and economic costs. Despite this fact, other drugs often get more public attention. *(Photograph courtesy of the Independence Center, Lincoln, Nebraska.)*

EPIDEMIOLOGY AND SOCIAL PROBLEMS

Apparent per capita consumption is derived by dividing the total amount of alcohol in gallons bought by the total population of people 14 years of age or older. In 1984, it was estimated that the alcohol consumption for the entire U.S. population 14 years of age and older was the equivalent of 2.65 gallons of pure alcohol per person. (This amount of alcohol would be found in approximately 50 gallons of beer, 20 gallons of wine, or more than 4 gallons of distilled spirits.) In 1987, apparent alcohol consumption was 2.54 gallons of pure alcohol. This was the lowest level since 1970 (U.S. Department of Health and Human Services [DHHS], 1990). The decline was primarily in the drinking of spirits. Spirits consumption dropped to 0.83 gallons per capita, which was the lowest since 1958. One reason for the decreased alcohol consumption that began in 1981 is that the public has become more aware of the risks associated with alcohol abuse. However, there has also been a decrease in the number of people in the age groups that are more likely to abuse alcohol. The segment of the population who are younger and drink more is growing smaller. On the other hand, the proportion of people over 60 years of age is increasing and these people have low rates of drinking.

Alcohol use is not evenly distributed. Ten percent of the drinking population consumes 50 percent of all alcohol sold. It is estimated that about 66 percent of Americans over 18 years of age drink. While the per capita consumption figures may seem large to most people, they are actually a reduction from earlier years in amount consumed. After a steady rise in alcohol consumption since 1960, an apparent downward trend occurred in 1981 (see Figure 3–1). Consumption of both beer and distilled spirits declined in 1984, although there was a slight increase in wine consumption (see Figure 3–2). This continued an upward trend in consumption of wine which began in the 1960s.

About one-third of Americans over the age of 18 are abstainers, one third are light drinkers, and one-third are moderate to heavy drinkers (Clark & Midnik 1982; Malin, Wilson, Williams, & Aitken, 1986). In every age group, men consume more alcohol than do women and there are more males than females who drink heavily. Whites of both genders are less likely to be abstainers than are other racial and ethnic groups. Asian-Americans and Native Americans have relatively high proportions of their groups who abstain. While there seems to be a trend toward more abstainers (Malin et al., 1986), preliminary reports indicate little change in the numbers of moderate and heavy drinkers. This means that the drinking groups may be becoming more extreme in their practices with more abstainers and fewer light drinkers.

FIGURE 3–1 Apparent U.S. per capita consumption of pure alcohol, 1977–1987. *(Adapted from* Seventh Special Report to Congress, *National Institute on Alcohol Abuse and Alcoholism, U.S. DHHS Publication No. ADM 90–1656. 1990, p. 14.)*

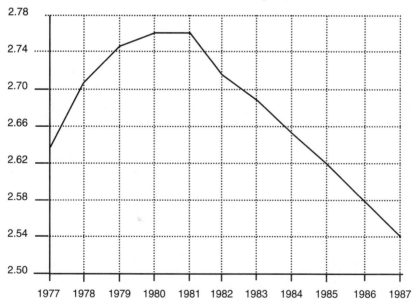

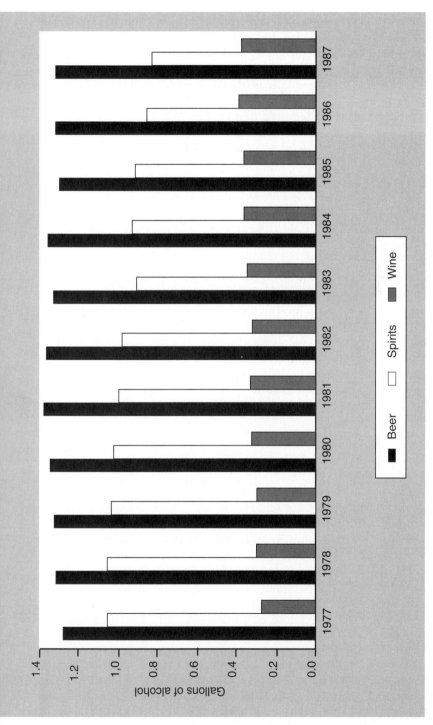

FIGURE 3–2 Apparent U.S. per capita consumption of beer, wine, and spirits, 1977–1987. *(Adapted from Seventh Special Report to Congress, National Institute on Alcohol Abuse and Alcoholism, U.S. DHHS Publicaton No. ADM 90–1656. 1990, p. 15.)*

There are suggestions that there has been a drop in alcohol-related mortalities in the United States. For example, Stinson and DeBakey (1992) found that there had been a decrease in deaths that could be directly attributed to alcohol and in deaths from diseases, injuries, and deleterious effects that could be indirectly blamed on alcohol. In a category they call "all deaths attributable to alcohol," deaths dropped from 49.8 per hundred thousand people in 1979 to 43.9 per hundred thousand in 1988. While there are probably multiple reasons for this drop in deaths, Westermeyer (1992) suggests it may be partly due to a drop in accidental deaths and deaths from cirrhosis in middle-aged men.

There are regional drinking patterns in the United States. Based on data from liquor sales and self-reports of drinking, 79 percent of persons over 21 years of age in the Northeast drink, while 72.2 percent of midwesterners drink. In the South, only 51.6 percent of the population over 21 years old use alcohol. The West falls somewhere in between with 66 percent of persons over 21 years of age using alcohol (U.S. DHHS, 1987).

There are important issues regarding drinking habits among people who are designated as belonging to special populations. Special population groups can be expanded to an unlimited number of groups. One book has fifteen special populations (see Lawson & Lawson, 1989). An overview of the epidemiology of women, adolescents, the elderly, and ethnic minorities will be presented in this chapter.

SPECIAL POPULATIONS

Women

It has been suggested that women may face different sources of stress in their lives than do men due to increased family demands. Shifts in stereotypical expectations and roles for the sexes have led to some major modifications in American society. Fewer households are composed of husbands as wage earners and wives as full-time homemakers. There has been an increase in households where both spouses are wage earners and in households that are headed by divorced, separated, or never-married women. Divorced mothers, for example, are the women most likely to be wage earners (Fellios, 1989).

Up until 1980, most national surveys of drinking included little information on women. In 1981 Wilsnack and her collaborators collected data that give a more accurate picture of women's drinking practices and problems (Wilsnack, Wilsnack, & Klassen, 1984; Wilsnack, Wilsnack, & Klassen, 1985; Wilsnack, Wilsnack, & Klassen, 1987). A comparison of their results with eight previous surveys of women's drinking shows no significant increase in women's drinking in the 10 years preceding the Wilsnack et al. survey. The majority of women continue to be either abstainers (39 percent) or light drinkers (38 percent). The one change in patterns from the 1970s is an apparent increase in consumption among middle-aged women (age 35 to 64) with both more drinkers and more heavy drinkers in this age group than have been found in previous surveys. Wilsnack et al. anticipated that there would be an increase in drinking or in heavier drinking among the younger age group (age 21 to 34) compared to previous surveys. No increase was found. In a separate study, Fillmore (1984) also found increases in consumption among middle-aged women. In addition, Fillmore found that women in their twenties, particularly those employed, had a higher rate of frequent heavy drinking than did earlier samples of women of the same age and background. Fillmore's findings are consistent with those of Hilton (1987, 1988), who also found overall stability in women's drinking over several years and several surveys, with the exception of the increase in the percent of heavy drinkers in middle-aged women. In another report, Fillmore (1987) found that the onset of both heavy drinking and drinking-related problems occurred earlier in the drinking careers of women than of men. While men reported chronic problems with alcohol in their forties and fifties, women reported chronic alcohol difficulties in their thirties. These comparisons of men's and women's chronic problems with alcohol suggest a reduced time frame between the onset of drinking and the occurrence of chronic problems in women when compared to men (U.S. DHHS, 1990). There have been several other issues associated with women's drinking:

Economic Status. A number of studies on drinking patterns in women provide information about who drinks what, when, and how. Lower socioeconomic and less well educated women are more likely to be abstainers. Half the women with household incomes of less than $10,000 a year and 68 percent of women with no more than an eighth-grade education are abstainers, compared with 39 percent for all women surveyed. Low-income women who do drink are more likely to drink heavily or to drink to intoxication. Women who are divorced or separated or who have never married are unlikely to be abstainers. However, very few women in this group are heavy drinkers. Many of these differences in drinking practices can be accounted for by age differences. Perhaps surprisingly, married women with paid employment are somewhat less likely than full-time homemakers to be heavy drinkers. Moderate drinking is more common among married women who work outside the home and especially so among those with part-time jobs.

Drinking of Significant Others. There is a close relationship between the amount women drink and the number of significant others (husbands, siblings, close friends) whom they perceive as frequent drinkers. If the women report that husbands or partners are frequent drinkers, then the women are more likely to report heavy drinking, drinking-related problems, or symptoms of alcohol dependence. On the other hand, if women describe their husbands as problem drinkers (rather than frequent drinkers), then those women are less likely to report that they themselves are dependent upon alcohol (Wilsnack et al., 1987).

Wife Battering. Russell (1982) found in 63 percent of battering cases wives reported that their husbands were sometimes, usually, or always drinking when they became violent. Leonard and Jacob (1988) found that many abused wives consider their husbands to be alcohol-dependent. Leonard, Bromet, Parkinson, Day, & Ryan (1985), in a study of male factory workers, discovered that physical conflict with wives was more than twice as likely among workers who met the criteria for alcohol dependency. Leonard et al. also discovered several interesting relationships when male factory workers were asked about alcohol problems, wife abuse, level of marital satisfaction, and general level of hostility. This relationship of alcohol dependence to spouse abuse was maintained, even after controlling for marital satisfaction, hostility, and social/demographic factors. A national telephone survey of more than 5,000 U.S. families found that the combination of blue-collar status, drinking, and approval of violence was associated with wife abuse (Kantor & Straus, 1987). In this study, the probability of violence tended to increase with frequency and amount of drinking (U.S. DHHS, 1990).

Reproductive Dysfunction. Wilsnack et al. (1984) found a strong association between levels of drinking and dysmenorrhea, heavy menstrual flow, and menstrual discomfort. Women who drink 1.5 ounces of ethanol a day or who experience at least five 3-ounce drinking episodes per week have higher rates of gynecologic surgery. Miscarriage, still birth, premature birth, birth defects, and infertility are associated with the highest levels of alcohol consumption.

Adolescents

Adolescents are another population who present special problems in the alcohol field. One study found that adolescents tend to self-report higher rates of alcohol use than do adults. In the same study, more adolescents reported their drinking to be a moderate to serious problem than did adults (Holland & Griffin, 1984). It is possible that the normal growth changes that adolescents experience can increase the risk for alcohol abuse. Any change, for example, voice change, rapid skeletal growth, acne, hair growth in the genital and other body areas, and menstruation, can be experienced by adolescents as threatening. Young persons become aware of new sexual roles that are both exciting and frightening. All this can make adolescents feel unsure of themselves and awkward in interpersonal relations.

It is in this context of growth and rapid change that adolescents are typically introduced to their first drink. How they are introduced to it seems to have long-term implications for the way they use alcohol. In one study, whether students took their first drink with parental knowledge predicted the rate of occurrence of alcohol problems later experienced in their college years. Those students who were introduced to alcohol with parental consent experienced fewer behavioral complications from their use of alcohol during their college years than did students who were introduced to alcohol without parental consent (Archambault, 1989).

Personality and relationship factors also seem to play a role in adolescent drinking problems. For example, those adolescents who are more detached from society and more involved with peer groups or themselves are more likely to move into heavy drinking (Archambault, 1989).

Although recent figures from the National Institute of Drug Abuse (1988) indicate a decline in adolescent use and abuse of alcohol, the proportion of users remains high. In 1987 two-thirds of high school seniors were current drinkers. More than one-third (and nearly half the males) indulged in occasional heavy drinking (U.S. DHHS, 1990). Figure 3–3 gives a graphic indicator of teenage drinking. The attitudes toward alcohol by these seniors were also alarming. For example, about one-third did not perceive a great risk in having four or five drinks nearly every day. About one-third still reported that most or all of their friends got drunk at least once a week. An even more alarming report was that 10 percent had their first drink by grade six (Johnston, O'Malley & Bachman, 1988, cited in U.S. DHHS, 1990).

Elderly

While adolescents have special risk problems with alcohol, those who are elderly also have special concerns. Like adolescents, the elderly are forced to deal with personal life changes that can be stressful. Hearing and vision losses may lead to reduced communication with others and the world around them. These physical limitations may reduce the availability of activities that help maintain self-esteem and self-worth. They also add to an increasing isolation from people who could provide support for alcohol-abusing older adults (Rivers, Rivers, & Newman, 1991).

Many of the elderly are depressed by the loss of family and friends. Many of the depressed may attempt suicide or may turn to alcohol and other drugs in attempts to deal with depression, loneliness, and isolation. Alcohol-abuse rates in people over 65 years of age are relatively low, but the incidence is higher among widowers, nursing home residents, and psychiatric patients (U.S. DHHS, 1990).

Elderly alcoholics differ from younger alcoholics in some significant ways. They may drink less on a particular occasion but drink more often. Their drinking is much less likely to be a pattern that requires detoxification and that includes severe withdrawal symptoms. Elderly alcoholics tend to be more psychologically dependent (and less physiologically dependent) than younger alcoholics. The interaction of drugs and alcohol is also different for younger and older alcoholics. Many of the elderly are on medications that can interact with alcohol. This presents a constant danger for many older

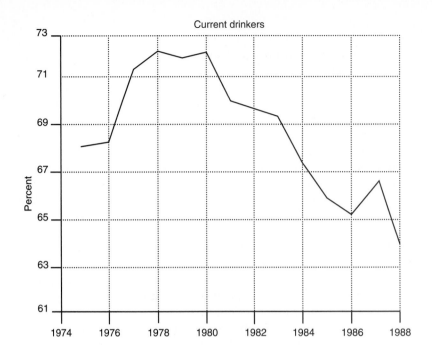

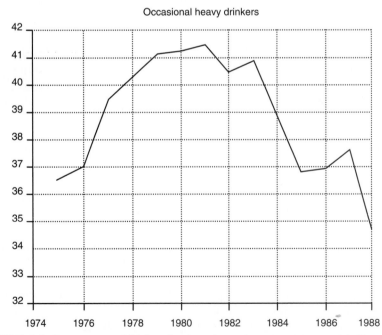

FIGURE 3–3 Percentage of high school seniors who were current drinkers (used alcohol in past 30 days) and percentage who were occasional heavy drinkers (took five or more drinks at a single sitting during the past 2 weeks), 1975–1988. *(Data from Johnston, O'Malley, and Bachman (1989) and cited in* Seventh Special Report to Congress, *National Institute on Alcohol Abuse and Alcoholism, U.S. DHHS Publication No. ADM 90–1656. 1990, p. 27.)*

drinkers. These interactions can lead to confusion, sedation, and possibly death (Lawson, 1989).

For many years it was generally assumed that alcohol abuse is reduced by old age or brought to a halt by the death of the abuser. Articles have been written describing alcoholism as a self-limiting disease (Drew, 1968), that is, a disease cut short by the death of the alcohol abuser. However, with the increasing number of people who are or who will live to be 65 years or older (by the year 2025, 17.2 percent of the U.S. population), elderly drinkers have become a concern. Significant risks for the elderly include health problems and reduced memory and attention span. Professionals have begun to focus on ways to prevent, intervene in, and treat alcohol abuse among this population.

There are two very different types of elderly problem drinkers: those who begin to abuse alcohol early in life and on into old age, and those who do not develop alcohol-related problems until their later years (Holzer et al. 1984; Williams, 1984). The early onset problem drinkers probably account for two-thirds or more of elderly alcohol abusers. The long-term alcohol abuse often results in severe medical problems, particularly diseases of the liver, heart, intestinal tract, and pancreas. The less than one-third of alcohol abusers who are late onset abusers usually drink in response to some late-life stress such as death of a spouse, retirement, reduced income, poor health, or geographic relocation.

Minority Groups

Drinkers from minority groups also present special issues in terms of alcohol abuse.

African-Americans. African-Americans, the largest minority in the United States (about 12 percent of the total population and 92 percent of the nonwhite population), have significant problems associated with alcohol use. Despite their relatively large numbers, very little research has been done on drinking among this population. Brown and Tooley (1989) review research on African-Americans and alcohol. They state that alcoholism is the number one health problem in the African-American community. Alcoholism and other health problems reduce life expectancies for African-Americans by almost 6 years when compared with whites.

Part of the African-American alcohol problem has been blamed on economic factors. In 1986, the African-American poverty ratio was 31 percent. The African-American median income is still only 57 percent of that of whites. Many African-American men drink because of unemployment and the inability to provide for themselves and their families. Another economic reality is that alcoholic beverages are readily available for sale in poorer African-American neighborhoods. For example, in some predominantly

African-American sections of Los Angeles there are as many as three liquor outlets per block as well as several beer and wine outlets.

Brown and Tooley cite a study in their review that describes the custom of African-Americans receiving weekly pay on Friday and then using the weekend to relax, visit, and drink. Alcohol is also viewed as a way to escape from personal problems. Brown and Tooley also compare African-American drinkers with abstainers. There are significant differences in psychological problems. Drinkers have more depressive symptoms than nondrinkers, and the amount of alcohol drunk is positively correlated with the degree of depression reported. While the sample size in this study was small (Neff, 1986) and generalizations should be made with caution, the investigation does suggest that drinking among African-Americans reduces tension and distress. It is used like a tranquilizer.

Two survey studies have found African-Americans of both sexes to have higher rates of abstention than do whites (Herd, 1989). Among drinkers, white men are more likely to be heavy drinkers than African-American men. The reverse is true for female drinkers, with African-American women more likely to drink heavily than white women (Clark & Midnik, 1982; Malin, Wilson, Williams & Aitken, 1986). Another study has found that there are significant age group differences in the drinking patterns of African-American and white males. The highest consumption rates for whites are in the 18 to 29 age group. Consumption is relatively low for African-Americans in that age range but rises sharply when these men move into their thirties (Caetano, 1984). Both of these findings regarding male and female drinking patterns and ages have been confirmed by other studies.

When African-Americans do abuse alcohol they are at high risk for certain alcohol-related causes of disease and death. In particular, liver cirrhosis and the associated disorders of fatty liver and hepatitis occur at high rates in African-Americans.

Geographic shifts in the African-American population are associated with increased rates of cirrhosis of the liver. For example, migrating to the urban North and the coastal South is related to increased cirrhosis death rates in nonwhites. In contrast, cirrhosis mortality rates remain low in the Deep South where there is a large and relatively stable rural African-American population. In this same Deep South area, cirrhosis deaths for whites rose more than they did among whites in the urban North during the same time period. It may be that the stresses and strains of adjusting to urban ghetto living and also losing the support of people and institutions in their former communities contribute to increased drinking, which leads to the increased deaths among African-Americans. Alcohol treatment programs in urban, northeastern states report increases in African-American patients, who are admitted at two to three times the rate of admissions in the population as a whole. In the Deep South, the number of African-Americans in treatment is generally proportional to their numbers in the population at large (Herd, 1985). This same study indicated that despite their late onset of drinking, African-Americans enter treatment at younger ages than do whites. Peak ages for admission of African-Americans is 35 to 44 years. The largest group for whites is between 45 and 54 years of age. As noted earlier, while African-American and white men have similar overall consumption levels, higher rates of all kinds of social and health complications occur in African-American men (U.S. DHHS, 1990).

As one might predict, the high problem rates are concentrated among those men who are more socioeconomically disadvantaged (Herd, 1989). These findings raise questions about the biological vulnerability of African-Americans to alcohol use and abuse and suggest more research is needed to decide the question of whether the more severe alcohol-related problems in African-American men are related to socioeconomic issues or to biological predisposition.

Hispanics. One of the major population shifts in the latter half of this century is the increase in the number of Hispanics in the U.S. population. In 1980 there were more than 15 million Hispanics in the United States, more than 6 percent of the total population. It should be understood that Hispanics are not a homogeneous group. They have diverse cultural, national, and racial backgrounds. However, taken as a whole, Hispanics suffer from several socioeconomic problems that may contribute to drinking problems. These factors may include high unemployment and failure to obtain better jobs. Twenty-two percent of Hispanic Americans had incomes below the poverty line in 1980 compared with 11 percent of non-Hispanic workers (Eden & Aguilar, 1989).

There are also traditional and social reasons why Hispanics may be susceptible to abusing alcohol. In traditional Hispanic cultures, drinking of alcohol is used to bind the community together and increase cohesion in the society. When alcohol use is an acceptable behavior in communities, it may be more readily available to help deal with the personal stresses. In Hispanic communities, many people are struggling with social and cultural adaptation. In addition, the concept of "machismo" suggests that consuming alcoholic beverages is an accepted behavior for males. It may be that even second- and third-generation males view drinking as the "macho" thing to do (Eden & Aguilar, 1989).

When Hispanics move into the broader culture and away from their families, they are faced with learning new social values. Social and cultural changes and the sense of cultural distancing occur. This distancing may be accompanied by feelings of betrayal, guilt, and doubt for persons who see themselves drifting away from their families of origin. In families where these changes are occurring, both the parents and the children may experience stress and may use alcohol to help deal with their problems.

Hispanic adolescents are particularly susceptible to risks associated with cultural changes. There may be wide differences, for example, in education, speech, and social values between parent and child. Again, the parents or children or both may use alcohol to deal with these difficult life-transition problems.

For newly immigrated Hispanics, social rejection by the larger culture may lead to lower self-esteem, which can increase psychological risks. Low feelings of self-worth can lead to using alcohol as a way to deal with those feelings (Eden & Aguilar, 1989).

The Sixth and Seventh Special Reports to Congress (U.S. DHHS, 1987, 1990) cite Caetano's research as the first truly representative nationwide survey of Hispanics. Caetano found that almost half (47 percent) of the Hispanic women in his study abstained while another 24 percent drank less than once a month. On the other hand, only 22 percent of the males abstained and 36 percent were heavy to moderately heavy drinkers, that is, they drank at least once a week and sometimes consumed five or more drinks at one sitting. Males tended to drink more heavily in their thirties than in their twenties, with consumption declining after 40 years of age. In both sexes there was a significant decline in consumption after age 60. Women showed a rise in consumption in their forties and fifties. In both sexes, increased drinking was associated with increased education and income levels.

Caetano's survey data were analyzed according to national origins. Mexican American men had the highest abstention rates and the highest rate of heavy drinking compared with Hispanics from Cuba, Puerto Rico, or other Latin American countries. Mexican American females drank more heavily than the other Hispanic groups but also had a high rate of abstaining. Puerto Rican women were primarily moderate drinkers and had the lowest rate of abstention and few heavy drinkers.

Hispanic men, unlike men in the general population, did not show a drop in their drinking between their twenties and thirties. Drinking problems remained high until their forties. Problem rates among Hispanic women in their twenties were high. The women reported rates for some problems (for example, importance of drinking, impaired control over alcohol consumption, health problems) that were not far below those reported for men in the same age groups. However, heavy drinking among men was eight times higher (Caetano, 1984). This suggests that health effects of abusive drinking for Hispanic females is greater than that for males. These findings are consistent with findings for alcohol abuse in women in general.

Native Americans and Alaskan Natives. No two minority groups in the United States have higher relative rates of alcoholism and alcohol problems than do Native Americans and Alaskan Natives (Hill, 1989). An overview of the rate of alcohol use among Native Americans shows that drinking rates vary considerably across different groups. Alcohol use among Native American tribes varies from abstinence to heavy use. A recent study of eleven tribes in Oklahoma found a wide range in proportion of alcohol-relat-ed deaths, from 1 percent to 24 percent (Christian, Dufour & Bertolucci, 1989, cited in U.S. DHHS, 1990). Utes, Ojibwas, and Standing Rock Sioux have drinking and heavy drinking rates that exceed drinking rates for the population as a whole. The Navajo have lower rates than the total U.S. popu-lation. Some writers suggest that the absorption rate for alcohol by Native Americans may be faster than that for other ethnic groups. Nonabusing Native Americans also have a high tolerance toward alcohol abuse in family members. These two factors may account for the higher rate of alcohol prob-lems in Native Americans (Hill, 1989).

While the 1.5 million Native Americans and Alaskan Natives constitute less than 1 percent of the total population, their problems with alcohol are highly disproportionate to their numbers. For example, Lex (1985) reports that the number of people discharged from Native American hospitals fol-lowing alcohol-related illnesses was three times the rate for the general popu-lation in 1979. Accidents, cirrhosis, alcoholism, homicide, and suicide occur most frequently in the younger age groups. In the Native American popula-tion, accidents account for 20 percent of deaths. Of these accidental deaths, 75 percent are alcohol related. Accidents are the leading cause of death in Alaska, accounting for 23 percent of all deaths in 1983, compared with 4½ percent for the United States as a whole. The 1983 accidental-death rate was 146 per hundred-thousand among Alaskan Natives compared with 82 per hundred thousand for all Alaskans and 39 per hundred thousand for the general U.S. population.

In another study, Rhoades, Hammond, Welty, Handler, and Amler (1987) found an estimated 75 percent of all traumatic deaths and suicides by Native Americans were alcohol related. Christian et al. (1989) found 9 per-cent of deaths among Native Americans in Oklahoma were due to alcohol while only 2 percent of whites' deaths were so classified.

Homicide is the cause of a little over 3 percent of deaths among Native Americans, more than double the rate in the U.S. population. An estimated 90 percent of Native American homicides are related to alcohol use (Lex, 1985). Suicide among Native American is also very high, almost double that for the population at large. An estimated 80 percent of all Native American suicides are alcohol related (U.S. DHHS, 1987, 1990). There is wide variabili-ty for suicide and all alcohol-related problems across tribes. Suicide rates are particularly high among Alaskan Natives, but these rates declined between 1975 and 1981, dropping from 43 percent to 18 percent of all Alaskan suicides.

As was noted about females in other special populations, Native American females seem to have severe problems as a result of alcohol abuse. That is particularly true of deaths from cirrhosis. Although Native American women drink less than do men, they account for nearly half of the Native American deaths from cirrhosis (Indian Health Service, 1988). They are also at high risk for problems with fetal alcohol syndrome if they drink while pregnant. (See Chapter 4 for more information on fetal alcohol syndrome.)

ECONOMIC FACTORS

A current projection of the economic cost of alcohol abuse and dependence suggests costs are expected to increase from $116.9 billion in 1983 to $150 billion in 1995 (Harwood, Kristiansen & Rachal, 1985, cited in U.S. DHHS, 1990). This projected increase is 2 percent per year and is based on the expected population increase of drinkers (and associated drinking problems) of the maturing "baby boom" generation and the consequent growth in workforce productivity. These projections are in 1983 dollars and do not allow for inflation. In the 1983 estimate, nearly $71 billion of the cost of alcoholism is designated as costs of lost employment and lowered productivity, and $15 billion is due to health care costs and treatment (U.S. DHHS, 1990).

One of the economic concerns about alcohol abuse is the cost of treatment. Does treatment of persons for alcohol problems have the potential for eventually paying off? Siegel, Haughland, Goodman, and Wanderling (1984) report cost comparisons between treatment of alcoholics and other mental health patients. They used a sample from Rockland County, New York, and found that while alcoholics were the largest percentage of those treated (39 percent), the cost of their care was only 22 percent of the total cost for care of alcohol and other mental health problems combined. The lesser cost was due to two factors. Alcoholics had fewer total inpatient days and received fewer days of the most costly outpatient service, full-day treatment. According to these researchers, on the average, alcohol services are less costly than treating mental health patients.

When other mental health disorders are compared to alcohol treatment, treatment costs seem favorable. However, the distribution of costs across alcohol patients is uneven. For example, Costello and Hodde (1981) found that five out of 100 patients account for 48 percent of total inpatient treatment costs over a four-year period. They also found that the high-expense patients tend to stay in inpatient treatment for long periods of time. Two of the five patients in their sample were still receiving inpatient care after four years. In Lincoln, Nebraska, a few patients account for a large number of the yearly admissions to a detoxification center. The problem has been so chronic that an attempt was made to reduce some of the repeaters by admitting them to a long-term, inpatient care program within the detoxification center.

The ultimate question about providing treatment is, Do the benefits from treatment offset the financial costs? Several studies suggest that alcohol treatment is cost effective. Up to a 40 percent reduction in the utilization of outpatient health care costs following alcohol treatment has been reported

(Brock & Boyajy, 1978). A 27 percent reduction in health care costs for treated alcoholics has been reported at Kaiser Permanente in California (Sherman, Reiff, & Forsythe,1979). Several other investigators have reported similar results, although the percentage reduction in overall health care costs varies considerably across studies. One study reports a reduction of annual health care costs of $864 per treated alcoholic in a health insurance plan (Holder & Hallan, 1981, cited in the U.S. DHHS, 1987). While the above findings show variability in degree of savings, it is clear that alcohol treatment is not only effective in many cases but also has been shown to reduce total health care costs. Treatment would appear to be one approach to cost containment in the total health care system.

SOCIAL ISSUES

Alcohol plays a major role in many kinds of social problems in the United States. For example, it is clear that alcohol plays a direct role in impairing the skill of drivers and increasing the probability of traffic accidents. In other social problems, like child and spouse abuse, alcohol abuse may not be the primary cause, but it may contribute significantly to the problem by reducing inhibitions that otherwise curb anger and aggressive behavior.

Traffic Accidents

Traffic accidents are the fifth leading cause of death in the United States and the leading cause of death among people under the age of 35 (U.S. DHHS, 1983). During 1984, motor vehicle accidents were the most common nonnatural cause of death in this country. During 1987, there were 46,386 people in the United States who died in automobile accidents. About half these deaths were alcohol related (National Highway Traffic Safety Administration, 1988). One estimate suggests that the risk of a fatal crash per mile driven may be at least eight times higher for a drunk driver (a driver with a blood alcohol content [BAC] of 0.10 or higher) than for a sober driver (Fell, 1987). The following story may be useful as an example of how alcohol can affect driving judgment. A deputy sheriff on routine night patrol came upon a car with its lights on and its motor revved up very high with the rear wheels spinning. It had been raining and the driver had run off the road into a muddy ditch. His wheels had no traction. When the deputy looked into the car, he saw the obviously intoxicated driver squinting ahead and "driving" the car in a deliberate manner. When the deputy knocked on the window, the driver looked at him in shocked surprise and slammed on the brakes to "stop" the car! While this story is humorous, it suggests the effect alcohol can have on a driver's judgment. This poor judgment is dangerous for the driver and for other people on the highway. The Fatal Accident Reporting System (FARS) contains data on all fatal traffic accidents in the

United States. FARS data show that the percentage of drivers with BACs equal to or greater than 0.10 (the legal BAC intoxication level in the United States) decreased from 46 percent in 1980 to approximately 38 percent in 1987 (U.S. DHHS, 1990).

Despite the above reduction, automobile crashes are still a serious factor in American society. Using the FARS data previously discussed, estimated Years of Potential Life Lost (YPLL) due to alcohol-related accidents can be calculated. This statistic is calculated by subtracting the actual age of death from the arbitrary number of 65 years of age. It was found that 11.9 percent of total YPLL was related to automobile accidents. More than half of these automobile accidents' YPLLs were related to alcohol use and abuse.

Fell (1983) looked at age groups and alcohol abuse among all licensed drivers. He found that 18-year-olds were involved in 5.5 percent of the alcohol-related accidents, although 18-year-olds made up only 2.2 percent of the drivers and drove less than 2 percent of the total miles driven by the entire sample. The 45 to 54 age group had six times as many drivers as the 18-year-olds and drove nine times as many miles. Compared with 18-year-olds, there were one-third as many alcohol-related fatal accidents in the 45 to 54 age group. The trend for younger drivers to have proportionately more alcohol-related accidents per miles driven has been a consistent finding for at least a decade. Alcohol is also a significant factor in pedestrian and bicyclist fatalities as shown by blood-alcohol tests. In the 41 percent of this group given blood tests, 42 percent had a BAC that exceeded 0.10. In 23 percent of the tests, the BAC level was 0.20 or higher.

The closing summary of the *Seventh Special Report to Congress* (U.S. DHHS, 1990) regarding traffic accidents is a nice, succinct statement of the state of affairs regarding traffic accidents and alcohol: "In summary, while the proportion of intoxicated persons (drivers, pedestrians, or bicyclists) killed in fatal crashes has been declining, approximately one-half of all crash fatalities have been alcohol related. Further, traffic crashes continue to be the single leading cause of death for people between the ages of 5 and 34 . . ." (p.165).

Other Accidents

A Maryland study (reported in the *Fifth Special Report to Congress,* U.S. DHHS, 1984) on workers who died in job-related accidents found that 11 percent had blood alcohol concentrations (BACs) above 0.08. Alcohol use was also related to other types of accidents. This study demonstrates that blood alcohol concentrations should be taken in all industrial accidents.

A study of the medical and social consequences of drinking among a large sample of railroad employees estimated that 19 percent of the work force were problem drinkers. Problem drinkers were defined as those per-

Alcohol is frequently a factor in automobile accidents, such as this one on a midwestern highway. *(Photograph courtesy of the Independence Center, Lincoln, Nebraska.)*

sons whose alcohol use caused harm to themselves or to others (Mannello & Seaman, 1979). According to the *Federal Register* (1986), between 1975 and 1984, alcohol-impaired or drug-impaired employees were implicated in 48 train accidents or incidents, which resulted in 37 deaths, 80 nonfatal injuries, and $34.2 million in damage.

Ten and one-half percent of the pilots fatally injured in general aviation accidents have measurable levels of alcohol in their bodies. Studies by several states indicate that 75 to 80 percent of boating accidents and deaths are alcohol related. In 35 to 38 percent of these fatalities, the victims are legally intoxicated. These and other data suggest that from one-third to two-thirds of boating fatalities may be alcohol related (U.S. DHHS, 1987).

Alcohol was involved in over two-thirds of the deaths by drowning, the third leading cause of accidental deaths in the United States, between 1975 and 1984 (U.S. DHHS, 1987). Alcohol impairs psychomotor skills, spatial orientation and breath-holding time. All of these impairments could contribute to drowning deaths.

Despite these presumed connections between alcohol and drowning deaths, the assumption of a causal connection between alcohol and drowning deaths should be accepted with caution. Howland and Hingson (1988), in a review of research on alcohol and drowning, concluded that it was not possible to establish a clear-cut connection between the two factors. The failure to establish a link was due in part to the flawed research where comparison with the population at large was not included in most studies (U.S. DHHS, 1990).

A review of medical records of seventy burn victims over the age of 14 found that 46 percent of them had been using alcohol. The majority of the accidents occurred in the home or near a motor vehicle. More than half of the male victims and about one-fourth of the female burn patients had been drinking. Half of the male victims were between 15 and 26 years of age. One way of establishing the rate of burns in alcoholics is to study treated alcoholics. Combs-Orme, Taylor, Scott, and Holmes (1983) found that the proportion of deaths by fire among treated alcoholics in St. Louis was twenty-six times the expected rate when compared to St. Louis mortality rates. Howland and Hingson (1987) concluded from their survey of data on alcohol use and fire-related fatalities that alcohol use in conjunction with smoking presents a serious risk for fire injuries (cited in U.S. DHHS, 1990).

Falls are a major cause of trauma. Alcoholics are five to thirteen times more likely than nonalcoholics to die from falls (U.S. DHHS, 1984). A study of 313 emergency room patients who had suffered accidental falls found that 60 percent had detectable levels of alcohol in their blood. Fifty-three percent of these fall victims had BACs above 0.20 (twice the legal limit to drive in most states). This study showed that the higher the BAC level, the more likely that the fall could be attributed to alcohol abuse. A more recent review of twenty-one studies published between 1950 and 1985 on alcohol use and falls found that the percentage of alcohol-related fatal falls ranged from 17 to 53 percent across those studies. Alcohol-related, nonfatal falls ranged from 21 to 77 percent (Hingson & Howland, 1987).

Crime

While it is generally believed that alcohol abuse and crime are closely related, establishing that connection has been difficult. One early homicide study in 1958 found that either the murderer or the victim had been drinking in two-thirds of the slayings reviewed. Later studies have confirmed that the majority of murderers or their victims or both had been drinking prior to the crime (U.S. DHHS, 1984). A later report indicates that more than half of the offenders involved in crimes (54 percent) had used alcohol just before the offense. Alcohol involvement is particularly frequent in cases of manslaughter (68 percent) and assault (62 percent). There is less alcohol involvement in property crimes (40 percent). A closer examination suggests that if property crimes are committed by professional criminals, alcohol is less likely to be involved than if the crimes were committed by unskilled perpetrators.

While there is a positive correlation between alcohol and crime, this relationship should be accepted cautiously. A direct causal relationship has not been established. The majority of criminals are not alcoholics, and the majority of alcoholics have never committed a serious crime (Collins, 1981). The relationship between alcohol and crime may be confounded with age and sex. Males are more likely to abuse alcohol and more likely to be arrested for a crime. Drinking levels are more likely to be higher in young males, and most police arrests are likely to be of young males. What is needed in this area of inquiry are comparison or control groups (e.g., non-alcohol-abusing groups) to see if there is a differential crime participation in alcohol-abusing and non-alcohol-abusing groups.

It is also difficult to assess the role of alcohol in rape. Rape is a very underreported crime, and intoxication may be offered as an excuse or as an extenuating circumstance by rapists. When rapists' drinking patterns were closely examined, it was found that they often drink heavily prior to the crime. The rate of alcoholism among rapists is two to three times that of the general population. Thus, as a group these individuals have significant alcohol problems. The role alcohol addiction plays in the actual disinhibition of behavior which leads to rape is unknown (U.S. DHHS, 1984). Room (1983) has shown that there is a strong association between drinking by both victims and perpetrators in cases of rape and homicide involving acquaintances and friends.

Suicide

Alcoholics have a relatively high rate of depression so it is not surprising that they also have high suicide rates. Whether the alcohol abuse leads to depression or depression leads to drinking is unknown (U.S. DHHS, 1983). Regardless of the specific dynamics, follow-up studies of alcoholics and retrospective studies of alcoholics show that alcoholics have very high suicide rates. Suicide rates among alcoholics vary from 8 percent to 21 percent (Kendall, 1983). Kendall's retrospective study suggests that alcoholics who commit suicide tend to be middle-aged and to have been drinking for 20 to 25 years. Collier and Malin (1986) report that suicide rates have declined for older males but increased for those in the 15- to 24-year-old age group. In the Kendall study, 74 percent of the males and half the females who attempted suicide were drinking shortly before the attempt. This suggests that alcohol may play a role in suicide attempts of individuals who are not alcohol addicted.

Welte, Abel, and Wieczorek (1988) have suggested that alcohol tends to be related to suicides that are impulsive. Studying suicides in a New York county from 1972 to 1984, they found that suicides with a detectable BAC received lower scores on a predictability scale. This scale gave points to the victim for leaving a suicide note, being diagnosed as depressed prior to the suicide attempt, having poor health, having had a prior suicide attempt, and being under psychiatric care. They also found that successful suicide victims who had been drinking prior to the attempt were more likely to have died of gunshot wounds (U.S. DHHS, 1990).

The Family

Alcohol abuse affects family life. In a 1982 survey, one-third of the people interviewed felt that alcohol caused problems in their families. It is sometimes difficult to document the precise ways alcohol can affect families. Separation and divorce rates among alcoholics are seven times that of the general population. Two out of five domestic-relations court cases involve alcohol. Most studies report that at least half of the spouse abuse cases are associated with alcohol. Parental alcoholism has an effect on children. Children from alcoholic homes are more likely to have school problems and to display antisocial behavior. A number of studies report that these children have lower self-esteem and more anxiety symptoms, are more aggressive, and display more psychosomatic symptoms. (See Chapter 10 for more information on children of alcoholics.)

Physical Consequences

The use (and particularly the abuse) of alcohol over a long period of time can lead to multiple health difficulties. A brief overview of the physiological effects of alcohol will help place in perspective the health problems caused by alcohol. (Chapter 4 covers health effects in detail.)

Alcohol's effects can range from the impairment seen in intoxication (an acute brain syndrome that is a reversible state) to life-threatening disease states. The organ most likely to show injury is the liver, the site where alcohol is largely metabolized in the body. An early stage of liver disease is fatty liver. This can progress to hepatitis, which is an infection of the liver that leads to jaundice (yellow skin). After an extended period of drinking, which is highly variable but usually several years, the structure of the liver may be changed. Scar tissue can develop and the liver's functional capacity can be reduced. This scarring is known as cirrhosis, often a fatal disease. Since the liver is essential for so many body functions involving metabolism and detoxification, other associated health problems can develop.

Excessive use of alcohol can also damage the gastrointestinal system, the muscles, and the pancreas. The cardiovascular system, the nervous system, and the endocrine system can also be affected. There is a strong association between chronic alcohol use and cancer of the stomach, large intestine, pancreas, and liver.

Many of alcohol's destructive effects result from damage done to the endocrine system. For example, fewer androgens are produced in alcoholic men. This often leads to a feminization of appearance, decreased libido and infertility. Women who abuse alcohol are affected with ovarian dysfunction. Alcohol can produce nutrition-related deficits in the body by its direct effects on nutrient uptake and by its effects on systems involved in vitamin production and distribution. These deficits can lead to altered protein metabolism and vitamin-related disorders such as anemia (U.S. DHHS, 1984).

SUMMARY AND CONCLUSIONS

It should be noted again that the vast majority of persons who use alcohol do so without ill effects to themselves or others. However, the relatively small percentage who abuse alcohol cause significant physical, social, and psychological problems for themselves, their families, and society in general.

As in all major problems, understanding the possible causes, interventions, treatment, and prevention of alcohol abuse and alcoholism is not simple. The following chapters present various dimensions of the alcohol problem. The complexity of the issue may at times be both confusing and overwhelming. Therefore it is necessary to explore the many factors that may contribute to the use and abuse of alcohol. The effects of alcohol on the body, genetic and physical theories of alcohol abuse, sociological theories, and psychological theories of alcohol use and abuse will be explored in depth in the chapters ahead to help understand the comprehensive nature of this problem. The ways alcohol problems are assessed and some of the major treatment approaches used will be presented and evaluated. Finally, the status of prevention in the alcohol field will be examined. This overview of the field should provide an understanding of the pervasive nature of alcohol problems and the difficulties faced in dealing with them.

REFERENCES

Archambault, D. (1989). Adolescence: A physiological, cultural and psychological no man's land. In G. Lawson & A. Lawson (Eds.), *Alcoholism and substance abuse in special populations* (pp. 223–245). Rockville, MD: Aspen Systems.

Brock, C. B., & Boyajy, T. G. (1978). *Group Health Association of America study: Alcoholism within prepaid group practice HMOs.* (Report to NIAAA No. 5H8AA01745). Washington, DC: U.S. Government Printing Office.

Brown, F., & Tooley, J. (1989). Alcoholism in the black community. In G. Lawson & A. Lawson (Eds.), *Alcoholism and substance abuse in special populations* (pp. 115–130). Rockville, MD: Aspen Systems.

Caetano, R. (1984). Ethnicity and drinking in Northern California: A comparison among whites, blacks and Hispanics. *Alcohol and Alcoholism, 19,* 31–44.

Caetano, R. (1989). Drinking patterns and alcohol problems in a national sample of U.S. Hispanics. In *Alcohol use among U.S. Ethnic Minorities: Proceedings of a confer-*

ence on the epidemiology of alcohol use and abuse among ethnic minority groups. (National Institute on Alcohol Abuse and Alcoholism Monograph No. 18., DHHS Publication No. ADM 89–1435), (pp. 147–162). Washington, DC: U.S. Government Printing Office.

Christian, C. M., Dufour, M., & Bertolucci, D. (1989). Differential alcohol-related mortality among American Indian tribes in Oklahoma. *Social Science and Medicine, 28,* 275–284.

Clark, W., & Midnik, L. (1982). Alcohol use and alcohol problems among U.S. adults: Results of the 1979 national survey. In National Institute on Alcohol Abuse and Alcoholism, *Alcohol consumption and related problems* (pp. 3–32). (DHHS Publication No. ADM 82–1190. U.S. Government Printing Office).

Collier, J. D., & Malin, H. (1986). State and national trends in alcohol related mortality: 1975–1982. *Alcohol Health and Research World, 10,* 60–64.

Collins, J. J., Jr. (1981). Alcohol use and criminal behavior: An empirical, theoretical and methodological overview. In J. J. Collins, Jr. (Ed.), *Drinking and crime. Perspectives on the relationship between alcohol consumption and criminal behavior* (pp. 288–316). New York: Guilford Press.

Combs-Orme, T., Taylor, J. R., Scott, E. G., & Holmes, S. J. (1983). Violent deaths among alcoholics: A descriptive study. *Journal of Studies on Alcohol, 44,* 938–944.

Costello, R. M., & Hodde, J. E. (1981). Cost of comprehensive alcoholism care for 100 patients over 4 years. *Journal of Studies on Alcohol, 42,* 87–93.

Drew, L. R. H. (1968). Alcoholism as a self-limiting disease. *Quarterly Journal of Studies on Alcohol, 29,* 956–967.

Eden, S. L., & Aguilar, R. J. (1989). The Hispanic chemically dependent client: Considerations for diagnosis and treatment. In G. Lawson & A. Lawson (Eds.), *Alcoholism and substance abuse in special populations* (pp. 205–222). Rockville, MD: Aspen Systems.

Federal Register (1986, January 9). *51*(6), p. 1226.

Fell, J. C. (1983). Tracking the alcohol involvement problem in U.S. highway crashes. *Proceedings of the 27th Annual Conference of the American Association for Automotive Medicine,* 23–42. Washington, DC: Center for Statistics and Analysis.

Fell, J. C. (1987). Alcohol involvement rates in fatal crashes: A focus on young drivers and female drivers. *Proceedings of the 31st Annual Conference of the American Association for Automobile Medicine,* 28–30. Washington, DC: Center for Statistics and Analysis.

Fellios, P. J. (1989). Alcoholism in women: Causes, treatment and prevention. In G. Lawson & A. Lawson (Eds.), *Alcoholism and substance abuse in special populations* (pp. 11-34). Rockville, MD: Aspen Systems.

Fillmore, K. M. (1984). When angels fall: Women's drinking as cultural preoccupation and as a reality. In S. C. Wilsnack & L. J. Beckman (Eds.), *Alcohol problems in women* (pp. 7–36). New York: Guilford Press.

Fillmore, K. M. (1987). Women's drinking across the adult life course as compared to men's. *British Journal of Addiction, 82,* 801–811.

Harwood, H. J., Kristiansen, P., & Rachal, J. V. (1985). Social and economic costs of alcohol abuse and alcoholism. (Issue Report No. 2.) Research Triangle Park, NC: Research Triangle Institute.

Herd, D. (1985). Migration, cultural transformation, and the rise of black liver cirrhosis mortality. *British Journal of Addiction, 80,* 397–410.

Herd, D. (1989). The epidemiology of drinking patterns and alcohol-related problems among U.S. blacks. In *Alcohol use among U.S. ethnic minorities: Proceedings of a conference on the epidemiology of alcohol use and abuse among ethnic minority groups.* (National Institute on Alcohol Abuse and Alcoholism Monograph No. 18, DHHS Publication No. ADM 89–1435). Washington, DC: U.S. Government Printing Office.

Hill, A. (1989). Treatment and prevention of alcoholism in the Native American family. In G. Lawson & A. Lawson (Eds.), *Alcoholism and substance abuse in special populations* (pp. 247–272). Rockville, MD: Aspen Systems.

Hilton, M. E. (1987). Drinking patterns and drinking problems in 1984: Results from a general population survey. *Alcoholism (NY), 11,* 167–175.

Hilton, M. E. (1988). Demographic distribution of drinking patterns in 1984. *Drug and Alcohol Dependency, 22,* 37–47.

Hingson, R., & Howland, J. (1987). Alcohol as a risk factor for injury or death resulting from accidental falls: A review of the literature. *Journal of Studies on Alcohol, 48,* 212–219.

Holder, H. D., & Hallan, J. B. (1981). Medical care and alcoholism treatment costs and utilization: A five year analysis of the California pilot project to provide health insurance coverage for alcoholism. Chapel Hill, NC: H-2 Incorporated.

Holland, S., & Griffin, A. (1984). Adolescent and adult drug treatment clients: Patterns and consequences of use. *Journal of Psychoactive Drugs, 7,* 79–89.

Holzer, C. E., III, Robins, L. N., Myers, J. K., Weissman, M. M., Tischler, G. L., Leaf, J. P., Anthony, J., & Bednarski, P. B. (1984). Antecedents and correlates of alcohol abuse and dependence in the elderly. In G. Maddox, L. N. Robins, & N. Rosenberg (Eds.), *Nature and extent of alcohol problems among the elderly* (pp. 217–244). (National Institute on Alcohol Abuse and Alcoholism Research Monograph No. 11, DHHS Publication No. ADM 84–1321). Washington, DC: U.S. Government Printing Office.

Howland, J., & Hingson, R. (1987). Alcohol as a risk factor for injuries or death due to fires and burns: A review of the literature. *Public Health Reports, 102,* 475–483.

Howland, J., & Hingson, R. (1988). Alcohol as a risk factor in drownings: A review of the literature (1950–1985). *Accident Analysis and Prevention, 20,* 19–25.

Indian Health Service (1988). *Indian health services chart series book.* (DHHS Publication No. 1988 0–218–547QL3). Washington, DC: U.S. Government Printing Office.

Johnston, L. D., O'Malley, P. M., & Bachman, J. G. (1989). *Illicit drug use, smoking, and drinking by America's high school students, college students, and young adults, 1975–1987.* (DHHS Publication No. ADM 89–1602). Rockville, MD: Alcohol, Drug Abuse and Mental Health Administration.

Kantor, G. K., & Straus, M. A. (1987). The "drunken bum" theory of wife beating. *Social Problems, 34,* 214–230.

Kendall, R. E. (1983). Alcohol and suicide. *Substance and Alcohol Actions/Misuse, 4,* 121–127.

Lawson, A. (1989). Substance abuse problems of the elderly: Considerations for treatment and prevention. In G. Lawson & A. Lawson (Eds.), *Alcoholism and substance abuse in special populations* (pp. 95–113). Rockville, MD: Aspen Systems.

Lawson, G., & Lawson, A. (Eds.) (1989). *Alcoholism and substance abuse in special populations.* Rockville, MD: Aspen Systems.

Leonard, K. E., Bromet, E. J., Parkinson, D. K., Day, N. L., & Ryan, C. M. (1985). Patterns of alcohol use and physically aggressive behavior in men. *Journal of Studies on Alcohol, 46,* 279–282.

Leonard, K. E., & Jacob, T. (1988). Alcohol, alcoholism, and family violence. In V. B. Van Hassett, R. L. Morrison, A. S. Bellack, & M. Hersen (Eds.), *Handbook of family violence* (pp. 383–406). New York: Plenum Press.

Lex, B. W. (1985). Alcohol problems in special populations. In J. H. Mendelson & N. K. Mello (Eds.), *The diagnosis and treatment of alcoholism* (2nd ed.) (pp. 89–187). New York: McGraw-Hill.

Malin, H., Wilson, R., Williams, G., & Aitken, S. (1986). 1983 alcohol health practices supplement. *Alcohol, Health and Research World, 10,* 48–50.

Mannello, T. A., & Seaman, F. J. (1979). *Prevalence, costs and handling of drinking problems on seven railroads.* Washington, DC: U.S. Dept. of Transportation. (NTIS No. PB 81–132516)

National Highway Traffic Safety Administration (1988). *Drunk driving facts.* Washington, DC: Author, National Center for Statistics and Analysis.

National Institute of Drug Abuse (1988). *National survey on drug abuse: Main findings.* (DHHS Publication No. ADM 88–1586. Rockville, MD: Author.

Neff, J. A. (1986). Alcohol consumption and psychological distress among U.S. Anglos, Hispanics and blacks. *Alcohol and Alcoholism, 21,* 111–119.

Rhoades, E. R., Hammond, J., Welty, T. K., Handler, A. O., & Amler, R. W. (1987). The Indian burden of illness and future health interventions. *Public Health Reports, 102,* 361–368.

Rivers, P. C., Rivers, L. S., & Newman, D. (1991). Alcohol and aging: A cross-gender comparison. *Psychology of Addictive Behaviors, 5,* 41–47.

Room, R. (1983). Alcohol and crime: Behavioral aspects. In S. H. Kadish (Ed.), *Encyclopedia of crime and justice* (vol. I) (pp. 35–44). New York: Free Press.

Russell, D. E. H. (1982). *Rape in marriage.* New York: Macmillan.

Sherman, R. M., Reiff, S., & Forsythe, A. B. (April 1979). Utilization of medical services by alcoholics participating in outpatient treatment program. *Alcoholism: Clinical and Experimental Research, 3,* 115–120.

Siegel, C., Haughland, M. A., Goodman, A. B., & Wanderling, J. (1984). Severe alcoholism in the mental health section: I. A cost analysis of treatment. *Journal of Studies on Alcohol, 45,* 504–509.

Stinson, F. S., & DeBakey, S. F. (1992). Alcohol related mortality in the United States, 1979–1988. *British Journal of Addiction, 87,* 777–783.

U.S. Department of Health and Human Services (1984). *Fifth Special Report to Congress* on *Alcohol and Health.* (DHHS Publication No. ADM 84–1291). Washington, DC: U.S. Government Printing Office.

U.S. Department of Health and Human Services (1987). *Sixth Special Report to Congress on Alcohol and Health.* (DHHS Publication No. ADM 87–1519). Washington, DC: U.S. Government Printing Office.

U.S. Department of Health and Human Services (1990). *Seventh Special Report to Congress on Alcohol and Health.* (DHHS Publication No. ADM 90–165). Rockville, MD: Alcohol, Drug Abuse and Mental Health Administration, National Institute on Alcohol Abuse and Alcoholism.

Welte, J. W., Abel, E. L., & Wieczorek, W. (1988). The role of alcohol in suicides in Erie County, NY, 1972–1984. *Public Health Reports, 103,* 648–652.

Westermeyer, J. (1992). Substance use disorders: Predictions for the 1990s. *American Journal of Alcohol and Drug Abuse, 18,* 1–11.

Williams, M. (1984). Alcohol and the elderly: An overview. *Alcohol Health and Research World, 8,* 3–9.

Wilsnack, R. W., Wilsnack, S. C., & Klassen, A. D. (1984). Women's drinking and drinking problems: Patterns from a 1981 national survey. *American Journal of Public Health, 74,* 1231–1238.

Wilsnack, R. W., Wilsnack, S. C., & Klassen, A. D. (1987). In P. C. Rivers (Ed.), *Alcohol and addictive behavior: Vol. 34. Nebraska Symposium on Motivation* (pp. 85–158). Lincoln: University of Nebraska Press.

Wilsnack, S. C., Wilsnack, R. W., & Klassen, A. D. (1985). Drinking and drinking problems among women in a U.S. national survey. *Alcohol Health and Research World, 9,* 3–13.

The Effects of Alcohol on the Body

_____ *chapter* 4

In order to understand the effects of alcohol on the body, it is first necessary to look at the chemical and pharmacological qualities of ethyl alcohol. Ethyl alcohol is the only alcohol that can be readily metabolized by the human body. This substance, also called ethanol, is an *aliphatic* sedative. Aliphatic is the term used to describe a compound in which an oxygen-hydrogen combination is attached to an *aliphatic hydrocarbon,* an organic compound formed solely of hydrogen and carbon atoms (Light, 1985).

Another important feature of ethyl alcohol is that it is a soporific or a sedative (Avis, 1990; Doweiko, 1990; Grilly, 1989; Julien, 1988; Julien, 1992). Sedatives differ from narcotics in that they induce sleep but do not reduce pain. Narcotics reduce pain but do not induce sleep. Alcohol, like all sedatives, is an irregular depressant of the central nervous system. A depressant is a substance that slows down or stops normal functions (Loomis, 1982).

Sedatives are said to be irregular because they affect only certain functions of the central nervous system. If alcohol affected all areas of the central nervous system equally, then vital life-sustaining areas would be affected when drinkers took their first drink. The irregular sedative action of alcohol means that the medulla, which controls life-sustaining functions like heartbeat, blood flow, and breathing, is not affected at lower dosages. Instead, the sedatives work first at the higher levels of the brain (the cerebrum), then the cerebellum, and finally, the spinal cord. So at relatively low levels of consumption, drinkers may feel less inhibited; at still higher levels, drinkers will be unsteady on their feet. A larger amount of alcohol knocks individuals out, and they become unconscious. A large enough amount of alcohol can kill them. (In a normal individual, a blood-alcohol content of 0.5 percent or 0.50 is life-threatening, according to Loomis (1982). A more extensive look at alcohol's cumulative effects is given later.)

Heavy drinkers (not just alcoholics) show an increased tolerance to alcohol and also to many so-called minor tranquilizers (Julien, 1992). These include Librium, Valium, and Miltown. The tolerance for hypnotics, including the barbiturates (e.g., Nembutal and Seconal) and the barbituratelike drugs (Quaalude), is also increased by heavy drinking. This pharmacodynamic tolerance results from changes in the target tissues upon which the drugs act, usually the central nervous system (Light, 1985).

As noted by Light, all of the drugs in the previously mentioned minor tranquilizers class are potentially addictive when abused for any substantial period of time. Such use not only leads to tolerance for the drug being used, but to tolerance for all similarly acting drugs. This cross-tolerance means a cross-tolerant drug will have less impact than if a similarly acting, cross tolerant drug had not been previously used or abused. (This cross-tolerance is one of the reasons that individuals facing surgery are asked about their alcohol and drug use.)

Constant use of the drug ethyl alcohol can lead to changes in at least two other types of tolerance, metabolic tolerance and pharmacodynamic tolerance. Metabolic tolerance essentially means that the liver cells become more efficient in removing alcohol from the body, that is, they do it more rapidly. This increased efficiency is due to physical changes in the liver cells, resulting in a more rapid metabolism of alcohol. (A more detailed description of liver metabolism will be given later.) Pharmacodynamic tolerance results from changes in the target tissues upon which the drug acts, usually the central nervous system (Segal & Sisson, 1985; Seixas, 1982). (A more extensive discussion of tolerance, alcohol dependence, and alcohol addiction is given in Box 4–1.)

INGESTION AND TRANSPORTATION OF ALCOHOL IN THE BODY

A brief overview of how alcohol is transported and distributed in the body once it is ingested may be helpful at this point. Alcohol is absorbed throughout the entire length of the gastrointestinal system, from the mouth to the rectum (Batt, 1989). (See Figure 4–1 for an overview of alcohol's absorption.)

For example, when alcohol is taken in by mouth, there are two ways it may be absorbed. It can be absorbed through the mucosa of the mouth, or it can be absorbed through the lungs. When alcohol is taken in by mouth, the

BOX 4–1
Alcohol Tolerance, Dependence, and Addiction

Because the concepts of alcohol tolerance, dependence, and addiction are so important in understanding alcohol problems, it seems appropriate to discuss these three concepts more extensively.

Alcohol Tolerance

Tolerance is usually defined as

> ... a *diminished response* to a particular dose of a drug (e.g., ethanol) *after* one or more administrations of this drug. ... Tolerance can also be said to be present if a larger *dose* of ethanol is necessary to produce a particular intensity of physiologic or behavioral response in an individual who has previously consumed ethanol as compared to the dose that was necessary to produce such response in an individual prior to the consumption of ethanol. ... (Tabakoff & Rothstein, 1983, pp. 187–188)

While this definition seems to be generally agreed upon by most authorities, other types of alcohol tolerance have also been discussed. For example, the distinction has been made between metabolic and functional tolerance. *Metabolic tolerance* refers to the body's adjustment so that it can increase the elimination rate of alcohol. *Functional tolerance*, on the other hand, refers to the fact that over time, alcohol has a decreased effect on drinkers' behaviors if they continue to use alcohol in a heavy and sustained manner. That is, the same amount of alcohol has less effect on the regular user's behavior than it does on a person just beginning to drink (Doweiko, 1990; Tabakoff & Rothstein, 1983). *Acute tolerance* and *chronic tolerance* are terms also frequently used to describe alcohol's effects. Acute tolerance refers to the amount of time that it takes an organism to clear its first single dose of ethanol from its body. Chronic tolerance is a tolerance to alcohol that develops *after* an organism has had one dose or after it has had repeated doses. Chronic tolerance refers to the fact that a particular dose of alcohol has less effect on an organism that has been consuming alcohol regularly than on a naive organism that is consuming its first dose. (The term *organism* is used here because much of the research on chronic and acute tolerance has been learned from laboratory animals.) (Tabakoff & Rothstein, 1983)

Alcohol Dependence

Alcohol dependence can be divided into *physical* and *psychological* dependence. Physical dependence is the reaction of the person or lower organism to the reduction or ceasing of alcohol intake. That is, physical dependence can generally be observed only when alcohol is withdrawn. The symptoms that indicate alcohol dependence are generally opposite to signs of acute intoxication. Physical dependence is thus defined by the characteristic withdrawal syndrome that occurs once the body has adapted to alcohol's effects. What seems to have happened is that the body has "learned" to function despite the presence of alcohol. If alcohol is now removed, it will take some period of adjustment before the body can function normally without alcohol. Alcohol withdrawal produces considerable discomfort and is avoided, if at all possible, by chronic drinkers drinking more alcohol. Doweiko (1990) suggests that the severity of alcohol withdrawal is intensified by a longer and more severe drinking history.

Psychological dependence is the consumption of alcohol by drinkers because they find its ingestion rewarding. Alcohol has the capacity to lead to state changes (temporary changes in how the person feels about, perceives, and reacts to the world), which some drinkers find positively reinforcing. The disinhibition, relief from anxiety, and euphoria that often accompany alcohol ingestion are examples of these state changes which could lead a drinker to become psychologically dependent on alcohol (Julien, 1988). It is, of course, possible to be psychologically dependent on alcohol without being physically dependent or to be physically dependent without being psychologically dependent, although the latter would probably occur less often.

Alcohol Addiction

This is a less specific and less well documented concept. It has multiple characteristics including the chronic consumption of alcohol, a compulsive need to continue to use the drug, the development of a tolerance to the effects of alcohol, and psychological and physical dependence on the drug (Walsh, 1973). Keller, McCormick, and Efron (1982) define alcohol addiction as

> a form of dependence on alcohol characterized by an overwhelming need to drink intoxicating amounts of alcoholic beverages. It is marked by a drive to obtain the gratification of alcohol intoxication or to escape mental or physical distress, and by *impairment of control over drinking* or *loss of control over drinking* ... Addiction has been attributed to learned or conditioned dependence activated by critical internal or environmental stimuli. It has also been attributed to a hypothetical alteration in cell metabolism consequent upon habituation to large amounts of the drug, with development of a withdrawal syndrome when the addict is deprived of the addicant. ... (pp. 6–7)

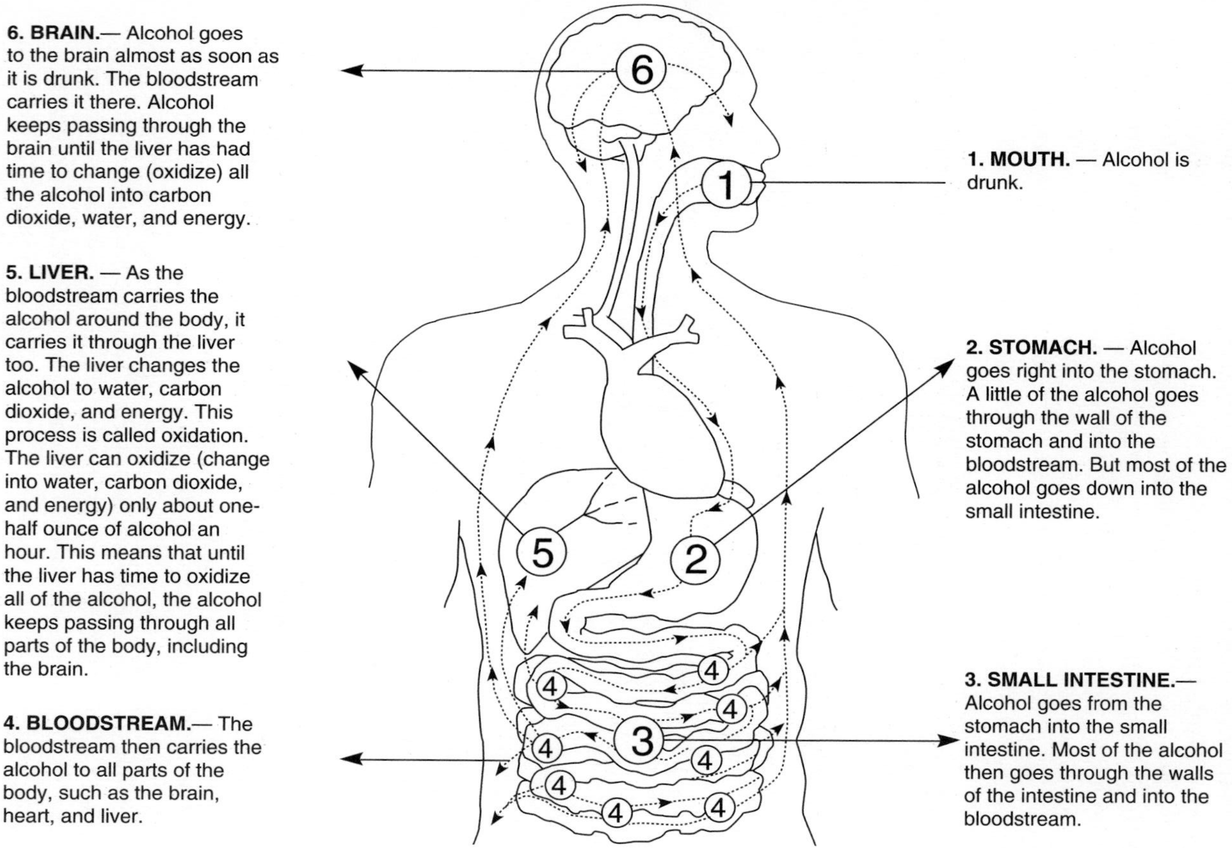

1. MOUTH. — Alcohol is drunk.

2. STOMACH. — Alcohol goes right into the stomach. A little of the alcohol goes through the wall of the stomach and into the bloodstream. But most of the alcohol goes down into the small intestine.

3. SMALL INTESTINE. — Alcohol goes from the stomach into the small intestine. Most of the alcohol then goes through the walls of the intestine and into the bloodstream.

6. BRAIN. — Alcohol goes to the brain almost as soon as it is drunk. The bloodstream carries it there. Alcohol keeps passing through the brain until the liver has had time to change (oxidize) all the alcohol into carbon dioxide, water, and energy.

5. LIVER. — As the bloodstream carries the alcohol around the body, it carries it through the liver too. The liver changes the alcohol to water, carbon dioxide, and energy. This process is called oxidation. The liver can oxidize (change into water, carbon dioxide, and energy) only about one-half ounce of alcohol an hour. This means that until the liver has time to oxidize all of the alcohol, the alcohol keeps passing through all parts of the body, including the brain.

4. BLOODSTREAM. — The bloodstream then carries the alcohol to all parts of the body, such as the brain, heart, and liver.

FIGURE 4–1 The way alcohol is absorbed in the body. (*Originally based on materials from the National Institute on Alcohol Abuse and Alcoholism, Alcohol Health and Research World (1988). Taken from Witters, Venturelli, & Hanson, 1992, p. 184.*)

so-called "mouth alcohol effect" may result, which means that a breath alcohol level taken immediately after the drink may be very high in the first two to four minutes after swallowing. (This effect is important since breath alcohol measures are calibrated to measure the blood alcohol level [BAL] or blood alcohol content [BAC] in legal actions like driving while intoxicated.) However, about 15 minutes after swallowing, there is almost no residual "mouth alcohol effect," that is, the breath alcohol measure now may accurately reflect current blood alcohol levels (Batt, 1989).

The absorption of alcohol from the stomach is very quick and this is particularly true when the alcohol is in relatively high levels of concentration. For example, distilled spirits, which contain 40 to 50 percent alcohol by volume (80 to 100 proof), produce rapid absorption. On the other hand, low alcohol-content beverages like beer (3 to 5 percent) or wine (12 percent ethanol by volume) are absorbed more slowly. Dilution by having food present in the stomach also slows absorption of alcohol from the stomach. But it is not only in the stomach that food affects absorption rates. When food is consumed with alcohol, it plays a dual role in reducing the rate of absorption. It dilutes the alcohol passed via the pyloric valve into the small intestine, so alcohol will be absorbed more slowly; and it delays the emptying of the stomach into the small intestine. In other cases, distilled spirits may cause a "pylorospasm," which means that alcohol is retained in the stomach and eventually absorbed from there. While these facts may seem like dull details, they are critical in understanding the effect of alcohol on an individual since the absorption rate determines the level of alcohol in the blood and the amount that reaches the brain. Taking food with alcohol means that alcohol is absorbed more slowly so that the rate at which the nervous system is affected is reduced. In addition, when alcohol is consumed and enters the bloodstream, the liver is working at its maximum rate (until the blood alcohol content is very low). In the first pass of alcohol-laden blood through the liver, a greater relative percentage of the alcohol will be metabolized at low blood alcohol levels than if the blood alcohol levels are high. A similar condition exists when several drinks are taken throughout the day as opposed to drinking the same amount all in one short time frame. In the first case, the liver's ability to deal with "first pass" amounts would be sufficient to keep most of the alcohol from the brain and hence reduce potential damage (Goldstein, 1983).

In terms of distribution, it should be remembered that alcohol goes throughout the body, especially to where there is water. Alcohol is not very soluble in fats, so the absorption rate in water is likely to be ten times the absorption rate in fats. The rate of distribution to various tissues varies according to the amount of their blood supply. Since the brain is generously supplied with blood vessels, alcohol reaches these tissues very rapidly while the concentration in adipose (fatty) tissue, which has a relatively smaller blood supply, is slower (Goldstein, 1983).

Ethyl alcohol is an irritant. When alcohol is consumed, it irritates the

When alcohol is consumed, one of its corrosive effects is gastric upset.
(Photograph courtesy of the Independence Center, Lincoln, Nebraska.)

lining of the entire digestive system. For example, heavy alcohol intake can
cause irritation of the mouth and the esophagus (Segal & Sisson, 1985).
Cancer of the mouth and esophagus are statistically correlated with the use
of both alcohol and tobacco. In terms of alcohol use, esophageal cancer is
twenty-five times more common among heavy drinkers (Light, 1985). So, the
irritant effect of alcohol on these ingestive pathways can be considerable
(Korsten & Lieber, 1985).

Alcohol can have pervasive effects on the body that are much more
complex than is immediately apparent. The presence of food in the stomach
inhibits absorption. Drinking alcohol on an empty stomach produces a
greater effect on individuals than alcohol consumed with or soon after a
meal because food slows the rate of absorption in the stomach and retards
the passage of alcohol into the intestine (Avis, 1990; Grilly, 1989; Light,
1985). This is the reason many authorities suggest that food be served at all
parties where alcohol is consumed. Food helps to reduce the rate of absorption of alcohol into the blood and helps to reduce the blood alcohol content. One more reason for slowed absorption rates in the stomach is that the
drying properties of alcohol can contribute to a shutdown of the blood supply to the stomach.

When the food content of the stomach is low or a great deal of alcohol
is consumed, alcohol directly disrupts the membranes in the stomach lining
or gastric mucosa. It "dissolves away the protective mucous lubricant secreted

by the mucosal *epithelial cells*. Not only are hemorrhagic lesions directly formed in the stomach lining by alcohol-induced damage, but the removal of the protective mucosa coat allows the hydrochloric acid (HCl) normally present in the stomach for digestive purposes to attack the stomach wall" (Light, 1985, p. 156). The irritation of the stomach lining increases the secretion of hydrochloric acid. The presence of hydrochloric acid in the digestive tract aggravates any abnormal condition present, for example, esophagitis, peptic ulcer, or hernia of the diaphragm. Alcohol also irritates the lower gastrointestinal tract because it increases the spontaneous motion of the tract and produces an outpouring of fluid. Thus, it is not unusual for the small intestine to become inflamed as a result of all of these alcohol-induced problems (Fenster, 1982; Light, 1985).

"Alcohol additionally stimulates excess production of HCl (by promoting gastric release in high concentrations) and delays emptying of the stomach contents. In high concentrations it also delays absorption from the stomach into the bloodstream, probably by inhibiting stomach motility. All of these factors prolong the corrosive effect of both alcohol and hydrochloric acid upon the stomach mucosa" (Light, 1985, pp. 156–157). Once alcohol reaches the small intestine, absorption is extremely rapid. This absorption is unaffected by the presence of food or the continued presence of alcohol (Goldstein, 1983; Light, 1985).

As previously noted, most of what is eaten is absorbed through the walls of the small intestine. The small intestine is about 9 feet long in the human adult. The inner lining or mucosa has a large number of very small fingerlike projections called *villi*. These small projections significantly increase the surface area available for absorption of food. The cells of the mucosa which line the intestine also have even smaller projections that help to increase the surface area that can absorb substances into the bloodstream. "As it does in the stomach, ethanol dissolves away the protective mucin coat and produces a variety of ultrastructural abnormalities in the cells of the intestinal lining. This can occur even in the presence of a nutritionally adequate diet" (Light, 1985, p. 60).

In alcoholics there can be a shortening of the intestinal villi. The chronic use of ethanol can produce hemorrhagic lesions at the tips of those structures. All of these effects cause serious disturbances in the absorption and transport of food and nutrients in the body. In part because of this failure to adequately take up nutrients, vitamin deficiencies are commonly seen in alcoholics, both with and without adequate food intake (Korsten & Lieber, 1985; Light, 1985). These deficiencies can occur from several causes.

1. Inadequate diet due to high caloric intake from the excessive drinking.

2. Decreased absorption of vitamins due to damage of the intestine and pancreas by alcohol.

3. Damage to the liver leading to the decreased ability to convert vita-

mins into the active cofactors needed by the body. (Cofactors are catalysts which speed up or slow down metabolic reactions while remaining relatively unchanged themselves.)

4. Increased requirements for certain vitamins because of the induced increases of these vitamins as cofactors resulting from the excessive amounts of alcohol that must be metabolized (Adapted from Light, 1985, p. 55).

"The most frequently seen vitamin deficiencies among alcohol abusers are due to poor intestinal uptake of thiamine (vitamin B1), ... (vitamin B12), and folate or folic acid" (Light, 1985, p. 55). Both vitamin B12 and folic acid are required for formation and maturation of the red blood cells, and they are both necessary for general cell replication. Folic acid is also needed in the synthesis of DNA, the carrier of genetic information in the cell nuclei. Deficiencies in the two vitamins cause severe anemia due to reduced blood cell counts. This anemia is often complicated by a corresponding iron deficiency resulting from acute bleeding of the upper stomach. Other organs and systems of the body are also injured or damaged by alcohol (Korsten & Lieber, 1985; Light, 1985; Segal & Sisson, 1985).

Pancreas

Acute hemorrhagic pancreatitis is a common condition in chronic alcoholics, with about 5 to 20 percent suffering from this problem. This condition is particularly prevalent in alcoholics during their middle years of life.

This is a first order medical emergency of life-threatening proportions. It is characterized by a sudden onset of intense pain in the abdominal area which resembles acute appendicitis. This is a recurrent condition and such an abrupt onset of an "acute abdomen" usually follows soon after a very large meal or an alcoholic binge. In many cases, this is followed by peripheral vascular collapse with profound shock having a 20 to 50 percent mortality rate! (Light, 1985, p. 61)

As Light points out, alcohol-related pancreatitis is a very dangerous disorder. Its cause is the death of cells in the pancreas, which is the result of the release of huge amounts of the enzyme *lysing*. This enzyme, secreted by the pancreas, dissolves tissue. An additional factor contributing to damage of the pancreas is that alcohol also leads to increased secretion of *pancreatic juice*. It is believed that the pancreas is attacked by its lysing enzyme and this leads to tissue destruction in the organ. Since pancreatitis tends to recur in alcoholics, there is recurring fat necrosis, edema, and calcification in this gland. This pathology results in the normal cells of the pancreas being replaced by fibrous tissue which, late in the disease process, can severely restrict pancreatic juice secretion (Korsten & Lieber, 1985; Light, 1985; Segal & Sisson, 1985).

While this damage to the pancreas can be life threatening, it is not the only way alcohol can disrupt pancreatic function. The *islets of Langerhans* which are located in the pancreas, can also be damaged by alcohol abuse. These cells in the pancreas secrete two hormones used to regulate sugar level in the blood. The *alpha cells* in the islets of Langerhans secrete glucogen, which aids in the conversion of glycogen (an animal starch stored in the liver) into a form of glucose, a type of sugar, which can be readily used by the body. Another substance, insulin, is released by *beta cells,* which are also located in the islets of Langerhans. Insulin is released in response to excessive sugar levels in the blood and, therefore, is responsible for maintaining optimal blood sugar levels in the body. If the islet cells are damaged too much, diabetes mellitus may occur. Another way the damage can be expressed is in recovering alcoholics who suffer from repeated occurrences of *reactive hypoglycemia*, which is caused by the delayed release of insulin following a meal and results in elevation of the sugar level of the blood (Light, 1985). The rise in sugar level then leads to a surge in insulin from beta cells, which accounts for a rapid "reactive" drop in sugar level and the hypoglycemia.

Liver

The liver is the largest organ in the body, weighing about 1.8 kilograms in the average adult (Light, 1985). The liver is involved in many of the detoxification processes that go on in the body, including detoxification of alcohol and the major tranquilizers like Thorazine. It is also involved in many of the digestive processes in the body, including the metabolism of alcohol. About 95 percent of all alcohol consumed is eliminated from the body through oxidation by the liver while the other 5 percent is eliminated through feces, urine, and sweat (Light, 1985; Segal & Sisson, 1985).

The first two steps in alcohol metabolism occur mainly in the liver, and the resultant energy enters the energy pathway that is used by many of the body's tissues. Through metabolism the liver converts alcohol to carbon dioxide and water and generates 7.1 calories for each gram metabolized. Thus, alcohol can generate considerable energy, and this energy source can substitute for other food sources. Light (1985) indicates that a pint of 85 proof whiskey has half the daily calories required for the average adult. As a result of this calorie source, alcohol abusers frequently do not eat properly, since most of their daily caloric needs are met by the alcohol they consume. (The presence of gastritis in many alcoholics may also contribute to low food consumption.)

Alcohol does not contain vitamins, minerals, or proteins and is often described as producing "empty calories" (food sources which do not contain essential nutrients like vitamins, minerals, and proteins but which do replace calories from foods containing these nutrients). Therefore, alcoholics frequently do not receive adequate daily nutrients. At the same time that they are suffering from malnutrition because of alcohol's empty calories, there is damage to liver cells caused by alcohol intake. This damage leads to an insufficient assimilation of vitamins and amino acids. Alcoholics often have abnormal intestinal absorption, and this occurs whether they have liver cirrhosis or not. Since alcohol has a tendency to preempt other foods metabolized by the liver because it is easier to metabolize than many other carbohydrates, foods which contain nutritious calories are not digested fully. For all of these reasons, even the food that is consumed by the alcoholic is incompletely utilized by the liver. This further complicates nutritional problems in the chronic abusive drinker (Light, 1985; Segal & Sisson, 1985).

Several steps are necessary in the metabolism of alcohol. Following uptake via the bloodstream from primarily the stomach and the small intestine, alcohol is transported through the portal vein to the liver. In the liver, alcohol is converted to acetaldehyde by alcohol dehydrogenase. Acetaldehyde, which is a highly toxic element in the body at high amounts, is then broken down rapidly by aldehyde dehydrogenase into acetate. Acetate then enters normal metabolic pools outside the liver and is eventually converted to carbon dioxide and water (Batt, 1989). The body cannot tolerate the acetaldehyde, the first step of alcohol metabolism. Under normal conditions, the acetaldehydes are broken down quickly, as already noted, by the enzyme aldehyde dehydrogenase. There is an enzyme inhibitor called disulfiram (Antabuse is the trade name) that prevents the action of aldehyde dehydrogenase. (There are other enzyme inhibitors but the one described here is the most frequently used.) This means that the very toxic acetaldehyde is no longer broken down and can build up in the body. If individuals take the enzyme inhibitor disulfiram and then drink they will become very ill. Symptoms include flushing, increased heart rate, pain and agitation, profuse sweating, nausea, and vomiting. All of these symptoms increase with the dosage level of disulfiram (at least up to a certain point) and the amount of alcohol ingested while the disulfiram is in the body (Peachey, 1989). This disulfiram reaction is potentially quite dangerous since the high initial blood pressure rise can be a precursor to a rapid drop in blood pressure, and the drinker can go into cardiovascular shock, which is life threatening. Because of its potential for difficulties in terms of the cardiovascular system, disulfiram is contraindicated for people with cardiovascular disease. For this and other reasons, it is also contraindicated for people with the following: cerebrovascular disease, severe chronic pulmonary disease, chronic renal failure, neuropsychiatric disease (including organic brain disease, psychosis, and depression requiring treatment), idiopathic seizure disorder, neuropathy, pregnancy, and chronic liver disease complicated by portal hypertension.

The liver can develop diseased conditions in the process of metabolizing alcohol. The least dangerous (and most readily reversible), fatty liver, follows just one session of abusive drinking. The most dangerous form is cirrhosis of the liver, and this is ultimately fatal if the person continues to drink (Fraser, 1989). However, in the early stages of the disease (i.e., fatty liver) it is reversible (Moore, 1986).

As previously noted, the earliest readily identified disease is called fatty liver (or more technically, steatosis). Upon examination, the liver (following just a single session of heavy drinking) shows fat deposits, which may be due to the fact that ethanol has supplanted fat as an energy source (Fraser, 1989; Moore, 1986). Fatty liver can be reversed without treatment, by ceasing to use alcohol and eating a nutritious diet.

If drinkers with fatty liver continue to drink, the next stage of alcoholic liver disease, alcoholic hepatitis, develops. Alcoholic hepatitis can produce jaundice, but more importantly, this disease can produce lesions in the liver that are precursors to cirrhosis of the liver. Treatment of alcoholic hepatitis is essentially the same as for fatty liver. Survival of the persons with this disorder can be dramatically improved by discontinuing or reducing alcohol consumption. For example, 7-year survival rates in one study were 50 percent when the person continued to drink and rose to 80 percent when drinking was reduced (Moore, 1986; Segal & Sisson, 1985).

For those people who develop cirrhosis, there is a scarring of the liver. Large parts of the liver become fibrous and thus are no longer capable of producing the enzymes needed to aid in food metabolism and detoxification of the body. If individuals continue to drink once this disorder develops, death usually follows. Thus, for people who have cirrhosis, abstinence from alcohol plays an essential role in survival (Moore, 1986; Segal & Sisson, 1985). While this disorder is not reversible, an individual who develops scarring of the liver and then abstains from alcohol may be able to live a normal life because the liver's capacity may be sufficient for normal nutrition. However, continued drinking after cirrhosis has been diagnosed can be a serious threat to life. Regrettably, even those who abstain and who live for five years or more following abstention have an increased risk of liver cancer, particularly if they have a history of hepatitis B (Fraser, 1989).

Cardiovascular System

Abnormal enlargement of red blood cells is the major blood disorder in alcoholics who do not have marked liver disease or folic acid deficiency. This enlargement of red blood cells is one of the causes of anemia that occurs in 7 to 19 percent of these alcoholics. Anemia in alcoholics can also be caused by

1. reduction of bone marrow production of red blood cells
2. folic acid deficiency caused by inadequate diet and/or poor uptake of folates in the intestine due to alcohol abuse
3. deranged iron metabolism related to fatty liver

Most of these problems are reversible if alcohol abuse ceases or is reduced. It should also be noted here that white blood cells are vulnerable to the toxic effects of alcohol ingestion, independent of liver disease and folic acid deficiency. This means that alcohol abusers may be more susceptible to a wider range of infections than are nonabusers (Moore, 1986; Segal & Sisson, 1985).

The effects of alcohol on the heart have been well documented. Large amounts of alcohol change myocardial cell metabolism and shorten the action potential in the myocardium (Kupari & Suokas, 1989). Reviews of the literature (see Moore, 1986) have concluded that alcohol consumed in moderate to heavy amounts daily for a year can induce damage to the heart muscle. The common result is enlargement of the heart. This heart disease is called cardiomyopathy because one or more of the heart chambers has become enlarged. Central to the beginning of heart muscle disease is a loss of contractile function in the heart muscle. This loss of contractability occurs "initially and predominantly in the left ventricle, the chamber that pumps oxygenated blood through the aorta to the rest of the body (The right ventricle pumps blood to the lungs.)" (Rubin & Doria, 1990, p. 277).

In general, cardiologists see the direct toxic effects of alcohol or its metabolites (e.g., acetaldehyde) as the cause of alcoholic cardiomyopathy or alcoholic heart disease. The major symptoms of alcoholic cardiomyopathy include shortness of breath and congestive heart failure. This leads to swollen ankles caused by fluid accumulation (called edema), chest pain, fatigue, and heart palpitations (unduly rapid action of the heart that is felt by the patient). This disorder is thought to be caused by the direct effect of alcohol and/or its metabolites (Van Thiel, 1983). However, alcohol-related disorders in other systems of the body can indirectly contribute to problems in the cardiovascular system. For example, acetaldehyde production from the oxidation of alcohol inhibits protein synthesis in the heart muscle. Another indirect effect is that alcohol consumption interferes with calcium absorption through cell membranes, and thus calcium binding (something needed in all muscles like the heart) is inhibited (Moore, 1986).

There have been some studies which suggest that moderate drinking may reduce the risk of heart disease. However, Moore points out that longitudinal data suggest that "teetotalers," particularly those who do not smoke, have the lowest heart disease mortality of any group.

THE CENTRAL NERVOUS SYSTEM

Acute Effects

As noted earlier, alcohol, like all the sedatives, is an irregular depressant of the central nervous system. A depressant is a substance that diminishes or stops normal functions. Ages ago it seems individuals became aware of the pleasurable effects of temporarily stopping some of the neurons from working. They found that changing their perceptions of the internal or external environment could be fun since it could take away the awareness of discomfort, cold, fear, or fatigue and it might rid them of individual and social guilt. However, they soon found that there were uncomfortable side effects.

The effects of alcohol on the individual at different blood alcohol content (BAC) levels have been nicely outlined by Santamaria (1989). At low levels of intoxication, persons may become less self-conscious and more talkative and have the tendency to lose emotional control. They may also be less socially discrete than normal. As the BAC rises to between 0.03 and 0.08, social judgment is impaired and individuals have difficulty understanding the importance of events. As the blood alcohol level continues to rise, thinking becomes more difficult and the ability to concentrate is disrupted. Individuals have difficulty learning and remembering. At this point, their judgment is poor and the lack of self-awareness leads to a false self-confidence. As the BAC continues to rise (between 0.05 and 0.08), muscle control is affected and there is mild incoordination. Note that all of these observable effects on thinking, judgment, concentration, and coordination (as well as vision) are at relatively low blood alcohol concentrations (below the 0.10 BAC that is used in most U.S. states for charging the person operating an automobile with driving while intoxicated).

As the BAC does approach 0.10, there is noticeably more impairment of coordination and movement. It is more difficult to enunciate words and sentences, and there is more difficulty in performing fine-motor movements and skilled actions. Noticeable lack of muscle coordination occurs at this point. As the level of intoxication rises, individuals become drowsy, then fall asleep, and then fall into a stupor. If they have even higher levels of alcohol in the blood, they may fall into a deepening coma, which may lead to suppression of the respiratory system and death. Falling asleep usually occurs around 0.30 BAC, while coma and death is likely when the BAC reaches 0.50 and above (Santamaria, 1989). A graphic illustration of how alcohol affects the body (taken from Julien, 1992) is given in Figure 4–2.

When, as in the preceding description, alcohol sedates the brain, it diminishes psychomotor activity levels. As individuals' blood alcohol levels rise, their psychomotor activity level goes down, and as a result, they are relieved, relaxed, and less anxious than they were before. However, as soon as the blood alcohol level starts to fall, the sedative effect begins to fade. Even if individuals drink as many as two drinks, the effect wears off very quickly after the second hour.

If alcohol had no additional physiological effects, there would be no such thing as alcohol abuse. Individuals could drink to get relief and their anxiety level would diminish. The drink would wear off and they would be back where they were. However, when individuals drink there are *two* oppos-

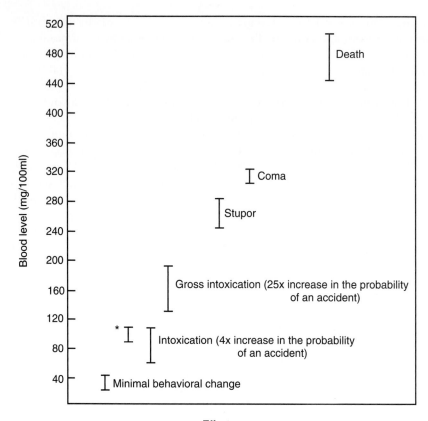

FIGURE 4–2. The correlation of the blood level of ethanol with degrees of intoxication. The legal level (*) varies by state: The range of values is shown. *(Taken from Julien, 1992, p. 78, and used with permission.)*

ing effects. There is the sedative effect described earlier and, at the same time, an agitating effect that has an opposite impact. Both the sedative and the agitating effects begin at the time the drink is consumed. However, the agitating effect is not felt immediately because it is at a much lower level of intensity than the sedative effect.

Usually the sedative effect will last two to three hours but the agitating effect from a single drink can last as much as twelve hours. As the sedative effect wears off (about two hours after consuming the drink), drinkers become more nervous and agitated than they were before they took a drink of alcohol. (This is sometimes called a psychomotor "rebound" effect.) Therefore, they have another drink and the perceived anxiety is again reduced. So a cycle is set up where there is increased tension, drinking, short-term sedative effect, longer-term agitating effect, higher tension, and drinking again, which can go on for some time—but not forever. Eventually, individuals reach a point where no matter how much alcohol they drink, they find it difficult to reduce the psychomotor activity level to a really low state. This is because the agitating effects from all the previous drinks add to one another (Segal & Sisson, 1985).

A chronic alcoholic was observed begging to be admitted to a hospital to deal with impending delirium tremens (d.t.'s) while each of his back pockets held a pint of whiskey. He had been intoxicated so long that he could no longer deal with the rebound effect by drinking more alcohol.

Alcohol's agitating effect is due to the pharmacology of the drug. It occurs in all individuals who consume the drug. The magnitude of the psychomotor effect is dependent upon how much the individuals have consumed and how long they have been drinking. Individuals suffering from a hangover from a social night on the town are suffering the same type of withdrawal from ethyl alcohol as chronic alcoholics who are experiencing seizures and full-blown delirium tremens, a condition in which the brain is tremendously agitated (Loomis, 1982; Segal & Sisson, 1985).

Chronic Effects

Thus far, the effects of alcohol on the central nervous system have been discussed as a reversible process. However, if alcohol is used for a sustained period of time (months and years) with heavy alcohol intake (BACs above 0.10 to 0.15), then damage to both the central and peripheral nervous systems can occur. In addition, psychophysiological reactions such as delirium tremens mentioned previously can also occur.

ALCOHOL-RELATED BRAIN DAMAGE

Brain disorders can be classified into the extremes of acute and chronic brain damage. Furthermore, J. W. Smith (1982) notes that research has isolated an intermediate, reversible stage of *alcohol-induced* brain damage.

Acute (and generally reversible) brain damage has a rapid onset. This type of damage could be expressed as simply acute intoxication, or it may result from withdrawal from alcohol and take the form of acute hallucinosis or delirium tremens. Delirium tremens has been described, perhaps erroneously, as a severe withdrawal reaction. However, as explained earlier, alcoholics who are drinking as much as they can consume can still go into delirium tremens. "Delirium" is the name given to the hallucinations, confusion, and disorientation that the alcoholic in this severe "withdrawal" state is suffering. "Tremens" on the other hand refers to the increased autonomic nervous system reaction, which produces tremulousness, agitation, rapid pulse rate, and fever. Persons suffering from this disorder are terrified, in a state of panic, and are sure horrible things will happen to them (Segal & Sisson,

1985). Patients in the throes of d.t.'s have been known to jump out of windows in reaction to their fear. Thus, they must be supervised closely during this reaction. Not only is the sensory input increased, but the motor output becomes tremendous, and individuals are literally unable to stop moving. They typically act as though someone is trying to kill them. The psychomotor activity level may reach the point of causing spontaneous generalized convulsions, which can result in shock and death.

The chronic brain syndrome is typically a slow-onset disorder with a progressive course. This disorder tends to be relatively irreversible (Segal & Sisson, 1985; J. W. Smith, 1982). Both acute and chronic brain damage show similar changes. For example, both stages show changes in memory and in complex intellectual processes (for example, calculation, comprehension, and new learning) (J. W. Smith, 1982) in addition to impaired judgment and labile or shallow affect.

Clinically, dramatic forms of acute brain syndrome *may* be presented without any detectable, permanent, structural changes in the brain (J. W. Smith, 1982). In contrast, the alcoholic chronic brain syndrome has long been associated with specific anatomical changes. These anatomical changes include progressive atrophy of the frontal lobes, which can be found at autopsy in chronic alcoholics. These same types of findings have been observed in living drinkers by using CAT scan procedures on young social drinkers (e.g., Cala et al., 1983) and on alcoholics (e.g., Muuronen, Bergman, Hindmarsh, & Telakivi, 1989). The clinical counterparts of the atrophy of the cerebral cortex are loss of memory for recent events, confusion, disorientation for time and place, and difficulty in concentration. Fitzhugh, Fitzhugh, and Reitan (1965) found that on tests of adaptive ability, alcoholics scored closer to brain-damaged subjects than to non-brain-damaged controls. J. W. Smith (1982) also found these same types of relationships in his clinical work.

J. W. Smith (1982) notes the earlier work of Bennett (1960), which establishes the diagnosis of an intermediate state of alcoholic brain disease. In this disorder, both clinical and electroencephalograph findings slowly revert to normal following abstinence from alcohol. Similar findings have been found in terms of improved psychological test performance and in partial reversal of cerebral atrophy (J. W. Smith, 1982). Thus, in many cases, alcoholic brain damage is fully or partially reversible. Sometimes it is difficult to detect changes in brain structure because of the tremendous adaptability of the brain. However, chronic alcohol abusers do show chronic, long-lasting, and seemingly irreversible changes in brain functions (Segal & Sisson, 1985; J. W. Smith, 1982).

Alcoholic Chronic Brain Syndrome (Dementia)

This disorder is associated with a rather diffuse loss of functioning brain tissue. It can be caused by several factors, including natural aging and chronic alcohol abuse. It may be indistinguishable from the disorder of a nonalcoholic, senile person. J. W. Smith (1982) cites dementia as the leading cause of first admissions to state mental hospitals. The exact rate of alcoholic dementia's occurrence is not known, although J. W. Smith believes it is more prevalent than has been previously suspected. While the specific rate and cause are unknown, dementia is an "insufficiency syndrome" based on the loss of functioning of brain cells. Since these neurons, like other nerve cells, have no way of regenerating themselves, their loss ultimately means a loss in cognitive function.

The onset of symptoms is gradual and insidious. The earliest symptoms may include fatigue, listlessness, loss of interest, depression, anxiety, or agitation. Personality changes such as irritability, social withdrawal, lack of consideration for others, petulance, and moral laxity also occur (J. W. Smith, 1982).

These symptoms may be present for months or years before any clear-cut confusion, disorientation, or recent memory defects are noticeable to others. However, when the disorder is present in full-blown form, individuals exhibit confusion, loss of memory for recent events, and general forgetfulness. This forgetfulness is most apparent in regard to financial matters, socially appropriate actions, and regard for the feelings of others. Affected individuals may be more readily offended by the actions of others and show sudden outbursts of anger or irritability. When symptoms develop gradually, many persons develop defense mechanisms to cope with them. For example, they may use confabulation to fill in the blanks left by memory deficits, although the confabulation will not be as gross and obviously false as that seen in Korsakoff's Psychosis (discussed later). Individuals may also use perseveration, denial, avoidance, jocularity, or other diversions to prevent others from discovering their loss in function (Segal & Sisson, 1985; Smith, 1982).

SECONDARY (ALCOHOL-RELATED) FACTORS
LEADING TO BRAIN DAMAGE IN ALCOHOLICS

Alcohol use can lead to an inadequate amount of oxygen reaching the brain. This condition can be caused by blood alcohol levels that are high enough to lead to coma by hypoventilation. (Note: At high blood alcohol levels, the function of the lungs is depressed, causing less oxygen to be available.) Another possible cause is the aspiration of vomit by chronic alcoholics, leading to a reduction of oxygen supply to the brain.

Hypoglycemia is another condition that can be produced by alcohol abuse. Since brain cells are dependent upon glucose and oxygen for survival, this disorder can also lead to brain cell death. Brain damage and death due to hypoglycemia have been recorded. Nutritional deficiencies of the B vitamins can also cause brain damage (J. W. Smith, 1982).

Korsakoff's Psychosis

This disorder is named after its discoverer. Briefly described, it is loss of recent memory sometimes accompanied by confabulation in alcoholics. Persons suffering from this disorder are chronic alcoholics, often with peripheral neuropathy, who may be recovering from Wernicke's syndrome (see next section) (J. W. Smith, 1982). Santamaria describes the psychological features of Korsakoff's disorder as follows:

1. The individual has poor memory for recent events. The person has considerable difficulty learning new information, regardless of its type and whether it is visual, auditory, or tactile.

2. Because immediate recall is still functioning, new information can be held briefly. For example, the brain-damaged person with this disorder can repeat six or seven digits without difficulty but cannot store the materials in short-term memory, so the information is lost in the span of a few seconds.

3. The affected individuals are often not aware that they have a memory problem.

4. There may be confabulation, that is, making up events to fill in for the material the patient cannot recall. Confabulation does not always occur; and in many cases where it does occur, it may be the result of memory difficulties. In some cases, actual past events are projected into a more recent setting and mixed with confabulation to make the brain-damaged person's story more believable to the listener (Santamaria, 1989).

This description matches closely a patient observed in Boston in the early-1970s. The patient described his visit to Boston after a long absence. After telling about several encounters with old buddies, he described his visit with these buddies the previous evening to several hangouts for chronic alcoholics in Boston's old "skid row" (Kelley Square). The only problem was that the old skid row area had gone through an urban renewal project and all of the places he had described had been torn down or renovated several years before his current visit to Boston! A neurological consultation confirmed the diagnosis of Korsakoff's Psychosis.

Santamaria indicates that the amnesia is associated with the bilateral destruction of certain structures close to the central axis of the brain, and the disorder is sometimes called "axial amnesia." The structures he lists as being affected are the hippocampus, the fornix, the mammillary bodies, and the thalamic nuclei in the Circuit of Papez. He also notes that there is often frontal lobe atrophy in these patients.

Korsakoff's Psychosis often emerges from the acute syndrome of Wernicke's Encephalopathy, as previously noted. While some cases of

Korsakoff's Psychosis do not have an obvious clinical history of Wernicke's Encephalopathy, post-mortem examination shows the same damaged areas in the brain as patients with established clinical histories of Wernicke's Encephalopathy (Santamaria, 1989).

Wernicke's Encephalopathy Syndrome

It is now generally agreed that thiamine deficiency is the primary causative factor in this disorder. The typical cases are chronic alcoholics between the ages of 40 and 60 who become confused and excited. While drowsiness may be present, the person is almost always rousable (Santamaria, 1989). At first, these individuals may be delirious or perhaps psychotic and frequently already have peripheral neuropathy. The staggering gait often associated with peripheral neuropathy is also frequently present. After a few days they develop double vision, *diplopia*. This is the first real clue to the diagnosis since both excitement and delirium may frequently occur in alcoholics without Wernicke's syndrome. Once double vision occurs, the affected person's mental state changes relatively rapidly to one of quiet, then progresses to somnolence and stupor. If therapeutic intervention is not undertaken rapidly, death will occur (J. W. Smith, 1982). Santamaria (1989) points out that in recent years there has been a more heterogeneous symptom pattern, and the cases seen have not been so clinically characteristic.

Peripheral Neuropathy

According to J. W. Smith (1982), alcoholic peripheral neuropathy is more common than peripheral neuropathy from all other causes. There is little doubt that it is caused by a vitamin deficiency, probably principally thiamine deficiency (Segal & Sisson, 1985). Peripheral neuropathy is a disease of the peripheral nervous system and can result in a weakness in the hands, arms, and feet. J. W. Smith (1982) suggests that it is not thiamine deficiency alone but also deficiencies in other B vitamins like niacin and pantothenic acid that cause the disorder.

J. W. Smith gives a clear picture of the symptoms of this disorder. The onset of symptoms is usually slow, extending over weeks or months. Occasionally, however, symptoms may occur rapidly over the course of a few days. Involvement is usually bilateral (to both sides of the body) and symmetrical (affecting both sides in equal manner). The first symptoms may be pain in the calf muscles or feet with burning, tingling, or prickling sensations in the lower limbs. Sometimes, the first symptoms may be numbness in the feet, and later these same sensations may occur in the hands and arms. The symptoms may start in the feet and gradually work themselves up, but it is not unusual for the hands and fingers to be involved. Treatment for this problem consists of abstinence from alcohol, a nutritious diet, and supplementary B vitamins. Thiamine has been emphasized in the past, but large doses of B vitamins, including niacin, pantothenic acid, and pyridoxine (in addition to thiamine) are recommended (J. W. Smith, 1982).

LESS FREQUENTLY OCCURRING CENTRAL AND PERIPHERAL NERVOUS SYSTEM DISORDERS

While the following disorders also occur in alcoholics, their rate of occurrence is probably lower than disorders noted previously.

Marchiafava-Bignami Disease

This involves primary degeneration of the corpus callosum. This disorder is related to alcohol use and not to a vitamin deficiency. Individuals with this disorder display confusion, excitement, ataxia (failure of muscular coordination), and apraxia (loss of the acquired ability to perform intricate skilled acts). They might be mistaken for patients with delirium tremens, except they do not experience hallucinations. The onset of the syndrome is usually sudden, but in some cases, it occurs gradually (J. W. Smith, 1982). The disorder is associated with coma and fits and usually has a fatal outcome (Santamaria, 1989).

Central Pontine Myelinosis

This disorder usually occurs in early chronic alcoholics with evidence of severe malnutrition. They have a fluctuating mental state with dullness progressing in one to two weeks to a deep coma (J. W. Smith, 1982). Paralysis of the limbs and of the face is common. This disorder is associated with severe demyelination of nerve fibers around the ventral part of the pons (Santamaria, 1989). This disorder almost always results in death, although there have been cases of recovery reported. It is thought to be caused by a thiamine deficiency.

ALCOHOL-RELATED SLEEP DISORDERS

Alcohol abuse also disrupts sleep. Using electroencephalogram (EEG) recordings, a large body of knowledge has been obtained about sleep and how alcohol affects it. Sleep has several levels or stages, usually described in terms of EEG readings and depth of sleep. In stage one sleep (Rapid Eye Movement or REM sleep), dreaming occurs. This stage is followed by stages two through four, moving to deeper levels of sleep. During a given night's sleep, a normal sleeper moves through stages one through four and returns to stage one (REM sleep) three or more times. Alcoholics studied while

BOX 4–2
Fetal Alcohol Syndrome (FAS)

D. Smith (1982) has traced the awareness of fetal alcohol syndrome (FAS) back to ancient Greece. It seems to be a disorder that the medical and lay communities keep rediscovering. D. Smith was one of the researchers who has most recently described the complete pattern of this disorder in research at the University of Washington. Thanks to his and his colleagues' efforts, this syndrome is now widely recognized as "a serious but preventable disorder" (D. Smith, 1982, p. 187).

In general, the mothers who gave birth to children with FAS have been chronic alcoholics. In many cases they also suffered from cirrhosis of the liver and delirium tremens. The type of alcoholic beverages consumed varied, but chronic consumption of large amounts of alcohol was a common denominator.

Those anomalies most characteristic of this disorder include prenatal growth deficiency, postnatal growth deficiency, developmental delay and/or mental deficiency, and fine motor dysfunction. The face shows characteristics which are relatively consistent across victims of this disorder. For example, D. Smith and his colleagues found microcephaly (abnormally small head with smallness of the cerebral hemispheres), short palpebral fissures (short eyelid fissures), midfacial hypoplasia (incomplete development of the midface), inner epicanthal folds (a congenital deformity consisting of a vertical fold of skin on either side of the nose) and minor ear anomalies in the head and facial area. They also found minor joint anomalies and abnormal palmar creases, as well as heart deformities.

While alcohol has been shown to be involved directly and immediately at the birth of several children, siblings born prior to a mother's abusive drinking did not have deformities. This finding further implicates alcohol abuse as the causal agent. A succinct summary of how alcohol affects these children has been given by Webster (1989).

> In general terms, the affected child is small-for-date at birth, with a small head and a peculiar looking face, and may show irritability associated with its own alcohol withdrawal. ... After birth there is a failure to thrive and one or more malformations may be identified. As a result, the child will probably be seen in one of the specialty clinics of a children's hospital. Eventually the child will be assessed

and will be found to have a low I.Q., and there may be other behavioral anomalies. Because of the difficulty in identifying heavy drinking, the child's problems are frequently not associated with the mother's consumption and the diagnosis of FAS is not made.

It is now appreciated that FAS represents only one pattern of possible alcohol damage. Children born to chronic alcoholics have an increased incidence of a variety of congenital disorders without necessarily having all the characteristics of FAS. As the range of malformations that can be induced by alcohol has been appreciated, the concept of an incomplete syndrome has become more accepted and the term FAS is being replaced by fetal alcohol effects (FAE) or alcohol-related birth defects. (p. 136)

Thus, when these children are born, they can be seen as being at high risk for birth defects and as developmentally delayed. As they grow, they show several developmental and long-range problems. They are likely to be physically smaller than children born to nonalcoholic mothers, and they may show slower progress in acquiring the basic developmental plateaus in walking and talking. They are also more likely to be mentally retarded or to show learning deficiencies of various types (D. Smith, 1982).

While children of alcoholic mothers have a much higher risk of being born with physical and psychological problems, mothers who are more moderate drinkers also place their children at risk. D. Smith indicates that a study at the University of Washington showed that babies of moderate-drinking women had an average birth weight of 160 grams less than children of nondrinking mothers. Moderate drinking was considered to be the equivalent of two martinis a day. Increasing drinking to four to six drinks a day led to noticeable mild physical effects and dysfunction. Webster (1989), while reviewing more recent research, indicates that the occurrence of alcohol-related birth defects varies with the drinking characteristics of the sample studied. After reviewing studies from the United States, France, and Sweden, he places the incidence of FAS at 1.1 cases per thousand live births and FAE at 3 to 4 cases per thousand live births. Among the offspring of chronic alcoholic females, the occurrence of FAS is 2.5 percent to as high as 40 percent. Webster suggests that prenatal alcohol exposure may be responsible for approximately 5 percent of all congenital malformations in western urban populations.

The prevention of this disorder lies in the education of potential mothers. Such education is frequently disseminated through the popular press and the medical profession, especially obstetricians and nurses working with pregnant mothers. A study conducted during the 1970s at the University of Nebraska–Lincoln (Shepherd, 1980) indicated that in a survey of mostly middle-class first-time mothers, almost all reported reducing or discontinuing alcohol use once they were aware of their pregnancy. However, a more recent paper by Peterson and Lowe (1992) reports that while the alcohol-education campaigns appear to be partially effective, most women drinkers (70 to 75 percent) continue to drink while pregnant. Between 3 and 10 percent of the drinkers report drinking levels that have been associated with harm to the fetus. Thus, there are some women who continue to place their unborn children at risk. These women may be disproportionately found in those individuals with less opportunity for education. Certainly, this would seem to be true in Native American populations, where a much higher incidence of FAS occurs compared to the population at large (see Chapter 3). Educational actions and the placing of warning information on alcoholic beverages seem to have made the public more aware of the danger of drinking during pregnancy.

drinking and 10 nights afterwards showed REM suppression. Increased tension and irritability have also been shown to be associated with REM-deprived sleep. Fragmentation of sleep by frequent short periods of awakening is also characteristic of alcoholics' sleep patterns. During periods of time that the alcoholic is experiencing hallucinosis, REM sleep occurs to the virtual exclusion of all other stages (J. W. Smith, 1982).

This survey of alcohol's effect on the body obviously does not provide a complete picture of how alcohol affects the body. For example, fetal alcohol syndrome was not covered within the body of this chapter. This is such an important topic that it has been set off in Box 4–2. This chapter does illustrate, however, the pervasive effect that alcohol has on body functions. Several physicians working in the alcohol area have indicated that a person who understands how alcohol affects the body has an excellent medical education. This is because so much of the body's functioning is affected directly and indirectly by the ingestion of ethanol. Each of the topics discussed here could be the basis for at least a single chapter in a book (see, for example, the three volumes edited by Crowe & Batt and cited in this chapter under various authors). There have been complete books written about some of the disorders. This chapter introduces the complexity of alcohol's interaction with body functioning in as nontechnical a fashion as possible. Persons who wish a more thorough, complex coverage of these issues are encouraged to use the references cited in the chapter to guide their further reading.

REFERENCES

Avis, H. (1990). *Drugs and life.* Dubuque, IA: Wm. C. Brown.

Batt, R. D. (1989). Absorption, distribution and elimination of alcohol. In K. E. Crowe & R. D. Batt (Eds.), *Human metabolism of alcohol, Vol. I: Pharmacokinetics, medicolegal aspects, and general interests* (pp. 4–8). Boca Raton, FL: CRC Press.

Bennett, A. E. (1960). Diagnoses of intermediate stage of alcoholic brain disease. *Journal of the American Medical Association, 172,* 1143–1146.

Cala, L., Jones, B., Burns, P., Davis, R., Stenhousen, N., & Mastaglia, F. (1983). The results of computerized tomography, psychometric testing and dietary studies in social drinking with emphasis on reversibility after abstinence. *Medical Journal of Australia, 2,* 264–269.

Doweiko, H. F. (1990). *Concepts of chemical dependency.* Pacific Grove, CA: Brooks/Cole.

Fenster, L. F. (1982). Alcohol and disorders of the gastro-intestinal system. In N. J. Estes & M. E. Heinemann (Eds.), *Alcoholism: Development, consequences and interventions* (pp. 136–143). St. Louis: C. V. Mosby.

Fitzhugh, I. C., Fitzhugh, K. B., & Reitan, R. M. (1965). Adaptive abilities and intellectual functioning of hospitalized alcoholics: Further considerations. *Quarterly Journal of Studies on Alcohol, 20,* 402–411.

Fraser, R. (1989). Structural changes in liver caused by ethanol. In K. E. Crowe & R. D. Batt (Eds.), *Human metabolism of alcohol, Vol. III: Metabolic and physiological effects of alcohol* (pp. 19–33). Boca Raton, FL: CRC Press.

Goldstein, D. B. (1983). *Pharmacology of alcohol.* New York: Oxford University Press.

Grilly, D. M. (1989). *Drugs and human behavior.* Needham, MA: Allyn and Bacon.

Julien, R. M. (1988). *A primer of drug action* (5th ed.). New York: W. H. Freeman.

Julien, R. M. (1992). *A primer of drug action* (6th ed.). New York: W. H. Freeman.

Keller, M., McCormick, M., & Efron, V. (1982). *A dictionary of words about alcohol.* New Brunswick, NJ: Rutgers Center of Alcohol Studies.

Korsten, M. A., & Lieber, C. S. (1985). Medical complications of alcoholism. In J. H. Mendelson & N. K. Mello (Eds.), *The diagnosis and treatment of alcoholism* (2nd ed.) (pp. 21–64). New York: McGraw-Hill.

Kupari, M., & Suokas, A. (1989). Effects of ethanol and its metabolites on the heart. In K. E. Crowe & R. D. Batt (Eds.), *Human metabolism of alcohol, Vol. III: Metabolic and physiological effects of alcohol* (pp. 49–60). Boca Raton, FL: CRC Press.

Light, W. H. J. (1985). *Alcoholism: Its natural history, chemistry and general metabolism.* Springfield, IL: Charles C. Thomas.

Loomis, T. (1982). The pharmacology of alcohol. In N. J. Estes & M. E. Heinemann (Eds.), *Alcoholism: Development, consequences and interventions* (pp. 93–108). St. Louis: C. V. Mosby.

Moore, D. T. (1986). Reversal of alcohol effects: Acute and chronic conditions. *Alcohol Health and Research World,* Fall, 52–59.

Muuronen, A., Bergman, H., Hindmarsh, T., & Telakivi, T. (1989). Influence of improved drinking habits on brain atrophy and cognitive performance in alcoholic patients: A 5 year follow-up study. *Alcoholism: Clinical and Experimental Research, 13,* 137–141.

National Institute on Alcohol Abuse and Alcoholism (1988). *Alcohol Health and Research World.* Washington, DC: Author.

Peachey, J. E. (1989). Disulfiram, ethanol and related reactions. In K. E. Crowe & R. D. Batt (Eds.), *Human metabolism of alcohol, Vol. II: Regulation, enzymology, and metabolites of ethanol* (pp. 201–218). Boca Raton, FL: CRC Press.

Peterson, P. L., & Lowe, J. B. (1992). Preventing fetal alcohol exposure: A cognitive behavioral approach. *International Journal of the Addictions, 27,* 613–626.

Rubin, E., & Doria, J. (1990). Alcoholic cardiomyopathy: Clinical, pathological and experimental aspects. *Alcohol Health and Research World, 14,* 277–284.

Santamaria, J. N. (1989). Effects of ethanol and its metabolism on the brain. In K. E. Crowe & R. E. Batt (Eds.), *Human metabolism of alcohol, Vol. III: Metabolic and physiological effects of alcohol* (pp. 35–47). Boca Raton, FL: CRC Press.

Segal, R., & Sisson, B. V. (1985). Medical complications associated with alcohol use and the assessment of risk of physical damage. In T. E. Bratter & G. G. Forrest (Eds.), *Alcoholism and substance abuse* (pp. 137–175). New York: Free Press.

Seixas, F. A. (1982). The course of alcoholism. In N. J. Estes & M. E. Heinemann (Eds.), *Alcoholism: Development, consequences and interventions* (pp. 68–89). St. Louis: C. V. Mosby.

Shepherd, W. P. (1980). *An evaluation of women's beliefs and behavior concerning alcohol during pregnancy.* Unpublished doctoral dissertation, University of Nebraska, Department of Psychology, Lincoln.

Smith, D. (1982). Fetal alcohol syndrome: A tragic and preventable disorder. In N. J. Estes & M. E. Heinemann (Eds.), *Alcoholism: Development, consequences and interventions* (pp. 187–192). St. Louis: C. V. Mosby.

Smith, J. W. (1982). Neurological disorders of alcoholism. In N. J. Estes & M. E. Heinemann (Eds.), *Alcoholism : Development, consequences and interventions* (pp. 144–167). St. Louis: C. V. Mosby.

Tabakoff, B., & Rothstein, J. D. (1983). Biology of tolerance and dependence. In B. Tabakoff, P. B. Sutker, & C. L. Randall (Eds.), *Medical and social aspects of alcohol abuse* (pp. 187–220). New York: Plenum Press.

Van Thiel, D. H. (1983). Effects of ethanol upon organ systems other than the central nervous system. In B. Tabakoff, P. B. Sutker, & C. L. Randall (Eds.), *Medical and social aspects of alcohol abuse* (pp. 79–132). New York: Plenum Press.

Walsh, M. J. (1973). The biochemical aspects of alcoholism. In P. G. Bourne & R. Fox (Eds.), *Alcoholism: Progress in research and treatment* (pp. 43–61). New York: Academic Press.

Webster, W. S. (1989). Alcohol as a teratogen: A teratological perspective of the fetal alcohol syndrome. In K. E. Crowe & R. D. Batt (Eds.), *Human metabolism of alcohol, Vol. I: Pharmacokinetics, medicolegal aspects, and general interests* (pp. 133–155). Boca Raton, FL: CRC Press.

Witters, W., Venturelli, P., & Hanson, G. (1992). *Drugs and society* (3rd ed.). Boston: Jones and Bartlett.

Physiological/Genetic Theories of Alcoholism

_____ *chapter 5*

The suggestion that alcoholism is a physiologically based phenomenon is quite old. Vigorous arguments were made against a physiological base for alcohol abuse as early as 1882 (Todd, 1882, cited in Jellinek, 1960). In the United States, Benjamin Rush, one of the signers of the Declaration of Independence, labeled alcoholism a disease. Jellinek traces the history of the disease-concept of alcoholism in his 1960 work. Some important historical events include the following:

1. Benjamin Rush, as Surgeon General of the United States, suggested that inebriety was a disease.

2. In 1870 the American Medical Association for the Study of Inebriety and Narcotics was formed. Two journals that emphasized that alcoholism was a disease were established in the late 1800s.

3. By the 1920s, there was increasing knowledge of the roles played by avitaminosis in chronic alcoholism.

4. Alcohol's effects on driving, traffic accidents, and performance were recognized by the 1930s. This led to interest in alcohol's effects on fatigue and efficiency.

This series of historical factors led to the working hypothesis of alcoholism as a disease. This idea was shared not only by researchers and caregiving professionals, but also by the public. The disease approach came to dominate diverse organizations dealing with alcohol problems. Those organizations included the "Yale Group" (predecessors of the Rutgers University Center on Studies of Alcohol), the National Council on Alcoholism, the Committee on Alcoholism of the American Medical Association, and the large lay organization called Alcoholics Anonymous (Jellinek, 1960).

RECENT RESEARCH AND THEORY

Thus, the disease concept of alcoholism with its implicit (and often explicit) assumption that alcoholism is physiologically based is a long-standing explanatory system. The 1970s and 1980s brought attempts to increase experimental control. Despite the more rigorous research methods, some of the overall research strategies utilized are limited.

Schuckit (1987) states that because biological research is in its early stages, most researchers have focused on relatives of individuals with more severe types of alcohol problems. This research strategy results in information on biological vulnerability being specific to severe forms of alcoholism. Much less is known about the biological vulnerability of people from families where less severe forms of alcoholism have occurred. The assumption made by researchers is that more severe alcoholism will be more readily detected across family members, while less severe types will not be as easily detected.

Several research strategies have been used to attempt to establish the role of inherited characteristics in alcohol problems. The strategies and the research evidence they have produced include familial studies, adoption studies, twin studies, and biological markers studies.

Familial Studies

Goodwin (1971) notes that, without exception, all studies of alcohol in families have found higher rates of alcoholism among the relatives of alcoholics than are present in the population at large. The fact that alcoholism runs in families does not necessarily mean that alcoholism is inherited. For example, the French language can be said to run in families, but no one would seriously argue that the ability to speak French is inherited. There are some converging data that do suggest that familial studies may be useful in clarifying the role of genetics in alcohol problems.

Gurling and Murray (1984) examined several studies based on interviews with family members to establish the presence or absence of alcoholism. These studies are summarized in Table 5–1.

There are some interesting aspects of this table. It should be noted that the rates of first-degree relatives are lower for mothers and sisters but higher for fathers and brothers. That alcoholism transmission via genetic factors is lower for women than for men is a general finding in the genetic research on alcoholism. However, there do seem to be higher alcoholism rates for the

TABLE 5-1 Frequency of Alcoholism in Relatives of Alcoholics

Authors	No. & Sex	FIRST-DEGREE RELATIVES (%)				SECOND-DEGREE RELATIVES (%)
		Fathers	Mothers	Brothers	Sisters	
Amark, 1951	203M	26	2	22	0	
Moore and Ramseur, 1960	100M	35	7			
Winokur and Clayton, 1967	69M	21	3	14	2	21
Winokur et al., 1971	156M	29	6	46	5	
Winokur and Clayton, 1968	45F	28	12	12	9	10
Schuckit et al., 1969	58F	27	5	27	13	
Winokur et al., 1971	103F	44	3	50	8	
Bleuler, 1955	50MF	22	6	12	8	7
Pitts and Winokur, 1966	62MF	16	2	12	1	

Source: Taken from Gurling and Murray (1984, p. 128) and used with permission.

mothers of female alcoholics than for the mothers of male alcoholics. Table 5–1 also shows that between 16 percent and 44 percent of alcoholics had fathers who were alcoholic. Between 2 percent and 12 percent had alcoholic mothers. The percentage of brothers who also had alcoholism present ranged from 12 percent to 50 percent, while sisters ranged from 0 percent to 13 percent.

While these findings are interesting, they do not mean that alcoholism is genetic. Theoretically, it would be possible to account for the close associations of alcoholism across family members as resulting from the harmful effects of having been reared in an alcoholic family. Gurling and Murray argue that if alcoholism is inherited, it would be the result of polygenetic influences (i.e., not a single gene) and thus indicate that alcoholism should be low in second-degree relatives because it would be highly unlikely that these relatives would all inherit all of the several genes needed to inherit alcoholism. The studies that include second-generation relatives indicate that alcoholism occurs relatively frequently in more distant relatives. These findings would suggest a strong role for family and environmental forces in the development of alcoholism.

Goodwin (1971), in his brief review of familial studies, notes that some researchers have attempted to control for environmental factors while utilizing a familial approach to alcohol genetic research. If, for example, the severity of alcoholism is the same in offspring whether the parents are abstainers or alcoholics, it might suggest an underlying genetic factor. Also, if some types of alcoholics differ in the rate they produce alcoholic offspring than do other types, it might imply an underlying genetic factor. In a very early study, Amark (1951) found that "periodic" and "compulsive" alcoholics are more likely to have alcoholic offspring than are those alcoholics with a supposedly less severe form of alcoholism. Other researchers have found that alcoholism is associated with other problems in families of alcoholics. These include depression, criminality, sociopathy, and "abnormal personality." A typical finding is that depression occurs more frequently in female relatives of alcoholics while sociopathy occurs more often in male relatives (Goodwin, 1971).

Despite the potential usefulness of showing that alcoholism runs in families, it is difficult to isolate environmental factors from genetic causation. For example, alcohol abuse and crime are highly related events. It might well be that the disruption of the family and not alcohol abuse per se leads to more social, behavioral, and emotional problems in alcoholic families. Despite these difficulties, there has been a continuing interest in the study of alcoholism and genetics using the familial strategy. Schuckit (Schuckit, Li, Cloninger, & Deitrich, 1985) used this method to identify close relatives of alcoholics who were nonalcoholic themselves. Schuckit's research sample is limited to men not considered to be at current risk for alcoholism. Subjects were male students and nonacademic staff ranging from 20 to 25 years of age who had responded to a questionnaire. Individuals who already had a "serious" alcohol or drug problem were excluded from the sample, as were those with other serious medical problems. The study identified a large number of relatives of many alcoholics rather than focusing intensely on a few families. These alcoholic family offspring and relatives were then compared to controls. This research strategy allows for a diverse, almost inexhaustible sample. A wide range of possible risk factors prior to the development of alcoholism can also be studied.

Subjects who drank but were nonalcoholic and who indicated they had an alcoholic parent were placed in the "Family history positive" (FHP) group and matched for demography and drinking history with similar men who reported no close alcoholic relative, that is, "Family history negative" (FHN) (Schuckit et al., 1985, p. 482). Once subjects were selected, they underwent extensive laboratory analysis. Over a series of visits, raters who were blind to parental history measured personality characteristics, metabolism of alcohol, subjects' physical reaction to alcohol, the function of the brain as measured by event-related potentials (ERPs), and cognitive and psychomotor performance.

Reactions to all the above tests were established for subjects while they were not drinking. Then both experimentals (FHP) and controls (FHN) were administered either a placebo or a 20 percent solution of ethanol. This administration was followed by a 5-hour monitoring of performance measures and biochemical markers. Utilizing this research strategy, Schuckit and his colleagues were attempting to establish whether there are any biological markers that indicate a predisposition to alcoholism. A genetic marker is defined by Hill, Steinhauer, and Zubin (1987).

> In genetic studies the term "marker" usually refers to a characteristic or trait given at birth through one's genetic heritage that endures as for example, whether one has type O or B blood. Usually, genetic markers have simple, unequivocal patterns on inheritance and heritable variations common enough to be classified as genetic polymorphisms. Of course, an enduring, heritable trait like type O or B blood is not necessarily a "marker" for a particular illness just because the frequency of the genetic marker is higher among a particular group of individuals having the illness. To be considered a "marker" the blood group or other variant should distinguish affected from nonaffected individuals, should distinguish relatives of affected individuals from individuals without such a family history and, additionally, should show linkage with affected status. That is, within families there should be a segregation of the marker with the disease status. . . . (pp. 225–226)

Schuckit et al.'s research goal was to identify biological-genetic factors that might interact with the environment to increase the risk for alcoholism. He summarizes his findings to date in several areas in a 1985 review of his research. Schuckit also reviews research by other investigators that he sees as related to the question of biological markers in high-risk drinking but nonalcoholic men.

Differences in Metabolism of Alcohol.   When alcohol is consumed, there seems to be no differences between FHP and FHN groups in terms of the rate at which peak alcohol levels are reached or the speed at which alcohol is removed from the system. There are some possible differences between the FHP and FHN matched pairs in the accumulation of acetaldehyde, the first product of the breakdown of ethanol by liver enzymes (described in Chapter 4). Schuckit and others speculate that a mild elevation in acetaldehyde could counteract some of the depressant effects alcohol has on the brain and reduce the sedation effects of alcohol at mild dosages. It is also possible that these higher acetaldehyde levels increase the probability of organ damage, particularly to the heart, liver, and brain. Acetaldehyde is also capable of joining with neurotransmitters to produce morphinelike substances. Some writers suggest that these morphinelike substances may play a central role in alcohol addiction. The research findings around biological markers are still not firmly established. The fact that there is genetic control of enzymes suggests this is a potentially fruitful area of research.

Personality and Neuropsychological Factors. In his studies of FHP and FHN sons of alcoholics, Schuckit and his colleagues have found few personality differences on tests like the Minnesota Multiphasic Personality Inventory (MMPI) and the Eysenck Personality Inventory. The only exception (and a very weak finding, according to Schuckit) is that the FHP subjects score higher on the MacAndrew subtest of the MMPI.

Other researchers have found that offspring of alcoholics have possible problems on the Halstead Categorizing Test and on memory and motor performance tasks. However, other environmentally related factors cannot be completely ruled out in most of these studies. Schuckit concludes there are very few differences on personality variables and few readily generalizable differences on neuropsychological test scores when sons of alcoholics are compared to controls.

Alcoholism Genetic Influences Mediated by Risk for Other Disorders. It is possible that the genetic influences that contribute to psychiatric difficulties such as schizophrenia, major affective disorders, and antisocial personality may be marked by primary alcoholism. One enzyme in particular, monoamine oxidase (MAO), has been shown to be lower in some patients with psychiatric disorders. Decreases in this enzyme have also been indicated in research with alcoholics. However, when alcoholics abstain, their enzyme levels may return to normal.

Using the FHP and FHN pairs, Schuckit et al. (1985) measured MAO levels prior to and following ingestion of alcohol. There was only a nonsignificant trend for lower MAO activity in the high-risk FHP men when compared to their controls. Similar research comparisons were made for dopamine B-hydroxylase (DBH), which has also been implicated in major psychiatric disorders. There were no significant differences between FHP and FHN males, but the FHP subjects did tend to show lower blood DBH following alcohol ingestion. After reviewing the literature on major depressive disorders and on hyperactivity, Schuckit concludes that both his research and the work of others indicate no clear link between genetic factors that increase the risk for primary alcoholism and factors mediating other major psychiatric disorders.

Acute Intoxication Characteristics and Alcoholism. There is some suggestion in the literature that individuals who have drinking problems have more difficulty estimating their blood alcohol levels than do controls who do not have alcohol problems. In addition, heavy drinkers may overestimate their cognitive abilities at high alcohol consumption levels. Schuckit and his colleagues conducted a series of studies designed to shed light on these tendencies with his high-alcohol-risk and low-alcohol-risk young men in a laboratory setting. ". . . A series of subjective and cognitive/psychomotor tests were given to higher-risk and lower-risk young men, and changes in responses were monitored after an ethanol challenge" (Schuckit et al., 1985, p. 484). Schuckit and his colleagues found that there was less subjective intoxication reported in the FHP than the FHN men. The FHP men also showed less impairment on some tests than did their controls, despite having the same blood alcohol levels. An additional finding was that the high-risk alcoholic men had lower levels of prolactin, a hormone believed to be secreted by the pituitary gland in response to alcohol ingestion. The high-risk alcoholic men also had lower levels of blood cortisol. These FHP males also reported that they required more drinks to get "tipsy." Schuckit suggests these results (and those of at least one other researcher) indicate that one source of risk for alcoholism may be a less-intense-than-normal response to alcohol. This lower response might deter high-risk drinkers from knowing when to stop drinking.

Alcoholism Risk and Electrophysiological Differences.   It might be that alcohol has a different effect on the nervous systems of subjects with high risk for alcoholism than it does on subjects with low risk. Previous research has shown that "acute administration of alcohol increases the latency and decreases the amplitude of the P300 [an electrical response of the brain which is measured as a part of an electroencephalogram (EEG)] and this has been used as one possible marker of differences between higher-and lower-risk groups on their neurological functioning before and after ethanol use" (Schuckit et al., 1985, p. 484). Current data are available that suggest that high-risk sons of alcoholics may show this P300 amplitude decrease without alcohol or when receiving a placebo. This could mean that individuals at high risk are not as able as others to pay attention to themselves and their surroundings. Thus they perceive themselves to be less intoxicated because they are unaware of their feelings, particularly while drinking.

These findings suggest a biological-genetic component that contributes to alcohol risk. However, it is difficult to isolate and eliminate environmental factors that may have played a crucial role in the risk level. Schuckit's work and his review of other research suggest that there are converging data that indicate that the study of familial alcoholism may contribute in very positive ways to the understanding of the genetic contributions to alcohol problems.

Adoption Studies

A productive method for separating environmental and genetic causal factors in alcoholism is to study people who have been separated from their biological parents at or shortly after birth (Goodwin, 1971). This group makes up a population that has received genes from one set of parents and has been reared by another set. While this may appear to be a straightforward procedure in theory, in practice it is difficult to carry out research using this method. Most adoption agencies in this country do not allow researchers access to adoption records. Even if records were accessible, they are unlikely to contain information on the biological parents' drinking histories. It is also difficult to trace biological parents, adopted parents, and adopted offspring in a country with a highly mobile population (Goodwin, 1971). For these reasons, there have been few attempts in this country to use the adoption strategy to study the genetic history of alcoholism. Gurling and Murray (1984) summarize several of the adoption studies in Table 5–2.

Table 5–2 presents four adoption studies (two are divided according to gender). Each of these studies needs to be examined closely in order to note some specific limitations and ramifications. Roe, Burks, and Mittelmann (1945), the earliest of the studies (see also Roe, 1945), utilized a sample of thirty-six adopted children whose fathers were described as "heavy drinkers." They compared the thirty-six adoptees to twenty-five adoptees whose adopted parents were psychiatrically normal. As can be seen in Table 5–2, there was no apparent genetic transmission of alcoholism in this study. (Note, for some unknown reason, Gurling and Murray [1984], the authors from whom this table is taken, included only fifty-nine subjects in their original table.) Cadoret (1990) has summarized the comparsions of the above two groups.

> At the time of follow-up, the adoptees ranged in age from 22 to 40 years. Approximately 7 percent of the adult adoptees of alcoholics drank "regularly" as opposed to 9 percent of the controls. There were no alcoholics in either

TABLE 5–2   Alcoholism in Adoptees

Authors	No. and Sex of Adoptees	FREQUENCY OF "ALCOHOLISM" IN ADOPTEES		
		With Alcoholic Biological Parent (%)	Without Alcoholic Biological Parent (%)	Ratio of Frequency of "Alcoholism" in Adoptees with and without Alcoholic Biological Parent
Roe et al., 1945	59MF	0	0	0:0
Cadoret and Gath, 1978	84MF	50[a]	1	50:1
Goodwin et al., 1973	133M	18	5	3.6:1
Bohman, 1978	812M	{39 Fathers 13		{ 3:1
		{29 Mothers 15.5		{ 1.9:1
Goodwin et al., 1973	96F	4	2	2:1
Bohman, 1978	1,993F	2.5	2.3	1.1:1

[a] 3 out of 6 opposed to 1 out of 78.

Source: Taken from Gurling and Murray (1984, p. 129) and used with permission.

group. It was further noted that, as adolescents, 2 of the 21 boys in the alcohol parent group had been in trouble for drinking too much, while 1 of 11 boys in the normal parent group had a similar adolescent drinking problem. Again, the difference is nonsignificant. . . . (p. 42)

Following Roe's initial study, little research was done in the United States using the adoption strategy until Goodwin and his colleagues' work in the early 1970s (Goodwin, Schulsinger, Hermansen, Guze, & Winokur, 1973). Since most Scandinavian countries keep far better demographic records than the United States, Goodwin et al. used the population register of Denmark to identify fifty-five sons of alcoholic parents who had been adopted. They compared the fifty-five males with seventy-eight control male adoptees. The researchers found few differences between the two sets of adoptees in the types of families in which they were reared. However, they did find that children adopted from alcoholic biological parents had received considerably more psychiatric treatment. More critically, they were four times more likely to be alcoholic themselves than were the adoptees of biological parents with no histories of alcohol problems.

In a smaller and more recent study by Cadoret and Gath (1978), six adoptees who had biological parents with drinking problems were compared with seventy-eight adoptees whose biological parents had no drinking problems. Three of the six adoptees from alcoholic biological parents developed alcoholism, but only one adoptee from nonalcoholic biological parents had a drinking problem. Both the Goodwin and the Cadoret and Gath studies have been criticized because of the arbitrary nature by which they assigned subjects to drinking categories. For example, when the categories of alcoholism and problem drinking are combined for the two groups being compared in Goodwin's study to make a "problem drinking" category, the differences between groups disappear. Thus the differences may be due to the arbitrary assignment of subjects to alcoholic and problem drinking groups.

In an extension of their 1973 research, Goodwin and his colleagues made comparisons between adopted children of alcoholic biological parents and those children's own brothers who were reared in the alcoholic home of their shared biological parents. The alcoholism rates between the two groups were quite similar. This finding suggests that family environment has relatively little effect on alcoholism rates. The risk for alcoholism in offspring was related to the severity of the parents' alcoholism, with severity being defined by the number of times the parents had been hospitalized. These findings suggest that alcoholism rates may be mediated by genetic factors.

For the research reviewed thus far, positive results have been found primarily in males. The adoption studies do not seem to support a clear-cut genetic factor in the transmission of alcoholism in females. The failure to find genetic contributions to female alcoholism has been a general finding regardless of the research strategy used (e.g., Cotton, 1979).

Cloninger (1987) has used the adoption strategy to begin to build a model of alcoholism(s) that includes the contributions of genetic factors. Cloninger's work represents an attempt to build a genetically based theory of alcoholism. Cloninger has developed a number of working hypotheses to deal with alcoholism. He asserts that the neurobiological systems involved in alcohol-seeking behavior (and the acquiring of a functional tolerance for this beverage) appear to be the same ones involved in the individual's ability to adapt to new stimuli in general. He notes that psychiatric studies of alcoholics have shown that there are different subgroups of alcohol abusers who differ in their personality factors and neuropsychological functioning and in how they abuse alcohol. These various subgroups also differ in the degree inheritance is involved in the etiology of their alcohol problems (Cloninger, 1987, p. 410).

These types of alcoholics have both developmental and personality differences, which are associated with different drinking patterns. For example, Cloninger sees those drinking in adolescence and early adulthood as being like Jellinek's delta subgroup: alcoholics who had not lost control but who could not abstain from alcohol entirely. Drinking at this point in development, according to Cloninger, is associated with the taking of risks, being impulsive, and displaying antisocial behavior, which can include bar fights and arrests for driving while intoxicated. Jellinek's other type, loss-of-control drinking, occurs in individuals who show guilt and fear of becoming dependent on alcohol. These loss-of-control alcoholics are also emotionally dependent, rigid, perfectionistic, and introverted. According to Cloninger, these types of alcoholics develop problems in late adulthood after a long period of heavy drinking that has been socially encouraged. Cloninger labels loss-of-control alcoholism as Type I alcoholism. Type II alcoholics are those with the inability to abstain. The characteristics of each of these types are given in Table 5–3.

Type I alcoholics include people who are passive-dependent. Cloninger (1987) further describes them as having

> (i) . . . high reward dependence (that is, one who is eager to help others, emotionally dependent, warmly sympathetic, sentimental, sensitive to social cues, and persistent). (ii) high harm avoidance (that is, one who is cautious, apprehensive, pessimistic, inhibited, shy, and susceptible to fatigue), and (iii) low novelty seeking (that is, one who is rigid, reflective, loyal, orderly, and attentive to details). (p. 411)

In comparison, the Type II alcoholics have characteristics that are associated with antisocial personality, the reverse of passive-dependent personality. These persons are seen by Cloninger as having

> (i) high novelty seeking (that is, one who is impulsive, exploratory, excitable, disorderly, and distractable), (ii) low harm avoidance (that is, one who is confi-

TABLE 5–3 Distinguishing Characteristics of Two Types of Alcoholism

CHARACTERISTIC FEATURES	TYPE OF ALCOHOLISM	
Alcohol-Related Problems	*Type I*	*Type II*
Usual age of onset (years)	after 25	before 25
Spontaneous alcohol-seeking (inability to abstain)	Infrequent	Frequent
Fighting and arrests when drinking	Infrequent	Frequent
Psychological dependence (loss of control)	Frequent	Infrequent
Guilt and fear about alcohol dependence	Frequent	Infrequent
Personality Traits		
Novelty seeking	Low	High
Harm avoidance	High	Low
Reward dependence	High	Low

Source: Taken from Cloninger (1987, p. 411) and used with permission.

dent, relaxed, optimistic, uninhibited, carefree, and energetic), and (iii) low reward dependence (that is, one who is socially detached, emotionally cool, rough-minded, and independently self-willed). (p. 411)

According to Cloninger's classifications, alcoholics can have widely varying combinations of personality traits and alcohol-seeking behaviors. Cloninger notes that these differences have been hypothesized as based on brain differences. The brain differences determine individuals' liabilities to find alcohol reinforcing and to increase the risk they have of developing tolerance and dependence on alcoholic beverages.

Genetic epidemiology is the study of the social and biological interaction that may affect the inheritance and development of familial disorders. Cloninger used genetic epidemiology to focus on the transmission of alcoholism through families. He utilized Bohman's sample (1978) to look at the transmission of Type I and Type II alcoholism in adoptees. The adoptees were designated as Types I or II based on the pattern of alcohol abuse exhibited by their biological parents. Those adoptees whose biological fathers or mothers had an adult onset of alcohol abuse with no criminal behavior that required extensive incarceration were designated genetically as Type I alcoholics. Type II alcoholics were children whose biological fathers had extensive criminal records and considerable treatment for alcohol problems as youths and as young adults. Only the fathers were considered in this case since not enough mothers could be identified as having alcohol problems.

When these two groups were compared, Type I alcoholism developed only if the genetic predisposition was associated with exposure to heavy recreational drinking. However, in the absence of either genetic risk or a high-risk drinking environment, the probability of alcohol abuse in the child was lower than the rate in the general population. The biological children of Type II alcoholics were at increased risk for alcoholism, regardless of the drinking environment in which they were reared. The risk of alcoholism in these adoptees was nine times that of sons of all the other fathers. These findings illustrate how the adoption strategy can be used to look at more specific hypotheses about the pattern of genetic transmission.

Twin Studies

The third major strategy for looking at the genetic transmission of alcoholism is the twin approach. Goodwin (1971) has outlined some of the strengths and weaknesses of using twin studies to better understand genetic transmission of alcoholism. This strategy is based on the assumption that identical and fraternal twins differ only in respect to their genetic makeup. Environments for both types of twins are assumed to be similar. If these assumptions are accepted, it would be predicted that genetic disorders would more often co-occur in both members of identical twins (i.e., be concordant) than in fraternal twins. For example, monozygotic (identical) twins have almost exactly the same genetic makeup; fraternal (dizygotic) twins share only about 50 percent genetic makeup. If it can be assumed that fraternal and identical twins have environments that do not differ significantly, then a comparison of co-occurrence in identical and fraternal twins should provide definitive information on the contribution of genetics to alcoholism. The environments of identical twins are often described as being quite different from fraternal twins and from the environments of other sibling relationships. Identical twins frequently are dressed alike and responded to in much the same way by adults. Additionally, it is relatively common for identical twins to develop idiosyncratic language, which may serve to further increase the similarity of their environment. Thus environmental similarities may be much more profound for identical twins than for fraternal twins or for siblings in general.

A Swedish study conducted by Kaij (1960) utilized 1,974 male twin pairs where at least one of the pairs was registered by a temperance board because of a conviction of drunkenness or some other indicator of alcohol abuse. The concordance rate for alcohol abuse in the identical twins group was 54 percent; in the fraternal twins the concordance rate was 28 percent. This difference in concordance rates for the two types of twin pairs was statistically significant. Kaij divided the alcohol abusers into subgroups based on severity. When this was done, the fourteen identical twin pairs classified as having the most severe alcohol problems showed a concordance rate of over 71 percent. There was no significant increase in concordance rates for the fraternal twins when one member of the pair was classified as having a severe drinking problem.

In a Finnish study, Partanen, Bruun, and Markkaners (1966) found less definitive support of a genetic predisposition to alcoholism. Using male twins, these researchers found no differences between monozygotic and dizygotic twins in terms of the consequences alcohol had on their lives. However, normal patterns (in terms of frequency and amount) were more concordant in identical than in fraternal twins.

As already noted, one of the main objections to twin studies as a basis for inferring a genetic transmission of alcoholism is that identical twins may have been reared under more similar circumstances than were other siblings. However, if twins are separated early in life and reared apart, there is the advantage of holding genetic factors constant while varying environmental factors. This would seem to be a strong test for the relative influence of genetic and environmental contributions to alcohol problems. Unfortunately, these ideal circumstances are difficult to find because of the low occurrence of identical twins. Furthermore, it is difficult to eliminate environmental factors.

Gurling and Murray (1984) report ongoing research on identical twins conducted at Maudsley Hospital in England. Their study includes twenty male and fifteen female identical twins and thirty-three male and eleven female fraternal twins. All the twins had undergone psychiatric screening and a standardized alcohol questionnaire. At the time of the report, research on identical twin pairs was more complete than on the nonidentical twin pairs. Zygosity had been established by ratings of physical resemblance and by a study of twelve blood groups. Gurling and Murray present their findings in terms of *alcohol dependence* because they found *alcoholism* to be more ambiguous and difficult to define. They use the Edwards and Gross (1976) definition adopted by the World Health Organization (WHO). This definition includes

1. a narrowing in the repertoire of drinking behavior
2. salience of drink-seeking behavior
3. increased tolerance to alcohol
4. repeated withdrawal symptoms
5. repeated relief or avoidance of withdrawal symptoms by further drinking
6. subjective awareness of a compulsion to drink
7. reinstatement of the syndrome when drinking reoccurs

Table 5–4 presents the pairwise concordance rates for the alcohol dependence syndrome examined in Gurling and Murray's research. While 38 percent of the twins were below 40 years of age and may yet develop alcoholism, the current data do not show the tendency to inherit alcoholism that was found in Kaij's (1960) study. It is important to note that Gurling and

TABLE 5–4 Pairwise Concordance for the Alcohol Dependency Syndrome in 56 Pairs of Maudsley Twins

	Males	*Females*	*Both*
MZ (identical) twins	5/15 (33%)	1/13 (8%)	6/28 (21%)
DZ (fraternal) twins	6/20 (30%)	1/8 (13%)	7/28 (25%)

Source: Table adapted from Gurling & Murray (1984, p. 133) and used with permission.

Murray have analyzed the data for only a portion of their sample. The present trend does indicate that there are no differences between fraternal and identical twins in terms of the concordance rate for alcoholism. At best, when these results are combined with those obtained by Kaij, the twin research at this point is equivocal in terms of supporting a genetic transmission of alcoholism.

Biological Markers Studies

Biological markers as a research approach have both potential strengths and limitations. Essentially, this type of methodology attempts to show that alcoholism is inherited by establishing an association between alcoholism and other inherited characteristics (Goodwin, 1971).

For example, Goodwin cites research showing that color blindness, cirrhosis, and alcoholism are associated. He notes that researchers have hypothesized that alcoholism is transmitted on the recessive X chromosome. While this early research has been provocative, other alternative explanations for the association have been proposed. For example, other researchers have found color blindness in alcoholics frequently disappears once they abstain for a period of time.

Hill et al. (1987) broaden the concept of markers for alcoholism to include performance and even personality-test profiles. In addition to biological markers which predict a vulnerability to alcoholism, markers for performance include neuropsychological performance and psychosocial functioning measures, that is, the degree to which one participates in families and family networks. They point out that in all types of markers, the ideal would be for the marker to occur in alcoholics but not in control subjects. The marker should also occur in high-risk individuals like blood relatives of alcoholics who do not have alcohol problems. Hill et al. point out that there is a difference between "episode" markers, which occur when persons are drinking abusively, and "vulnerability" markers, which are present preceding alcoholic drinking and which remain during recovery.

The markers described by Hill and her colleagues include both physiologically based, psychologically based, and ecologically based factors associated with vulnerability. At the time of their report, Hill et al. had only preliminary information on their multiplex family study. In a multiplex family, one alcoholic family member is detected, at least one other sibling is affected, and one sibling is not affected by the disorder. This strategy allows researchers to partial out the acute effects of the alcoholism. Using this approach, Hill et al. found MMPI test responses to be useful as markers with high-risk subjects having elevated profiles on the psychopathic deviate scale and the schizophrenia scale when compared to controls. The researchers also found that event-related potentials differed across control and at-risk groups. The at-risk groups (both alcoholics and their nonaffected siblings) had longer brain potential latencies than did controls, that is, they showed brain wave patterns that were significantly different.

Some of the biological marker research was covered in the discussion of Schuckit's family strategy research. It is clear that being able to isolate nonbiologically based and biologically based factors (like evoked potential responses) in high-risk but not yet alcohol-dependent individuals offers an excellent way to study physiologically based precursors to abusive drinking. These markers may also be important as a focus of prevention efforts, since a high-risk prevention strategy can be effectively utilized (see Chapter 13).

IMPLICATIONS OF GENETICS RESEARCH/THEORY FOR TREATMENT AND PREVENTION

Tarter and Edwards (1986) suggest that the most powerful predictor of problematic drinking is a history of familial alcoholism. They further suggest that what is inherited may also be expressed through behavior. As Tarter and Edwards state: "Potentially, therefore, a genetic vulnerability may also be expressed behaviorally, although this need not necessarily be the case ... " (p. 347). These authors believe that the expression of genetic vulnerability may provide meaningful guidelines for intervention by treatment and prevention personnel.

Treatment and Genetic-Behavioral Vulnerability

Tarter and Edwards speculate that the limited effectiveness of current alcohol programs may be due to their failure to look closely at the effects that genetic, behavioral vulnerability may have on alcoholism. For example, they note that previous research using the MMPI indicates that persons who display a problem with depression during treatment have the most successful outcome. A poorer outcome is associated with persons having elevations on hypomania (a measure of maniclike behaviors) and the psychopathic deviate scale (a measure of antisocial behavior and lack of conscience). In the latter case, patients are characterized by high energy output—even hyperactivity—and poor control of impulses. These individuals also have interpersonal superficiality and low tolerance for frustration. They have difficulties sticking with tasks and dealing with authority figures and are nonconforming and emotionally impoverished. According to Tarter and Edwards, many of these characteristics are the same ones that are said to comprise vulnerability to alcoholism. It should be noted that Tarter and Edwards' research focused on males, so their conclusions are not meant to pertain to women.

Tarter and Edwards review Vaillant and Milofsky's (1982) research and note parallels with the MMPI profiles discussed earlier. Vaillant and Milofsky list four factors that were positively associated with recovery from alcoholism: (1) acquiring substitute behaviors; (2) acquiring external control; (3) having a source of increased hope; and (4) developing new relationships with people. Tarter and Edwards believe that alcohol treatment centers might profit from focusing treatment on the acquisition of substitute behaviors. The subjects in Vaillant and Milofsky's research effectively utilized the substitute behaviors of chain smoking, compulsive hobbies, and meditation. One effect of these behaviors is that they stabilize the level of arousal individuals experience. Subjects learned these substitute ways of dealing with tension and stress following alcohol treatment. This finding suggests that there are coping strategies that can help people deal with the behavioral, affective, and arousal problems that make them vulnerable to alcoholism.

Tarter and Edwards (1986) suggest that alcoholism may be only one of many ways that genetically based vulnerabilities may be expressed. If environmental supports for drinking are absent or if alcohol is unavailable, alcoholics might choose to abuse other drugs like minor tranquilizers. In brief, Tarter and Edwards believe that outcome in alcoholism is influenced, to some extent, by the predisposing behavioral characteristics of individuals in treatment. By implication, treatment centers need to be more aware of these predisposing characteristics and design treatment programs to deal with them. One of the broad-based interventions Tarter and Edwards suggest is to incorporate cognitive control over behavior into treatment programs. For example, since biologically predisposed persons seem to require larger amounts of alcohol to feel intoxicated, they may need to learn cognitive monitoring of blood alcohol levels. Since many alcohol abusers seem to have social adjustment difficulties (and they drink to help deal with these problems), social skills training needs to be provided. Relaxation training might reduce the emotional lability and anxiety some studies have reported as preceding alcoholic drinking. Improved cognitive controls to help reduce impulsive tendencies would seem useful in poorly controlled alcoholics. Finally, teaching alcoholics to regulate stimuli input may also be helpful. Alcoholics tend to want to augment stimulus input, which makes them more tense. Meditation training has proven effective in providing relaxation. One report suggests sensory deprivation facilitates deep relaxation. This may be another way of helping alcoholics with their tension. Overall, Tarter and Edwards make the point that alcohol treatment programs do not focus on behavioral predisposition in most therapeutic communities. This failure to orient treatment to behavioral predispositions has been due in part to the fact that they are not well understood. Yet, they seem to be similar in nature to temperament, a characteristic that can be inherited.

Behavioral Predisposition and Prevention

Tarter and Edwards also suggest that an awareness of genetic vulnerability to alcoholism should help in the development of prevention programs. (See Box 5–1 for a discussion of the pharmacogenetic approach and its role in both prevention and treatment.) The authors' discussion of prevention is more general than their consideration of treatment. They do, however, point out some areas where prevention and early intervention might be useful. They assert that specific risk factors occur during preadolescent development. Those factors could be modified by some type of clinical intervention. Early in life, high-risk populations (for example, children of alcoholics) could be subjected to behavioral techniques to

> improve self-control ... reduce aggressivity and impulsivity ... increase social skills ... [These] ... would appear to have substantial prophylactic benefits ... (p. 353).

The needs for these types of interventions are based on genetic etiology. They are, however, quite similar to prevention procedures suggested by theorists and researchers who approach prevention in children of alcoholics from a psychosocial orientation.

THE GENETIC APPROACH—CRITICISM AND EVALUATION

The role that genetics plays in the etiology of alcoholism has been argued for several years. Tolor and Tamerin (1973) criticized the research of Goodwin et al. (1973) on a number of grounds. The most serious criticism was aimed at the grouping of drinking severity. Tolor and Tamerin saw this as arbitrary. Their critical question was, Did the significant differences found between adoptees from alcoholic biological parents and those from nonalcoholic biological parents depend upon how problem drinking was defined? Eighteen percent of the experimental group (adopted children of alcoholics) were designated as alcoholics while 5 percent of the controls were said to be alcoholic. Fourteen percent of the controls and 9 percent of the experimental subjects were defined as problem drinkers. If the categories of problem drinker and alcoholic are combined into one category (yielding a category that would fit many researchers' notions of alcoholism), 27 percent of the experimentals and 19 percent of the controls would be designated problem drinkers or alcoholics. When combined in this manner, it becomes meaning-

BOX 5–1
The Pharmacogenetic Approach— A Brief Outline

The pharmacogenetic approach to genetic foundations for alcoholism hypothesizes that there are some underlying differences in the way that potential alcoholics metabolize alcohol. Pharmacologically, the drug ethanol is simply not metabolized the same way by individuals with a predisposition for alcoholism as it is by those with low risk for the disorder (Gurling & Murray, 1984). Early research by Ewing, Rouse, and Pellizzari (1974) indicated that some Orientals show a flushing response to alcohol intake, which looks similar to that shown by alcohol drinkers who are on disulfiram regimens. This led to the theory that individuals might differ in their ability to secrete the enzymes alcohol dehydrogenase and aldehyde dehydrogenase. Aldehyde dehydrogenase rapidly breaks down acetaldehyde into acetic acid, which can be readily metabolized by the body. This rapid breakdown assures that acetaldehyde, which is highly corrosive in large amounts in the body, does not build up in the drinker's bloodstream. It is thought that some individuals (and some racial groups, like Orientals) may produce aldehyde dehydrogenase in lower amounts than do other people. When individuals who produce less aldehyde dehydrogenase drink, they can show sweating, flushing, vomiting, and other effects that are reflective of corrosive levels of acetaldehyde in their bodies. This may explain the fact that the Chinese have low alcoholism rates. Because of the corrosive effects of high alcohol intake they may curtail their drinking at lower blood alcohol levels than the general population in the United States.

Paradoxically, acetaldehyde is also thought to be involved in the development of addictive, opiatelike substances, which could explain a genetic predisposition to alcohol. That is, acetaldehyde could be one of the mechanisms whereby people become addicted to alcohol. Whether acetaldehyde plays a prominent role in reducing or increasing risk to alcoholism is still undetermined. However, Gurling and Murray (1984) indicate that "any genetic predisposition to alcoholism at a biochemical level is likely to be more complicated than the simple effects of acetaldehyde" (p. 134). They go on to suggest that genetic variations in human membrane properties might account for some of the differences in tolerance noted between high-risk and low-risk drinkers. These same membrane differences may help account for differences in the severity of withdrawal symptoms. They may also increase the risk of Korsakoff's Psychosis and cirrhosis of the liver. Gurling and Murray see the genetic contribution to alcohol problems as yet to be established. However, they point out that it took several years of different approaches to genetic research to firmly establish that schizophrenia was in part genetically determined. It would be reasonable to expect a similar time span for genetic research in the alcohol area to be fully established. In areas where genetic risk has been established, there are some clear guidelines for treatment and prevention.

less to treat the two groups as representing different populations. Thus, it is suggested that the arbitrary assignment to alcoholic and nonalcoholic categories by Goodwin and his colleagues may be responsible for an artificial difference between the two groups of subjects.

Gurling and Murray (1984) have raised questions about the genetic transmission of alcoholism in a review of their own data on co-occurrence in identical twins. They state: ". . . it is clear that our preliminary findings do not show the same tendency for alcohol dependence to be heritable, as Kaij found in Sweden. Indeed the concordance for both MZ [monozygotic] and DZ [dizygotic] twins is similar to the prevalence of alcohol dependence in first-degree family members" (p. 133).

Peele (1986) has written a significant paper on the implications and limitations of the genetic model of alcoholism and other addictions. He reviews several of the difficulties that confront the genetic model of alcoholism. He notes that two Danish prospective studies have generally been inconsistent. Even the studies that have found differences in acetaldehyde levels in offspring of alcoholics and nonalcoholics are clouded by the fact that measurements of acetaldehyde are difficult to make and highly unreliable. It may be that the acetaldehyde differences between alcoholic and nonalcoholic genetic groups are the result of a difficult measurement process.

The research on the ability of subjects to accurately estimate blood alcohol levels indicates no differences between alcoholic and nonalcoholic offspring. In general, there seem to be different outcomes by different researchers in the area of evoked brain potentials and in personality characteristics. Each set of researchers seems to find either different patterns of evoked potentials or differing personality types in alcoholics. Peele asserts that this makes generalizations of genetically based findings difficult.

Peele is particularly persuasive when he points out that genetic theories can make little sense out of the differences between social groups. He cites Vaillant's findings that ethnic differences play a greater role than genetic history in clinical outcomes. For example, return to controlled drinking seems to be related more to ethnic grouping than to genetic history. Peele also observes that the incidence of alcoholism is influenced by social class and gender. In the latter case, the results indicate that the genetic transmission of alcoholism is generally limited to males.

Goodwin and other researchers have conceptualized inherited alcoholism as a distinct and separate variety of alcoholism. However, Peele states:

> ... the ... findings [are] that the same socially based differences in alcoholism rates pertain as well for less severe gradations of alcohol misuse. That is, those same ethnic and gender groups that have a high incidence of problem drinking ... also display a high incidence of alcoholism. ... It simply strains scientific credulity to imagine that the same factors which act to determine alcohol misuse also operate through separate genetic paths to influence alcoholism. Moreover, epidemiological studies such as Vaillant's and the Cahalan group's have always found more severe forms of alcohol dependence to merge imperceptibly and gradually with lesser degrees of problem drinking, so that a distinct, pathological variety of alcoholism does not stand out along a population curve of those who have drinking problems. ... (1986, p. 66)

The data on the presence or absence of a pure, inherited alcoholism are conflicting. It seems reasonable that an inherited predisposition might interact with the environment to increase individuals' risks for alcohol problems. What can be said at this point is that alcoholism, if it is inherited, does not follow a simple Mendelian pattern. Whether it will be possible to isolate the degree of risk a given individual may have from a family history of alcoholism may depend on the improvement of measurement instruments and a more specific, generalizable definition of alcoholism and/or problem drinking.

REFERENCES

Amark, C. (1951). A study in alcoholism. *Acta Psychiatrica et Neurologica, Supplement 70.*

Bleuler, M. (1955). Familial and personal background of chronic alcoholics. In: O. Diethelm (Ed.), *Etiology of chronic alcoholism* (pp. 110–166). Springfield, IL: Charles C. Thomas.

Bohman, M. (1978). Some genetic aspects of alcoholism and criminality. *Archives of General Psychiatry, 35,* 269–276.

Cadoret, R. J. (1990). Genetics of alcoholism. In R. L. Collins, K. E. Leonard, & J. S. Searles (Eds.), *Alcohol and the family: Research and clinical perspectives* (pp. 39–78). New York: Guilford Press.

Cadoret, R. J., & Gath, A. (1978). Inheritance of alcoholism in adoptees. *British Journal of Psychiatry, 132,* 252–258.

Cloninger, C. R. (1987). Neurogenetic adaptive mechanisms in alcoholism. *Science, 236,* 410–416.

Cotton, N. S. (1979). The familial incidence of alcoholism. *Journal of Studies on Alcohol, 40,* 89–115.

Edwards, G., & Gross, M. M. (1976). Alcohol dependence: Provisional description of a clinical syndrome. *British Medical Journal, 1,* 1058–1061.

Ewing, J. A., Rouse, B. A., & Pellizzari, E. D. (1974). Alcohol sensitivity and ethnic background. *American Journal of Psychiatry, 131,* 206–210.

Goodwin, D. W. (1971). Is alcoholism hereditary? *Archives of General Psychiatry, 25,* 545–548.

Goodwin, D. W., Schulsinger, F., Hermansen, L., Guze, S. B., & Winokur, G. (1973). Alcohol problems in adoptees raised apart from alcoholic biological parents. *Archives of General Psychiatry, 28,* 238–243.

Gurling, H., & Murray, R. (1984). Alcoholism and genetics: Old and new evidence. In J. S. Krasner, J. S. Madden, & R. J. Walker (Eds.), *Alcohol related problems: Room for manoeuvre* (pp. 127–136). New York: John Wiley.

Hill, S. Y., Steinhauer, S., & Zubin, J. (1987). Biological markers for alcoholism: A vulnerability model conception. In P. C. Rivers (Ed.), *Alcohol and addictive behavior: Vol. 34. Nebraska Symposium on Motivation* (pp. 207–256). Lincoln: University of Nebraska Press.

Jellinek, E. M. (1960). *The disease concept of alcoholism.* New Haven, CT: Hillhouse Press.

Kaij, L. (1960). *Studies on the etiology and sequels of abuse of alcohol.* University of Lund, Sweden, Department of Psychiatry.

Moore, R. A., & Ramseur, F. (1960). A study of the background of 100 hospitalized veterans with alcoholism. *Quarterly Journal of Studies on Alcohol, 21,* 51–67.

Partanen, J., Bruun, K., & Markkaners, T. (1966). *Inheritance of drinking behavior.* New Brunswick, NJ: Rutgers University Center on Alcohol Studies.

Peele, S. (1986). The implications and limitations of genetic models of alcoholism and other addictions. *Journal of Studies on Alcohol, 47,* 63–73.

Pitts, F. N., Jr., & Winokur, G. (1966). Affective disorder VII: Alcoholism and affective disorder. *Journal of Psychiatric Research, 4,* 37–50.

Roe, A. (1945). Children of alcoholic parents raised in foster homes. In *Alcohol, science and society. Quarterly Journal of Studies on Alcohol,* 378–393.

Roe, A., Burks, B., & Mittelmann, T. (1945). Adult adjustment of foster children of alcoholic and psychotic parentage and the influence of the foster home. In *No. 3, Memoirs of the Section on Alcohol Studies, Quarterly Journal of Studies on Alcohol.*

Schuckit, M. A. (1987). Biological vulnerability to alcoholism. *Journal of Consulting and Clinical Psychology, 55,* 301–309.

Schuckit, M. A., Li, T. K., Cloninger, R., & Deitrich, R. A. (1985). Genetics of alcoholism. *Alcoholism: Clinical and Experimental Research, 9,* 475–492.

Schuckit, M. A., Pitts, F. N., Reich, T., King, L., & Winokur, G. (1969). Two types of alcoholism in women. *Archives of General Psychiatry, 20,* 301–306.

Tarter, R., & Edwards, K. (1986). Antecedents to alcoholism: Implications for prevention and treatment. *Behavior Therapy, 17,* 346–361.

Tolor, A., & Tamerin, J. S. (1973). Comment on the study by Goodwin et al., and a response. *Quarterly Journal of Studies on Alcohol, 34,* 1341–1347.

Vaillant, G., & Milofsky, E. (1982). The etiology of alcoholism: A prospective viewpoint. *American Psychologist, 37,* 494–503.

Winokur, G., & Clayton, P. (1967). Family history studies I.: Two types of affective disorder separated according to genetic and clinical factors. *Recent Advances in Biological Psychiatry, 9,* 35–50.

Winokur, G., & Clayton, P. (1968). Family history studies IV: Comparison of male and female alcoholics. *Quarterly Journal of Studies on Alcohol, 29,* 885–891.

Psychological Theories:
Predispositional

_____ *chapter* 6

One way to view the development of alcohol abuse is that it is due to some underlying psychological process that predisposes persons to alcoholism. In other words, instincts or events shape individuals' personalities, and that personality formation is responsible for difficulties with alcohol abuse. It is this assumption that has guided, in part, the search for the "alcoholic personality." While the search for the alcoholic personality has been abandoned by most researchers because no clear-cut personality type associated with alcoholism has been discovered (e.g., Cox, 1987, 1988), the presence of preexisting personality issues still plays a role in some clinical treatment approaches. This personality predisposition has been theoretically explained in a number of ways. Three possible psychodynamic conceptions of how personality factors may predispose individuals to alcoholism will be examined: *psychoanalytic theory* (based on the writings of Sigmund Freud); *dependency theory* (which is related to psychoanalytic theorizing); and *power theory* (which also has its roots in psychoanalytic theorizing and is based on the research and theorizing of McClelland and his colleagues).

PSYCHOANALYTIC THEORY

Because of its historical influence on the development of a theoretically based approach to intervention with alcohol problems (Barry, 1988; Cox, 1987, 1988) and because it still plays an important role in alcohol treatment in some psychiatrically oriented treatment settings, this theory will be examined closely. It is also true that in the so-called "talking therapies" of mental health professionals, the psychodynamic orientation is the predominant one in which most have been trained. Clinicians are still guided by the psychodynamic orientation, despite the fact that many professionals believe it has little empirical support (Wilson, O'Leary, & Nathan, 1991).

The interpretation of psychoanalytic theory has been undertaken by several authors. The present discussion is based on Blum and Blum's (1969) application of the theory to alcohol use and abuse. First, a brief overview of the general theory of psychoanalysis is necessary to provide background for applying the theory to the alcohol field. Following the outline of the overall theory, the ways various writers have modified the theory to account for alcohol abuse and alcoholism will be described. (An understanding of this theory will also be helpful in reading Chapters 9, 10, and 11, which utilize psychodynamic concepts.)

Psychoanalysis was developed by Freud in Vienna during the latter part of the nineteenth century and the early part of the twentieth century. The central tenet of psychoanalytic theory and treatment is the presumption that unconscious conflicts that cannot find expression in socially approved action cause mental illness (where the person suffers psychological discomfort) or delinquent behavior (where the environment around the person suffers). Suffering persons are unaware of the unconscious conflicts and the ways these affect their actions, thoughts, and feelings. They must act in accordance with their unconscious need (even though that need may not lead to long-term satisfaction) or rationalize their actions or feelings.

The most general description of unconscious conflict is of two opposed forces balanced against each other. One of these forces strives for expression, the other for repression. Since these forces are unconscious, suffering persons are unaware of the two opposed forces. They are aware only of the resultant symptom from the conflict. One way to view these unconscious forces is as needs that seek fulfillment. These needs are usually expressed in interpersonal relations. The needs that oppose fulfillment are those that are expressed as a prohibition and as feelings of guilt and shame. These are the forces which deny pleasure for the sake of prudence and morality.

As individuals move through developmental stages, they learn to inhibit impulses until the appropriate manner of satisfaction is available; for example, a child learns to wait for food without throwing a tantrum. Whenever there is excessive repression of needs or when there is unrestrained expression, there is *neurotic* behavior. The aim of psychoanalytic therapy is to bring out these unconscious childhood conflicts, so they can be relived and bring the opposing forces into a better balance. By creating a better balance between opposing forces and needs, neurotic behavior is relieved.

It is important to bring these unconscious conflicts out into the open because persons act in accordance with their unconscious needs, no matter what situation they are in. In the treatment setting, these unconscious needs and desires from childhood are expressed as positive and negative emotions toward the therapist. (These emotional conflicts are frequently associated with inadequate resolution of developmental stages, as will be discussed later.) The transferring of childhood conflicts on to the therapist is called *transference*, either positive (having positive, affectionate, and loving or sexual feelings toward the therapist) or negative (having hostile, angry, and aggressive feelings toward the therapist). These reactions are transferred from the unresolved conflicts of childhood to the therapy setting. The unconscious repetition of feelings from the past and their analysis by the therapist and patient leads to an understanding of the origin of these feelings.

In the analysis of transference, persons learn about the origins of their childhood feelings and begin to better understand why they react the way they do to others. They learn that while these behaviors were once effective in getting attention and affection from other people, they are now ineffective or self-defeating and perhaps even painful. The feelings patients develop toward the therapist and, more importantly, the feelings they fail to develop because they cannot allow themselves to experience feelings, provide clues to their present behavior. Analysis of transference is a basis for understanding why patients react the way they do to intimacy, disappointment, or delayed gratification, for example, and why they handle their dependency needs and frustrations the way they do.

The analysis of transference is complicated by *resistance*. Resistance prevents the full development of transference and it prevents persons in treatment from showing emotions such as hate or love as strongly as those emotions were originally experienced. Since these feelings are hidden because they are too dangerous and frightening to express, it is important for the psychoanalytic therapist to analyze the resistance.

Analysis of resistance makes patients aware of their psychological fears and blind spots. According to Blum and Blum (1969), analyzing resistance is more important to treatment than analyzing the unconscious urges that resistance is designed to keep out of awareness.

The psychoanalyst uses the method of *free association* to make unconscious drives and needs more accessible to awareness. Through this process, persons learn to allow anything that comes to mind to be spoken aloud, no matter how irrelevant it may seem. Free association is an uneven process because of resistance. Resistance can occur during free association in the forms of blocking, distorting, or falsifying threatening thoughts or suppressing dangerous thoughts that come into consciousness. Despite resistance, free association has proven to be an excellent way for persons to rediscover repressed and forgotten childhood experiences and memories. It allows patients (with help from the therapist) to make connections between seemingly unconnected experiences.

Dream analysis is another way of getting at unconscious material. While sleeping, defenses are relaxed and unconscious material may be expressed.

Even though defenses are relaxed during sleeping, they still operate at some level and distort the experience so that the *manifest* content of a dream may not be closely tied to unconscious drives and needs. The expression of needs and drives are disguised, even in dreams. The analyst can help patients see the relevance of their dream material by interpreting the *latent* content of the dream.

Another important aspect of psychoanalytic theory is Freud's ideas about development and how early experiences affect adult personality. Vinacke (1968) gives an abbreviated summary of Freud's developmental stages and their impact on personality:

> Freud presented a detailed conception of developmental processes. In fact, he emphasized the paramount importance of childhood events to such an extent that later experience was regarded as having comparatively little effect on personality. . . . Freud regarded development as proceeding through successive psychosexual stages, in which libido [instinctual life energies] becomes attached to particular forms of gratification. Broadly conceived, these occur first in pregenital ways, followed by a quiescent or latency period, finally leading to genital expressions.

> *Pregenital Stages*

> During the first year of life, an *oral stage* exists in which primary gratification is centered on the mouth. It is featured by pleasures of sucking and stimulation of the mouth and lips; a little later, satisfaction is gained, also, from incorporating objects by eating. From ages 2 to 4, gratification shifts to an *anal stage,* [and the child] enjoys the acts of urination and defecation—an expulsive phase—and later enjoys holding back his waste products, partly because of the internal stimulation and partly because the parents value their release—a retentive phase. Beginning at about age 3 and extending to age 5, the infant passes into a *phallic stage,* associated with pleasures in the genital region. It is marked by sexual and aggressive feelings. These first three stages are narcissistic, that is, oriented primarily toward the infant's own sensations and needs. There is the implication that libido does not have a fixed mode of gratification, but shifts from one area to another. Beginning at about age 5, . . . there is a shift away from narcissistic gratifications; the libido diminishes in intensity, and the *latency stage* begins. This is a period of psychosexual quiescence. . . . It is a period of acquiring skills and knowledge, of perfecting socialized patterns of behavior. . . . Clearly, this period corresponds to the early school years and to the acceptance of parental standards.

> As puberty approaches, accompanied by the beginnings of sexual maturity, there is a shift to the *genital stage*. It continues into adolescence and ends with the adoption of adult modes of behavior. This period is marked by an increasing orientation to other people. Emotional attachments to genuine love objects, apart from the self, become increasingly important. Of course, members of the opposite sex figure centrally in the genital period, but the upsurge

of libido signifies great reserves of energy which can be directed in a variety of directions as well. The interests and emotions of the adolescent are varied. In later phases of the genital stage, adult characteristics become well established and emotional attachments are consolidated.

Fixation and Regression

The foregoing stages are not sharply separate, but merge into each other. Furthermore, experiences at one stage are not lost at the next; rather, personality is a progressive development in which each stage represents, so to speak, a strand in the final pattern. But, normally, there *is* a change to the next stage. It happens, however, that the emotional effects of one stage may be especially pronounced and only incompletely abandoned. If these components of personality endure strongly, a *fixation* may result, and if it is too strong, there may be a condition conducive to neurosis. The experiences at any stage are likely to be anxiety-provoking, and the child may have difficulty coping with them. He may, therefore, have a tendency to cling to the gratifications associated with a particular stage. A fixation of this kind is an arrest in emotional development, providing a refuge, so to speak, from later anxieties. If frustration becomes acute, the person may seek again for the satisfactions—largely at an unconscious level—of an earlier stage. This recurrence of infantile behavior is called *regression*. The difficulties attendant on socialization lead to at least some degree of fixation and some tendency toward regression in everyone. In short, development is uneven at best.

Adult Character

Although a wide variety of consequences of early experience could be listed, the Freudian position commonly recognizes only a few major patterns. They stem from fixations at the several stages just described. Without describing them thoroughly, we can briefly summarize some of the principal features. *Oral character* is one marked by preoccupations and interests with the mouth—smoking, eating, kissing, and so on. There is a tendency to be dependent on others for providing support for self-esteem. *Anal character* includes some combination of excessive parsimony, obstinacy, and orderliness. Traits of the *phallic character* are aggressiveness, impulsiveness, attempts to dominate others, vanity, and exhibitionism. Finally, traits especially typical of the *genital character* are those we associate with the mature, well-organized person: realistic, coping with problems, sublimated impulses directed toward constructive goals, healthy and socially approved sexual behavior, and so on. (pp. 385–386)

Within the framework of Freudian theory, fixation at the oral stage is often used to explain alcoholic behavior because alcoholics do so many things that remind psychoanalysts of infants. For example, they derive pleasure from the bottle and the feeling of satiation followed by sleep or unconsciousness. The orthodox Freudian views the bottle of alcohol as a substitute

Satiation and sleep (like a baby) is one way of seeing an alcoholic's role from the psychoanalytic point of view. *(Photograph courtesy of the Independence Center, Lincoln, Nebraska.)*

for the mother's breast, the symbol of security, which was either too available, not available enough, or inconsistently available, resulting in the fixation at the oral stage. Persons who adhere to the psychoanalytic view suggest that the frustration children feel because of their parents' mismanagement of their oral needs results in anger toward the parents, which in turn generates guilt. Therefore, the anger is turned inward. For individuals with this experience, drinking serves the triple purpose of punishing the self, satisfying oral needs, and lessening inhibitions in expressing hostility toward symbolic parents, such as spouses or authorities. Fixation can also take place in the anal stage if children's needs are mismanaged when they begin to assert selfhood and learn sphincter control. Alcoholics with this background are likely to show traits of aggressiveness, cruelty, obstinacy, and rebelliousness. Since the anal period is a later developmental stage than the oral period, the prognosis for this type of alcoholic is better than for the "oral" alcoholic. According to the psychoanalytic view, the main conflict experienced by alcoholics who are fixated at the anal stage of development is a conflict over homosexual impulses. This is the type of alcoholic who is most likely to make homosexual advances while under the influence of alcohol. Anal alcoholics are viewed as more psychosexually advanced than oral alcoholics, who have little capacity to be interested in anyone other than themselves.

Fixation at the phallic stage of development is characteristic of the type of alcoholic who is friendly and easy to get along with and who forms many superficial relationships. This type of alcoholic experiences feelings of sexual inadequacy, anger, and low self-esteem. Alcohol provides some relief from the anxieties that grow out of these conflicts. Also, psychoanalysts agree that any given alcoholic can have symptoms which reflect a combination of one or more of the three types just described, since a partial fixation can exist in more than one stage.

Some Freudian theorists suggest that alcohol addiction is a substitute for masturbation. Masturbation is viewed as the one great habit that is a primary addiction. Blum (1966) uses the concept of psychic energy to describe addiction. According to this view, individuals with median levels of psychic energy will be relatively resistant to alcohol addiction, since they are not tempted by the temporary release effect of alcohol and they are not disabled by the consequent depressant effect of alcohol. Persons with an excess of psychic energy will be more affected by the depressing effect of alcohol and will drink heavily to maintain psychic balance. Addiction is not likely so long as their psychic energy is not exhausted. Individuals who have too little psychic energy will be more affected by the release effect of alcohol since alcohol frees lower brain centers from higher cortical control.

Classic psychoanalytic theory emphasizes orality and homosexuality in the genesis of alcoholism. More modern versions of the theory take a broader view of the origins of alcohol problems. Levy (1958) is a representative of this latter group. He lists seven functions that alcohol serves for the individual.

1. Discharge—to release unconscious, repressed material
2. Narcotizing—to protect the ego from anxiety-provoking stimuli
3. Oral gratification—to recreate infantile feelings of being powerful, immortal, and lovable
4. Masochistic—to punish the self by the immediate discomfort of a hangover or by such long-range punishments as losing a job, ruining a career, or breaking up a marriage
5. Hostile—to release aggressive hostile urges (The long-range effects of alcohol can also serve to punish those closest to the alcoholic.)
6. Identification—to identify with manhood in general
7. Homosexual—to make it easier to express such urges

Unlike orthodox psychoanalytic theorists, Levy does not feel that there is any special link between alcoholism and homosexuality.

In addition to notions about the basis of alcoholism, some psychoanalytic theorists are also concerned with definitions and classifications of alcoholism. Knight (1937) distinguishes between what he calls "symptomatic" and "reactive" alcoholics. He defines symptomatic alcoholics as individuals who drink only incidentally and for whom alcohol is not the major problem. Reactive alcoholics are those whose drinking is triggered by a traumatic event. Both types of alcoholics are classified as neurotic patients. The symptomatic alcoholic's excessive drinking is a reaction to a past experience that could not be integrated and was, therefore, repressed. Reactive alcoholics drink in response to a seemingly intolerable or insolvable life situation. Alcoholics who fall into these two categories are viewed as relatively easy to treat by the classic psychoanalytic method because their symptoms cause them suffering and they seek relief from their misery.

Within the psychoanalytic framework, there is a group of patients whose difficulty is not viewed as neurotic nor as necessarily caused by unconscious conflict. Individuals in this group have alcohol problems that stem from a maldevelopment of their personality and from an arrested emotional growth at an early level. These are the psychotics and people with character disorders. Individuals with character disorders present particular difficulties for treatment in the psychoanalytic scheme. This is because the people around these individuals suffer more from the patients' problems than do the patients themselves. This is in contrast to neurotic patients who suffer mostly from their own problems. Asocial acts of individuals with character disorders are directed first to the outside rather than towards themselves.

In Knight's classification of alcoholics, individuals with character disorders are classified as "essential" alcoholics. Acting out is an especially common behavior pattern for essential alcoholics, and lack of motivation for change is an especially common attitude. The main difficulties with treating essential alcoholics as seen by the psychoanalytic school are (1) it is very hard to get them to want to change; (2) it is difficult to get them to reduce their acting out episodes (e.g., delinquent behavior while drinking); (3) it is difficult to overcome the damage done to personality at a very early age in emotional development.

In psychoanalytic treatment, the aim with the reactive or symptomatic drinker (neurotic patient) is to remove the blocks to full emotional development by helping them achieve insight. With essential alcoholics (character disorder), the goal of treatment is to start the maturational process by having the therapist provide them with structure and direction that they can internalize and in this way achieve the inner strength that they need for resocialization and self-control. In most cases involving psychoanalytic treatment of alcoholics, a chaotic course must be expected with an alteration and intermingling of internalized and acted out conflicts. Alcoholics have seldom developed the capacity to withstand frustration and generally cannot wait for gratification that might be coming in the future. They want gratification now. Successful classical psychoanalytic treatment that is based on learning to wait and learning to delay impulse gratification until it is safe and appropriate is an extremely difficult, if not impossible, undertaking for most alcoholics. A desire to provide alternative methods of dealing with alcoholics has prompted many changes in psychoanalytic treatment of this group of patients.

In the early days of psychoanalytic treatment, it was believed that alcoholics could be cured in a matter of months. However, as the theory became more sophisticated and as research with alcoholics accumulated, it became apparent that the early optimism was unwarranted.

Simmel (1929) was one of the early pioneers in work with alcoholics based on psychoanalytic theory. Simmel attempted to treat alcoholics as in-patients at the Tegel Clinic near Berlin. His treatment program consisted of regular psychoanalytic interviews and an institutionalized setting intended to provide the maternal care and discipline that he presumed his patients had lacked during infancy. The institutional staff was trained to give symbolic and direct gratifications with suitable amounts of frustration. Presumably, Simmel's method fostered emotional growth, redirection of asocial impulses, and self-control.

The idea behind the psychoanalytic sanitarium at Tegel was to replace the patient's own "bad" mother with a new and better mother who would succeed where the first one had failed in furthering personality development. A similar philosophy has guided efforts at the Menninger Foundation. The Menninger Foundation and the Tegel Clinic were among the first to attempt to use psychoanalytic methods with alcoholics as in-patients. Treating alcoholic patients in a hospital setting departs from the strict psychoanalytic method, which traditionally consists of daily 50-minute interviews during which the therapist remains as anonymous as possible. In the hospital setting, the therapist's real personality cannot remain unknown to the patient since there are daily patient-therapist encounters, both planned and incidental, in which the patient can get an idea of the therapist's character.

At the Tegel Sanitarium, the patients' destructive aims, which were viewed as being intended for their mothers and neurotically directed against themselves by drinking, were redirected against the therapist. The patients were permitted to act out killing, devouring, or castrating fantasies on acceptable substitutes, for example, by cutting off branches in the garden or smashing coffee services. At a later point, self-understanding had to replace acting out, and the destructive relationship had to be resolved by means of analysis. Ideally, the patients learned that their behavior represented the unconscious conflict between their irrational and rational self, and that they had projected this conflict onto the therapist. When patients reached this point in the treatment process, they were ordered to bed for a while with special nursing care to insure that their unconscious needs received the utmost fulfillment. They were allowed to be little children again, to lay in bed, and to have a kind mother feed and tend them. This situation, in turn, was utilized in psychoanalytic sessions where its meaning for patients was explored.

From the psychoanalytic point of view, the sanitarium plays an important role as a symbol of the mother's womb. The treatment is based on the principle of allowing patients to regress to an early stage of emotional development and then providing them with the gratification they originally missed. They are then encouraged to progress to a more mature level of development. In psychoanalytically oriented regression treatment, nursing care is of the utmost importance, because it provides the right kind of nurturance and rebirth and replaces a "bad" and depriving mother with a "good" mother.

Knight (1938) has treated alcoholics at the Menninger Clinic. He advocates that an especially affectionate bond be encouraged between the alcoholic and the therapist. He points out that alcoholic patients cannot endure a passive, withdrawn attitude. Therefore, unorthodox techniques must be used. He recommends that these patients' great need for affection be met rather than just analyzed and interpreted. In addition, Knight feels that the emotional relationship with the therapist acts as a partial substitute for drinking for the alcoholic. Even though the primary requirement for successful psychoanalytic treatment is unflagging motivation on the part of the patient, Knight has treated involuntary patients who have been committed to the Menninger Clinic. The present trend among psychoanalytic professionals appears to be to fit the treatment to the patient by making changes in method, as seems appropriate, instead of rejecting patients who do not fit the notions of being suitable for the particular type of therapy.

One of the weaknesses of classical psychoanalytic theory's application to alcoholism is that many of the predictions made for alcoholism are the same ones made for neurotic behavior in general. To have utility for prediction, this theory should be able to differentially predict neurotic behavior from alcoholism. Currently, classic psychoanalytic theory does not differentially predict the two types of behavior.

DEPENDENCY THEORY

From this theoretical perspective, strong dependency needs are viewed as the underlying cause of alcohol abuse. The strong dependency needs are seen as beginning in childhood as a result of the parents' behavior toward the child. The infant's needs are met either inconsistently, too much, or not at all. The person whose needs were not met in childhood has increased dependency needs in adulthood. Males with this type of childhood history begin to display exaggerated masculinity, including aggressive and antisocial behavior, during adolescence. These same behaviors may also be seen in preadolescence. From this theoretical perspective, such behaviors are a reaction formation against underlying dependency needs. Prealcoholic individuals have strong dependency needs but are ashamed of them. They want maternal care, yet they want to be independent. This situation produces a dependency conflict. The facade of being self-reliant is an attempt to cover up dependency needs.

Drinking is seen as a masculine behavior. As such, drinking helps persons to maintain an image of independence and self-reliance. Williams (1976) points out that drinking also helps satisfy dependency needs by providing feelings of warmth, comfort, and omnipotence, which help recreate the maternal care situation. Overall, drinking is motivated by dependency needs.

Blane (1968) presents a more elaborate description of dependency theory. He agrees that the source of dependency needs may be expressed in several ways. While Blane sees dependency needs as having central importance in the alcoholic's personality, this does not mean that the dependency will be openly expressed. The ways that alcoholics solve the conflict over their dependent wishes is the crucial factor. Blane sees at least three ways that alcoholics can resolve their dependency needs, each resulting in a different set of behaviors. Blane suggests the theory only for males since he sees different dependency needs in women.

One type of alcoholic is *openly dependent* on other people. These individuals seem to have strong dependency needs, and they seek direct gratification of their needs. These alcoholics expect other people to meet their needs, and they get them to do so. They take initiative only to meet their dependency needs, a behavior that Blane describes as passive mastery of life. These overtly dependent men can express their dependency in two ways. Some take a direct route. They show little evidence of having attempted to be independent in adolescence and remain close to home and parents. In adulthood, they often remain at home in a childlike relationship with their parents or significant others in their family. For example, one alcoholic was thrown out of his mother's home because she insisted that he quit drinking. Despite this, he continued to drink and slept in his car parked in the front yard of his mother's home for several months prior to seeking treatment. This individual and many homeless and transient individuals fall into this category. They usually team up with someone who helps meet their dependency needs as they travel from place to place.

A more indirect path is taken by overtly dependent men who have, in the past, made an intense effort to achieve an independent male role. As the requirements for independent status increase in the areas of marriage, jobs, and rearing children, however, these individuals become tense and anxious as they try to meet these adult challenges. At the same time, strong dependent needs remain unmet. These men may surrender to dependency and turn increasingly to alcohol while abandoning their adult responsibilities.

No matter which way overt dependency is reached, these individuals present problems when they are admitted to treatment settings. Overtly dependent persons can be both enjoyable and difficult, depending on the ways the caregiver must interact with them. On treatment units, these patients may be very pleasant and agreeable—ideal persons to have on the ward because they make no waves. However, they do not attempt to progress in treatment or to complete treatment in an expeditious manner because they find that hospitalization meets their dependency needs. Ward personnel can deal with this passive acceptance of care by establishing definite and clearly stated limits on dependency demands. Blane also suggests that therapists adopt an impersonal but warm, professional attitude with these patients.

An attempt may also be made to spread the fulfillment of dependency needs of these patients across several staff members and to use treatments, such as group therapy, where close dependency relationships are less likely to occur. Blane does not recommend the use of insight-oriented therapy for this type of alcoholic. Instead, he suggests that it is crucial for the treatment process that case management procedures focus on the patient's way of handling and expressing dependency needs.

The second type of alcoholic in Blane's scheme is the *counterdependent* alcoholic. These individuals avoid expressing any dependency needs and avoid dependency relationships. These men feel that they can take care of themselves and typically deny any problem with alcohol abuse. They take great pride in physical and "masculine" achievements, especially drinking "like a man."

They do try to satisfy dependency needs, usually in indirect and covert ways, for example, through maudlin friendship in bars. Their dependency on alcohol is also an illustration of this indirect expression of dependency needs. There is a fear that expressing dependency needs will destroy their identity as men. These individuals have displayed counterdependent masculine behavior from childhood up to adulthood. They have displayed leadership roles and have had considerable athletic accomplishments and other achievements culturally defined as masculine. They may also have been involved with daring exploits, such as reckless driving, fighting, and occasionally, criminal activity. While they may have many friends, they have few relationships that involve openly dependent relationships. They are often people who cannot tolerate inactivity and who seek out action.

Because they wish to avoid dependent relationships of all kinds, counterdependent alcoholics are not often seen in alcohol treatment centers. Those in treatment were usually forced into it by the judicial system or pressured into it by employers or family. While they are in treatment, they avoid admitting any problem with alcohol.

The caregiver finds these patients difficult. They defy routine and are eager to leave the treatment setting as soon as possible. While they are in treatment, they are anxious and overreact to situations on the ward. This is because they find themselves in a dependent relationship in treatment, something they have tried to avoid all their lives. Treatment personnel must use considerable care and skill in managing these patients' aroused anxiety. Blane suggests telling counterdependent alcoholics that following the routine of the ward is difficult and requires self-discipline. This strategy frequently appeals to this type of patient's counterdependent defense. The counselor and other caregivers may also find it useful to turn to these individuals for help with other patients. Counterdependent alcoholics often become ward leaders and centerpoints for patient morale. By assuming a counterdependent stance as leaders, these alcoholics also satisfy their dependency needs by helping to care for other people. Care must be taken that counterdependent patients do not take over the caregiving role or lead the patients in directions that may be counterproductive to ward goals.

The third type of alcoholic, the *dependent-independent* alcoholic, is viewed by Blane as falling midway between the extremes of the two outlined previously. These alcoholics fluctuate between denying and expressing dependency wishes. Because of the fluctuation, their behavior can be both frustrating and aggravating to treatment personnel. These alcoholics may act very dependent on those around them and the next minute deny that they need anything at all from others. Though seeking advice, direction, and emotional support at one point, they may later resent advice and insist they can handle their own affairs.

Because of the constant fluctuation in their stance toward dependency, these individuals suffer more pain and anxiety than do those who have selected the counterdependent or dependent solution to their dependency needs. Therefore, they are more motivated to come to treatment voluntarily. They are also more flexible than the other two types of alcoholics, which is a favorable prognostic sign for their eventual recovery.

Despite their motivation and their flexibility, these individuals are not always easy to treat. They show an uneven path toward recovery and can exhibit the more difficult characteristics of dependent and counterdependent alcoholics. Blane indicates that treatment personnel cannot use or gratify either side of these persons' dependency style. Thus, they may be difficult patients.

Other dependent-independent patients alternate between being overtly dependent and counterdependent, which can be bewildering to the treatment staff. In this circumstance, the caregiving staff must take care to maintain consistency in their reactions to the patients. In general, these unresolved dependency needs make this type of patient ideal for psychotherapy. This is true despite the fact that alcohol caregivers may see this type of patient as so contrary as to be an unacceptable referral to long-term psychotherapy. Caregivers are often surprised to find that when referral is suggested, they get an immediate positive response from this type of patient.

As noted earlier, Blane's theory is presented as being applicable to men only. He sees dependency needs of women as often directly expressed and accepted both by females and the people around them. Being dependent does not lead to guilt, and their ability to accept dependency relationships without conflict is a positive factor in therapy.

POWER THEORY

McClelland and his colleagues began their study of power theory and alcohol abuse at Harvard during the 1960s. Since the publication of their book in 1972, there has been little extension of their theoretical position, despite its potential for offering an important theoretical picture of alcohol abuse. This position also offers some tentative suggestions for treatment approaches that differ in significant ways from those pursued in treatment programs based on Alcoholics Anonymous. Thus, despite the failure of the theory to move into the mainstream of thought in terms of alcohol abuse, it is a potentially useful and different perspective on the problem.

Power theory is based on 10 years of programmatic research by McClelland and his colleagues. The theory, like dependency theory, focuses on men. The descriptions of the dynamics for women are quite different from that of men. The theory maintains that men who have accentuated needs for *personalized power* drink excessively. Aggressiveness and the tendencies of prealcoholic men to be assertive, to seek thrills, and to engage in antisocial activities are indications of power concerns (Williams, 1976).

Men with personalized power needs seek to overcome their doubts about their own potency as males. They suppress all feelings of weakness. They want to establish personal domination over other people and try to gain it without regard for the feelings and needs of others. The world is seen as a competitive place where one must win out over competitors.

McClelland et al. (1972) used TAT-like cards to study personalized power with alcoholic males. They found that personalized power fantasies increased at high levels of alcohol consumption. They concluded from these findings that alcohol intake makes the drinker feel stronger and increases his desire to dominate others. Men with high needs for personalized power may receive direct gratification from these personalized power fantasies. In other words, men with personalized power needs feel weak and they drink because it allows them to feel powerful. According to McClelland et al., the origin of these personalized power needs is unclear. The researchers hypothesize that it may be due to some type of power conflict, that is, men are expected to be strong but are undercut, and their power needs are compensatory in nature.

The evidence for power theory is based on several lines of research. McClelland and his colleagues were interested in investigating drinking behavior in general rather than simply focusing on problem drinking. They needed a theory that would explain both normal and problem drinking. McClelland maintained that the best way to conduct research on drinking was to make the research as close to real-world conditions as possible. One strategy he and his collaborators followed to assure that the research was based on real-life phenomena was to collect data in natural surroundings— the cocktail party.

Parties were sponsored at several fraternity houses on a college campus. Partygoers were told that McClelland was interested in studying the effects of partying on fantasy behavior. He was, of course, interested instead in the effects of alcohol use on the fantasies of his subjects. The bartender kept an unobtrusive check on the amount consumed by each drinker. Participants were asked to write a story in response to TAT-like cards at the beginning, middle, and end of the party. For comparison, the researchers also sponsored nonalcoholic parties where soft drinks were served and musical entertainment was provided. These control sessions allowed McClelland to isolate the effects of alcohol on fantasy.

McClelland et al. summarized their findings by saying that the examination of these stories (which were scored following a prescribed procedure—see McClelland et al., 1972) did not support the widely held psychiatric belief that drinking leads to oral gratification or dependency fantasies. These researchers also found that anxiety was not reduced following small amounts of alcohol intake (one to three drinks). It usually took five to six drinks before anxiety thoughts were reduced. What they did find were systematic increases in thoughts of power following drinking. Examples include thoughts of aggression, sexual conquest, strength, and influence.

These power concerns were expressed in two ways in the stories. One type was a need for power that was concerned with having the influence to help others. McClelland et al. labeled this as *social power*. It is altruistic. The other type of power is called *personal power* and is both more selfish and more self-aggrandizing. It is dominance over others, at their expense, for example, defeating someone in an athletic event. McClelland et al. found that, in general, two or three drinks increased fantasies of socialized power. Personal power fantasies began to rise and to dominate fantasy with five or six drinks.

These researchers found the same type of themes on an individual level using TAT-like cards with working-class men who were asked to make up stories. The men with strong power concerns and a low level of restraint in their fantasies tended to be heavy drinkers. This personal power, that is, seeking to increase one's power, reputation, or glory without reference to the needs of other people, was associated with heavy alcohol intake. Those who sought power out of a concern for the good of some cause (social power), tended to be light drinkers.

In cross-cultural studies of heavy drinking, McClelland found that folk tales (which he assumed reflect what people in a culture think about) in societies where there was heavy drinking tended to contain themes of physical assertiveness. These themes were mentioned frequently. The word *not*, titles of respect, and fear or anxiety phrases representing inhibition of aggression were not found as often in the folk tales of heavy-drinking societies.

McClelland's work, as noted earlier, has been conducted primarily with men. Power theory does not seem to apply to women in the same way that it does to men (as discussed later). In men, McClelland clearly sees that the motivation to drink and, in particular, to drink excessively is tied to power needs. He argues that the notion that men drink because of anxiety is inconsistent with his cross-cultural analysis of folk tales. Societies that expressed more anxiety in their folk tales actually drank less alcohol.

According to McClelland, neither folk tales nor individual fantasy behavior supports the assumption that men drink to attain feelings of being cared for. McClelland asserts that what other writers and researchers have labeled counterdependency and aggression in males may be more directly interpreted as evidence for a personalized power need. He also suggests that the frequently described tendencies of some alcoholics to seek the companionship of powerful and strong people need not be seen as an expression of dependency. Instead, it can be viewed as an attempt to borrow strength from these stronger people.

In brief, McClelland sees men as drinking to feel stronger. When personalized power is a central concern, they will drink more heavily. When alcohol is used in small amounts by restrained people, thoughts of social power are increased. When more alcohol is used in less-restrained settings by impulsive people, increases in personalized power are reported.

The cuing of thoughts of power in males in every society by the ingestion of alcohol is probably due to physiological changes associated with alcohol intake. Alcohol causes a burning sensation in the throat and stimulates secretion of adrenalin, which has mobilizing effects across the entire body. It also enters the bloodstream and supplies a quick source of energy. These sensations of increased strength brought about by drinking alcohol can lead to fantasies of increased power in some men to a greater or lesser degree.

Since alcohol produces these sensations in all men when they drink, what type of man drinks excessively? According to McClelland, it is the type who has a strong need for personalized power and who uses alcohol as an outlet to fulfill this need for power. McClelland cites his research with working-class males as an indicator that men seeking personalized power can use alcohol, along with several other outlets, to satisfy power needs. These other outlets include accumulating prestige supplies (a big, powerful car, for example), gambling, and acting out aggressive impulses.

Why does personalized power become so prominent in males? The culture stresses male strength and daring. Body build may also play a role; physically larger boys are more likely to be aggressive, and aggressive boys have an increased probability of becoming alcoholic, according to McClelland. Assuming this theoretical position is correct, how can excessive drinking be dealt with? The simplest way, according to McClelland, seems to be to socialize these men's power drives. He points to the cross-cultural finding that societies with clear hierarchies of authority, which demand that power and authority be carefully circumscribed and directed, tend to be relatively sober societies. In a more individualized way, alcohol abuse might be curtailed by having excessive drinkers focus on achieving prestige supplies as substitutes for alcohol. Such individuals may also benefit from joining an organization that helps others, that is, by directing their power needs toward social power. This point is very similar to one of the Twelve Steps of Alcoholics Anonymous. McClelland's main conclusion is that what alcoholic males experience has a common core in all societies. It is simply the experiencing of personalized power that underlies this type of alcohol use.

Power Theory and Women

McClelland's power theory has also been applied to females. However, research suggests that it is not clear that women show power needs as a basic motivation to drink. Instead, there is a suggestion that alcohol's ability to make females feel more womanly motivates some women to use and especially to abuse alcohol.

Wilsnack (1973) has conducted much of the research with women using McClelland's theory and research strategies. Based on subjects' responses to an interview questionnaire, she found that women do not show an increase in power concerns after using alcohol. Instead, female alcoholics tend to value the maternal role more highly than do nonalcoholic females. These women alcoholics had a more masculine style, inferred from their descriptions of themselves as misbehaving in school as children and from their being more confrontive with people. They also had an unconscious male identity, as measured by responses to the Franck Test. Female alcoholics also have had more obstetrical-gynecological problems, such as the inability to conceive. Wilsnack suggests that these types of problems could potentially raise doubts in these women about their femininity. Women also reported that a specific incident precipitated their drinking (something not noted in males). The majority of women in the Wilsnack study usually mentioned divorce, obstetrical or gynecological problems, or children leaving home as the specific precipitating event. All of these events potentially threaten women's sense of adequacy as females.

It may be that the above reports by women in Wilsnack's study are the result of alcohol abuse and are not necessarily personality factors that preceded alcohol abuse. However, a second study by Wilsnack focusing on younger women (21 to 32 years of age) confirms some of the original findings. In a partylike setting, female subjects were asked to write stories about TAT cards in a sober condition and while drinking. Several coding systems designating dependency, power, and femininity were used to analyze these stories.

The data analysis indicated that there were no changes in the dependency measures or in social power after the use of alcohol. Drinking reduced personal power fantasies (whereas it increased them in males) and increased feelings of womanliness. Heavy drinking females in a sober condition gave responses that led to higher scores on personal power than for light or moderate drinkers. These same heavy-drinking females scored in the masculine direction on the womanliness coding. These findings support the notion that women with an insecure feminine identification drink heavily. This implies that women drink in order to feel more feminine. One way of seeing power concerns as consistent across both males and females is that both men and women use alcohol to enhance feelings that are consistent with sex role expectation.

As noted previously, these psychodynamic approaches are not well grounded in empirical research. Despite the lack of research support, psychoanalytic theory continues to play an important role in some settings, particularly in those individual therapy cases seen by psychoanalytically oriented psychotherapists. In many cases, modified, somewhat more structured versions of the psychodynamic approach have been very effective in programmatic treatment of alcoholics. However, in the main, there is not a great deal of vigorous alcohol-related research or theorizing occurring in the United States at the present time using psychodynamic approaches.

REFERENCES

Barry, H. (1988). Psychoanalytic theory of alcoholism. In C. D. Chaudron & D. A. Wilkinson (Eds.), *Theories on alcoholism* (pp. 103–141). Toronto: Addiction Research Foundation.

Blane, H. T. (1968). *The personality of the alcoholic: Guises of dependency.* New York: Harper & Row.

Blum, E. M. (1966). Psychoanalytic views of alcoholism: A review. *Quarterly Journal of Studies on Alcohol, 27,* 259–299.

Blum, E. M., & Blum, R. H. (1969). *Alcoholism: Modern psychological approaches to treatment.* San Francisco: Jossey-Bass.

Cox, W. M. (1987). Personality theory and research. In H. T. Blane & K. E. Leonard (Eds.), *Psychological theories of drinking and alcoholism* (pp. 55–89). New York: Guilford Press.

Cox, W. M. (1988). Personality theory. In C. D. Chaudron & D. A. Wilkinson (Eds.), *Theories on alcoholism* (pp. 143–173). Toronto: Addiction Research Foundation.

Knight, R. P. (1937). The dynamics and treatment of chronic alcohol addiction. *Bulletin of Menninger Clinic, 1,* 233–250.

Knight, R. P. (1938). The psychoanalytic treatment in a sanatorium of chronic addiction to alcohol. *Journal of American Medical Association, 111,* 1443–1446.

Levy, R. I. (1958). The psychodynamic function of alcohol. *Quarterly Journal of Studies on Alcohol, 19,* 649–659.

McClelland, D. C., Davis, W. N., Kalin, R., & Wanner, E. (1972). *The drinking man: Alcohol and human behavior.* New York: Free Press.

Simmel, E. (1929). Psychoanalytic treatment in a sanitarium. *International Journal of Psychoanalysis, 10,* 70–89.

Vinacke, W. E. (1968). *Foundations of psychology.* New York: American Book Company.

Williams, A. F. (1976). The alcoholic personality. In B. S. Kissin & H. Begleiter (Eds.), *The biology of alcoholism: Social aspects of alcoholism, Vol. 4* (pp. 243–274). New York: Plenum Press.

Wilsnack, S. C. (1973). The needs of the female drinker: Dependency, power or what? In M. Chafetz (Ed.), *Proceedings of the Second Annual Conference of the National Institute on Alcohol Abuse and Alcoholism: Psychological and Social Factors in Drinking and Treatment and Treatment Evaluation* (pp. 65–83).

Wilson, T. W., O'Leary, K. D., & Nathan, P. (1991). *Abnormal psychology.* Englewood Cliffs, NJ: Prentice Hall.

Psychological Theories: Social Learning

_____ *chapter 7*

The previous chapter on predispositional theories focused on how preexisting psychological traits may predispose an individual to have psychological problems. In brief, these theories suggested that the existence of certain personality factors may predetermine alcohol problems. We now turn to a theoretical system that focuses more on the learned association between alcohol and the reduction of tensions with which an individual must cope. More specifically, this chapter focuses on social learning and cognitive approaches to alcohol use and abuse. It is organized into the following subsections: (1) an overview of some basic learning concepts that will help the reader follow the issues discussed; (2) the older learning approaches to alcohol use and abuse; (3) the more recent conceptualizations of alcohol use and abuse from the learning perspective; (4) the ramifications for intervention and treatment that early and late models may have for the alcohol field; and (5) evaluation of the status of the learning approach in the alcohol field.

CLASSICAL AND OPERANT CONDITIONING: BASIC CONCEPTS

One way of seeing alcohol problems is as learned behavior. Like all learning, the learning of how to use (and to abuse) alcohol is a complex process. For example, the reduction of underlying emotional discomfort or tension is a motive for drinking. Alcohol, a depressant drug, temporarily (but immediately) reduces tension and makes the tense person feel more relaxed. Alcohol can also make the person perform more effectively in social situations, which can be a very positive outcome. Effectiveness in a social situation and reduced tension are said to be "reinforcing," that is, to have positive consequences for the drinker. Therefore, drinking alcohol is **reinforced** by the pleasant outcomes it offers.

Alcohol use can be learned through two specific procedures, *classical* and *operant* conditioning or learning. (We learn much of what we feel and do through these two procedures, so it should be remembered that these apply to all learning, not just the learning of how to use alcohol.) *Classical* or Pavlovian conditioning has to do with the learning of emotional responses through body systems not usually under our control (e.g., the smooth muscles, pulse rate, and blood pressure, which are controlled by the autonomic nervous system). An example would be a person who is claustrophobic and who has panic reactions when in closed places like an elevator. Individuals frequently are unaware of this type of learning and are sometimes unaware of why they respond the way they do. These reactions may well have been conditioned (learned) early in life, perhaps before language. Somewhere the fear response has occurred in the presence of something or someone threatening, and the fear has been learned or conditioned to that situation. It may be that some people have an overreactive autonomic nervous system, and such fear responses are more easily learned or conditioned in these individuals. These individuals may, over their lifetime, develop fear responses to a wide range of psychological, social, and physical situations. While these people are generally fearful, they may feel they need to put on a competent, even aggressive front. As a result, they almost overdo by being the best workers or getting the most done at their jobs or with their friends. However, they may have many conditioned fears, and these become even more overwhelming as they take on more challenges and become more tense. Eventually, as a result of their performance, these individuals are asked to take on more responsibilities (be the supervisor, become the head coach, or move up to vice president). At this point, they feel overwhelmed by the level of tension and the multiplication of their fears. Alcohol can quickly reduce these fears and make the overly tense person feel comfortable again. In learning terms, drinking alcohol is said to have reduced "drive" (the inner conflict and tension the person feels). Thus, for a tense individual, drinking leads to a positive outcome—tension reduction and relaxation. In learning terms, the more often drinking is reinforced by tension reduction, the more likely a person is to respond by drinking in the future.

Another way of seeing drinking is as an operantly conditioned response. In *operant* learning, it is not the involuntary responses of the individual that are central. Instead, it is the voluntary responses, those a person consciously chooses to make. While classical and operant learning will be discussed as if they were separate, they usually operate together in an individual. In operant learning, behavior is shaped by choosing to give those responses that pay off in getting us to a given goal.

Most of the learning goals that are voluntary among humans involve social reinforcers. For example, choosing to sit down and read this book is not due to hunger or thirst (motivational factors used with lower animals) but is based on such long-term goals as getting a degree or a better job. The short-term goals may involve doing well on the upcoming examination in a course on substance abuse. These goals have little to do with survival, but instead are linked to gaining social reinforcers, for example, success. How a person gets to this point involves the learning of a number of *discriminations* (decisions about when and how to respond to a certain situation or task) and the pairing of those discriminations with effective *responses* (the things a person can choose to do to reach a goal or to accomplish a task). Many of the discriminations individuals learn tell them how and when to respond. There is also *response generalization*—learning that some responses are effective in a wide range of settings. Often, individuals choose between a widely generalized response or a more subtle discrimination in the choice of the response. For example, smiling at people usually leads to a reciprocal positive (and reinforcing) response. However, smiling at someone who is very angry or who is in the midst of grief may be misinterpreted, and a negative social reaction (e.g., a punch in the eye, or tears from the grieving person) may occur. It is interesting that individuals are able to develop quite precise and subtle discriminations of how to react to social situations and how to obtain social reinforcers. However, all people face situations for which their learning histories have not quite prepared them. An example might be meeting prospective in-laws. In these awkward social situations it is possible to understand just how subtle and complex an individual's learning history is. The individual has met people before in many settings but never when they might be forming an alliance that is completely new to them.

From the learning perspective, alcohol use is seen as initially undertaken in a social setting. For a while people may not find that alcohol has much impact on them or their interactions with others. Eventually, for some individuals, alcohol takes on a very reinforcing role. For example, it could be that some individuals find that alcohol helps them deal with the awkward social situation of meeting the future in-laws. It makes the individuals feel more relaxed, wittier, and better able to handle social situations. If this occurs in a wide range of interactions, individuals may learn to drink when faced with any "difficult" social situation. It is quite possible that alcohol will make some people more effective in social interactions. That is one of the reasons that the cocktail party is so popular. It allows strangers without a friendship history to chat freely and openly with each other. Like all things, a cocktail party is not "good" or "bad." The use of alcohol becomes risky when it becomes a highly generalized response to one specific social situation or to a wide range of social situations.

One of the important ramifications of looking at alcohol from a learn-

From the social learning perspective, alcohol use is seen as initially undertaken in a social setting, like these two fishermen enjoying a beer.
(Photograph courtesy of the Independence Center, Lincoln, Nebraska.)

ing perspective is that individuals must be taught (and must learn) new
responses to those situations they formerly handled by drinking. One of the
most rapid ways to learn both positive and negative behaviors is through *modeling*. For example, alcohol use can be learned through modeling the behavior of others who drink. Drinkers may adopt the behavior of those people
whom they would wish to be like and whose praise they seek. These models
are said to have high *social reinforcement value* for the beginning drinker.
Drinking offers a clear and distinct way to identify with and share in the
behavior of a valued person. That is, being like the other person is reinforcing; it meets a need (making the drinker feel good about himself) and may
lead to drinking as a behavior that helps meet that need in the future.

Another important learning concept is the process of *response extinction*.
If a person makes a response that is not rewarded, the likelihood of that
response being given in a similar situation in the future is reduced. Even
those responses that have been well-learned or well-conditioned will eventually be reduced and eliminated if they are no longer rewarded. Extinction
results from the person learning that the response given is no longer effective in reaching a goal or receiving a reward. If a response was always reinforced, a person easily recognizes when the response is no longer being
rewarded. If it was only occasionally rewarded, the person has more difficulty
learning that the response will no longer lead to a reward. This difference in
the rate of extinction is related to *schedules of reinforcement.*

Many responses that are acquired are learned under partial reinforcement conditions. For example, a college male may find that attempting to kiss a female may not be rewarded every time. It may be reinforced only half the time. When a response is acquired under partial reinforcement conditions, it is much more resistant to extinction than if it had been reinforced every time (continuous reinforcement). It may be that drinking behavior as a response to feeling tense is acquired under partial reinforcement, since it may make persons relaxed some of the time but more tense at other times. If so, this might explain why it is difficult to extinguish the drinking response to tension arousal in many people.

Most organisms work for reinforcements under schedules of reinforcement. There are generally three conditions under which organisms respond for reinforcements. These "rules of the game" dictate which response is necessary to get a reinforcement under different conditions. Under conditions of continuous reinforcement, each and every response leads to a reward or reinforcement. Under the ratio schedule of reinforcement, the organism must give a certain number of responses before a reinforcement occurs. Under an interval reinforcement schedule, the number of responses made does not matter; reinforcement is based on when the response is made. Reinforcement is obtained if the response is made at a certain time. There are fixed interval schedules (for example, getting paid once a week) and variable interval schedules of reinforcement. This relatively brief background on learning principles leads to an examination of the older learning approaches to alcohol use and abuse.

LEARNING APPROACHES TO ALCOHOL USE AND ABUSE: OLDER MODELS

There are two basic approaches to alcohol use and abuse from the learning theory perspective. The first is the drive reduction model, which assumes that anxiety reduction by the intake of alcohol leads to excessive use of alcohol by an individual. Conger (1956) indicated that drinking becomes habitual because it leads to drive reduction (in this case, the reduction of anxiety). So, to the degree that alcohol reduces tension, worry, and anxiety, it serves as a source of reward to the individual. The second major learning approach to alcohol use and abuse is labeled several different ways by various writers. A general title would be a social learning approach to alcohol use and abuse. Here, in basic learning terms, alcohol abuse is dependent upon a specific operant response (drinking alcohol) becoming a general response for dealing with life's problems. Ullman and Krasner (1969) note that, in the social learning approach, the chief focus is on the inappropriate behavior of drinking.

While these two basic approaches to alcohol use and abuse are helpful in thinking about alcohol and learning, it is important to remember that tension reduction and social learning are frequently occurring at the same time. In some cases, writers actually combine the two into a single theory. These two basic approaches can be expanded even further with the inclusion of cognitive factors, as discussed later.

Individuals engage in abusive drinking even though it may cause them physical and social difficulties. One could ask why individuals would continue to drink when it causes them so much difficulty. Conger (1956) argues that two factors should be considered in explaining this apparently paradoxical behavior. The first is the immediacy of reinforcement. Immediate reinforcements are more effective than delayed reinforcements. (This learning principle is called "the gradient of reinforcement.") It may be that, in the long run, the immediate reduction of anxiety more than compensates for the punishment the person suffers. The second factor is the amount of drive and conflict. If individuals' anxiety levels are high enough, the anxiety-reducing effects of alcohol may be more reinforcing than the social punishment they receive. Conger's approach uses Mowrer's two-factor theory of avoidance behavior. The underlying drive state (a classically conditioned response) can be relieved by drinking alcohol. The drinking of alcohol is an operant response that reduces the drive level of the classically conditioned response of anxiety (Wilson, 1987a). These early learning theorists saw heavy drinking as a learned response to stressful, conflict situations with the drinking response being reinforced by the anxiety-reducing properties of alcohol. Behavioral theory or social learning theory assumes that learning is based on conditions that are present in the individual's environment. These early theorists saw alcohol as being a very potent positive reinforcer in that it immediately reduces the strength of the individual's drive. The immediate nature of alcohol's tranquilizing effect is the basis of the explanation for individuals continuing to drink despite the disastrous, far-reaching consequences of their drinking.

Bandura (1969), one of the leading social learning theorists, believes that the search for personality dynamics underlying alcoholism is futile, because any personality can be taught to misuse alcohol under the proper social conditions. He asserts that behavioral scientists can more profitably spend their time investigating the learning conditions and reinforcements that are associated with drinking behavior.

As suggested earlier, many theorists assume that learning theories of reinforcement cannot account for alcoholism, because the devastating social and physical consequences are so much greater than the temporary relief value obtained from alcohol. Bandura states that this type of argument overlooks the fact that behavior is more powerfully controlled by its immediate consequences (temporary relief obtained from drinking) than by delayed consequences. Thus, individuals may persistently engage in behavior that is immediately reinforcing but potentially self-destructive. Bandura's position is that the thoughts of future adverse conditions that will result from drinking may be sufficiently strong to inhibit drinking when the individual's drive for escape is relatively weak. However, thoughts of future effects will not do much to inhibit the drinking of a person who experiences a high level of adverse stimulation and who has a well-established pattern of responding to stress by drinking alcohol.

The early theorizing about the relationship between learning and alcohol was based in part on several animal learning experiments. Masserman and Yum (1946) were the first researchers to report findings that suggest that alcohol may have fear-reducing effects. These researchers set up a situation where cats learned to perform complex manipulations in order to secure food. After those behaviors were learned, electric shock rather than food was administered to the cats at the goal. The effect was that the instrumental manipulatory and approach responses were inhibited. The cats were given small doses of alcohol, and the approach manipulations necessary to obtain food were immediately reinstated. During the series of shock trials, the cats developed a preference for milk cocktails containing 5 percent alcohol to plain milk. They went back to their original preference for nonalcoholic drinks when the adverse stimulation was discontinued.

Conger (1951) designed an experiment in which he trained one group of laboratory rats to approach the lighted end of an alley to obtain food. He trained another group of rats to avoid the lighted end of the alley in order to escape electric shocks. Following the training period, the effects at the end of the alley were reversed for the two groups. In order to test whether alcohol reduces punishment-induced avoidance behavior (avoid lighted end of alley in order to escape shock) or increases approach tendencies in an approach-avoidance conflict (group first received food, later received shock), Conger administered alcohol injections to half the rats in each group and placebo injections to the other half. He found that avoidance responses of the rats that received alcohol injections were significantly less than those rats without alcohol. While it is obvious that the findings with animals cannot readily be generalized to humans, using animal models allows testing in a preliminary fashion of some hypotheses about the relationship between alcohol and learning principles.

These older learning approaches suggested that excessive alcohol consumption was maintained by the positive reinforcement the alcoholic obtained from the depressant and anesthetic properties of alcohol. Furthermore, individuals who are subjected to environmental stress are more prone to consume anesthetic doses of alcohol than are those individuals who experience less stress and for whom alcohol has only weak reinforcing value. After persons have used alcoholic beverages on a prolonged and heavy basis, alterations in the metabolic system take place. According to learning theorists, these alterations provide a second support system for excessive drinking behavior, which is independent of the original functional value of alcohol. After individuals become physically dependent on alcohol, a reduction in alcohol intake brings on extremely aversive physiological reactions. Therefore, they must drink large quantities of liquor to alleviate distressing physical reactions and to prevent their reoccurrence. Since the drinking of intoxicants promptly alleviates these adverse physical reactions, drinking behavior is automatically and continuously reinforced.

Even though both positive reinforcements that typically go along with social drinking and the reduction of adverse stimulation may account for inebriation, Bandura (1969) says that an adequate theory of alcoholism must encompass other variables that the alcoholic learns in the social environment. This is so because most individuals who are subject to stressful experiences do not become alcoholics. He notes that many theorists emphasize the role of personality disturbances as causative factors in alcoholism. However, when the marked variations in cultural and subcultural alcoholism rates are taken into account, it becomes obvious that this explanation is inadequate.

Bandura notes that if one accepts the notion that some form of "neurosis" is the underlying factor in alcoholism, one would have to conclude that the Jews, Mormons, Moslems, Italians, Chinese, and members of other cultural groups who have exceedingly low alcoholism rates are lacking in oral deprivations, self-destructive tendencies, latent homosexuality, and similar disorders. It would also seem to follow that these types of conditions would be highly prevalent among the Irish, because they surpass all other ethnic groups in terms of chronic alcoholism. Needless to say, few respectable theorists would entertain this type of thinking. Bandura states that perhaps the most striking evidence that alcoholism primarily represents a learned pattern of behavior rather than a manifestation of some predisposing, underlying pathology is the strikingly low alcoholism rates among the Jews who experience no less, and quite probably more, psychological stress than members of ethnic groups noted for their drinking. Social learning theorists point to these ethnic and subcultural differences in the use of intoxicants as evidence of the important role that the social learning of drinking behavior plays in the development of alcoholism. (Chapter 8 discusses the role of cultural socialization in alcohol use and abuse more thoroughly.)

A variety of features in the social environment influence the learning of drinking behavior. At a general level, these features are reflected in the cultural norms that define the reinforcements associated with the use of alcohol. There is considerable evidence that the consumption of alcohol is significantly influenced by the drinking mores of a given social group. For example, if becoming intoxicated is accepted in the culture as ordinary, is the object of humor, and is thought of as a sign of manliness, then excessive drinking behavior is reinforced. Members of cultures that are highly permissive toward the use of intoxicants or who consider drinking to be a competitive activity have a higher incidence of drunkenness than individuals reared in cultures that, for religious and other reasons, demand sobriety. In the same vein, in cultures such as the United States where the total population is made up of a large variety of ethnic and religious groups, the prevalence of chronic intoxication varies according to the types of social learning conditions that are associated with class status, religious affiliation, racial and ethnic background, occupation, and place of residence.

Social learning theorists hold that although cultural and subgroup mores obviously play an influential role in determining the extent of excessive drinking, cultural norms alone do not explain the relatively low incidence of addictive drinking in social groups that positively sanction the use of alcoholic beverages. Cultural norms by themselves also do not explain the occurrence of chronic alcoholism in cultures prohibiting intoxicants. This group of theorists explains the foregoing, in part, by the fact that cultural and subgroup mores are, to a large extent, transmitted through the modeling behavior of socializing agents (for example, the behavior a parent displays to a child). Therefore, members of a particular class do not necessarily undergo equivalent learning experiences. In addition, if the culture has clearly defined ways of using alcohol, then learning to discriminate when and how to use alcohol appropriately is easier. Thus, the reinforcements are likely to be more consistent.

Social learning theorists view drinking behavior as most often being initially acquired under nonstress conditions. However, a habitual social drinker will experience stress reduction on many occasions. Once drinking is thus intermittently reinforced, drinking behavior will be readily elicited under frustrating or aversive conditions. Therefore, according to this view, alcoholism typically results from habituation after prolonged heavy social drinking that has been acquired within the context of familial alcoholism.

According to the early theoretical positions, adverse stimulation and its quick reduction through the depressant action of alcoholic beverages plays a central role in the development and maintenance of addictive drinking. These theorists emphasize that conflict, boredom, frustration, and other stressful conditions may prompt a wide variety of reactions. Such reactions include aggression, dependency, withdrawal, regression, inebriety, or constructive coping behavior. Persons who exhibit constructive coping behavior will typically be judged as "normal." "Neurosis," "deep seated personality disturbances," and other names are frequently used to describe disease processes of individuals who have acquired one or more of the former patterns of coping behavior. Assigning these pathologies to symptoms does not constitute an explanation of the behavior, since the main evidence for their existence is the behavior that they are called on to explain.

Instead of underlying processes, early social learning theories saw alcoholics as people who, through modeling and reinforcement experiences, had acquired alcohol use as a widely generalized and dominant response to adverse stimulation. This "tension reduction theory" indicated that people drank alcohol to reduce stress. Recently, early social learning theories have come under considerable criticism because research has indicated that alcohol has variable effects on tension and anxiety. In one person, alcohol may increase tension and agitation while in another person it may increase depression. In addition, it is obvious that alcohol has variable effects in the same individuals at different times depending on their psychological states, their surroundings, and other psychosocial factors. While Wilson (1987a) insists these differing outcomes are not as damaging as some people have suggested, the findings do run counter to a central assumption of the theory that alcohol is consumed to reduce stress.

Wilson finds the basic two-factor theory used by Conger (1956) to be an inadequate formulation. The theory implies that reduction of a classically conditioned response (anxiety) leads to an increased probability that persons will drink alcohol when they become tense in the future. Wilson and others have come to believe that increasing the role of cognitive factors in the learning explanation of alcohol use and abuse provides a more complete explanation. This broader and more complex theoretical perspective of the relationship between alcohol use and learning is discussed in the next section.

LEARNING APPROACHES TO ALCOHOL USE
AND ABUSE: NEWER MODELS

Wilson (1987a, 1987b, 1987c) has traced the evolution of learning theory in the alcohol field. Wilson sees the controlled laboratory studies of the 1960s as providing a major breakthrough in understanding alcohol problems from the learning perspective. Pomerlau, Pertschuk, and Stinnet (1976) say that this research

> employed an operant-conditioning paradigm in which a quantifiable behavior, such as bar pressing, produced a predetermined amount of alcohol as a consequence. In specially designed research wards, the drinking behavior of volunteer alcoholics (screened to exclude those for whom further drinking was medically contraindicated) was studied objectively over an extended period of time. Predrinking, drinking, and postdrinking intervals were designated, with some studies lasting up to several weeks. Observations of social behavior as well as psychiatrically relevant behavior were typically conducted using one-way mirrors and closed circuit television. (p. 852, cited in Wilson, 1987c, p. 73)

One of the most controversial approaches taken in the 1960s was administering alcohol to alcoholics on a research ward. However, being able to observe their reactions to alcohol use under controlled conditions provided new insight into the causes, consequences, and factors related to alcohol use. The results of these observations were inconsistent with some of the core concepts of disease theory. (For a discussion of Jellinek's disease conception of alcoholism, see Chapter 2 and beginning of Chapter 5.) The research indicated that drinking was at least partially determined by the consequences of its ingestion for the drinker. Being positively reinforced, being punished, or being put in a situation where no reinforcement was available (time out from reinforcement) was found to be effective in controlling drinking in alcoholics. Further, it was found that having alcohol in the bloodstream did not necessarily lead to the loss of control of drinking by the alcoholic subjects. This latter finding challenged one of the core concepts of the disease theory of alcoholism, that drinking alcoholic beverages always leads to the loss of control of drinking in the alcoholic.

When this laboratory research was examined more closely, intoxication in these experimental ward alcoholics was determined (in part) by the psychological rewards and punishments surrounding drinking. It was established that the rate at which alcoholics drank was determined by the payoffs and punishments that existed in the environment where the drinking occurred. It was concluded from this ability to control drinking in alcoholics that if environmental control and proper learning circumstances were present, even chronic alcoholics could return to normal drinking (Wilson, 1987c).

Based on the findings from these laboratory studies and other clinical studies, new learning-based approaches to treating alcoholics were developed. One of the learning-based and research-based clinical approaches to the intervention and treatment of alcoholism was the work of Hunt and Azrin (1980, first published in 1973). This research followed an operant model in which voluntary responses of the alcoholic were positively and negatively reinforced. More specifically, alcoholics' social, vocational, recreational, and family satisfactions in the community in which they lived were rearranged in what was labeled a community reinforcement approach to alcoholism.

As noted, Hunt and Azrin developed their procedures based on operant learning principles as applied to alcohol abuse. These researchers suggested that one way of deterring alcohol abuse might be to find the natural negative events that operate in the person's environment to deter drinking. Once these natural deterrents were isolated, it might be possible to use operant procedures to maximize the effectiveness of the natural deterrents. Hunt and Azrin saw alcohol abuse as interfering with certain life satisfactions of the drinker. These included social censure from friends and family, being fired from a job, and having difficulty with social interactions and recreational activities. In operant terms, the alcoholic might be seen as having an omission or postponement of reinforcers. Hunt and Azrin reasoned that time out from reinforcement needs to be maximized with the alcoholic so that the consequence has a more potent impact on behavior. (Time out from reinforcement is a widely used technique, although it is not always labeled. For example, preschool children who enjoy playing with their classmates may be taken to the quiet room because they have been disruptive to the group.

These children could be seen as having a time out from reinforcement, i.e., the enjoyment they get from playing with their classmates.)

In Hunt and Azrin's research, eight institutionalized alcoholics were placed in a program with the community reinforcement program rearranged so that a time out from family, social, and vocational reinforcers of not using alcohol would occur if the alcoholic drank. In addition, a carefully matched control group received the usual treatment available at the institution. The experimental group was told at the beginning of the program that staying sober was improved if the alcoholic had a steady, satisfying job. Vocational counseling was set up to help the person find a satisfactory job. Family and social adjustment were also labeled as factors that helped to maintain sobriety. Counseling in these areas was also undertaken.

In the vocational counseling, subjects were asked to (1) prepare a resume; (2) read a pamphlet on how to get a job; (3) call friends and relatives on the phone and tell them they were seeking a job; (4) call the major plants and factories in the area; (5) place a job-wanted ad in the newspaper; (6) rehearse the job interview; (7) place applications; and (8) interview for any available jobs. The vocational counselor was present to assist the alcoholic in all these tasks and even to escort the client to the job interviews. Once the alcoholic indicated he had found a satisfactory job, he was discharged from the hospital.

Marital counseling had three goals. First, it provided reinforcement for the alcoholic to be a fully functioning marital partner. Second, it provided reinforcement for the spouse to maintain the marital relationship. Finally, it attempted to make drinking incompatible with improved marital relationships. Counselor-couple sessions were initially conducted in the hospital and, following discharge, were continued at home. The focus of the counseling sessions was establishing reciprocal agreements, a list of specific activities that the couple would perform to make each other happy. The activities were directed at specific marital problem areas and included (1) preparing meals; (2) listening to the partner with undivided attention; (3) picking up children at school; (4) redistributing the finances; (5) engaging in sexual activities of a specific kind or for a minimal period of time; and (6) visiting relatives and spending a night out together. These activities were frequently undertaken with couples who were resistant to engaging in an intense examination of their marriage. Many of the couples also had minimal initial motivation to reestablish relationships with their mate. Despite these difficulties, Hunt and Azrin found procedures that seemed to overcome these difficulties, at least to some extent. Once the procedure of reciprocal agreements was established between husband and wife, several of the couples were able to draw up their own agreements for situations and relationship issues that were not covered in the original agreement.

Social counseling was thought to be of central importance in the study because many of the alcoholics had narrowed their acquaintances to a small number of friends. Most of these friends were drinkers who also abused alcohol. Therefore, drinking was a prerequisite for maintaining these social relationships. The alcoholics were counseled to schedule social events with friends, relatives, and community groups where the drinking of alcoholic beverages was not tolerated. Interactions with friends who were known to have an active drinking problem were discouraged. Obviously, many of the alcoholics had few friends who were not abusive drinkers. To deal with this issue, a former tavern was converted into a self-supporting social club for the recovering alcoholics. The social club provided a jukebox, live music, and dances. No alcoholic beverages were served, and anyone who had been drinking prior to arrival was not allowed in the club. In this manner, the alcoholics experienced a much-improved social life that was not contingent on alcohol use and abuse.

One of the central factors in the research was the community maintenance that followed treatment. For the first several months following discharge, the alcoholics were visited in their homes by their counselor.

Hunt and Azrin found that the mean percent of time spent drinking, being unemployed, being away from home and institutionalized was more than twice as high for the control group compared with the community-reinforcement group. These results raise the question of whether the outcome can be accounted for by the time out from reinforcement. It seems possible that the procedures used in the research raised the positive reinforcement density for the community reinforcement group. They may have either stayed sober or drank very little because they were enjoying the other social reinforcements in their life. The community-reinforcement group did have higher reinforcement density, as assessed by increased amount of time at work, increased time with families, increased salaries, and increased social life. In addition, the subjects frequently spontaneously stated that they were more satisfied with their lives. In many cases, time out did not occur because the community-reinforcement alcoholic never drank. These nondrinking subjects indicated that they anticipated a time out from reinforcement if they were to drink. When discussing the factors that facilitate and inhibit drinking, Hunt and Azrin state:

> Opposed to these factors that facilitate drinking are various influences that serve to inhibit drinking and which can be conceptualized as negative reinforcers. The major types of negative reinforcers correspond roughly to the major types of positive reinforcers. Under excessive alcohol consumption many of the subjective sensations become unpleasurable such as nausea, dizziness, incoordination and sexual impotence. Unpleasant social reactions rather than approval may result from one's friends, family, legal authorities, and employers who then reject the alcoholic. The deterrent value of these negative reinforcers on a given individual will depend on whether they are operative on him (does he have a family or job), on the magnitude of the negative reinforcer (how much is lost when losing a job or family) and the immediacy with which the

negative reinforcer follows the act of drinking (how much does the employer tolerate drinking). (1980, p. 340)

This overview of Hunt and Azrin's research illustrates how learning concepts can be applied to the issue of alcohol abuse. Their work is an example of how learning concepts can be used to conceptualize alcohol problems.

The work of Miller and Mastria (1977) is another example of an attempt to conceptualize alcohol problems from a learning perspective. Miller and Mastria have developed a theory based on the "functional analysis of *problems in living*, not on any one theoretical framework. It assumes that, on the basis of our current knowledge, no one theory of alcoholism is satisfactory and that alcohol abuse is probably related to numerous sociological, physiological, and psychological factors. It further assumes that treatment techniques should be derived from the current problems of the alcoholic, not from a theoretical frame of reference" (1977, p. 2).

Despite their insistence that treatment should not be undertaken from any specific theoretical perspective, Miller and Mastria clearly base their "functional-practical" approach on a social learning model. They state that they see alcohol abuse as being learned and as being maintained by numerous antecedent (preceding) and consequent (outcome) events. Treatment is directed at specific factors in the abusive drinker's life, which occur shortly prior to drinking (antecedents) or soon after excessive drinking (consequences). The antecedent events can be psychological, sociological, or physiological in origin. People may drink to deal with unpleasant emotional or cognitive states; to be more relaxed and uninhibited in social relationships; or, as in the tension reduction model discussed earlier, to avoid the unpleasant effects of withdrawal from alcohol.

Miller and Mastria focus assessment and intervention procedures on the events that are presently associated with abusive drinking. These "maintaining factors" are the ones that must be dealt with in order to do something about the drinking problem. Those things that may have predisposed the person to have an alcohol problem are of less interest to Miller and Mastria than changing the contingencies, the factors that are currently maintaining the drinking. The factors that help to maintain excessive drinking are numerous and include emotional, social, cognitive, situational, and physiological events. Miller and Mastria view these events as cues for drinking. For example, boredom, social isolation, or environmental factors may set the conditions where a person will use alcohol. Alcohol enhances social interactions for shy individuals, and alcoholics frequently feel more comfortable in social situations if they drink. (One individual could not go to a job interview without first having several drinks. Needless to say, he was never hired.)

Drinking behavior is also affected by *modeling*. Modeling in its simplest form can be said to occur when persons behave like those around them. Watching other people drink and trying to emulate them has frequently led to some very destructive drinking behaviors by college freshmen and new inductees into a fraternity. Essentially, modeling is learning by example. The drinking habits of the group with whom one associates are extremely important since modeling and social reinforcements sought from peers are major ways persons establish drinking patterns.

While the short-term consequences of drinking can be positive in interpersonal relationships, long-term abusive drinking generally leads to problems in social relationships. Heavy drinkers are frequently hostile and verbally abusive toward others. Thus, many alcoholics find that the only response they get (particularly when drinking) is a negative one. In the alcohol abuser, a negative response will usually maintain drinking as effectively as will a positive social response.

In Miller and Mastria's model, emotional factors play a key role in abusive drinking. They note that the tension reduction theory (that alcohol reduces anxiety) has been shown to be inadequate. These authors state that the relationship between alcohol abuse and stress is a complex one. They do suggest that alcoholics may frequently use alcohol to deal with all types of interpersonal difficulties, including assertiveness problems. The logical answer to these problems is to help the alcoholic learn more effective ways of coping with such situations. This might include specific training in assertiveness, how to conduct oneself in a job interview, etc. Having these types of skills might make the interpersonal situation less emotionally arousing for the alcohol abuser.

Situational factors play a role in drinking because drinking behavior becomes associated with certain cues, such as time of day. One recovering alcoholic still gets the urge to drink around 6:00 P.M. because the pubs in his home country opened at that hour. He carries soft drinks in his car to help deal with this time-cued thirst. Other alcoholics may associate drinking with being in a social group or at a party. When drinking is cued by time, other activities can be scheduled. In the case of social events, the individual must simply be exposed to similar events where no one drinks. Recovering alcoholic alumni groups frequently hold "dry" dance-parties for members and their guests.

The impact of cognitive factors on alcohol abuse was not well established within social learning theory when Miller and Mastria reported their work. They viewed the indirect measurement of thinking and cognition as unrealistic since thought cannot be directly observed. However, being good clinicians, they were aware of the alcoholics' self-reports that negative thoughts about themselves, or guilt-related thoughts, keyed drinking. The increasing role of cognitive factors in social learning approaches to alcohol are discussed later in this chapter. As will be seen, this new cognitive approach incorporates the role of negative thinking in abusive drinking.

Physiological factors like pain can also cue drinking. Many alcoholics report that they use alcohol to deal with headaches, backaches, or other discomfort. Using alcohol is also a way to avoid withdrawal symptoms that can be quite uncomfortable and painful. As previously noted, earlier learning theories of alcohol use and abuse viewed the use of alcohol to avoid withdrawal symptoms as a secondary maintenance system for drinking.

This approach demands a specific statement of treatment goals and the therapeutic procedures that will be used. Miller and Mastria concentrate on teaching alcoholics better ways of adjusting to their environments. In this system, the client is intensely involved in setting goals for treatment and establishing and implementing the treatment plan.

Teaching the alcoholics is accomplished by showing them alternatives to alcohol abuse. The goal is to help the alcoholic achieve self-management and cope with life more effectively. The techniques they use in treatment include training in one or more of the following: relaxation, assertion, social and marital skills, self-control, occupational skills, and sexual relationships. Hunt and Azrin's and Miller and Mastria's research and writings serve as illustrations of how learning principles can be utilized to establish an intervention-treatment program for alcoholics.

THE RECENT DEVELOPMENTS APPLYING BANDURA'S SELF-EFFICACY THEORY TO ALCOHOL PROBLEMS

There has been an increasing awareness that the direct relationship once thought to exist between alcohol and the reduction of negative feelings (for example, anxiety, fear, discomfort) is too simple to cover all the outcomes that seem to occur when a person drinks alcohol. More recent conceptualizations have focused on "cognitive mediators." These are cognitive processes that may modify and channel the effects of alcohol. For example, depending on the cognitive set at the time, alcohol might lead to a euphoric or a depressive reaction from the same person at two different times, or it may produce happiness or sadness in varying degrees across different people.

The cognitive mediator theory that has been utilized most frequently with alcohol problems is the self-efficacy theory of Bandura. Bandura's theory has been applied in several ways to alcohol problems.

Self-efficacy is a general theory of behavioral change and comes out of Bandura's reconceptualization of social learning theory (e.g., see Bandura, 1986). As originally presented, the theory was designed to be a behaviorally based theory of human behavior in general. It was not directed specifically to addiction problems. Much of Bandura's early work in social learning was done with individuals with snake phobias. The theory has become increasingly important to the addiction field in general and to alcohol problems specifically. This is due to its application to alcohol treatment and, especially, relapse prevention.

Self-efficacy refers to an individual's sense of self-control. Within this theory, anxiety and avoidant behaviors are related to perceived self-efficacy. The perception of control is the important point. This is a theory that focuses on expectations about what one can and cannot effectively accomplish, not about one's actual skills or abilities. These expectations are not static. Expectations change as a function of experience. More specifically, "self-efficacy is concerned with judgments about how well one can organize and execute courses of action required to deal with prospective situations that contain many ambiguous, unpredictable, and often stressful elements" (Bandura, 1981, pp. 200–201).

Self-efficacy is a cognitive process since it deals with perceived judgments (expectations) that people make about their competence to perform in specific situations. It is important to note that Bandura differentiates self-efficacy from self-esteem and self-concept. Self-efficacy refers to persons' expectancies or perceptions that they can perform in a *specific* situation, while the other two terms are more global in nature (Marlatt, 1985). As applied to alcohol and other addiction problems, the concept of self-efficacy has embraced both treatment issues (Rollnick & Heather, 1982) and relapse prevention (Marlatt & Gordon, 1985). More research and writing has been done on relapse prevention.

Rollnick and Heather (1982) have discussed the application of Bandura's self-efficacy theory to abstinence-oriented alcoholism treatment. They point out that Bandura's theory focuses on a set of expectations that can hypothetically account for the success or failure of all types of therapy. Expectations are not viewed as static or one-dimensional. Bandura made an important distinction between expectations of outcome and efficacy expectations. Expectations of outcome are "a person's estimate that a given behavior will lead to a certain outcome," while efficacy expectations are described as "the conviction that one can successfully execute the behavior required to produce the outcomes" (Bandura, 1977, p. 193, cited in Rollnick & Heather, 1982, p. 243). In another instance, Bandura suggests that "individuals can believe that a particular course of action will produce certain outcomes, but if they entertain serious doubts about whether they can perform the necessary activities, such information does not influence their behavior ..." (Bandura, 1977, p. 193, cited in Rollnick & Heather, 1982, p. 243). If persons have the desire to change their behavior, the magnitude of efficacy expectations will determine how much work will be done and how long they will sustain their efforts to change in the face of obstacles and stressful situations. In the case of alcohol abuse, individuals must want to change their behavior *and* have high expectations that they can modify their behavior in order to succeed.

In their application of Bandura's theory to abstinence-oriented alcohol treatment, Rollnick and Heather illustrate how the theory might be applied to alcoholism treatment. They note that the application of the model to treatment requires the identification of the expectancies created or reinforced in treatment. Outcome expectancies for alcohol treatment appear to have positive and negative aspects. The expectancy of life-long abstinence (the prescribed behavior) leads to persons dealing with their drinking problems (the desired outcome). There is also the negative expectancy that if they return to drinking they will relapse.

Efficacy expectations also seem to have positive and negative aspects. Attention is directed to developing the alcoholics' feelings of personal mastery of managing to remain abstinent. At the same time, there is the reinforcing of the expectancy that individuals have a weakness and will be unable to cope with further drinking. Thus, for treatment to be successful, patients must endorse the positive side of each expectation—believe that life-long abstinence is the desired solution—and, at the same time, develop a sense of personal mastery of self-efficacy necessary for achieving the goal of life-long abstinence. In the typical alcohol treatment program, counselors and therapists must simultaneously convince alcoholics of the need for life-long abstinence and, at the same time, enhance self-efficacy in relation to this goal.

A problem seen by Rollnick and Heather is that some alcoholics may not be able to accept the abstinence outcome (and may not have an expectancy that they will abstain from alcohol for the rest of their lives). Failure to accept the goal of abstinence and failure to have a high expectancy of abstinence for life is seen as a hindrance to treatment for some alcoholics. Rollnick and Heather suggest matching patients with treatment regimens that stress different outcomes, for example, a return to controlled drinking or Marlatt's programmed relapse.

In terms of efficacy expectations, most abstinence-oriented treatment programs use verbal persuasion to suggest to patients that they can deal with the drinking problems that have been so overwhelming for them in the past. Typically, this is accomplished by patients listening to the achievements of another alcoholic and expressing their own desires to cope with their problem. For treatment to be successful, the counselors must use verbal persuasion to convince alcoholics that abstinence can be achieved, that is, persuade the drinkers they have self-efficacy.

Burling, Reilly, Moltzen, and Ziff (1989) looked more closely at self-efficacy (as measured by a modified form of the Situational Confidence Questionnaire [SCQ] based on Bandura's theory). Their findings were consistent with the predictions of self-efficacy theory. In a behaviorally oriented Veterans Administration hospital inpatient program, SCQ scores (self-efficacy) increased with time in treatment and were higher among abstainers than among relapsers at follow-up. The study did not find that high self-efficacy at discharge was related to positive treatment outcome. The failure of this prediction appeared to be due to the fact that abstainers had lower self-efficacy scores on admission than did relapsers. ("Hitting Bottom," to use AA terms, might be a major factor here. See Chapter 12.) The abstainer group had to increase their self-efficacy scores a larger amount to be even with those patients who eventually relapsed. One possibility for the relatively high self-efficacy scores of the relapsers at admission is that those patients underestimated the difficulty of learning how to cope with their problem. Perhaps they felt they did not need that much help. It appears that this underestimation led to a lack of motivation to learn the coping skills needed to maintain abstinence.

Another unexpected finding in Burling et al.'s study was that patients who showed greater change in self-efficacy during treatment had higher abstinence rates at follow-up. Abstainers had a twofold increase in self-efficacy during the course of treatment compared with relapsers. This finding suggests that changes in self-efficacy during treatment may be a salient prediction of outcome.

In the substance abuse area self-efficacy has had the most extensive impact on the issue of relapse (e.g., Marlatt & Gordon, 1985). Marlatt (1985) has noted that self-efficacy plays a powerful role in coping with high-risk situations. More specifically,

> The probability of relapse in a given high-risk situation decreases considerably when the individual harbors a high level of self-efficacy for performing a coping response. If a coping response is successfully performed, the individual's judgment of efficacy will be strengthened for coping with similar situations as they arise on separate occasions. Repeated experiences of success strengthen self-efficacy and reduce the risk that occasional failure or slips will precipitate a relapse. . . . The degree of change in self-efficacy is tied in with the specific circumstances of coping (or failing to cope) with a particular high risk situation. Bandura notes . . . that the extent of increase in self-efficacy associated with successful performance depends on such factors as the perceived difficulty of the task, the amount of effort expended, the degree of external aid received, and the situational circumstances under which the response is performed. Similarly, performance failures may not lead to significant decreases if the failures are discounted on the grounds of insufficient effort, adverse situational conditions, despondent mood, or debilitated physical condition. (Marlatt, 1985, p. 133)

Marlatt cites a study by Rist and Watzl (1983) in which 145 female alcoholics were asked to provide self-efficacy ratings of how difficult it would be not to drink in various social pressure situations involving alcohol. The subjects also completed a questionnaire designed to measure degree of assertiveness in drinking situations and self-efficacy ratings prior to and following social skills training. The social skills training was part of a 3-month treatment program. The patients who relapsed at three months following treatment were those who rated drinking as significantly more difficult to refrain from at pretreatment (lower self-efficacy) than did patients who were still abstinent. These findings are not consistent with Burling et al.'s research (1989), discussed previously.

RELAPSE PREVENTION: A SUMMARY OVERVIEW

Relapse prevention has been discussed a great deal in the literature in reference to self-efficacy theory. Marlatt and Gordon (1985) describe how self-efficacy might be operationalized to deal with relapse by alcoholics and other substance abusers. They outline a program to prevent relapse and/or to minimize the impact of relapse on abstinent alcoholics. The sense that one can handle any threats of relapse obviously increases self-efficacy.

Telling persons how to deal with a relapse is viewed by some professionals as indicating to alcoholics they will relapse, and this leads to a self-fulfilling prophecy. Marlatt (1985) points out that fire drills and lifeboat drills are conducted for ship passengers to prevent disasters should the worst happen. The same could be argued for alcohol relapse prevention. How to deal with a relapse should be seen as a part of an ongoing treatment program.

Involving clients in working out their relapse prevention program is emphasized. The overall goal is to increase their awareness of the choices they have in dealing with their problem. There is also a focus on developing individualized coping skills and self-control abilities. All of these factors contribute to a sense of mastery and self-efficacy. The teaching of these skills is done gradually, at a pace that allows mastery without clients being overwhelmed by too much too soon. (Thus the sense of mastery also helps build self-efficacy.)

Marlatt utilizes two types of intervention strategies to prevent relapses: specific intervention strategies and global self-control strategies. Specific intervention strategies are procedures directed at immediate precipitants of relapse. Global self-control strategies are designed to help modify clients' lifestyles and to deal with covert threats to relapse. The procedures used in both strategies can be subsumed under the categories of skill training, cognitive reframing, and lifestyle intervention.

Skill training involves learning both cognitive and behavioral responses to deal with high-risk situations. Cognitive reframing techniques have several uses. They help clients to see the habit change process as a learning experience. They help in introducing coping imagery to deal with urges and cravings. They help in restructuring how clients see the initial relapse. This latter use involves coping with what Marlatt calls the Abstinence Violation Effect (AVE). This effect is the sense of failure and guilt, or the feeling that everything gained in recovery is lost as a result of a drinking slip.

An examination of the specific intervention and global self-control strategies suggested by Marlatt gives a clearer picture of how relapse prevention techniques are operationalized. *Specific intervention strategies* involve teaching clients to recognize the high-risk situations that may trigger a relapse. These must be individualized because the risks are different for each person. It is important for clients to recognize as early as possible in a chain of behaviors that the behaviors are leading them closer to high-risk situations which may trigger a relapse. The earlier that individuals are aware of the risks, the sooner they can intervene by using coping skills and by using these cues as both warning signals and as reminders to engage in alternative or remedial actions. Clients should be taught to monitor their reactions, check their sense of competency, and use relapses and descriptions of previous relapses to alert themselves to modify their behavior. They should be taught relaxation, stress management, and efficacy-enhancing imagery as coping responses. In the face of decreased self-efficacy and the perception of positive outcome from drinking (alcohol will make them feel better), efficacy-enhancing imagery helps again. Education about the immediate positive and the long-term negative delayed effects of alcohol use may also be beneficial. Two other procedures that help clients limit the impact of a relapse are (1) contracting with them that should they drink, they will limit alcohol's use; and (2) using a reminder card that tells them what procedures to follow if they slip.

Another training device sometimes used to anticipate relapse is "programmed relapse," that is, letting clients drink in the presence of the counselor so they discover that they can go back on the wagon after this programmed slip. To deal with the AVE, cognitive restructuring is involved. Clients are taught to see the slip as a mistake and not a total failure. They learn to attribute blame to the situation and not to themselves. These examples are not exhaustive, but give some of the major preparations for preventing and limiting relapse with these risk sources.

Global self-control strategies help clients establish a broader framework for resisting relapse. To deal with lifestyle imbalance, clients are trained to develop a balanced daily lifestyle and to utilize "positive" addictions such as jogging or meditation. To deal with the clients' desires for indulgences, substitute indulgences like recreational activities or massage may be utilized. Global self-control strategies used to deal with urges and craving for alcohol include coping imagery, stimulus control techniques, labeling, and detaching oneself from the feeling state (that is, recognizing that the urge to drink will occur and that it will eventually pass). Individuals must deal with rationalization and denial by becoming aware of these defenses and treating them as aids to alert themselves about drinking risks. To deal with high-risk situations, alcoholics should make up relapse "road maps" that show where risks are likely to occur and how to avoid those situations. Avoidance strategies can then be used.

Unfortunately, the research on self-efficacy and alcohol abuse has been relatively limited. While the theory has been thoughtfully applied to alcohol and other types of substance abuse, the research base is still being developed. Burling et al. (1989) suggest that the theory could be quite useful to substance abuse in general and may have an even more specific impact on alcohol problems and recovery. Certainly, Marlatt and Gordon's (1985) work indicates that self-efficacy theory has applications that may be helpful in making patients more specifically and systematically prepared to deal with high-risk relapse situations. It also offers an alternative way of viewing relapse, which differs from disease or AA-based treatment approaches. For example, the self-efficacy approach sees a single lapse as something for which alcoholics should prepare for rather than as the road sign of failure. For a more extensive discussion of self-efficacy theory, the reader is referred to Marlatt and Gordon (1985).

Learning theory, in general, and social learning theory, in particular, have become increasingly influential in the alcohol field. Hunt and Azrin (1980) and Miller and Mastria (1977) outline in a practical format how social learning theory can be applied to the treatment of alcohol problems. These writers and others have moved learning approaches to a more central position in alcohol treatment. However, in the United States, learning-based treatment programs are still rare. Wilson (1987c), in commenting on the impact of behavioral research, suggested that the alcohol field was insular and resistant to research and its application. Since the mid-1980s, many of the principles drawn from family therapy research have been applied in alcohol treatment centers. This would suggest that research findings can and will be accepted by alcohol treatment personnel. A significant roadblock to utilizing research findings in treatment programs is that many of the learning concepts and terms are foreign to the typical alcohol counselor. Individuals are badly needed who can translate the research findings and train the alcohol counselors to use learning principles in treatment. Since the 1960s, much has been learned about how to apply learning principles to alcohol treatment (Wilson, 1987c). However, until learning approaches have been applied in a wide variety of alcohol treatment settings and have been evaluated across a wide variety of patients, it is potential and not achievements that will characterize this approach.

REFERENCES

Bandura, A. (1969). *Principles of behavior modification.* New York: Holt, Rinehart and Winston.

Bandura, A. (1977). Self-efficacy: Toward a unifying theory of behavioral change. *Psychological Review, 84,* 192–215.

Bandura, A. (1981). Self-referent thought: A developmental analysis of self-efficacy. In J. H. Flavell & L. Ross (Eds.), *Social cognitive development: Frontiers and possible futures* (pp. 200–239). Cambridge: Cambridge University Press.

Bandura, A. (1986). *Social foundations of thought and action : A social cognitive theory.* Englewood Cliffs, NJ: Prentice Hall.

Burling, T. A., Reilly, P. M., Moltzen, J. O., & Ziff, P. G. (1989). Self-efficacy and relapse among inpatient drug and alcohol abusers: A predictor of outcome. *Journal of Studies on Alcohol, 50,* 354–360.

Conger, J. J. (1951). The effects of alcohol on conflict behavior in the albino rat. *Quarterly Journal of Studies on Alcohol, 12,* 1–29.

Conger, J. J. (1956). Alcoholism: Theory, problem and challenge. II. Reinforcement theory and the dynamics of alcoholism. *Quarterly Journal of Studies on Alcohol, 17,* 291–324.

Hunt, G. M., & Azrin, N. H. (1980). A community-reinforcement approach to alcoholism. In D. A. Ward (Ed.), *Alcoholism: Introduction to theory and treatment* (pp. 330–343). Dubuque, IA: Kendall/Hunt.

Marlatt, G. A. (1985). Cognitive factors in the relapse process. In G. A.Marlatt, & J. H. Gordon (Eds.), *Relapse Prevention* (pp. 128–200). New York: Guilford Press.

Marlatt, G. A., & Gordon, J. H. (Eds.). (1985). *Relapse Prevention.* New York: Guilford Press.

Masserman, J. H., & Yum, K. S. (1946). An analysis of the influence of alcohol on experimental neurosis in cats. *Psychosomatic Medicine, 8,* 36–52.

Miller, P. M., & Mastria, M. A. (1977). *Alternatives to alcohol abuse: A social learning model.* Champaign, IL: Research Press.

Pomerlau, O., Pertschuk, M., & Stinnet, J. (1976). A critical examination of some current assumptions in the treatment of alcoholism. *Journal of Studies on Alcohol, 37,* 849–867.

Rist, F., & Watzl, H. (1983). Self-assessment of relapse risk and assertiveness in relation to treatment outcome of female alcoholics. *Addictive Behaviors, 8,* 121–127.

Rollnick, S., & Heather, N. (1982). The application of Bandura's self-efficacy theory to abstinence oriented alcoholism treatment. *Addictive Behaviors, 7,* 243–250.

Ullman, L. P., & Krasner, L. (1969). *A psychosocial approach to abnormal behaviors.* Englewood Cliffs, NJ: Prentice Hall.

Wilson, G. T. (1987a). Cognitive processes in addiction. *British Journal of Addiction, 82,* 343–353.

Wilson, G. T. (1987b). Cognitive studies in alcoholism. *Journal of Consulting and Clinical Psychology, 55,* 325–331.

Wilson, G. T. (1987c). Laboratory research on alcohol use and abuse: Past trends and future directions. *Advances in Behavior Research and Therapy, 9,* 73–90.

Sociocultural Factors in Alcohol Use and Abuse

 _chapter 8_

The attitudes, norms, and values learned from society affect the ways individuals perceive and react to all factors in their society. Learned attitudes, norms, and values affect how individuals react to and use alcohol. A number of writers have discussed sociocultural variables and their effects on alcohol use and abuse.

Bennett (1988) indicates that anthropology and sociology are the disciplines that have contributed most heavily to the understanding of sociocultural factors in the use and abuse of alcohol. She sees most of anthropology's work in the alcohol area as being interdisciplinary with psychology, sociology, and psychiatry. One of the key writings, _Drunken Comportment: A Social Explanation,_ by MacAndrew and Edgerton (1969), is a collaboration between the first author, who is a psychologist, and the second, who is an anthropologist. This is an important book in terms of reinforcing anthropological views that drunken behavior is culturally defined. The definitions that particular cultures and subcultures use for drunken behavior are derived from the social and cultural expectations, sanctions, and norms that societies have regarding alcohol. MacAndrew and Edgerton go on to state ". . . however great the differences may be between persons' sober and drunk comportment—and there can be no doubt that these differences are often very great indeed—it is evident that both states are characterized by a healthy respect for socially sanctioned limits" (p. 85).

Chafetz and Demone (1962) suggest that alcohol's ability to change people's perspectives may be one way to understand its increased use. These authors state that some people feel alcohol use is directly related to anxieties. Primitive cultures contained the potential for considerable anxiety, but the sources of that anxiety were relatively few. For example, if early man stumbled upon some new wild animal, its potential danger or usefulness could be ascertained fairly quickly. Today, threats from the environment are also faced. Because of the increased complexities of life and rapidly expanding boundaries of knowledge and communication, sources of anxiety are more numerous and less directly known. Another way of stating this is that stimuli are less controllable and predictable. Therefore, life is less controllable and predictable.

Bacon (1963) suggests that one function of alcohol in modern complex society is "social jollification" (p. 87). He notes that it is to be expected that as a society becomes more complex, there will be an increase in meetings for pleasure. This expectation is met in our society. There has been an elaboration of recreation in modern technological societies. With this elaboration and extension, there has been an elaboration of alcohol's role in what Bacon calls social jollification or pleasure association. Modern societies are more self-contained and independent than were primitive societies, and individuals are less aware of people around them and those persons' activities. Modern people are also more competitive and aggressive in their relationships than were people in primitive societies. However, the human need for unsuspicious, pleasant, and relatively easy joint gatherings still exists. Bacon says one way to fulfill this need is to break down hostilities, indifference, and ignorance between people, that is, to try to get people to relax. Drinking alcohol provides a quick, fairly sure way of achieving this relaxation. Alcohol is also a way to establish a trustworthy, noncompetitive friendship between two people. The cocktail party and the sharing of a social drink are examples of the positive function alcohol plays in a modern complex society.

While alcohol can play a positive role, it also has the possibility of producing dysfunctional behavior. Bales (1983) looks at both the positive and negative effects of alcohol use. He draws a number of comparisons between alcohol's role in primitive and modern societies. He asserts that most modern individuals have increased anxieties, and the depressive function of alcohol has become more significant in dealing with those anxieties. At the same time, complex modern society requires more discrimination, caution, timing, cooperation, and acceptance of responsibilities than did primitive societies. Alcohol taken in excess can diminish the skills needed to carry out these more advanced activities. Drinking pervades all aspects of a complex society and is primarily loosely organized around people's recreation. For that reason, prevention of alcohol problems is more difficult in a complex society than in a simple one. In addition, alcohol can more rapidly affect individuals' participation in a complex society than it can in a simple one. Alcohol's power to destroy effective personality functioning is greater in a complex society. That is, self-esteem, social competence, and ability to deal with frustrations are more negatively affected by alcohol abuse in a complex society. How individuals feel about themselves is also more negatively affected.

AN OVERVIEW OF THE SOCIOCULTURAL MODEL

Heath (1980, 1982, 1987) has had a continuing interest in the sociocultural model of alcoholism. In his critical review of the sociocultural model (1980), he outlines the theoretical and empirical bases for the model. Heath says that the model is consistent with the broadly held social science view that human behavior is the complex result of an interplay of biological and historical factors. This includes an interaction of culture, society, and the individual. The research on which this model is based comes mainly from anthropology (which used research based on field work in alien societies) and sociology (which used research based on surveys of minority populations). Unfortunately, most of the studies used to support the sociocultural model of alcohol use and abuse do not come from studies designed to investigate alcohol. Rather, the findings have been serendipitous in studies originally designed to investigate something else. Studying alcohol use in its "natural context" is a fairly recent occurrence.

Most of the descriptive work for the sociocultural model has been done by anthropologists. Sociologists and psychologists have contributed to the theoretical and conceptual aspects of the model. Heath cites some key studies that have contributed to the model including (1) Horton's (1943) study of preliterate societies; (2) Bales's (1983) research on cultural differences of alcoholism and its rates in societies; and (3) Jessor, Graves, Hanson, and Jessor's (1968) study of a triethnic community.

From these and other studies, Heath concludes that it has become apparent that drinking is "embedded in a matrix of social and cultural factors such as values, attitudes, and expectations learned from significant others" (1980, p. 40). Studies of alcoholic use across cultures establish that the number of problems created in a society is not directly related to the frequency of drinking or the amount of alcohol consumed in that society. (Note that the distribution of consumption model does suggest there may be such a linkage; see Chapter 13.)

By looking at subcultural variance within a larger society, Heath established these propositions: (1) ritual and symbolism affect drinking habits in important ways; (2) ambivalence towards alcohol can pose hazards for individuals living in such a subculture; and (3) groups attach convivial, utilitarian, and other expectations to the use of alcohol.

Heath maintains that while it is useful to study cultures in order to better understand alcohol use and abuse, the approaches taken by some researchers can lead to misleading interpretations. For example, comparing alcoholism rates of two countries like France and Italy and then attributing any differences in alcohol abuse to the way that those cultural groups view alcohol would be superficial. It is necessary to have more data showing how and why these cultural groups view alcohol use differently before an understanding of the cultural underpinnings of alcohol use and abuse can be reached.

Anthropologists, in particular, have frequently used another type of cross-cultural approach to study alcohol use and abuse. The co-occurrence of particular traits, institutions, or other cultural factors are correlated with alcohol use patterns in a large number of societies. When significant correlations are found between cultural items and the quantity and frequency of alcohol used, such findings suggest culturally, socially, or individually significant associations.

Horton's (1943) work is the best known of these types of studies. Horton suggested that the primary function of alcoholic beverages in preliterate societies was a reduction of anxiety. His conclusion was based on the analysis of fifty-six societies in which alcohol use patterns and their relationship to several indices of anxiety were available. Although Horton's research is still considered a pioneering effort because of its methodology, Heath (1980) maintains that Horton's conclusions have been rejected.

Field (1962) reworked Horton's original data and determined that it was not fear but the absence of supportive kin groups (with stability, permanence, and formal structure) that made the difference in the ways alcohol was used in the cultures Horton studied (cited in Heath, 1980). Barry, Bacon, and Child (1965) used a larger sample of societies and more rigorous methodology. Their findings emphasized the relationship of drinking to dependent-independent conflicts in society. Heath (1980) presents these examples of cross-cultural studies to point out that different researchers using similar data sources have come to different conclusions about the relationship of alcohol to factors in primitive societies.

Heath summarizes some of the issues that need further study in the sociocultural area. He notes, ". . . we should try to learn how others view alcohol and human behavior . . ." (1980, p. 13). While Heath views the major success of the sociocultural model as providing information about human variations in the use of alcoholic beverages, he sees the need for more rigorous scientific study on how others view alcohol. More rigorous research might provide, for example, a better understanding of why individuals conform or fail to conform, or why the degree of intoxication relates to socially expected forms of behavior. It might also be possible to learn how people, in general, view "alcoholism" in a society. This knowledge might provide the basis for a better focus on education and prevention efforts in the United States and other modern countries.

In another paper, Heath (1982) notes that the way people use alcohol is related to the attitudes, norms, and values they hold toward alcohol use. The ways people view alcohol can range from abstinence and the condemnation of all drinking to enthusiastic connoisseurship or frequent heavy drinking of alcoholic beverages. For some, alcohol is a staple part of the diet. Alcohol can be used as a tonic or medicine for specific ills. In some groups, sociability without alcohol is unthinkable since alcohol is used as a social lubricant. Others use alcohol in highly ritualized settings.

Most members of any society share drinking customs in the same way they share other customs. These customs affect drinking patterns and the types of alcohol consumed in a given society.

Sociocultural variances in the use of alcohol have major importance in relation to drinking problems and their outcomes. The nature of drinking problems is affected in large part by the nature of the drinking. For example, in a society where members drink daily, there may be high rates of cirrhosis and other medical problems but few accidents, fights, homicides, or other violent behavior associated with alcohol. A population where the majority of the members are binge drinkers usually shows the latter complex of problems.

The rate at which these problems occur within a society is significantly affected by the belief and behavior patterns related to alcohol. A society that views drinking as ritually significant is not as likely to develop alcohol-related problems as is a society that does not view alcohol in this way. A cultural group that sees alcohol primarily as a way to deal with stress or to show strength is at high risk for developing alcohol problems. Heath maintains that these cultural variances have implications for intervention, treatment, and prevention and must be taken into account in planning any of these programs for a given society.

Heath uses the public's common perceptions of alcohol use patterns of the Jews and the Irish-Americans as a case example. He points out that Jewish drinking patterns have for centuries been perceived as moderate and unproblematic. Jews learn to drink at a young age in the supportive family context and both moderation and religious rituals are emphasized. The Irish differ significantly from the Jews in their approach to and use of alcohol. Their drinking usually does not begin until adolescence. The first drink usually occurs in an all-male setting where heavy drinking is emphasized. The ritual use of alcohol by Jews contrasts with the Irish convivial "drinking like a man." Instead of the consecration of the Jewish drinking situation, competition is the main feature of Irish drinking. These contrasting drinking patterns lead to different admission rates to alcohol treatment centers. The Irish show high admission rates and the Jews show low admission rates.

According to Heath, examinations of drinking patterns by American sociologists are 20 to 35 years old. New evidence indicates that Jews are now showing more alcohol-related problems. Irish drinking patterns have also changed somewhat.

According to Heath, in the Jewish culture there has been a reduction in the number of Jews following Orthodox religion. This has lowered the ritual and sacred use of alcohol by Jews. There has also been a progressive loosening of family cohesion that has led to the weakening of family norms and family models of alcohol use. These and other factors have led to the adoption of Gentile patterns of business and social interactions including alcohol use. Some writers argue that Jewish alcoholics of the past were underidentified by family and social agencies. However, draft records for World Wars I and II show that, proportionately, Jews, indeed, did have fewer alcoholics and alcohol abusers than the population as a whole and had significantly fewer abusers than the Irish. Whatever the truth of the matter, sociocultural variables have been seen as important factors in Jewish drinking.

A similar sociocultural emphasis has been put forth for the Irish. Heath outlines the "sociological reappraisal" (1982, p.433), which suggests several new ways of looking at the Irish's drinking. Heath points out that the continuity of drinking in the Irish culture is significant. Drinking problems are expected among Irish men.

Heath notes that as members of a cultural group are socialized in alcohol use, they are usually taught what their society "knows" about drunkenness. When alcohol is introduced to those persons, they then act in ways that confirm their previously learned knowledge.

Social and personal problems are thought to cause alcohol problems in many cultures. For example, anomie (used to refer to a person's loss of traditional norms or the inability to achieve the norms of society) has been explained as a cause for alcohol abuse. Persons who experience anomie are seen as marginal individuals who use alcohol to reduce the isolation they feel or to help them cope with that isolation.

Problems associated with alcohol abuse are not only psychological. They can also be economic, political, or social. While poverty is frequently suggested as a cause of alcoholism, it is interesting that consumption levels are often associated with the amount of expendable income in a societal group.

Anthropological investigation of different cultural groups' uses of alcohol continues. However, Heath's assessment of the additional data on new groups indicates that he does not feel that the additional information changes the primary generalizations one can draw about alcohol use from cross-cultural research.

> Despite the significant increase in societies among which drinking beliefs and behaviors have been described, there is no reason to revise some of the most significant generalizations that derive from cross-cultural study of the subject:
>
> 1. In most societies, drinking is essentially a social act and, as such, it is embedded in a context of values, attitudes, and other norms.
> 2. These values, attitudes, and other norms constitute important sociocultur-

al factors that influence the effects of drinking, regardless of how important biochemical, physiological, and pharmacokinetic factors may also be
in that respect.

3. The drinking of alcoholic beverages tends to be hedged about with rules
   concerning who may and may not drink how much of what, in what contexts, in the company of whom, and so forth. Often such rules are the
   focus of exceptionally strong emotions and sanctions.

4. The value of alcohol for promoting relaxation and sociability is emphasized in many populations.

5. The association of drinking with any kind of specifically associated problems—physical, economic, psychological, social relational, or other—is
   rare among cultures throughout both history and the contemporary
   world.

6. When alcohol-related problems do occur, they are clearly linked with
   modalities of drinking, and usually also with values, attitudes, and norms
   about drinking.

7. Attempts at prohibition have never been successful except when couched
   in terms of sacred or supernatural terms. . . . (1987, pp. 45–46)

There is also consistency across time in the drinking patterns of certain
cultural groups that have problems with alcohol and those that do not. The
characteristics of those that have problems with alcohol will be discussed at
this point.

REASONS FOR DIFFERENT RATES
OF ALCOHOLISM ACROSS CULTURES

There have been several explanations for cultural differences in rates of alcoholism and alcohol problems. For example, Bales (1983) outlines factors that
may contribute to the cultural differences in rates of alcoholism. He notes
that a high rate of consumption in a society does not necessarily mean that
the society will have the physical and social complications associated with
alcoholism in American culture. Bales states that there are three general ways
culture and social organization can influence rates of alcoholism.

"The first is the degree to which the culture operates to bring about
acute needs for adjustment, or inner tensions, in its members" (1983, p.
212). For example, the culture can induce guilt, create conflict, and suppress
aggression and sexual tension in its members. Bales uses the Irish peasants to
illustrate how this might work.

The English, who wished to keep the Irish an agricultural people sub-
servient on the land (most of the farms were owned by absentee British land-
lords), took every penny they could get from the Irish farmers. As a result,
the Irish were always on the edge of hunger. Because they raised so few
foods, the potato blight led to several famines.

The small farms had room for only one extended family made up of retired grandparents, the farmer, his wife, and children. Labor was delegated according to gender, with boys helping their fathers in the fields and girls helping their mothers with household tasks. There was a strict separation of sexes both within the home and in society as a whole. The "boys" could not marry until their father gave up the farm and retired. Then, only one boy, usually the oldest, could farm. Others would have to find jobs as apprentices or immigrate to other countries.

Males had to stay away from females because of the severe restrictions placed on premarital sexual intercourse by the church and by the peasantry. In effect, the "boys" were dependent upon their fathers for spending money and were deprived of sexual contacts by church and societal restrictions. Even social contacts between the two sexes were limited. Since a farm would not support more families, love relationships were discouraged. Instead, "boys" met at farmhouses and taverns. Drinking and physical horseplay were their major activities. Persons who did not drink in these all-male groups were regarded with suspicion. They were suspected of wandering around with the intention of molesting girls. In this type of culture, there was a great deal of suppressed sexuality and aggression. These suppressed tensions found their expression in drinking.

When the Irish moved to America, the old roles were no longer workable. Fathers seemed to become impotent figures, and mothers became the dominant parent. Mothers bound their sons to them in traditional Irish ways. However, in the United States this relationship made it difficult for sons to successfully attain the independent status of adults. In a study of alcoholic patients of Irish descent, Bales found this mother-son dependence and conflict in 60 percent of the cases. He suggests that these conflicts might explain the motivation for alcohol use and abuse in America by Irish males.

The second way in which culture and social organization can influence rates of alcoholism is by "the sort of attitudes toward drinking which the culture produces in its members" (1983, p. 212). Bales outlines four different types of attitudes that a culture may generate in its members.

The first is an attitude that calls for complete abstinence. This attitude is usually based on religion. The use of alcohol is not allowed under any circumstances. Bales uses the Moslem culture as a large-scale example of this attitude. Moslems do not drink because it is forbidden by a command from Mohammed. This ruling appears to be based upon the dangers to social order and alcohol's role in aggression and its effect on sexuality. While there is little empirical evidence on drinking rates among Moslems, there is considerable evidence that the drinking taboo has been unevenly observed. Some Moslems have used all types of rationalizations to escape the spirit and letter of the law, including mislabeling the contents of some wine containers, insisting wine is allowed or that the taboo applies only to excessive drinking, and smuggling and using alcohol privately.

One of the difficulties of total prohibition, both in the Moslem faith and in America during the prohibition era, is that it is difficult to maintain total prohibition of use. Obtaining a genuine acceptance of total prohibition is extremely difficult. The breaking of the drinking taboo in a prohibition society appears to be an ideal way for members to express dissent and aggression. This is especially true when group consensus is weak and aggression is strong. Advocating total prohibition sometimes results in the opposite of what is desired. For example, parents who abstain and forbid their children to drink frequently have children who develop alcohol problems. Another societal example is the difficulty the United States had when it attempted to ban alcohol (in an attempt to enforce total abstinence). Not only did a great deal of drinking occur, but also a whole system of bootlegging, smuggling, and organized crime developed around the illegal delivery of alcoholic beverages (see Chapter 1).

The second attitude is the ritual attitude. Like the complete abstinence attitude, it also has its base in religion. Alcoholic beverages (sometimes a specific one) are prescribed for use in religious ceremonies. Orthodox Jews present one of the best examples of the test of the ritual attitude's utility. These Jews drink regularly and in a ritualistic manner. Despite the fact that most of them use alcohol on many occasions, they are seldom arrested for drunkenness and have few admissions to psychiatric hospitals for alcoholic psychoses. Comparison tables of various ethnic groups in America almost invariably place Jews lowest in terms of having alcohol problems.

Other hypotheses for the Jews' lack of alcohol problems could also be entertained. In most societies in which they have lived, they were weak politically and thus had to be sure that they had their wits about them or be sure that drunkenness did not set off persecution. Bales (1983) believes that it is the lifelong ritualistic use of alcohol that impresses on these people the sentiments and emotions to use alcohol in moderation. Wine stands for several sacred things in the Jewish culture. For example, it is described as "the word of God" and the "commandment of the Lord" (p. 218). The Torah (the Jewish faith's sacred body of law), Jerusalem, and Israel are all compared to wine. Wine must be ritually pure and untouched by an idolater before it is used in religious ceremonies. The use of wine is bound up in the control of appetites exemplified in the dietary laws of the Jewish people. Thus, in the Jewish culture, attitudes toward drinking are clearly connected to attitudes toward the sacred and the mind and emotions of the person. Bales sees this as the central reason why drunkenness in an individual is perceived as so deplorable by Jews. To be drunk is to be profane; it is a perversion of the sacred use of wine. Therefore, the idea of becoming drunk, particularly for personal reasons, creates a strong counter-anxiety that also helps the Jew avoid insobriety.

The third of Bales's types "can be called a convivial attitude toward drinking. Drinking is a social rather than a religious ritual performed both because it symbolizes social unity or solidarity and because it actually loosens up emotions which make for social ease and goodwill. This is what is called 'social drinking'" (p. 216). Bales views this attitude as a mixed type of drinking. It has the symbolism of solidarity seen in ritual drinking. It also leans toward the utilitarian (the fourth type, discussed next) in terms of the good feelings expected from drinking. This drinking attitude leads to purely utilitarian drinking in its most highly developed form. Here, the Irish culture is a good example. Bales notes that while drinking is a part of gatherings such as Irish marriages, the guests do not drink as a part of the marriage ritual, but only afterwards in the marriage celebration. This drinking does lead to social unity or solidarity and does loosen up emotions, making people more relaxed in the wedding setting. However, alcohol is also used in business transactions. Here, it moves over into the utilitarian attitude described next. Another example of this type of drinking attitude is the cocktail party, which is usually aimed at making people less socially inhibited and more comfortable with each other.

Finally, Bales describes the utilitarian attitude towards drinking. "This includes medicinal drinking and other types calculated to further self-interest or exclusively personal satisfaction. It is often 'solitary drinking,' but not necessarily so. It is possible to drink for utilitarian purposes in a group and with group approval. The distinction is that the purpose is personal and self-interested rather than social and expressive" (p. 216). As noted earlier, the Irish frequently use alcohol in the business world. When haggling over the price of cattle in Ireland, a buyer may take the seller to a tavern to soften him up. In Ireland, the bargaining for marriage is very important because the agreement made can decide the amount of the bride's dowry. In this match-making, the participants treat (buy drinks) back and forth until both sides are intoxicated. One side hopes to be less intoxicated and to strike the best side of the bargain. Another aspect of this utilitarian attitude is the perception the Irish have of intoxicated people. Laborers envy intoxicated persons returning from the fair because these persons are in a better state than they are. Bales says that drinking to get over a hangover is a pure example of individuals indulging in utilitarian drinking. Alcohol in this case is regarded as a medicine. Bales cites Morewood (1838), an Irish historian, who indicated that whiskey was first introduced into Ireland as a medicine for preserving health and a panacea for all disorders. These disorders ranged from colic and dropsy to fever and various types of stones in the body.

The final way that culture and social organization can influence rates of alcoholism is by "the degree to which the culture provides suitable substitute means of satisfaction" (Bales, 1983, p. 212). In this case the people in a culture are assumed to be under tensions. Unless the society allows ways other than alcohol abuse to deal with these tensions, some members of the society will become alcoholic. One of the most common substitutes for alcohol is other mood-changing drugs. The Jews have a high rate of drug addiction.

Some Moslems use hashish and are addicted to strong teas. Other groups use trancelike state changes to meet the need to reduce tension. Still others use elaborate mystical rituals.

While noting that the maladjustments individuals must face differ markedly across cultures, Bales cautions against the idea that there are some few concrete solutions that might work in all cultures to reduce tension. He asserts that anything that can reduce the acute tensions of individuals and steer them away from utilitarian attitudes toward drinking or anything that provides substitute satisfactions to replace the rewards of drinking should reduce alcoholism rates in a society or culture.

Studies indicate that various ethnic, national, and religious groups have different drinking habits and customs and that, within each group, the attitudes toward drinking and drunkenness can vary considerably. The records of alcohol treatment facilities indicate significant differences in the percentage of alcoholic patients drawn from different ethnic or religious groups. Irish-Americans are strikingly overrepresented while Jewish-Americans are underrepresented. If differences do exist in the way that different national ethnic groups use alcohol, finding out how each ethnic, national, and religious group teaches its members to use alcohol becomes important. If some groups have difficulty with alcohol abuse and others do not, and if clear differences emerge in the ways the abusing and nonabusing groups teach their members to use alcohol, then the different socialization skills might be important. Therefore, studying groups that have low rates of alcohol problems might provide some possible strategies for reducing alcohol problems in other groups. Conversely, looking at commonalities in alcohol-abusing groups might point out some things that should be eliminated in a society's teachings about alcohol. A review of groups with low rates of problems and groups with high rates of problems will be presented to see if there are any commonalities.

DRINKING AND SOCIALIZATION IN LOW-RISK GROUPS

As previously stated, Jews have a low rate of alcoholism. But other psychological disorders do occur among Jewish people. This suggests that the elements of traditional Jewish life that "protect" against alcoholism are rather specific and are not simply reflective of such things as family solidarity or emphasis on control. If they were, there should be no differences in the occurrence (rate) of alcohol problems and, for example, mental health problems.

The percentage of alcohol users among Jews is comparatively high. The members of this group start to use alcohol at a very early age and drink all kinds of alcoholic beverages, although wine is the most common. Acceptable settings for alcohol use include houses of worship, ceremonies such as weddings, other religious events, and rituals in the home. Moderation in drinking is encouraged, and drunkenness is rare. For a Jew to violate propriety while drinking is severely disapproved. Most Jews strongly approve of these negative sanctions. There is no notable feeling of ambivalence attached to the use of alcohol in the Jewish culture.

Most of these impressions were based on research that occurred in the 1940s, 1950s, and 1960s. A more recent national sample study by Greeley, McCready, and Theisen (1980) looked at drinking patterns among Jews, Italians, Chinese, Swedes, and a comparison group of drinkers from England. The Greeley et al. study found that Jews were low (compared to the other groups) in the percentage of people who reported drinking twice a week or more, in the percentage of people consuming three or more drinks of liquor in a sitting, and on rankings involving serious drinking problems. At the same time, this study found the Jews to have the highest percentage of "nonabstainers" (90 percent of Jews reported using alcohol).

Glassner and Berg (1985), in a more recent chapter on Jewish-American drinking, have attempted to outline the reasons that Jews have fewer problems with alcohol. They note that less than 1 percent of the Jewish population is alcoholic while 7 percent of the general population is alcoholic. These writers isolate four factors that they see as protecting the Jewish people from alcoholism.

First, alcohol problems are seen by Jews as non-Jewish. There is a prevailing and widespread belief among Jews that alcoholism does not happen to Jews. That is, alcoholism is defined as an "outgroup" characteristic. Jewish identity with sobriety may be one of the reasons for low alcoholism rates in this group.

Secondly, Jews are exposed to moderation practices as children. Through the ceremonial and ritual use of alcohol, Jewish children are continually exposed to "prescriptive norms" (see the material on Mizruchi and Perrucci's prescriptive and proscriptive norms later in this chapter). As Jewish children grow up, alcohol is associated with special, indeed often sacred, occasions. Glassner and Berg suggest that sobriety and drinking are the norm in Jewish homes as children grow up. "Our interviews suggest that Jews perpetuate this association and its connection with ritual, not only by affiliation with religious life, but also by restricting drinking to special secular occasions and by cataloguing drinking as a symbolic part of festive eating" (p. 97).

Isolation by peers is another protective factor in Jewish drinking. In Glassner and Berg's study, three-fourths of the Jews interviewed indicated that nearly all their friends were Jewish. This tendency to move in the direction of Jewish things and Jewish people protects Jews from abusive drinking, according to these writers. Jews who do become intoxicated are likely to be scorned or pitied. Since Jews value their interactions with each other, such pity and scorn is an effective moderator of abusive drinking. In addition, by their being with other Jews while using alcohol, the drinking behavior of older Jews becomes a model for younger generations.

Finally, the development of an avoidance repertoire to deal with alcohol use helps protect Jews from alcoholism. The fact that Jews share common drinking histories, symbolic associations, and uniformity of opinion about appropriate drinking behaviors allows Jews to say an affirmative "No!" when asked to drink more than they wish. Avoidance repertoires that might be used at parties include taking one mixed drink and adding mixer for the rest of the evening, saying one cannot drink because of work demands, and being occupied with other tasks while others are drinking.

In general, there is agreement among investigators that the ritual and symbolic features of Orthodox Jewish drinking patterns leads to the low rate of alcoholism among Jews. The social ostracism faced by inebriants is also a factor in controlling and preventing drunkenness and alcoholism. Studies by Snyder (1962) have shown that very low rates of alcoholism are also common among Jews who do not have strong ties to traditional Jewish culture. He concludes that Jews learn how to drink in a controlled manner as a result of ceremonial use of alcohol and that they learn how not to drink inappropriately through exposure to broad patterns and ethnocentric ideas and sentiments.

The Italians and Italian-Americans both have relatively low rates of alcoholism, despite the fact that the per capita consumption of wine in Italy is second only to that of France. Wine is a normal part of the daily diet in Italy, where alcohol is consumed almost exclusively with meals. Children drink at a very young age, and no special meaning is attached to their drinking—it is considered a part of their normal routine. Italians meet with indifference a refusal to drink. They have strong negative attitudes about drunkenness, and severe social sanctions are attached to such behavior.

The drinking practices and attitudes of the Italian-Americans have undergone some changes. Less than 10 percent of this group drink alcoholic beverages exclusively with meals. Drinking for pleasure and relaxation, as a part of social situations, has increased and incidents of excessive drinking occur more frequently than in Italy. The Italian-Americans seem to be losing the protection against alcoholism afforded by Italian traditions, but their rate of alcoholism is still comparatively low (Lolli, Serianni, Golder, & Luzzatti-Fegiz, 1958; Williams & Straus, 1950).

More recent data seem to confirm low rates of alcoholism and alcohol problems among Italians and Italian-Americans. However, whether or not Italians have problems with alcohol seems to be based on which type of problems are being examined. De Lint (1976) and Simboli (1985) both point out that the Italians living in Italy have one of the highest rates of cirrhosis of the liver of all European countries. However, drunkenness is rarely observed and there are few social problems associated with alcohol use. In fact, it has been established by Lolli et al. (1958) that the occurrence of drunkenness is markedly lower in Italy than among Italian-Americans in the United States. At the same time, the incidence of cirrhosis of the liver in Italy has been reported to be about one-seventh the rate in the United States, despite Italy's relatively high rate when compared to European countries (Simboli, 1985).

In a study of Italian-Americans living in San Francisco, Simboli found that almost all Italian-Americans in his sample were users of alcohol. Most felt that alcohol sustained their health. His participant observation, survey, and key informant approach never revealed any Italian-Americans who were intoxicated or disorderly. There was a move away from wine drinking to other types of alcoholic beverages from the first to the third generation of Italian-Americans. Only one informant, in the third generation, indicated that many people in her generation had alcohol problems. Simboli believes that the more Italian-Americans are acculturated into U.S. society, the more likely they are to have alcohol problems.

Despite the shift away from traditional drinking habits that have accompanied the moving away of many Italian-Americans from Italian communities, Italian-Americans still have relatively low rates of alcohol problems. Greeley et al. (1980), in their study of a large national sample, also found that most Italian-Americans used alcohol but that relatively few had alcohol problems.

The reasons for the Italian-Americans' lack of significant alcohol problems, despite their extensive use of the beverage, is not easy to understand. It is probably not true that if one is exposed early in life to alcohol by a culture that uses alcohol extensively, one automatically is "inoculated" against alcohol problems. Simboli (1985) points out the complex relationship between Italian acculturation and drinking.

> The fact is that the drinking behavior of nonacculturated Italian-Americans inherently involves a complex of cultural relationships which includes personality, norms, beliefs, values, attitudes and social structure. For example, it has been shown in studies on Southern Italians in Italy and in the United States that Italian family solidarity is a major cultural trait, as compared with other family systems in the United States and many Northern European Countries. . . . Most of these studies suggest that family honor and togetherness is highly valued in Italian culture. . . ." (p. 73)

Simboli further suggests that the Southern Italian social structure, which was transplanted to the United States, invoked social controls that dealt quickly and directly with any family member who engaged in any behavior (like being intoxicated) that would shame the family.

The Chinese are another group with low alcoholism rates. As with the Jews and Italians, the Chinese learn to drink at an early age and their consumption of alcoholic beverages is high. They drink at meals and at all kinds of ceremonial occasions. In Chinese culture, drinking serves as a social catalyst. Therefore, it is approved so long as it cements social relationships, but is disapproved when it tends to destroy group harmony. Public drunkenness is deplored, and its occurrence is rare. The Chinese community keeps a check on its members so that when a serious drinking transgression occurs, the offender is ridiculed and loses face, a serious personal punishment for members of this culture.

Sue, Kitano, Hatanaka, and Yeung (1985) report on the drinking patterns of Chinese in California. They found that the Chinese-American males have the highest rate of abstention (54.7 percent) and have one of the lowest rates of heavy drinkers (8.4 percent). Chinese females had an even higher rate of abstention (73.8 percent), and no Chinese-American females were found in the heavy drinking category. Sue et al. suggest that because of the low rate of heavy drinkers, alcoholism may be a relatively minor problem among Chinese-Americans.

After comparing the alcohol consumption and demographic patterns of Chinese-Americans with Japanese, Koreans, and other California drinkers, Sue et al. drew three general conclusions.

1. Chinese-Americans have a low rate of consumption when they are compared to Caucasians and other Asian groups.

2. Chinese women reported far less drinking than did Chinese men, which was consistent with the male-female ratio of drinking in all Asian groups.

3. Those Chinese-Americans in the 18 to 29 age group consumed the most alcohol.

After surveying and comparing several studies in addition to their own, Sue et al. came to the following conclusion. "There appears to be a U-shaped curve among many of our Chinese-American acquaintances. A high proportion are abstainers, whereas another high, but smaller proportion are heavy drinkers. It may follow the saying that most of them don't drink, but those who do drink will drink you under the table'" (p. 369).

The Italians, Jews, and Chinese share to some degree the following characteristics regarding drinking behavior and the rules surrounding it: (1) gradual socialization of children in the use of alcoholic beverages; (2) relatively low social pressure to drink; (3) negative sanctions against excessive drinking; (4) positive, accepting attitudes toward moderate, nondestructive drinking; (5) a well-established consensus on the customs of drinking; and (6) freedom from ambivalence in the drinking situation.

DRINKING AND SOCIALIZATION
IN HIGH-RISK GROUPS

In contrast to the groups already discussed, study after study has shown that Irish-Americans have one of the highest rates of alcoholism. According to

Bales (1983), Irish-American drinking behavior can be explained by a combination of family, economic, and attitudinal factors that prevailed in Ireland during the time the Irish-Americans' forefathers lived there. (These have already been discussed in greater detail.) Ireland was a generally poor, agricultural country where family and economic conditions resulted in the strict separation of the sexes and in marriages occurring late in life. Men spent much of their time together and found their outlet for aggression in sexuality and drinking, a major activity. Drunkenness was a fairly frequent occurrence and was tolerated with good humor or even a kind of sympathetic encouragement. Drinking often took place outside the home in uncontrolled settings. Drinking was more or less a prerequisite for being accepted as a member of the group; a person who did not accept an offered drink was considered suspect by the host.

Irish-American attitudes toward drinking seem to play a significant role in the multitude of problems associated with alcohol in this group. The Irish-Americans stress congenial and utilitarian attitudes toward drinking. In other words, the goal of their drinking is to promote fun and pleasure, physical states of well-being, and gratification of self-interests such as release of inner tensions. Overall, the drinking situation for a member of the Irish-American culture contains a high degree of ambivalence.

Bales gathered much of this material between the mid-1940s and the 1960s. Recent studies on Irish drinking have indicated that this group's drinking patterns are still marked by considerable social complications (for example, fights, arguments, and difficulties in relationships). But the actual severe drinking described in earlier research may have been in error, at least in Ireland. Stivers (1985) points out that there is a higher rate of alcoholism among Irish-Americans than among the Irish living in Ireland. De Lint (1976) indicates "that the Irish in Ireland have relatively low rates of alcoholism despite their customary preference for so-called utilitarian drinking" (p. 329).

Stivers (1985) suggests that hard drinking by the Irish-Americans was a way of establishing ethnic identity, of distinguishing the Irish-American from other ethnic groups. Drinking was a way for the Irish-American people to affirm their nationalism. In the United States, the hard drinking of the bachelor groups in Ireland was transformed into political-machine club and street drinking in the large American cities. Hard drinking became symbolic of Irish identity (and not just Irish male identity).

> Hard drinking had all the appearance of a religious obligation—the obligation to be Irish and to promote one's Irishness. The implication was that the more one drank, the more Irish one became. The habitual drunkard was at least a true believer and at worst a religious fanatic. On the social level, hard drinking was encouraged by saloon keepers and liquor dealers for socioeconomic reasons, and by politicians for political reasons in their quest for a power base. (Stivers, 1985, p. 116)

Whether Stivers' appraisal is correct or not, the Irish-Americans continue to be relatively heavy drinkers and to have a higher rate of alcohol-related problems than other American groups. Greeley et al. (1980), in a study employing a large national sample, came to the following conclusions regarding Irish-American drinking. "Of all American groups, the Irish are the least likely to be [abstainers], the most likely to report drinking twice a week or more, and the most likely to consume three or more drinks of hard liquor at one sitting. . . ." (p. 3). (It is interesting that these writers do not see the Irish as having more serious alcohol problems than the population at large. They see the comparison of the Irish with immigrant groups like the Italians and the Jews, who both have low rates of alcohol problems, as the reason that the Irish-Americans have been characterized as having severe alcohol problems.) Greeley et al. examined and compared Irish-American drinkers to Jewish, Italian, Swedish, and a comparison group of British drinkers. They found that recent Irish-American drinking patterns matched closely the drinking patterns found 20 to 30 years earlier. They found the Irish-American subculture remarkably durable, surviving across three generations.

In a separate investigation, Ablon (1985) discovered in her study of Irish-American families that "many historical characteristics appeared to be remarkably persistent, despite the seeming acculturation and homogenization of the Irish in American society . . ." (p. 403). Ablon's examination of American families in her sample led her to pose some reasons for drinking by Irish-American males.

> In this cultural milieu in which divorce is not a thinkable alternative, I suggest that excessive drinking on the part of husbands enmeshed in this life pattern of massive social control, generally passed on and enforced by wives and mothers, is a culturally familiar and ambivalently condoned mode of registering their complaints without actually endangering their marriages. Women register *their* complaints through refusal to have sex and through their domination of their spouses and children. Thus, the drinking patterns of Irish men may best be understood through an examination of the behavior of family members as they relate through a complex of social and cultural expectations. This behavior is part of a self-perpetuating cultural paradigm that continues to produce families beset with alcohol problems. . . . (pp. 405–406).

Whatever the reasons, the Irish-Americans seem to have developed some specific expectations regarding alcohol use and abuse. Later, some possibilities of commonalities between the Irish and other alcohol-abusing groups will be examined.

Excessive drinking is prominent in France, and that country has high alcoholism rates. Although viticulture is very important to the national economy, it cannot be viewed as the cause of the high alcoholism rates; Italy is just as economically dependent on the wine industry yet has low alcoholism rates.

There are large differences between French and Italian customs and attitudes toward drinking and drunkenness. The drinking of alcoholic beverages is viewed favorably by most Frenchmen, but they do not have any of the controls like the Jewish and Italian customs that limit consumption. The French do not limit their drinking to mealtime as the Italians do. Drunkenness is tolerated to a great extent. Eighty percent of French men and women view drinking as good for one's health, and 88 percent think drinking alcoholic beverages is indispensable or useful. Further examples of the French attitudes toward drinking are the slogans found on menus in France, such as "the wines of France give self-assurance."

Regular drinking is not really a matter of choice for a French man or woman, it is a social obligation. Drinking alcoholic beverages is so entwined with the French culture that if individuals refuse to drink, they are at least subject to ridicule, they may be held in suspicion, and frequently they are the object of contempt. There is an immense production of alcoholic beverages in France and frequent and large consumption. However, French alcoholism manifests itself more in physical disorders than psychological or social disruptions. The French culture contains attitudinal supports for all kinds of drinking. That is to say, there is very little ambivalence in the French drinking patterns.

The fact that national attitudes may continue to influence alcoholism rates, even when people of certain nationalities immigrate to faraway shores, is discussed by Jellinek (1957), one of the pioneers in alcohol studies. He notes that in Argentina, a viticultural country where there is a large population of Italian extraction, Italian and Spanish cultural attitudes prevail. These attitudes and customs "put the brakes" on drunkenness and alcoholism. In contrast, in Chile, another viticultural country, the cultural influences of France, Ireland, Lithuania, and Yugoslavia prevail, so the attitudes and sanctions against drunken behavior are weak. Chile ranks high among countries with the largest alcoholism problems.

Studies conducted in the United States have found that religious affiliation may adversely affect drinking behavior, especially affiliation with groups that believe in total abstinence. In certain religious groups, such as Mormons, Baptists, and some Methodists, alcohol is taboo and it is believed that drinking to any extent leads to personal problems and all kinds of social disorganization, including crime and immorality. In these religious groups, the social pressure for absolute abstinence is often severe.

In the United States, the social pressures to drink are pervasive. When young adults are removed from their family ties, as when they go off to college, enter military service, or move out into their own apartments and start working, they often encounter conflicting sets of values about alcohol use. The effects of such cultural conflicts on drinking behavior among college students have been studied.

College students make up the population most often studied in the social science field. This is not because they are the most representative or desirable sample, but because, as a group, they are more available to researchers. It is generally possible to study them over periods of time while they attend college.

Straus and Bacon (1953) studied the drinking behavior of over 16,000 college students throughout the United States and related their findings to the students' religious affiliations. For example, of the Jewish students who drank: 67 percent had been "tight" (that is, slightly intoxicated), 45 percent had been drunk, and 18 percent had passed out. These findings contrast with the Mormon students who drank: 88 percent had been "tight," 74 percent had been drunk, and 40 percent had passed out. (Figures reported were for the students' lifetime experience with alcohol.)

Straus and Bacon employed a social-complications scale in their study to determine what constituted a problem drinker. The scale included damage to friendships, accidents, and other difficulties that were associated with drinking. On this scale, they found that the Mormon students made up a proportionately larger number of problem drinkers than did students from other religious groups who drank.

To look further into religious groups and drinking behavior, Skolnick (1958) used Straus and Bacon's records and compared the drinking practices of four groups of students: Jews, Episcopalians, Methodists, and a group of students not affiliated with any particular religious group but who had backgrounds of abstinence. Skolnick found that, in terms of frequency of intoxication over their lifetimes, Jews rated lowest—considerably lower than the other three groups, who ranked almost equally. Using Straus and Bacon's Scale of Social Complications, Skolnick found that 4 percent of the Jews, 39 percent of the Episcopalians, 50 percent of the Methodists, and 57 percent of the nonaffiliated reported problems with drinking.

The data from these studies indicate that when individuals with Protestant backgrounds of strict abstinence drink, there is a relatively high likelihood that they will become problem drinkers. One explanation for this finding is that such individuals drink with ambivalence since they violate religious and familial training. As a result, they experience feelings of anxiety and guilt. Skolnick asserts that teaching total abstinence implants a repugnance to drinking and drunkenness. It tends to identify the act of drinking with personal and social disorganization. According to Skolnick, such teaching suggests a pattern of insobriety when drinking. When individuals with this type of strict abstinence background drink, all they have ever learned about drinking leads them to follow a pattern of insobriety, which is the very behavior most deplored by their religious and family training.

Members of the groups with high rates of alcoholism (Irish-Americans, French, and Protestants from abstinence backgrounds) share some common characteristics, although the agreement among all groups is not always consistent.

1. There is high social pressure to drink.
2. There are inconsistent or nonexistent social sanctions against drunkenness.
3. The goals of drinking are utilitarian or convivial.
4. There are ambivalent attitudes and feelings toward moderate drinking.

CONCEPTUAL REASONS FOR CULTURALLY LEARNED ABUSIVE AND NONABUSIVE DRINKING

Several theoretical positions have been set forth that attempt to explain the relationship between drinking behaviors and cultural patterns. Ullman (1958) postulates that any group or society that has drinking customs, values, sanctions, and attitudes that are well-established, known to and agreed upon by all, and consistent with the rest of the culture will have a low rate of alcoholism.

On the other side of the coin, Ullman theorizes that when there are conditions where individuals do not know what is expected of them or when the expectations vary from one situation to another, they will have ambivalent feelings about alcohol and, as a result, the rate of alcoholism will be high. In other words, Ullman says that the psychological product of unintegrated drinking is ambivalence, and that conflicting attitudes about drinking in the culture are related to high rates of alcoholism.

Studies of Italians, Jews, Chinese, Irish-Americans, and Protestants from abstinence backgrounds support Ullman's notions. However, the French seem to have all of the characteristics outlined by Ullman as necessary for a low rate of alcoholism, yet their alcoholism rate is very high. Blacker (1966) deals with this inadequacy in Ullman's theory by noting that the absence of a proscriptive norm against excessive drinking may be more important than the presence of consensus in the tolerance of excessive drinking for explaining the higher French rate of alcoholism.

Mizruchi and Perrucci (1962) examine the drinking practices of several cultural groups with respect to proscriptive and prescriptive norms. Proscriptive norms are those that direct people to abstain from, avoid, and reject all forms of behavior associated with a particular type of potential activity. Prescriptive norms direct participants to act in a particular way by spelling out the forms of behavior that the group's members must perform.

Mizruchi and Perrucci theorize that when deviant behavior occurs in a society with highly proscriptive group norms, it is likely that behavior will be highly pathological. If deviant behavior occurs in a society with prescriptive group norms, it is likely to be at a low level of pathology. In other words, if a culture spells out that its members are to absolutely avoid all drinking behavior but the members drink, there is a high likelihood that they will have alcohol problems. On the other hand, if a culture has established clear-cut rules and regulations for drinking behavior and its members drink, there is a low likelihood that they will have alcohol problems.

Studies of Protestant and Mormon groups by Straus and Bacon (1953) and Skolnick (1958) support Mizruchi and Perrucci's theory. The norms governing drinking in these groups are primarily proscriptive; the studies show that when members of these groups drink, the incidence of serious alcohol-related problems is high.

The findings about Mormons and abstaining Protestants can be contrasted with the studies of Jews, people who have highly prescriptive norms and, correspondingly, a low rate of alcoholism. Mizruchi and Perrucci's theory can account for low and high rates of alcoholism in a number of cultural groups. But their theory, like Ullman's, fails to explain the high rate of alcoholism among the French, whose drinking norms are neither highly prescriptive nor highly proscriptive. Although the theory is incomplete, it does provide what appears to be a fruitful approach to explain and predict rates of alcoholism.

Blacker (1966) adds to Ullman's hypothesis. According to Blacker, in a group or society that has drinking customs, values, sanctions, and attitudes that are well-established, agreed upon by all, consistent with the rest of the culture, *and are characterized by prescriptions for moderate drinking and proscriptions against excessive drinking* (Blacker's amendment in italics), the rate of alcoholism will be low.

With the addition of Blacker's amendment, Ullman's theory continues to account for Italian, Jewish, Chinese, Irish-American, and Protestant alcoholism rates. It also accounts for the French alcoholism rates, since the French have few proscriptive norms against excessive drinking. If Blacker's formulation proves valid, it follows that groups with high alcoholism rates can reduce their difficulties with drinking by developing a better balance in their prescriptive and proscriptive norms for drinking behavior.

Before ending discussion of theories about the relationship between cultural norms and drinking behavior, it should be noted that the nature and quality of sociocultural variables as they influence drinking practices may change over time and with acculturation. For example, unstable and erratic norms of people in the United States seem to have modified the drinking practices and attitudes of Italian-Americans, even though Italian traditions predominate. In the modern world, each culture has easy access to others and, as a result, there has been some exchange of attitudes toward drinking. For example, the Italians imported the cocktail party from America. As a result, more Italians are drinking for personal and utilitarian reasons. The interchange between countries of norms regarding drinking practices may very well affect alcoholism rates in the future.

THE IMPACT OF SOCIOCULTURAL FACTORS ON TREATMENT AND PREVENTION

The complexity of the socialization process around alcohol use across various cultural subgroups makes it clearer why alcohol treatment and prevention programs are often ineffective. A review of cultural subgroups also allows for the development of some tentative working assumptions about how to prevent alcohol problems and some of the difficulties experts face.

For example, the subcultural groups reviewed here who have low rates of abusive drinking seem to be groups who carefully prescribe how alcohol is to be used and who have group consensus as to how alcohol should be used. They are free from the ambivalence toward alcohol use that seems to characterize the broader American culture. These low-abusing groups also have clear-cut prohibitions against abusive drinking, and these seem to be a part of their subgroup's agreed upon way to use alcohol. Indeed, the nonabuse of alcohol is often one of the ways that these subgroup members express their group membership.

These factors suggest that to get a major cultural change in the use of alcohol in the United States, we may need to establish a broad cultural acceptance of alcohol use and "prohibit" (via cultural and group pressure) abusive use. Such changes will take years and involve a systematic and carefully orchestrated approach to convince people that there are ways we can and should use alcohol in a moderate and low-risk manner.

Such shifts in thinking are difficult to manage but not impossible. If one looks at the way the U.S. public views drunk driving now compared to how it was viewed in 1970, one can see a considerable change in the attitudes, norms, and feelings about this social and legal problem.

Given the current focus on drunk driving and the renewed interest in health in this country, teaching people to use alcohol in a healthy, safe, and moderate manner might be easier now than in earlier years. However, ambivalence still is the hallmark of American approaches to alcohol. Finding some way to build a consensus about safe alcohol use will necessarily involve a massive educational campaign focused from several directions (for example, health and fitness, drinking and driving, competitive performance in the workplace, drug-free environments, and protection of children and youth). Such a campaign would take years to implement and would be resisted by the liquor industry (in the same way the reduction of cigarette smoking was and is resisted by the tobacco industry). Thus, under the best of conditions, prevention programs will be difficult to implement. However, understanding the particular positions of various subgroups toward alcohol and how the society as a whole has been socialized to use alcohol is critical in planning prevention efforts that reach their targeted groups. (For more on prevention approaches and strategies, see Chapter 13.)

The treatment of alcohol problems is characterized by high rates of referral and treatment failures and by repeated relapses of those who successfully complete a treatment program. (See Chapters 9, 10, 11, and 12 for a more complete discussion of various treatment approaches to alcohol problems.) In terms of cultural subgroups and differing socialization, it may be helpful to know about the differing socialization histories. It may also be important to assess the possible impact that a person's socialization history may have on planning a patient's treatment program. Very few alcohol treatment programs currently plan a treatment program to meet those needs that are a direct result of the client's socialization history.

Ablon (1985) is one of those researchers who has made some suggestions about the clinical relevance of her findings with Irish-Catholic families in Southern California. She first notes that her subgroup tends to deny that excessive drinking is a problem and to avoid mental health and alcohol services. Alcohol abuse is seen as helping to deal with family problems and as a means of maintaining homeostasis (equilibrium) in the whole family. For these reasons she believes, in the case of the Irish, intervention and treatment should be directed at the family level.

Her specific recommendations include the following:

> A primary task would appear to be the development of basic and trusting communication patterns between spouses, difficult as this might be, relatively late in their life and marriage cycle. Within the context of a more explicitly loving and trusting relationship, sexual dysfunction as a major issue can be broached. As a "naturally occurring" program in the Church environment, the Catholic Marriage Encounter has proven of great help to those few who have experienced it. This program focuses on the establishment and maintenance of candid spousal communication. It is family-oriented, nonconfrontive, and culturally acceptable. Thus, it seems to be tailor-made for the Irish-American population. (pp. 406–407)

Treatment for other cultural subgroups needs to be equally tailored to their socialization histories and to the realities of effectively intervening with these groups. While there is not much attention paid to this issue in the majority of treatment programs, it is obvious that an important determiner of alcohol problems and the outcome of their treatment is the patient's socialization history.

REFERENCES

Ablon, J. (1985). Irish-American Catholics in a West Coast metropolitan area. In L. A. Bennett & G. M. Ames (Eds.) *The American experience with alcohol: Contrasting cultural perspectives* (pp. 395–409). New York: Plenum Press.

Bacon, S. D. (1963). Alcohol and the complex society. In D. J. Pittman & C. R. Snyder (Eds.), *Society, culture, and drinking patterns* (pp. 78–93). New York: John Wiley.

Bales, R. F. (1962). Attitudes toward drinking in the Irish culture. In D. Pittman & C. Snyder (Eds.), *Society, culture, and drinking patterns* (pp. 157–186). New York: John Wiley.

Bales, R. F. (1983). Cultural differences in rates of alcoholism. In D. A. Ward (Ed.), *Alcoholism: Introduction to theory and treatment* (2nd ed.) (pp. 211–224). Dubuque, IA: Kendall/Hunt. (First published in the *Quarterly Journal of Studies on Alcohol, 6,* 1946, 480–484.)

Barry, H. B., III, Bacon, M. K., & Child, I. L. (1965). A cross cultural study of drinking. *Quarterly Journal of Studies on Alcohol.* Supplement 3.

Bennett, L. A. (1988). Alcohol in context: Athropological perspectives. *Drugs and Society, 2,* 89–131.

Blacker, E. C. (1966). Sociocultural factors in alcoholism. *International Psychiatry Clinics, 3, Summer.* Boston: Little Brown.

Chafetz, M. E., & Demone, H. W. (1962). *Alcoholism and society.* New York: Oxford University Press.

De Lint, J. (1976). The epidemiology of alcoholism with specific reference to socio-cultural factors. In M. W. Everett, J. O. Waddell, & D. B. Heath (Eds.), *Cross-cultural approaches to alcohol: An interdisciplinary perspective* (pp. 323–330). Chicago: Aldine.

Field, P. B. (1962). A new cross-cultural study of drunkenness. In D. J. Pittman & C. R. Snyder (Eds.), *Society, culture, and drinking patterns* (pp. 48–74). New York: John Wiley.

Glad, D. C. (1947). Attitudes and experiences of American-Jewish and American-Irish male youth as related to differences in adult rates of inebriety. *Quarterly Journal of Studies on Alcohol, 8,* 406–472.

Glassner, B., & Berg, B. (1985). Jewish Americans and alcohol: Processes of avoidance and definition. In L. A. Bennett & G. M. Ames (Eds.), *The American experience with alcohol: Contrasting cultural perspectives* (pp. 93–107). New York: Plenum Press.

Greeley, A. M., McCready, W. C., & Theisen, T. (1980). *Ethnic drinking subcultures.* New York: Praeger.

Heath, D. B. (1980). A critical review of the sociocultural model of alcohol use. In T. C. Harford, D. A. Parker, & L. Light (Eds.), *Normative approaches to the prevention of alcohol abuse and alcoholism.* (Research Monograph No. 3 DHHS Publication No. (ADM) 79-847 (pp. 1–36). Washington, D.C.: Government Printing Office.

Heath, D. B. (1982). Sociocultural variants in alcoholism. In E. M. Pattison & E. Kaufman (Eds.), *Encyclopedic handbook of alcoholism* (pp. 426–440). New York: Gardner Press.

Heath, D. B. (1987). A decade of development in the anthropological study of alcohol use: 1970–1980. In M. Douglas (Ed.), *Constructive drinking: Perspectives on drink from anthropology* (pp. 16–69). New York: Cambridge University Press.

Horton, D. (1943). The functions of alcohol in primitive societies: A cross-cultural survey. *Quarterly Journal of Studies on Alcohol, 4,* 199–320.

Jellinek, E. M. (1957). The world and its bottle. *World Health, 10,* 4–6.

Jessor, R., Graves, T. D., Hanson, R. C., & Jessor, S. L. (1968). *Society, personality and deviant behavior: A study of a triethnic community.* New York: Holt, Rinehart & Winston.

Lolli, G,. Serianni, E., Golder, G. M., & Luzzatto-Fegiz, P. (1958). *Alcohol in Italian culture.* Glencoe, IL: The Free Press.

MacAndrew, C., & Edgerton, R. B. (1969). *Drunken comportment: A social explanation.* New York: Aldine.

Mizruchi, E. H., & Perrucci, R. (1962). Norm qualities and differential effects of deviant behavior: An exploratory analysis. *American Sociology Review, 27,* 391–399.

Morewood, S. (1838). *A philosophical and statistical history of the inventions and customs of ancient and modern nations in the manufacture and use of inebriating liquors.* Dublin: W. Curry, Jr. & Co., and W. Carson.

Simboli, B. J. (1985). Acculturated Italian-American drinking behavior. In L.A. Bennett & G.M. Ames (Eds.), *The American experience with alcohol: Contrasting cultural perspectives* (pp. 61–76). New York: Plenum Press.

Skolnick, J. H. (1958). Religious affiliation and drinking behavior. *Quarterly Journal of Studies on Alcohol, 19,* 452–470.

Snyder, C. R. (1962). Culture and Jewish sobriety: The ingroup-outgroup factor. In D. J. Pittman & C. R. Snyder (Eds.), *Society, culture, and drinking patterns* (pp. 188–225). New York: John Wiley.

Stivers, R. (1985). Historical meanings of Irish-American Drinking. In L. A. Bennett & G. M. Ames (Eds.), *The American experience with alcohol: Contrasting cultural perspectives* (pp. 109–129). New York: Plenum Press.

Straus, R., & Bacon, S. D. (1953). *Drinking in college.* New Haven, CT: Yale University Press.

Sue, S., Kitano, H. H. L., Hatanaka, H., & Yeung, W.-T. (1985). Alcohol consumption among Chinese in the United States. In L. A. Bennett & G. M. Ames (Eds.), *The American experience with alcohol: Contrasting cultural perspectives* (pp. 359–371). New York: Plenum Press.

Ullman, A. D. (1958). Sociocultural backgrounds of alcoholism. *Annals, 315,* 48–54.

Williams, P. H., & Straus, R. (1950). Drinking patterns of Italians in New Haven: Utilization of the personal diary as a research technique. *Quarterly Journal of Studies on Alcohol, 11,* 586–629.

Intervention, Assessment, and Individual Treatment

_____ _chapter_ 9

This chapter focuses on the issues of detecting, assessing, and diagnosing alcohol abuse and alcoholism. It also examines the differences between alcohol abusers and other treatment populations such as the mental health client. Approaches to individual counseling and psychotherapy for alcohol clients are overviewed. Each of these topics are complex issues still under debate in the alcohol field.

DETECTION, ASSESSMENT, AND DIAGNOSIS

Detection, assessment, and diagnosis are perhaps some of the least-developed areas in the alcohol field. Jacobson (1983) comments on the debasement of the diagnostic process for alcoholism and suggests that the static nature of the alcoholism field has hindered the development of diagnostic approaches. He suggests that the traditional stereotype of alcoholism as a sin has been swapped for a disease stereotype, assuming that all alcoholism is the same. While the disease concept is certainly more humanitarian than viewing alcoholism as a sin, it has led to stagnation in conceptualizations of alcohol abuse and alcoholism. In many cases, according to Jacobson, the field has moved from a rational position on alcoholism to an emotional one. A premature closure on the concept of alcoholism has been demanded before a complete understanding of the dimensions of this complex problem has been achieved.

Jacobson (1989) suggests that *alcoholisms* (1976, 1983) should be discussed instead of *alcoholism*. Many of these concerns have been elaborated in Chapter 2, where the definitions, typologies, and models of alcoholism were discussed. The assumption one takes about alcohol abuse and alcoholism tends to dictate how detection, assessment, and diagnosis are approached. *Detection*, according to Jacobson (1989), refers to the process of identifying individuals who have major life problems with alcohol or alcoholism. Here the decision question is a binary one, that is, is this individual an alcoholic or not. A broader phrasing of the question would be, is the person suffering from an alcohol problem or not? An example of using a standardized procedure to make a binary diagnosis is the work of Smart, Adlaf, and Knoke (1991). They used the CAGE Scale, a four-item self-report screening test, to help to decide whether a person was a problem drinker or not. They found this short scale to be potentially useful for making population surveys of drinking problems.

Detection is relatively easy for intake counselors at an alcohol treatment center. Since most individuals who come to alcohol centers have come there through pressures from others or from life circumstances having to do with the abuse of alcohol, it is quite probable that the majority will have an alcohol problem, and it is easier to determine. However, in other settings (an employee assistance program and a university-based alcohol assessment and referral service are two examples) detection may be more difficult.

Within an employee assistance program, the counselor-diagnostician is often faced with multiple psychological, physical, interpersonal, economical, and substance abuse problems. Work problems can also be affected by traumatic events in an employee's life. Frequently, drinking may be temporarily increased around these life problems and may be reduced when the problem is solved or managed. Therefore, treatment may need to be aimed at the life circumstances that may be causing the problem. Deciding whether an individual's central problem is alcohol abuse can be a difficult one in this setting (see Box 9–1).

Considerable abusive drinking occurs in the college setting. There is usually a rise in drinking during the college years, then a drop-off following college. However, some of the heavy drinkers in college have alcohol problems that continue and even accelerate after college. Detecting these problematic drinkers and separating them from others who are drinking at a similar high rate but who will not have long-term problems presents a challenge. In both of these cases, detection can be very difficult. Most programs follow a conservative course, that is, risking more false positives (saying a problem exists when it does not) than false negatives (saying a problem does not exist when it does.)

While detection asks for an either/or decision, *assessment* assumes a

BOX 9–1
An Alcohol Assessment Example

This is a description of a case seen by an examiner working in an alcohol assessment center at a major university in the United States. The description includes (1) diagnostic instruments given the client, (2) information provided by the client through an interview, and (3) assessment results, i.e., how the examiner uses the test data and client history to come up with recommendations for treatment.

Diagnostic Instruments

Four assessment instruments were given. The *Alcohol Expectancy Questionnaire* (AEQ) (Brown, Christiansen, & Goldman, 1987), which is a measure of an individual's expectancies about alcohol across life situations, will be described first. Individuals' expectancies for how alcohol may be used to deal with life may make them vulnerable to abusing alcohol to help cope with the conflicts and stresses of life. The AEQ has scales measuring six major areas of expectancies about alcohol and life functioning: (1) global positive changes; (2) enhanced sexual performance and experience; (3) physical and social pleasure; (4) increased social assertiveness; (5) relaxation and tension reduction; and (6) arousal and power.

The second instrument administered was the *Alcohol Use Inventory* (AUI) (Skinner & Allen, 1983). This lengthy questionnaire provides information on the social, psychological, interpersonal, physiological, and behavioral aspects of personal alcohol use. As such the instrument provides information on the nature and extent of alcohol dependence and patterns of alcohol use.

The third instrument given was the *MacAndrew Alcoholism Scale* (MAC) (Davis, Colligan, Morse, & Orford, 1987). This scale is a forty-nine-item, forced-choice, true-false subscale, which is self-administered. It was developed from the Minnesota Multiphasic Personality Inventory (MMPI), which is typically given to alcohol abusers to measure psychopathology (e.g., Graham & Strenger, 1988). (The MMPI was also given in this case, but since the focus in this example is alcohol assessment instruments, the MMPI results will not be discussed here.) It is possible and appropriate to use the MAC subscale without the full MMPI, particularly if the Lie subscale of the MMPI (used to determine if subject is being untruthful on the test) is also administered. Research suggests that high scores on the MAC (over 25 on the raw score) reflect the risk of addiction rather than addiction to alcohol per se.

Rotter's *Incomplete Sentence Blank* (ISB) (Churchill & Crandall, 1955) was the last test administered. This semiprojective test is made up of a series of incomplete sentence stems (for example, I like . . .; I am very . . .) designed to provide information concerning test takers' current life situations, relationships, goals, fears, and ambitions.

In addition to these test instruments, an extensive individual interview was part of the assessment. This interview focused on drinking history , social-psychological issues, and the social and family history of the person.

Information Obtained From Interview

A 34-year-old white male was being evaluated to determine the appropriateness for his treatment in a local mental health facility that also treated substance abuse clients. He had sought service as a result of his separation from his wife. The purpose of the evaluation was to establish whether he had problems with alcohol and/or drugs.

The client reported that he had his first drink at age 12; from age 14 on, every time he drank he passed out. He reported drinking in a regular pattern as a freshman in high school. This pattern included drinking to intoxication each Friday and Saturday night. He weighed about 130 pounds and would drink about six beers in a short time span. He drank more frequently in his junior year of high school. However, his drinking from Monday to Thursday was limited to two to three beers each evening.

After graduating, he worked for a railroad company. He limited his drinking to one or two beers during the week, but his Friday and Saturday drinking rose to eight or nine beers. He reduced his drinking somewhat when he moved away from home (the move was made to get away from his drinking buddies and to attend junior college). However, he soon returned to eight or nine drinks a night when he drank, and he now started using spirits in addition to beer.

The client stated that his father was alcoholic and that he was afraid he would become like his father. The client admitted using marijuana since early adolescence and that he was using it up until the time tested. He had also sold marijuana.

Assessment Data

The client endorsed items on the AEQ that suggested that he expected alcohol to enhance physical and social pleasure, to increase social assertiveness, and to reduce tension and aid relaxation. He also saw alcohol use as leading to feelings of arousal and power. The MAC score was 29, indicating that he was at high risk for addiction. The scales of the AUI also suggested he was abusing alcohol and that the level of that abuse was quite high. The ISB suggested that he had problems expressing feelings appropriately, particularly in his marital relationship. He indicated sadness and depression over his current life circumstances. He also admitted that he was frequently tense. In general, he saw his future as being sad and difficult. He feared being alone in life and mentioned the importance of his marital relationship and his relationships with his relatives. He seemed to have a strong need to be with and be supported by people, which may suggest dependency needs.

This information suggests the presence of a severe and long-term alcohol and drug problem. The only missing element, which might be looked for in this case, was a drinking and driving arrest. While the client had not been arrested, he admitted that he had driven under the influence of alcohol fifty or more times during the past 2 years.

Treatment Recommendations

The client seems to see himself needing close relationships and being a drinker who is easily influenced by friends. This information, combined with the fact that he has a severe alcohol problem, suggests that hospitalization that would remove him from the influence of his drinking environment would be wise. This inpatient treatment would allow him to "dry out." A factor that also weighs in support of inpatient treatment is that the alternative—outpatient treatment—is more likely to be successful if the client has a strong family support system, with support from the spouse being especially important. This client does not have this family support network. The close cohesion that tends to develop among alcohol inpatients who are helping each other deal with their problems might be very helpful to him during his early days away from alcohol.

Because this client feels that alcohol is helpful with so many life issues, as measured by the AEQ, extensive alcohol education about the limitations and dangers of alcohol use and abuse would also seem important for him. The high score on the MAC suggests he is at high risk for alcohol addiction. This risk combined with a family history of alcoholism validates the need for immediate and intensive treatment.

The information obtained by the battery of tests used with this client also can be obtained from other instruments, and other methods are probably equally useful. The present alcohol assessment example may also be more extensive than those used by some alcohol agencies. But multiple-instrument, in-depth assessments may be preferred for several reasons. For example, a thorough inquiry forces clients to confront their drinking from several perspectives and is an excellent way to get them to come to terms with their problems early in treatment. Also, a broader, more intensive assessment is potentially useful in planning specific treatment programs for clients. The assumption underlying this approach to assessment is that treatment can and should be as individualized as possible.

continuum of severity on one or more evaluation dimensions. Severity on these dimensions can vary. According to Jacobson (1989), there is an implicit assumption that alcoholism is progressive since the continua are usually anchored in terms such as mild, moderate, and severe, or early, middle, and late, alcoholism. Problem drinking, in general, could also be discussed in this way.

In assessment, the interest is in establishing the severity of alcohol problems on several dimensions that reflect individuals' functioning. Some individuals may show almost no disruption of their home or work life but show rapid physiological deterioration due to alcohol. Still other persons may show problems in home life but not elsewhere. With only these few gross dimensions, it can be seen how changes along each dimension might lead to differing assessment outcomes. In evaluating individuals' functioning, evaluators need to take into account each of these dimensions. At the present time in the alcohol field, such subtle approaches to assessment are seldom used. Instead, broad, crude categories are used, partly because treatment procedures that could readily take advantage of subtle differences in potential patients simply do not exist. More recently there has been an increasing awareness of the importance of doing a comprehensive assessment. Westermeyer (1992) suggested that in the future there will be more emphasis on the need for phased assessments, reassessments over time, and special assessments for certain clients. It is possible that the appropriate assessment at the right time could improve treatment effectiveness and produce a better cost/benefit ratio.

Diagnosis, as Jacobson notes, can be used as simply a labeling process. However, he feels that a diagnosis should include "the use of scientific and skillful methods to establish *the cause and nature* of a sick person's disease . . . by evaluating the history of the disease process; the signs and symptoms present; laboratory data; special tests. . . . The value of establishing a diagnosis is *to provide a logical basis for treatment and prognosis*" (from Thomas, 1977, p. 11, cited in Jacobson, 1983, p. 380; Italics added by Jacobson).

Jacobson, in his 1983 review, discusses Rudie and McGaughran's (1961) Essential-Reactive Alcoholism Scale. Information can be obtained on eight specific subscales using a structured interview format that takes a half hour or less. Information is provided on dimensions of personality, behavior, alcohol and drug use, social interactions, and variables hypothesized as relevant to a psychoanalytic conception of alcoholism. Two types of alcoholism are recognized in this scale, even though they represent only the end points of a continuum. *Essential alcoholics* bear a strong resemblance to the description of the sociopath. *Reactive alcoholics* show relatively good adjustment in most areas of their lives, but they abuse alcohol in reaction to some real or perceived life crisis. Both the wording and scoring of the interview instrument is distinctly sexist, and Jacobson and his colleagues have been in the process of rewriting some of these objectionable items. One of the exciting potential uses of this instrument is the possibility of matching patients to specific treatments in order to provide more positive outcomes following treatment.

Jacobson cites a study by Treffert, Ansfield, and Hughes (1974) as support for the utility of the Alcoholism Scale. As proof of the instrument's potential, he also cites unpublished research done by himself and his colleagues which isolates patients at the detoxification stage of treatment who are at high risk for recidivism. However, the outcome studies to show that this instrument is effective in predicting treatment outcome and relapse prognosis are not yet available.

According to Jacobson, the second instrument that is diagnostically useful in planning treatment is the Alcohol Use Inventory (AUI). This 147-item instrument is a forced-choice, self-administered questionnaire. A graphic description of patients' syndromes can be obtained from a profile sheet. Three conceptually different domains include styles of alcohol use, negative consequences of drinking, and perceived consequences of alcohol use. Wanberg, Horn, and Foster (1977), the authors of the scale, specifically state how certain scores on subscales relate to treatment strategies.

Despite Jacobson's work and the work of others, the detection, assessment, and diagnosis of alcohol problems is still a global phenomenon with few specifics as to how to use the assessment and diagnosis to better focus treatment efforts. The processes of assessment and diagnosis also have a primary role in the intervention into the lives of individuals who have alcohol problems. The assessment procedure itself has frequently been a very powerful intervention process. In many cases, the evaluation itself has long-term therapeutic effects, witnessed by the fact that some clients never come back but later say that the assessment session led to a change in the way they approached and used alcohol.

INTERVENTION

Intervention with alcohol patients requires both some general and specific knowledge about how alcohol patients function and how they arrive at treatment. Intervention sets the stage for a patient's eventual treatment (or failure to accept and complete treatment). It is particularly important to be aware of some differences between alcohol patients and mental health patients in terms of confrontation, motivation, and referral issues. These issues, along with some factors that increase the probability that alcohol patients will begin and continue treatment, require some in-depth discussion.

There are some important differences between most mental health clients and alcohol clients. In general, mental health clients come to treatment because they are suffering from psychological discomfort of some sort. They are usually self-referred. It has been their choice to seek treatment. Therapists trained to treat mental health patients frequently note that patients must be motivated to change. When clients' motivation wanes and premature termination occurs, therapists will usually note that the clients are not psychologically uncomfortable enough to complete treatment or are not yet ready to commit to the psychological changes that therapy may demand. Mental health therapists most frequently view motivation for treatment as coming from the client rather than from outside forces.

In contrast, alcohol patients most frequently come to treatment because someone else has pressured them. Very few seek treatment without some outside pressure. Alcohol patients are most likely to deny the presence of any problem, particularly regarding the use of alcohol. Many professionals see alcoholics' lack of motivation for treatment as one of the major obstacles to effective therapy. For many years, motivation for treatment was viewed as a stable condition, which an alcoholic either did or did not have. More recently, motivation has been seen as a fluctuating interplay of needs, pressures, perceived ways of getting satisfaction, and balances between the relationship of all people involved in the treatment process. Poor motivation for treatment may be seen as just another aspect of the total problem to be met in whatever ingenious ways therapists can devise.

Some professionals who have what Koumans (1969) calls a "hidden agenda" of expecting clients to play the role of a passive recipient of care from all-knowing caregivers will not have their expectations met with alcoholics and alcohol abusers. Alcohol patients frequently come to treatment angry, hostile, and very defensive. They deny their need for help and often are very unpleasant to deal with in the early stages of treatment. They are also under duress since (as noted previously), in the majority of cases, they have been directly or indirectly coerced into treatment. For this reason, getting them into treatment and keeping them there is frequently very difficult.

When confronting alcohol clients about their problem, it is important to know and use approaches that will facilitate their entry into treatment. Effective approaches include (but are not limited to) the following:

1.   Before confronting alcohol clients about their problem, therapists must be sure to have their facts in order. Whenever possible, it is usually better to have a group confrontation including significant others in alcoholics' lives. When several people are involved in the confrontation, each person must agree on the facts and agree not to be swayed by arguments raised by

the alcohol abuser. Timing of the intervention is crucial. Chafetz, Blane, and Hill (1970) suggest that the most effective time to intervene is at a point of crisis in an abuser's life that has been precipitated by alcohol abuse.

2.   Therapists also should interact with alcohol clients with warmth and concern. Alcohol abusers have had plenty of experience with anger and with hostile people. On the other hand, care and genuine concern by another person are reactions they do not expect. It is possible that this strategy may upend alcoholics' expectancies that they will be harshly treated during the intervention process.

3.   The behaviors and observations made by therapists should be described in very specific terms. No punches should be pulled, and communications should be as clear and precise as possible. Therapists *should not* assume the role of a prosecutor—they should be human and matter-of-fact. In particular, the possibility of coming across as judgmental should be avoided. In brief, the confrontation with the alcoholic should stick to the facts and the procedures that have general consensus among those participating in the interview, whether, caregivers, family, or employers.

4.   Clients should not be allowed to rationalize their drinking-related behavior. When the clients deny the behavior or say: "I drank because of . . . (my wife, my job, no money, poor health)," one response might be "I understand that things are bad for you and that it is easy for you to drink when you feel that way. A lot of people use alcohol to make them feel better when they feel the way you do. However, alcohol is clearly causing problems in your life and you must stop drinking to deal with those problems."

5.   The client's drinking behavior should be placed in the larger context of alcoholism or alcohol abuse. This can be done by using the third person, for example, "A lot of people who drink because of problems find that they sometimes drink more than they mean to, or get drunk when they didn't expect to. Or they find that they have done things they would never do while they are sober. Some people discover they have forgotten things that happened to them while drinking."

6.   It should be established that drinking is the *source* of many of the clients' problems, not the *result*. What is being said to clients here is that a lot of their problems would get better if they stopped drinking. Saying something like "Do you know what alcoholism is? It is when alcohol begins to cause serious problems in your life" may be very effective in confronting alcoholics.

7.   If denial continues, the following strategy might be used: "You say that drinking has never been a problem for you. Has a friend or family member or coworker ever said you drink too much?" This approach reminds the client that several people feel he has a problem. It makes the client's denial more difficult to maintain.

8.   Hope should be expressed about the treatment of alcoholism, giving specific information about what patients can expect. However, therapists should be realistic. It should be pointed out that treatment will not be easy or a surefire cure, but that people who work hard in treatment can show dramatic changes in their lives. Something might be said such as: "I know it is hard for you to understand that the things you are doing are signs of an illness called alcoholism—an illness that could happen to anyone—but there are lots of things people can do about their drinking problems, and people do recover."

9.   It should be established that outside help is needed. Therapists should try to find out what clients know about the services available. Something like the following might be said: "Lots of people recover, but you can't do it alone. It is very unusual for someone with a severe drinking problem to say, 'I am going to quit drinking for good,' at least not without help. Maybe you know that because you have already tried to stop drinking on your own. That is just the nature of the problem." Available agencies might then be reviewed with the client.

10.   Several options should be left open for action in the future. For example, therapists might say, "Maybe you are not ready to do anything right now if you like your life the way it is, but if you decide you would like it to be different, remember you can change it. I'm going to leave you something you might want to read. If you decide you would like to do something about your drinking, I'd be happy to talk with you about it again or arrange for you to talk to someone who has recovered from an alcohol abuse problem. If you are interested, they could tell you about AA and about those meetings. They might also take you to a meeting later if you want to. In the meantime, here is my name and telephone number. Just give me a call when you feel like it."

(Many of the above suggestions are taken from training resources developed in the early 1970s by the National Institute on Alcohol Abuse and Alcoholism [NIAAA] for nurses and other caregiving professionals.)

Whether the above intervention approaches will work is dependent upon a number of factors, including the degree of crises individuals are suffering and the amount of leverage that can be applied by significant others in their lives. If individuals can be convinced they have an alcohol problem, making an appropriate referral or getting them to the best program is still very difficult. Referral failures and their causes is the next topic.

Baekeland and Lundwall (1977) have reviewed the literature on engaging alcoholics in treatment and keeping them there. As these authors note, even if alcoholics are detected and confronted, an inappropriate referral to a treatment agency is often made. The main sources of referral to alcohol clinics are patients' families, physicians, hospitals and service agencies, and the legal system. Often agencies that have clients with alcohol problems fail to refer them to treatment. An example is the failure of a hospital to refer an individual with multiple surgical interventions for pancreatitis to an alcohol clinic, even though an alcohol evaluation seems to be warranted.

Even if alcoholics are referred to an alcohol treatment agency, the majority do not get there. Chafetz et al. (1970) found that only 5 percent of alcoholics seen in a metropolitan hospital emergency room actually made it to treatment. Workers in one alcohol assessment center discovered that alcoholics referred by a physician only three blocks away never made it to the center. The referral rate improved when a taxi was called and the alcoholic was driven to the center. (Between the assessment center and the physician's office were many pubs and taverns, and the alcoholics seemed to always need to stop off for one last drink before coming to the center!)

According to Baekeland and Lundwall (1977), a number of factors have been found to contribute to referral failures. In hospital emergency rooms, anger in the voice of the referring physician (usually a reflection of negative attitudes toward the patient, [Milmore, Rosenthal, Blane, Chafetz, & Wolf, 1967]) and delays in scheduling first appointments have been shown to lead to referral failures (Mayer, 1972). The impact of these two factors on alcoholic referrals can be understood when the usual psychological state of referred alcoholics is recalled. Blane (1968) describes alcoholics as persons who (1) feel inferior and worthless; (2) have fears of new situations that present challenges, particularly those relationships that make demands on them; and (3) display ambivalence, denial, and low frustration tolerance. It is no surprise that with these situational and self-esteem issues alcoholics find it difficult to handle rejection and harsh confrontation with authority figures.

Making sure individuals are seen by someone who will help them negotiate the bureaucracy can combat referral difficulties (Chafetz, 1967). When it is not possible to get individuals into treatment, maintaining contact with them prior to admission, even through letters or phone calls, increases the probability that they will reach treatment eventually (Koumans & Muller, 1965; Koumans, Muller & Muller, 1967). Baekeland and Lundwall (1977) also suggest that involving an AA member early in the referral process may increase the likelihood that persons suffering from alcohol problems will utilize that organization.

Once alcoholics get to treatment, there are many who drop out. Dropout rates are lower for inpatient treatment, ranging from around 13 percent to 40 percent, while rates for outpatient treatment range from 52 percent to 75 percent (Baekeland & Lundwall, 1977). Inpatient treatment may require more motivation and commitment from alcoholics. However, more intense and continual support is available, from fellow patients and from the therapists on the unit, in inpatient treatment. This support and care is more intermittently available in outpatient treatment.

In their review of studies of dropouts from inpatient programs, Baekeland and Lundwall found that the patient "who drops out of an inpatient treatment program seems to be one who is in a more advanced stage of alcoholism, has more passive aggressive and psychopathic features, is more apt to deny his hostility, suspicion, and interpersonal problems, and depends on alcohol for relief of feelings of resentment, anxiety or depression" (p. 178).

In their overview of ten outpatient studies of dropouts, Baekeland and Lundwall note commonalities across several studies on several patient characteristics. It should be noted that the methodology in these studies differs in many ways. Several studies indicate that lower socioeconomic factors (for example, low education, income, and occupational status) are related to treatment dropout. In some of the studies, social isolation is predictive of patients dropping out of outpatient treatment. Factors such as not living with one's spouse or being single are associated with dropout rates. An ambivalent or negative attitude toward treatment is associated with an increased dropout rate. Also, individuals who have difficulty accepting help from others and who want to solve their own problems are frequent dropouts. Poor motivation is associated with dropouts in several studies of outpatient alcoholics.

In looking at treatment dropouts, Baekeland and Lundwall state that offering a wide range of treatment options and attempting to match patients with the best possible treatment available in a particular therapeutic setting is the wisest course. Unfortunately, it is not yet firmly established just what interventions and treatment approaches are best for individuals at high risk of dropping out. It is probably true that just making a greater effort within current programs would reduce the dropout rate to some degree. However, for some potential dropouts, a more carefully crafted set of procedures dealing specifically with the patients' characteristics that increase dropout risk needs to be developed. Pattison (1981) and others suggest that better matching of patients to treatment settings would be helpful.

There are some hints that the model under which alcoholic patients will be treated in the future may be modified somewhat. The disease model which has dominated the treatment scene in the United States for the past five decades may be altered to integrate more behavioral approaches. This has already changed at the doctoral training level and one can only wait and see if the changes filter down to the alcohol counselors who actually do the treatment. These changes, if they occur, may be gradual. There will be more emphasis on identifying environmentally based cues, which elicit drinking and self-help strategies that allow the client to manage drinking urges. The disease model's emphasis on changing beliefs and on identifying emotionally with other recovering people (and using them as a self-help group) will continue to be used (Morgenstern and McCrady, 1992).

The remainder of this chapter will deal with individual treatment of alcoholics. The three chapters that follow this one focus on family therapy, a relatively new but rapidly expanding treatment approach for alcoholics; group psychotherapy, one of the most popular approaches to treatment of alcoholics; and Alcoholics Anonymous, a grass-roots program that has received considerable (and justified) praise for its program to help alcoholics in their recovery.

INDIVIDUAL COUNSELING AND THERAPY

Deciding the best approach to take with alcoholics is still being debated. There are no hard and fast answers as to what works well. Some people believe that a psychoanalytic approach has little to offer alcoholics. However, one psychiatrist has a reputation for being very effective with alcohol clients by using a psychoanalytic orientation. There do not seem to be any theoretical positions that are universally accepted. Rather, the phases of treatment seem to be more predictable and somewhat independent of the therapist's theoretical background.

While there are several approaches to individual alcohol treatment, two will be summarized here. These two authorities, Blane and Zimberg, are discussed because they offer two of the most thorough general descriptions of individual alcohol treatment available; and both researchers have a very pragmatic and practical approach to treatment.

Blane's Description of Individual Therapy

Blane (1977) divides the general treatment process of alcoholic clients into three phases: the initial phase; the middle phase; and the late phase, which includes termination.

Initial Phase. Blane indicates that the initial phase of therapy includes the first three to five sessions. He outlines five aims which must be accomplished during this phase.

1. *Relationship and relationship building.* Therapists must take an active role in building a relationship with clients. They must convey to patients a sense of competency, respect for their integrity, and acceptance of them. Warmth, kindness, and interest must be combined with the ability to set firm limits. An action-oriented approach that includes doing something relevant for patients is often necessary. A friendly, nonjudgmental, but forthrightly confrontive approach is recommended. For example, patients might be asked a question about whether they are willing to pay the price to remain abstinent. Other therapists stress the psychological aspects of establishing a relationship, for example, making patients aware of their feelings of hostility, helplessness, and fear.

2. *Pretherapy factors that affect treatment.* The expectancies that patients bring to treatment must be dealt with here. If patients have been detoxified several times without referral to long-term treatment, extra effort might be

A counselor conducting individual therapy in an alcohol treatment center.
(Photograph courtesy of the Independence Center, Lincoln, Nebraska.)

required to establish a treatment alliance. Other clients who may have done well for some time and then had a slip, and still others who are afraid of a slip may present themselves for treatment. Frequently, therapists may find out what elements in a specific client's past therapy were effective and utilize those. In other cases, crisis intervention may reduce the possibility of more serious problems. In general, says Blane, if patients have been successfully treated in the past, it is probably unwise to attempt to improve on the strategies used before without trying them first.

In successful treatment, therapists frequently meet patients who are angry and challenging and who are daring them to prove that they can provide effective treatment. There is considerable gain for patients in being the champion of failure. Therapists must confront this challenge by indicating to patients that they must take treatment seriously if it is to be successful. Blane maintains that if patients fail to take responsibility for their own treatment (and if therapists have no leverage such as families and employers), then those persons probably will not be good candidates for therapy.

Persons who have been in many different treatment facilities but who did not receive proper care are a different type of case. These individuals are usually discouraged and are beginning to feel they cannot change. Therapists have the responsibility to help these patients restructure their perceptions of treatment so that they have hope.

Still another factor that must be dealt with occurs when patients have been transferred from one therapist to another. In this case, patients may expect rejection and may feel a real loss of the previous relationship. Therapists must deal with clients' feelings of loss and can even use those feelings as a springboard to help them deal with grief and losses in general.

A final pretherapy factor that affects therapy exists in cases where a residential program refers persons to follow-up treatment. Entering treatment at this point may prevent regression and loss of treatment gains. Since patients have been primed for therapy by the residential experience, therapists may be direct and to the point in explaining that unless treatment continues, patients may lose many of the gains made during residential treatment. This is also a time when therapists can select a crucial bit of unfinished business from the residential treatment setting to work on with patients.

3. *Drinking or not drinking.* While drinking versus nondrinking can be viewed in a number of ways, today therapists generally favor no drinking during treatment. However, each drinking violation during therapy should be dealt with on its own merits. While therapists vary considerably, confronting clients about their drinking during a therapy session may be helpful in establishing why they drink prior to the session. Therapeutic contracts can be set up with one issue being that clients will not be seen if they show up intoxicated. If they are intoxicated, an explanation of why they will not be seen should be presented in a matter-of-fact, nonjudgmental manner before they are sent home.

4. *Goal-setting and confrontation.* There are two broad sets of goals that need to be dealt with in the initial phase of therapy. The first is to help alcohol patients function, live more comfortably, and become more aware of themselves and their environment. Abstinence is not the central issue here. The second goal emphasizes the attainment of abstinence and then the treatment of other problems that patients have. The first goal is likely to be prominent when persons entering therapy are no longer drinking; the second goal is likely to be more frequent when patients enter treatment and are still drinking.

When abstinence is the central goal, *confrontation* is used to make patients concretely aware that they have an alcohol problem and must not drink. Depending on the treatment setting's philosophy, confrontation can range from unrelenting scare tactics by poorly trained staff members to well worked out psychoeducational procedures that help ease patients into therapy. While more explicit concrete confrontation makes beginning clinicians more comfortable, it is in direct opposition to an approach that utilizes individual differences to plan treatment programs that fit patients' needs.

Blane suggests that treatment goals in this phase can be viewed as being either substitutive, proximal causative, or distal causative. The substitutive goal is to replace drinking behavior with other activities and behavior patterns that will occupy the time formerly used for drinking alcohol, for example, AA, work, hobbies, and family projects. Therapists who adhere to a proximal causative goal usually focus on psychological factors that brought about drinking episodes. Such therapists are not centrally interested in historical factors (for example, childhood) as things that must be resolved in treatment. Distal causative therapists are open to personal historical information from clients and are interested in the continuities between present and past. These therapists devote much time in early interviews to obtaining a family history that includes patients' views of each member of their families, their earliest memories, and their recurrent dreams.

5. *Therapeutic contracts.* While many therapists proceed with treatment without an explicit patient-therapist contract, others feel a contract helps the therapeutic process. More specifically, a contract helps avoid unconscious abuse of the therapeutic relationship by therapists (for example, letting unconscious, personal issues enter into the treatment of the patient). A contract also makes the therapeutic time more focused and productive. It can help resolve patients' resistance and acting out earlier in the therapy process (it allows the therapist to confront the client who displays these characteristics).

Mutual consent is important to therapeutic contracts and usually consists of an offer by therapists with definite terms that are accepted by patients. The specific content of contracts varies across therapists with factors such as the type of patient (for example, manipulative versus anxious and frightened) and the theoretical orientation of the therapist dictating the specific form and content.

Middle Phase.   Blane lists several general aims and issues for the middle phase of treatment. This phase begins when the following have been accomplished: (1) the drinker is abstinent, or drinking does not disrupt therapy; (2) a positive relationship has been established between therapist and patient; (3) the therapeutic contract has been established; and (4) the goals of treatment have been tentatively established. The greatest amount of therapy time is spent in this phase. The focus is on exploring, understanding, trying out, and working through various problems in the patient's life.

Blane outlines a detailed approach to treatment in this phase. The discussion here is limited to his description of how therapy might proceed using the substitutive, proximal causative, and distal causative focuses in treatment. It should be noted that each of these three approaches uses strategies from the other two. Blane highlights the major emphasis of therapy with alcoholics.

Substitutive treatment in the middle phase tends to focus "on getting the patient involved in a supportive social and interpersonal network that emphasizes the value of abstinence" (1977, p. 134). Therapists either encourage patients to seek out the support network or actually introduce them to it. The system could, and frequently does, include AA and similar groups, the clergy, former alcoholics, and other individuals who might be interested and potentially supportive of abstinence. In therapy, the central concern is on how the support system is working for patients. How involved are patients in the system and what are their feelings about shifting from an alcoholic to a sober life? There is a continued focus on abstinence, with therapists trying to isolate the situations and circumstances that led patients to drinking. This is done with an eye toward environmental manipulation to reduce the risk of drinking. There is very little concern with deep psychological functioning. There is a discussion of the problem, complaints, and rationalizations that led to drinking. The positive aspects of support systems are reinforced (for example, family life, work, and interpersonal functioning). According to Blane, in situations where conflict exists in these areas, therapists help patients to reduce the conflict.

From the substitutive position, therapists aim to make abstinence as important in patients' lives as alcohol once was. Patients must now become as obsessed with staying sober as they once were with drinking.

The proximal causative focus differs for "reactive" and "essential" alcoholics. Reactive alcoholics are usually seen as drinking in reaction to a psychological problem or some type of stress or loss in their lives. Once these persons' psychological problems have been dealt with, the need for drinking heavily is no longer present and drinking subsides. Essential alcoholics are seen as having long-standing, characterological problems and long-term problems with impulse control. They usually have an extended history of drinking and need to abstain to function effectively.

During the middle phase of therapy from a proximal causative position, a drinking problem can sometimes be clearly tied to a loss in the reactive alcoholic's life. In such cases, treatment is centered on the loss, and drinking is discussed only when it disrupts treatment. Therapy may include grief, or it may involve working on clients' grieving processes. In other cases, the loss may not be as clear-cut. For example, threats to self-esteem can come from business losses or from a midlife crisis. The main therapeutic aim with these patients is to get them to see the effects of the loss on their emotional life. Since affective reactions to loss are usually repressed, it is difficult for patients and those around them to see that abusive drinking is related to the loss. That is, since patients may not always consciously experience emotional upheaval, it is more difficult for them to connect alcohol abuse with the loss. Instead, they may view drinking as necessary in their job, for example. Reactive alcoholics seldom see their drinking as a way to handle anxiety.

Blane says that the relationship between anger and guilt that patients are feeling, and their anxiety and their depression, must be established in relation to the loss. Patients are asked to ventilate their feelings. Therapists help them discriminate and label feelings of love, anger, and guilt and show them that feelings do not equate with acting on the feelings.

Because reactive alcoholics have usually been relatively problem-free prior to the loss, Blane maintains that therapy should usually be directed to the specific conflict at hand, that is, their loss and the resolution of feelings around it. Generally speaking, the more specific the loss and the shorter the period of destructive drinking, the shorter the period of therapy needed.

The proximal causative focus in the middle phase differs for essential alcholics. The major change is a greater focus on the drinking behavior and trying to find ways to cope with life problems other than through the use of alcohol. The goal is to help individuals deal with present conflict in a flexible manner so that they can select the best alternative to deal with issues.

During this phase, therapists are sensitive to patients' use of rationalization, denial, and projection, the most common defenses used by alcoholics. Because many alcoholic patients are passive and unresponsive in therapy, the use of reflection and nondirective or direct questioning may be necessary to get them to examine their feelings and thoughts.

Blane says that since rationalization is more accessible to conscious understanding, therapists should center their confrontation strategies on that defense. Letting patients know that rationalization is masking a reason for drinking often makes them feel that therapists know them better than anyone else. This helps to build the therapeutic alliance. As patients accept their rationalization for drinking, it is easy for therapists to intervene with a raised eyebrow or a quick comment that can keep them focused on an emotionally laden topic.

Blane suggests that denial in treatment should usually be accepted and not challenged. From his perspective, denial around an emotionally laden topic usually indicates that anxiety is very high. It may be necessary to delay exploration of some emotionally laden areas until clients are less anxious, that is, until they are less defensive and are denying the conflictual area to a lesser degree.

Blane also maintains that projection should be handled carefully. Confrontation of this defense should usually be undertaken only when there is a strong therapeutic alliance. Therapists do well to avoid becoming a central object in patients' projective systems (such as persecutor or benefactor). To avoid this, Blane recommends a consistent, honest, open, and nonjudgmental attitude with patients.

The last treatment condition of the middle phase is the distal causative condition. When this approach is taken it may mean little therapeutic emphasis is placed on patients' drinking behavior except when their attitudes toward drinking misrepresent reality. (Blane uses the example of clients saying drinking is no problem, that they can take it or leave it.) It is generally agreed that this approach (psychoanalytically oriented therapy) is appropriate for only a small percentage of alcoholics who come to treatment. Blane estimates that about 5 percent of the total alcoholic population can profit from this treatment orientation. In general, most psychoanalytic practitioners suggest that the typical psychoanalytic therapy be modified for alcoholic patients. (An early modification of the psychoanalytic approach to therapy is outlined in Chapter 6). The distal causative condition is an example of the application of predispositional theoretical approaches in the alcohol field. Blane notes that working with alcoholics from a psychoanalytic orientation may require dropping some of the central points in the usual psychoanalytic treatment approach. For example, one analytic therapist suggests that transference not be interpreted with alcoholic clients. This is because transference is usually centered around unconscious childhood material and alcohol therapy is oriented toward current functioning.

A commonly recommended technique in alcohol treatment is assigning tasks of a psychological, behavioral, or interpersonal nature. Blane indicates that homework is frequently assigned in substitutive treatment and in therapy emphasing proximal causative conditions. Homework can range from working on ways to learn to deal with anxiety through systematic desensitization to planning each day the night before with a special emphasis on times during the day when the temptation to drink is aroused. Being more caring and supportive of one's spouse or learning to control anger in certain situations are other types of homework assignments.

There are several treatment techniques frequently used with alcoholic clients. Reversing the roles of patients and therapists is useful when patients feel therapists have failed them in some way. Other useful techniques include role playing and armchair problem solving. These homework assignments and special techniques are useful adjuncts to the usual one-on-one psychotherapy used in the middle phase of treatment.

Blane maintains that the most critical point during the middle phase of treatment is dealing with a drinking episode. It is crucial because the way the drinking episode is handled determines whether treatment will be successful. Usually, the drinking episode is a means of testing the relationship between therapist and patient. The episode may signal a premature termination of therapy. Blane says that therapists must convey to patients that a drinking episode does not lead to the termination of therapy by the therapist; it is an issue to be dealt with as a regular part of treatment. One therapist tells outpatients early in therapy that he will still continue to see them if they have a relapse during treatment. He also explains that he will not see them if they are drinking at the time of therapy sessions, and he tells them that monitoring abstinence is critical for success in therapy. Another contractual agreement sometimes made with patients is that if they cannot maintain sobriety as an outpatient, they may have to go to inpatient treatment. This is an issue when strong supports for drinking are present in patients' daily lives.

In work more recent than Blane's, Marlatt and Gordon (1985) propose some methods that are very promising for preventing and managing relapse. Since relapse is a reality factor patients must deal with, a drinking episode may offer the opportunity to strengthen them against future drinking slips.

Late Phase and Termination. Blane notes that this is a relatively untouched area. It is difficult to establish when therapy is completed and when it is time to terminate treatment. In the later stages of treatment, the gains made in the middle stage are pulled together, and the new behaviors and coping patterns are extended to widely different situations. Blane suggests the following criteria as indicators that patients have reached this late stage of therapy:

> ... the patient (1) reports spontaneous engagement in new activities, interests, and behavior; (2) handles unique, potentially conflictual situations in an adult and self-satisfying manner; (3) accepts setbacks without becoming anxious or depressed, or without acting out; (4) knows and experiences feelings as they occur; (5) when conflicted, examines and works through the conflict himself or in a nondefensive way with the therapist; and (6) shows a growing desire to try things on his own and be independent of the therapist. To expect these criteria to manifest themselves as baldly as this listing indicates would be unrealistic; the therapist must be alert to signs and cues that indicate their presence and he may explore these signals with the patient as they occur. (1977, p. 145)

Obviously, to reach the level of functioning that these criteria suggest, therapy has to have been going on for some time. It is difficult to determine just how long therapy should continue. Most therapists doing individual therapy suggest that at least a year is necessary, with optimal length being between 1 and 2 years (Blane, 1977). Length of treatment may be seen as a general guideline for when patients have reached the late phase of treatment. (One can readily see that this length of treatment far exceeds the usual 30-day program of inpatient treatment. One to 2 years may become a more probable length of treatment if more patients are forced by insurance limitations to seek outpatient care.)

Discussion of termination sometimes leads to regression by patients. Usually therapists can explain that this is typical and that long-term gains will continue to be maintained. The usual strategy used to prepare clients for termination is a gradual lengthening of the time between sessions, for example, moving sessions from once a week to every other week to once a month, and finally the breakoff of therapy entirely. Since many alcoholics are very dependent, it is important to deal with termination at the appropriate time. Unless there is clear evidence that there are some unfinished issues, therapy should be brought to a close.

In his discussion of individual therapy with alcohol clients, Blane indicates that therapy can be conducted alone, with a group, or as family therapy. Individual therapy may also follow inpatient treatment (varying from detoxification to the typical 30-day inpatient program). Alcoholics Anonymous is also an important adjunct to any form of alcohol treatment.

It should be noted that some therapists do not see individual treatment as the treatment of choice for most alcoholics. These therapists maintain that group therapy offers much more to alcoholics than can be obtained in individual therapy. Deciding which therapy modality is best is, in reality, probably dependent on the individual patient and the specific therapist. Group therapy (covered in Chapter 11) meets many of the confrontation and support concerns that therapists have with alcoholics. On the other hand, if patients have difficulty talking about personal issues or if these issues need more intense work, individual psychotherapy may be the preferred method.

Zimberg's Description of Individual Therapy

Writing on individual therapy with alcoholics, Zimberg (1982) notes that the art of alcoholism psychotherapy is learning where to intervene in alcoholics' lives and defenses and where to leave things be. There are aspects of alcoholics' defenses and lives that should either be left alone or redirected by therapists. (For example, the patient who has been obsessive about drinking can turn this defensive tendency toward maintaining sobriety by working on all the things that will help achieve this goal.) Wallace (1982), in an excellent discussion of therapy with alcoholics, suggests that the preferred defense structure of alcoholics need not be suddenly changed but can become an effective tool to use in therapy.

Zimberg (1982) outlines the following principles that should be recognized when working with alcoholics:

1. Establish contracts that tell alcoholics that abstaining from alcohol is the goal of treatment. Alcoholics should be told that the initial efforts have to be directed at keeping them sober.

2. Therapists must recognize that there will be intense transference with alcoholic patients. This transference will involve much dependency, manipulative behavior, and testing of limits on the part of alcoholics.

3. Therapists must also recognize the countertransference that they may develop toward alcoholic patients. Alcoholics' behavior can be provocative, and therapists can react with anger, frustration, and impatience to this acting out behavior. One way of reducing this tendency is for therapists to recognize their own limitations. Therapists cannot keep alcoholics sober—they can only build on alcoholics' own commitments to maintaining sobriety. (Therapists must also remember, although it is often difficult, that the acting out and drinking are a part of the problem. Therapists would not stop seeing neurotic clients because they acted neurotically; the same is true for alcoholics).

Therapists should be aware that alcoholism therapy moves through several stages. The first stage is the beginning of therapy where alcoholics do not want to give up alcohol but are usually forced to consider that option because of outside pressure. While acknowledging that they cannot drink

BOX 9–2
Controlled Drinking—A Continuing Controversy

Controlled drinking is a term generally used with individuals who have been diagnosed as alcoholic and who then are able to return to moderate drinking. The idea that some people have the ability to return to moderate drinking after abusing alcohol has been known for some time (Miller, 1983; Peele, 1992). However, the notion of alcoholics returning to controlled drinking is in conflict with the disease model (as usually interpreted in this country), because the disease model says that once an alcoholic has the disease of alcoholism that person can never return to moderate drinking. That is, any attempt at drinking will exacerbate the problem, resulting in loss of control, abusive drinking, and eventually, death.

Because the disease model has been so prominent, and because so many alcoholics express a desire to return to drinking, which is seen as ultimately destructive in this model, total abstinence has been the dominant goal in alcohol treatment. However, most of the research suggests that the goal of abstinence (which is supported by those using the disease model) is not achieved by the majority of people treated in disease model programs. For example, in one report, total abstinence for individuals coming out of traditional disease model programs was 12 to 45 percent (depending on the study reviewed) and averaged 26 percent (Miller, 1983). On the other hand, this same reviewer found that in controlled drinking studies patients showed an average success rate of 65 percent.

More recently, however, individuals who had previously supported controlled drinking as a treatment option for all types of alcohol problems have become more conservative. These social-learning-based researchers now recommend an abstinence goal for the majority of people who seek alcohol treatment (Peele, 1992). Nathan (1986) has summarized the position of many of these previous advocates.

> The consensus among informed observers is that alcoholism treatment with controlled drinking as a prime treatment goal is neither efficacious nor ethical when offered to chronic alcoholics. . . . the weight of the available data now suggests both that we have not developed treatment programs that can reliably teach chronic alcoholics to become controlled drinkers and that status as a controlled drinker is not in the best interests of most chronic alcoholics. (p. 44)

The problem in using controlled drinking may be finding the types of patients who can benefit from a program designed to teach moderate drinking. The general characteristics of those who can effectively use controlled drinking treatment seem to be known.

. . . Successful controlled drinkers are generally found to be younger (under 40), less addicted individuals with fewer life problems related to alcohol and fewer than 10 years of problem-drinking history. Those who succeed in moderation also tend not to regard themselves as alcoholic and not to subscribe to disease concepts of alcoholism. (Miller, 1983, p.77)

Unfortunately, the assessment procedures to match clients with moderate drinking treatment programs are not in place and there are not, as indicated by Nathan, programs that can reliably treat chronic alcoholics using this approach. However, for individuals early in their drinking careers who need to become more aware of alcohol's effects on them this may be an important technique. Often younger drinkers will not accept referral to programs which require that they declare themselves alcoholic. They may be able to learn from the self-control procedures used in the typical moderate drinking program. At the same time, it should be remembered that we are still not very successful in treating alcohol problems with the procedures currently available. That is, we need all the treatment options we can find and use effectively. Research and continued clinical monitoring of moderate drinking under carefully controlled conditions should assure that we do not arbitrarily throw out a helpful procedure.

At present the probability of a person with chronic alcohol problems, treated in most traditional alcohol treatment programs, becoming a controlled drinker is not great. The chances of such a patient achieving controlled drinking is perhaps one out of ten or, at best, two out of ten. These odds suggest that controlled drinking is not the goal of choice for the chronic alcoholic treated in most currently available programs.

safely, alcoholics most often really want to find a way that they can drink safely. Because of the failure to fully commit to abstinent lives, this first stage is very unstable and can end by patients returning to drinking or by patients achieving an attitudinal change toward alcohol. In the latter case, alcoholics have accepted that they must live without alcohol and have learned new ways to deal with the stresses of life.

The second stage is fairly stable with alcoholics developing effective internal controls over the impulse to drink. Zimberg indicates that this stage has been achieved by most successful AA members. Although sober, they have no insight into their psychological problems. This stage represents a relatively good recovery for alcoholics, since they feel they have control over alcohol and they can direct some of their grandiosity into rescuing other alcoholics.

The third stage occurs when alcoholics do not have to drink. According to Zimberg, this is achieved through development of insight into their personality conflicts. Zimberg suggests that psychoanalytically oriented psychotherapy and the development of understanding are required to reach this stage. This is called insight in psychoanalytic therapy, that is, an understanding of themselves and how the use and abuse of alcohol fits into their lives. Zimberg further indicates that not all alcoholics want to or need to reach this stage, but some may choose to work on their problems at this depth.

Zimberg suggests a fourth stage as a theoretical possibility—the return to social drinking. He notes that predicting who can do this is very difficult. Others agree and would not suggest that this alternative be considered a goal of therapy with the overwhelming majority of alcoholics. (See Box 9–2 for a discussion of this controversial issue.)

As can be seen throughout this chapter, individual therapy with alcoholics is a very complex undertaking. Treatment of alcoholic patients should involve not only individual but also group therapy and support groups like Alcoholics Anonymous. Whenever appropriate and possible, patients should be involved in family therapy. It should be remembered that in psychotherapy alcholics and therapists are putting back together lives that have been affected in several spheres. This can include psychological, sociological, physiological, and economic issues. Therapists working individually with alcoholics must frequently be excellent case managers who draw upon outside resources to provide the best possible care available.

REFERENCES

Baekeland, F., & Lundwall, L. K. (1977). Engaging the alcoholic in treatment and keeping him there. In B. Kissin & H. Begleiter (Eds.), *The biology of alcoholism: Vol. 5. Treatment and rehabilitation of the chronic alcoholic.* (pp. 161–195) New York: Plenum Press.

Blane, H. T. (1968). *The personality of the alcoholic: Guises of dependency.* New York: Harper & Row.

Blane, H. T. (1977). Psychotherapeutic approach. In B. Kissin & H. Begleiter (Eds.), *The biology of alcoholism: Vol. 5. Treatment and rehabilitation of the chronic alcoholic.* (pp. 105–160). New York: Plenum Press.

Brown, S. A., Christiansen, B. A., & Goldman, M. A. (1987). The Alcohol Expectancy Questionnaire: An instrument for the assessment of adolescent and adult alcohol expectancies. *Journal of Studies on Alcohol, 48,* 483–484.

Chafetz, M. E. (1967). Motivation for recovery in alcoholism. In R. Fox (Ed.), *Alcoholism: Behavioral research, therapeutic approaches* (pp. 110–117). New York: Springer.

Chafetz, M. E., Blane, H. T., & Hill, M. J. (1970). *Frontiers of alcoholism.* New York: Science House.

Churchill, R., & Crandall, V. (1955). The reliability and validity of the Rotter Incomplete Sentences Test. *Journal of Consulting Psychology, 19,* 345–350.

Davis, L. D., Jr., Colligan, R. C., Morse, R. M., & Orford, K. P. (1987). Validity of the MacAndrew Scale in a general medical population. *Journal of Studies on Alcohol, 48,* 202–206.

Graham, J. R., & Strenger, V. E. (1988). MMPI characteristics of alcoholics: A review. *Journal of Consulting and Clinical Psychology, 56,* 197–205.

Jacobson, G. R. (1976). *The alcoholisms: Detection, assessment and diagnosis.* New York: Human Sciences Press.

Jacobson, G. R. (1983). Detection, assessment and diagnosis of alcoholism: Current techniques. In M. Galanter (Ed.), *Recent developments in alcoholism: Vol. I: Current concepts in diagnosis* (pp. 377–413). New York: Plenum Press.

Jacobson, G. R. (1989). A comprehensive approach to pretreatment evaluation: I. Detection, assessment and diagnosis of alcoholism. In R. K. Hester & W. R. Miller (Eds.), *Handbook of alcoholism treatment approaches* (pp.17–53). New York: Pergamon.

Koumans, A. J. R. (1969). Reaching the unmotivated patient. *Mental Hygiene, 53,* 298–300.

Koumans, A. J. R., & Muller, J. J. (1965). Use of letters to increase motivation for treatment in alcoholics. *Psychological Reports, 16,* 1152.

Koumans, A. J. R., Muller, J. J., & Miller, C. F. (1967). Use of telephone calls to increase motivation for treatment in alcoholics. *Psychological Reports, 21,* 327–328.

Marlatt, G. A., & Gordon, J. H. (Eds.). (1985). *Relapse prevention.* New York: Guilford Press.

Mayer, J. (1972). Initial alcoholism clinic attendence of patients with legal referrals. *Quarterly Journal of Studies on Alcohol, 33,* 814–816.

Miller, W. R. (1983). Controlled drinking: A history and a critical review. *Journal of Studies on Alcohol, 44,* 68–83.

Milmore, S., Rosenthal, R., Blane, H. T., Chafetz, M. E., & Wolf, I. (1967). The doctor's voice: A postdictor of successful referral of alcoholic patients. *Journal of Abnormal Psychology, 72,* 78–84.

Morgenstern, J., & McCrady, B. S. (1992). Curative factors in alcohol and drug treatment: Behavioral and disease model perspectives. *British Journal of Addiction, 87,* 901–912.

Nathan, P. E. (1986). Outcome of treatment for alcoholism: Current data. *Annals of Behavioral Medicine, 8,* 40–46.

Pattison, E. M. (1981). Differential diagnosis of the alcoholism syndrome: Clinical implications of empirical research. In E. Gottheil, A. T. McLellan, & K. A. Druley (Eds.), *Matching patients and treatment methods in alcoholism and drug abuse* (pp. 3–31). Springfield, IL: Charles C. Thomas.

Peele, S. (1992). Alcoholism, politics, and bureaucracy: The consensus against controlled-drinking therapy in America. *Addictive Behaviors, 17,* 49–62.

Rudie, R. R., & McGaughran, L. S. (1961). Differences in developmental experience, defensiveness and personality organization between two classes of problem drinkers. *Journal of Abnormal and Social Psychology, 62,* 659–665.

Skinner, H. A., & Allen, B. A. (1983). Differential assessment of alcoholism: Evaluation of the Alcohol Use Inventory. *Journal of Studies on Alcohol, 44,* 852–862.

Smart, R. G., Adlaf, E. M., & Knoke, D. (1991). Use of the CAGE Scale in a population survey of drinking. *Journal of Studies on Alcohol, 52,* 593–596.

Thomas, C. L. (Ed.). (1977). *Tabor's cylopedic medical dictionary.* Philadelphia: F. A. Davis.

Treffert, D. A., Ansfield, P. J., & Hughes, G. B. (1974). Different strokes for different folks: An analysis of specific treatment in two sub-groups of alcoholics. (Research Grant No. MH. 18441-02) Final Report to National Institute of Mental Health.

Wallace, J. (1982). Working with the preferred defense structure of the recovering alcoholic. In S. Zimberg, J. Wallace, & S. B. Blume (Eds.), *Practical approaches to alcoholism psychotherapy* (2nd ed.) (pp. 23–36). New York: Plenum Press.

Wanberg, K. W., Horn, J. L., & Foster, F. M. (1977). A differential assessment model for alcoholism: The scales of the Alcohol Use Inventory. *Journal of Studies on Alcohol, 38,* 512–543.

Westermeyer, J. (1992). Substance use disorders: Predictions for the 1990s. *American Journal of Drug and Alcohol Abuse, 18,* 1–11.

Zimberg, S. (1982). Principles of alcoholism psychotherapy. In S. Zimberg, J. Wallace, & S. B. Blume (Eds.), *Practical approaches to alcoholism psychotherapy* (2nd ed.) (pp. 3–22). New York: Plenum Press.

Alcohol and the Family: Family Therapy

_____ *chapter 10*

Alcohol has a long history as a disrupter of family life in this country and elsewhere (Jackson, 1954; Steinglass, 1977). However, the idea that the family unit might be a point of intervention and prevention of alcohol abuse is of fairly recent origin. This chapter focuses on alcohol and its impact on family function. It will cover the clinical issues underlying alcohol's disruption of the family, methods of and approaches to intervention, and the long-range impact on members of alcoholic families.

One of the earlier overviews of alcohol and family therapy research was written by Steinglass (1977). He also did a review of 25 years of alcohol and family therapy research from 1950 to 1975 (1976). These two important papers help define some of the major concepts of family therapy and alcohol problems. A more recent review by McCrady (1989) summarizes the research between 1975 and 1989. These three articles nicely outline what is now known about the impact that family intervention may have on alcohol problems. Treatment of the family with alcohol problems is a very complex issue.

The first focus of this chapter is the family as "patient," the unit at which treatment is directed. This is a very different orientation from that found in individual treatment and also differs from group therapy (particularly in level of intimacy).

Here the family is seen as a unit in which each individual plays certain roles. The well-adjusted family allows shifts in roles and shows well-established boundaries between family members and between the family as a unit and the outside world. Family therapy focuses on issues of interaction. The notion that a family unit attempts to maintain equilibrium or homeostasis (that is, a balance of forces) helps distinguish family therapy from individual therapy. Steinglass (1977) outlines six "key concepts" that distinguish family therapy from other therapy modalities.

1. The Family as a System.   The family is seen as a unit where the activities of each member have an impact on the behavior of the entire family and where the family in turn affects each individual and has an impact on each member's behavior. Thus, from a family therapy perspective an individual's behavior has to be understood in terms of how all the members of the family contribute to that behavior and in terms of how that behavior affects all of the people in that family.

2. The Homeostasis Concept.   This is the notion that families tend to reach and maintain balance and stability. Families are seen as having built-in ways to resist change in their established stability. Unfortunately, stability is not always a healthy phenomenon in families since pathological patterns are as resistant to change as those of healthy family adjustments. In fact, chronic alcohol abuse is one of the pathologies around which a family can stabilize and thus resist change. An example of how various forces within the family tend to provide feedback and thus maintain even pathological balances can be seen in the family where the alcoholic sobers up. Since the family's adjustment and ways of interacting have been "balanced" around the alcoholic's drinking, when the drinking stops the family must seek a new adjustment, a new way of balancing its interactions. However, once a family has established a balance, it is difficult to leave that adjustment because it requires multiple changes or new roles and ways of interacting by everyone else in the family. Change is usually threatening in human interactions, especially multiple changes. Therefore, there is pressure by the family to revert back to the previous ways of relating because it is less difficult and more comfortable for the family as a whole. For example, a person may encourage the alcoholic spouse to go along to parties or to bring alcohol into the home so it is more readily available.

Children, who may have been able to play a more central role as the nondrinking parent's advisor and supporter, may act out to increase psychological pressure on the drinking parent. (These actions are not carried out in a conscious way; it is the unrecognized discomfort of the family members that leads to these actions.) These are examples of efforts to return to the homeostasis or equilibrium that the family has previously learned to use in relating to each other and carrying out its many tasks.

3. The "Identified Patient" (or Scapegoat).   Another way of viewing psychopathology from a family perspective is that the "identified patient" (the alcoholic, in this case) plays a central role in managing potential pathology in one or more of the other family members. For example, a nondrinking spouse who is potentially a depressed person may have to find other ways of adjusting while dealing with the problem of an alcoholic. From a family therapy perspective, the partner's alcoholism helps the nondrinker to deal with depression. When the alcoholic quits drinking, the nondrinking spouse will become depressed. It is also possible that drinking can help put off other troubling issues of a pathological nature in the family. These may include acting out behavior by children (fights at school, shoplifting, sexual promiscuity during adolescence, lying, and stealing) in reaction to the parent ceasing to drink. Frequently, children try to be "extra good" and supportive during the drinking days despite receiving little attention. In other cases, incest may be ignored while the drinking is occurring because the problems around alcohol are so great.

4. Communication Patterns. Communication among family members has received major attention by family therapists. Some family therapists suggest that the only goal of therapy should be improving the communication patterns of family members. Communication patterns can involve both verbal and nonverbal behavior. Verbal and nonverbal behaviors of all family members are greatly affected by alcohol abuse. In some families, there is a total reduction of communication while the abusing member is drinking because everyone is on "pins and needles," afraid that they will cause the alcoholic to become violent or to drink more. When the alcoholic is not drinking, communication patterns may still be subdued and less open because family members are afraid that they may say or do something that will set off drinking by the alcoholic member. Another possible change in communication can be the exchange of more hostile and aggressive verbal and nonverbal behavior while the alcoholic is drinking . One area of particular interest to recent researchers is the differences between sober and drinking interactions in alcoholic families. These have been shown to be qualitatively and quantitatively different (Jacob, 1987).

5. Behavioral Context. In individual therapy, the focus is on the unconscious-conscious internal conflicts of clients and how these affect their behavior. Behavioral therapy places little emphasis on underlying conflicts. Behavioral therapists focus on the individual and the consequences behavior has for that individual. Family therapists work with more than one individual. They are interested in internal, individual processes and also in how individuals' behaviors are related to those around them. It is the other members of the family and the setting in which the interactions occur that set what Steinglass calls the "context for behavior" (1977, p. 266). The family context can predetermine the behavior of any single member by limiting the number of behaviors the person can successfully or appropriately express. Some clinicians believe that alcoholic families limit the expression of feelings and the discussion of the drinking problem itself. These particular family-based context limitations are of particular interest to family therapists. (These changes in behavioral context are also of interest to those therapists working with children of alcoholics; see Brown, 1992.) If they are seen as potentially harmful to the family unit (and they generally are seen that way by family therapists), then these issues may become the focus of intervention. In brief, the family therapist is interested in more than the quantity and frequency of drinking. The drinking behavior must be examined in terms of the context in which it occurs and how it affects the interactions and relationships of family members.

6. Boundaries.   Every person in an interaction has a boundary, that is, a point that separates them from the other person or persons with whom they are relating. People in families have boundaries that separate them from other members of the family unit. The family unit has boundaries that separate it from the broader community. Boundaries are discussed in the family therapy area in terms of permeability. High permeability boundaries exist when there is an easy exchange of communication. When there is low communication, boundaries are rigid. It should be noted that boundaries are ways individual members of the family can maintain their individuality. Having boundaries that are too permeable can lead to the loss of self by a family member. In alcoholic families, it may be that the boundaries between the drinker and the nondrinking spouse become less permeable and more rigid; in turn, it may be that the boundaries between the nondrinking parent and oldest child become more permeable so that topics not usually shared by a parent with a child are shared. The support and care that is no longer available to the parent from the spouse is sought from the oldest child. It can be readily seen how alcohol may tend to distort and modify boundaries between members of an alcoholic family. In the same way, boundaries between the alcoholic family unit and the broader community can also become more rigid, and the alcoholic family can become increasingly more isolated and have poorer communication with the outside world. This isolation means that the family can become shut off from potential sources of support and help in the community. It is also possible to have boundaries that are so permeable between the family and the broader community that the family loses its sense of integrity and togetherness. When these types of open boundaries occur, the family may lose its effectiveness as a family unit. As Steinglass indicates, "Alcoholic families have been characterized as having extremely rigid boundaries leading to a characteristic sense of isolation within the community" (1977, p. 267).

These key concepts as outlined by Steinglass highlight the complexity that family therapists face when they attempt to intervene in and to change the family. Family therapy as an important and central intervention strategy for families with alcoholic members is a relatively recent treatment approach in the alcohol field (Steinglass, 1976, 1977). A grasp of how the family treatment approach evolved will help in understanding this approach.

A BRIEF OVERVIEW

Steinglass (1977) outlines the development of family therapy in the alcohol field. A review of his outline provides one of the most economical ways of understanding the history of alcohol and family therapy.

The initial interest in family issues and alcoholism began in the 1930s. This early interest focused on the role of family factors in the etiology of alcoholism. Family issues were seen as a possible source of alcoholics' abusive drinking. Little attention was given to family interactions and how they might be affecting drinking. The general consensus was that knowing families helped one understand alcoholics, but treatment was still focused on the alcoholic. Specific family patterns that helped to cause alcoholism were emphasized (for example, a spouse constantly nagging the drinker). It was also suggested that families where alcholism was present were more alike than different and, by inference, these families should be grouped together and treated by alcohol professionals. This treatment was seen as necessary to help the alcoholic recover.

Because of these emphases on family interaction as an explanation for an individual member's drinking and because of the idea that family issues should be dealt with by alcohol counselors, alcohol therapists tended to be isolated from the later developments in family therapy. Alcohol treatment of families tended to maintain this fairly narrow focus of looking at how the family's actions might maintain drinking in the alcoholic, while the general family therapy field moved ahead, focusing more on communication and interaction patterns of all family members as contributors to problems in the whole family. These developments in the alcohol field, beginning in the 1930s and lasting until the development of family therapy in the mid-1950s, were important precursors of family treatment of alcohol problems (Steinglass, 1976, 1977).

A second phase in the development of family therapy with alcoholics was the focus on the alcoholic marriage. (It should be noted that in almost all of the early work in family therapy with alcoholics, the husband was the alcoholic.) The role played by wives in initiating and maintaining their husbands' drinking was of central concern. There were two opposing views as to why wives acted to initiate and maintain drinking in their husbands. Clinicians (psychiatrists and social workers) maintained that women married alcoholic males to help themselves deal with their own preexisting psychopathology. Some women's psychological needs were met by marrying alcoholics. Sociologists, on the other hand, saw wives' behaviors as being the result of pressures placed on them by the drinking. For example, wives might not trust their alcoholic husbands' new sobriety because the husbands had tried and failed to stop drinking so many times before. These doubts led wives to be reluctant to give up their assumed roles of functional heads of the family because they feared another failure. They made attempts to sabotage their husbands' sobriety as a way to avoid giving up their roles.

These explanations for wives' behaviors were still in terms of their effect on the alcoholic's drinking. However, there was some movement toward an interactional model. Many of the explanations were filled with value judgments. Whalen's (1953) work was one of the more extreme examples.

Whalen reported on four "types" of wives of alcoholics who presented themselves to her agency. Whalen implied that these types were prototypical for marriages where alcoholism played a major role. Unfortunately, this assertion received widespread acceptance in much of the literature of the time (summarized by Rodgerson, 1974). Whalen's work is of historical interest and it also shows the dangers of overinterpreting observational data from limited samples in clinical settings.

Whalen's first type is "Suffering Susan." This type of wife chooses her alcoholic husband to insure that she will be miserable. She has low self-esteem and self-worth. Her severe mistreatment by an alcoholic husband helps to confirm her self-image as an unworthy person who must accept all of these family problems as inevitable circumstances. The motivation is to maintain a self-image of being inadequate and unable to change her life.

"Controlling Catherine" is the second type of "alcoholic wife." This person marries an inept, unassertive male because she basically distrusts and dislikes all men. She wants to control the marriage relationship and gains increasing control as her husband's alcoholism progresses. She is openly critical of her husband, but she has invested in maintaining his drinking because his alcoholism has obvious advantages for her.

Whalen's third type is "Wavering Winnifred." She is basically weak, insecure, and has her own intensive dependency needs. She chooses a weak, inadequate husband because he is unlikely to leave her. She is secure in the relationship so long as she feels he cannot get along without her. She will threaten to leave and at times she will waver in her affection for her husband, but she will not leave him. She does little to help him with his alcohol problem because his alcoholism ties him to her.

The final Whalen type is "Punishing Polly." Generally speaking, she is a rival of men and is both envious of and resentful toward males. She will risk marriage only to men who are inadequate and vulnerable. She is frequently a career woman who marries a younger man and then constantly belittles him. The only way he is allowed to rebel is by getting drunk. "She controls everything, giving him anything but his manhood" (Rodgerson, 1974).

According to Whalen's types, much of the motivation for the married male alcoholic's continued drinking is placed on the neurotic needs of his wife. The "normal female," who may have chosen her mate based on many positive characteristics that later changed, is noticeably absent. Whalen's conclusions are based on studies of clinical samples. When clinical samples are used, only those persons who are "having troubles" and are seeking professional help are included. Those women who are living in alcoholic marriages and who do not seek treatment may be leading well-adjusted lives despite their husbands' alcohol problems. This group of women is not included in studies like Whalen's that use clinical samples. Whalen's data do not include the possibility that even in women who have problems with alcoholic husbands, there may be several adaptive stages. A developmental or longitudinal perspective is necessary to understand the development of coping strategies in alcoholics' wives. Whalen's work also ignores the chance that alcohol abuse itself may lead to drastic shifts in the relationships between husband and wife. Jackson (1954) discusses this possibility.

Jackson's work represents the sociological approach to alcoholic marriages, even though she used a clinical sample. Her reports on alcoholic marriages are based primarily on her observations of wives who attended weekly Al-Anon meetings over a three-year period. While her results, like Whalen's, are based on clinical observations, she reached quite different conclusions. She found little evidence that deep-seated neurotic needs led to alcoholic marriages by the wives she observed. Instead, she saw the wives sharing a similar set of adjustment stages in reaction to their husbands' drinking. Jackson suggests that Whalen did not see different types of wives; she saw wives at different stages in their adjustment to the alcoholic marriage. Jackson outlines seven stages the wives in her study experienced.

1. During the first stage, the husband's abusive drinking begins. The drunken episodes create tension and embarrassment. The wife is indecisive and the husband is embarrassed. Both spouses try to deny that there is a problem, and they try to be perfect between each drinking bout. This prevents them from facing any of their problems. If the wife talks about his drinking, the husband is resentful but promises to never drink again.

2. Drinking is increased in the second stage, and the family becomes more socially isolated. The wife covers up her husband's drinking in an attempt to prevent his employer and the community from knowing about it. Family interactions become more intense, conflicted, and centered around drinking. The wife develops self-pity, and the alcoholic becomes more resentful. Both partners try to find reasons for the drinking, but this cannot be adequately accomplished. The wife attempts to control her husband's drinking by using punishments and rewards (e.g., withholding sexual access). At this point the wife looks most like Whalen's "Suffering Susan."

3. In the third stage, the family gives up and becomes disorganized. The wife resents her husband and begins to doubt her own sanity. There are increasing problems with the children, and violence frequently occurs. Sexual activity between the couple almost completely ceases. At this point, outside agencies may be contacted for help. This action may lead to the wife feeling guilty since she feels she should be able to handle these problems on her own. The wife and family are puzzled, fearful, and helpless. The wife resembles "Wavering Winnifred" at this point.

4. During the fourth stage, the wife takes charge of the family. The husband becomes just another child she must look after and manage. As she succeeds in meeting each new problem, she gains increasing confidence in her abilities. She may take a job and/or seek outside help for the family drinking problem. The family becomes more stable, and the children have fewer problems. These behaviors resemble Whalen's "Controlling Catherine."

5. During this stage, the wife and children leave the alcoholic. This is not without difficulties with the husband and considerable emotional conflict and self-doubt on the wife's part. However, she quickly gains confidence as time goes on.

6. In this stage, the mother and children reorganize their lives without the alcoholic. This process is frequently quite successful.

7. In the final stage, the alcoholic husband is allowed to return to the family only if he has clearly demonstrated he can remain sober. If he does return, this final stage can be filled with difficulties as he begins to reassert himself in those family areas which his wife has controlled for a time.

Whalen and Jackson's clinical-sociological approaches to alcohol's effect on the family illustrate Steinglass's alcoholic marriage phase. The next phase Steinglass outlines is an important transition point in the development of family therapy in the alcohol field. Concurrent therapy for alcoholics and their spouses marked an adaptation of group therapy procedures by treating the alcoholic and the spouse in separate therapy groups but during the same time periods.

The first reported work on this phase was done by Gliedman and his colleagues (Gliedman, 1957; Gliedman, Nash, & Webb, 1956; Gliedman, Rosenthal, Frank and Nash, 1956). These researchers merely extended group psychotherapy into the treatment of alcoholics and their spouses at the same time.

The majority of research on group psychotherapy using concurrent therapy for alcoholics and spouses was done by Ewing and his colleagues at the University of North Carolina Medical School. Thirty-two married alcoholic men and sixteen of their wives participated in a study in which they all followed the same treatment center schedule for group therapy. This experimental arrangement allowed a comparison of therapy outcome between the alcoholic males whose wives participated and those whose wives did not.

Ewing, Long, and Wenzil's (1961) long-term follow-up of these participants is impressive. Compared with alcoholics whose wives did not participate in therapy, alcoholics whose wives were also in treatment (1) stayed in treatment longer, (2) had significantly improved control of drinking, and (3) had major improvement in "marital harmony." Unfortunately, it is difficult to sort out what is cause and what is effect in this type of research. For example, it could be that the differences in drinking rates and improvements in marital harmony were due to the fact that the alcoholics with participating wives stayed in therapy longer. Despite this shortcoming in the research, Steinglass (1977) notes that keeping alcoholics in treatment is no small accomplishment. Other researchers have reported the same types of results as Ewing and his colleagues. Most treatment centers now try to provide some type of marital or family therapy to improve treatment effectiveness.

The adaptation of family therapy to alcoholism treatment was the next phase in family therapy in the alcohol field. Substance abuse treatment and family therapy had developed quite separately for a number of years. Alcohol-based treatment of families dealt with the pragmatic issue of how to increase success rates for alcohol treatment by using adaptations of existing individual and group therapy procedures. At the same time, family therapy techniques were being developed by professionals working with other human problems. Family concepts of symptom development and family-oriented therapy interventions were being established.

These new family therapy ideas were developed around diverse "family-based" problems, for example, schizophrenia, psychosomatic disorders, and dysfunctions of adolescents. As Steinglass notes, "Although somewhat puzzling in retrospect, alcoholism and drug abuse was almost ignored both theoretically and clinically" (1977, p. 275). Family therapy was not the only psychiatric area that ignored alcohol abuse. Until the 1960s and 1970s alcohol problems were generally seen as a nuisance, with many psychiatric training programs having strong prejudices against working with alcoholics. Similar negative attitudes were present in psychology and, to a lesser extent, in social work.

Ewing and Fox (1968) were two of the earliest writers to suggest that alcoholism is a family disorder that should be treated in a family context. They presented the notion that family emotional homeostasis is maintained by alcohol abuse in the family. From this point of view, the family must be seen as the client, and work must be done on changing family members' interactions in order to treat the alcohol problem. In particular, it is important to work with husband and wife to change the two halves of the homeostatic dyad, that is, to produce a relationship where both can learn to interact with each other without the presence of alcohol.

If one person (the alcoholic) changes, the change may lead to resistance in the untreated nondrinking spouse. Steinglass, Davis and Berenson (1975) had families predict what their interactions would be when the alcoholic member was drinking. For example, families might predict depression, fighting, and emotional distancing between family members. These researchers found that families' predictions or expectations of their interactions during drinking episodes were not necessarily correct. A family might instead be observed to show increased warmth, more care toward one another, and more animation when the alcoholic was drinking (Steinglass, 1977). These findings reinforced the idea that the alcoholic's drinking might be highly adaptive for the family. Steinglass looks at alcohol use in terms of how it affects family interactions and how it is integrated into family life. He points out "that alcohol, by dint of its profound behavioral, cultural, societal and physical consequences might assume such a central position in the lives of some families as to become an organizing principle for interactional life within those families" (1977, p. 279). For this type of family system, the presence or absence of alcohol is the single most important determiner of family interaction.

The logical outcome of seeing the family in this manner is to treat the family unit as the patient rather than focus on the alcoholic (the identified patient). When therapy is undertaken using this model, the focus is on the interaction between family members since it is these interactions that must be modified and changed. This differs from other psychiatric therapeutic approaches, which focus on changes within the patient. In this approach, the treatment goals are to improve the function, flexibility, and ability of the family to grow as a whole.

The family therapy approach is focused on finding the specific manner in which drinking behavior is serving an adaptive role for the individual and family. The maladaptive outcomes of drinking can usually be readily seen. Once the adaptive roles have been pinpointed, therapy focuses on finding ways for the alcoholic to show the adaptive behavior while sober and to learn appropriate alternative behaviors to replace drinking.

Conjoint family therapy (conjoint meaning pertaining to two or more in combination) is the next to last phase in the development of therapy with alcoholic families. Here interviewing is conducted with the married couple or with two or more members of a nuclear family (father, mother, children) or extended family (father, mother, children, and grandparents).

Steinglass reviews a clinical report by Meeks and Kelly (1970) who applied Satir's (1967) family therapy model to alcoholic families in an aftercare program. Meeks and Kelly dealt with issues such as clarifying interaction conflicts, improving and opening up communication, and developing an understanding of how intrapsychic issues affected interpersonal conflicts. While their work involved only five couples, they concluded that conjoint family therapy showed promise.

Steinglass' last phase involves multiple couples and multiple families.

Here, a large number of people may be involved in therapy at the same time. There have been clinical reports of as many as sixty individuals in multiple-family therapy. However, more research has been conducted on group therapy with multiple couples.

Steinglass and his colleagues report on their research using the multiple-couples group therapy approach. This program recruited ten middle-class intact couples who had stable economic and family lives despite the fact that one member was abusing alcohol. An important departure from traditional therapy with alcoholics was that the drinking member was not required to be abstinent. The therapists used the intoxicated behavior of the alcoholic as an adjunct to treatment. Therapy was directed at the couple, not specifically at the alcohol abuser. Treatment focused on the interactions between alcohol use, intoxicated behavior, and how the couple related to each other. Improved family functioning, not the reduction of drinking, was the primary treatment target. All ten couples finished the demanding treatment regimen and reported that the program had an important emotional impact on them. It is important to note that the alcohol abusers in each couple were patients who had failed several times in previous treatment programs. The therapists found that the in-hospital experiences, which were a part of this treatment program, speeded up the recognition of the relationship between drinking behaviors and the interaction between husband and wife.

This overview of the development of group therapy for alcoholic families sets the stage for understanding how clinicians utilize family therapy.

TWO APPROACHES TO FAMILY THERAPY

There are several orientations to alcohol treatment using family therapy. Each one differs, more or less, from the others. Summary presentations of Dulfano's (1985) and Kaufman's (1985) work illustrate how two family therapists approach family therapy with alcoholics and illustrate what clinicians deal with.

Dulfano's Approach to Family Therapy

The family is seen as a system from the family therapy perspective. When two people marry, they bring differing expectations to the marriage. These differing expectations must be resolved so that each member maintains individual identity. The family begins with the spouse dyad. When children are born, spouses must learn new tasks, and new patterns of relationships are established. Any change in any part of the family affects other units in that structure. There is always a feedback loop so that when the role of one member changes, it effects changes in other members. These changes lead to different interactional patterns in the other members, which then can lead to further changes in the member who originally showed the change. Thus, throughout the life history of the family, there is a constant need for change and compromise. The family must be able to adjust to these changes and at the same time maintain the stability needed by individual members of the family reference group. As families develop their own rules, they provide a social group in which people learn to love, to care for other people, and to satisfy their own needs. According to Dulfano, the growth and development of the individual is dependent upon this primary social system.

Alcohol can drastically affect this social system. For example, the interactions of the spouse subsystem (husband and wife) can be built around the drinking partner's alcohol problem. The changes in the parent subsystem may affect other subsytems of the family such as the children. Because of the loss of one functioning adult (the alcoholic), children may assume adult responsibilities at inappropriately early ages. The nonalcoholic spouse may, due to the pressure of dealing with family responsibilities, assign some parental responsibilities to an older child. These actions distort role models, and the roles that children normally play in the family are lost. Both the nondrinking parent and the children lose some of their "turf" in the family and the normal nurturing relationships for both adults and children may be abandoned.

When the children find that their needs are not met, they may find satisfaction in their roles as pseudoparents. In order to protect these roles, they may encourage younger children to remain more immature. From these examples of changes, it can be seen how alcohol problems can distort family relationships. These distortions lead to an environment in which there is little trust and in which it is difficult to learn how to be appropriately close to another person. Such conditions can have a long-range impact on the children of alcoholics, which may be played out in their adult lives and be transferred across generations to their own nuclear families. These issues are covered in more depth later in the chapter in the discussion of children of alcoholics.

Generally speaking, when a family begins therapy, alcohol has already been built into its equilibrium. While the removal of alcohol abuse may be desirable, its removal becomes a threat to all members of the family, not just the alcoholic. As Dulfano indicates, "There are all the problems of helping the individual alcoholic change his behavior, plus the problem that if such change does occur, the family system may respond with homeostatic transactions that encourage the reappearance of alcoholic behavior. Only structural change will remove the unacknowledged pressure on the alcoholic to remain an active alcoholic" (1985, p.136).

Dulfano stresses that each intervention with an alcoholic family has to be individually designed. However, he does suggest the following therapeutic contract:

(1) Focus on helping the alcoholic stop drinking, making him responsible for it and by doing so removing alcoholism from its central place in the family; (2) at the same time target for change those family transactional patterns that are trapping all family members in growth-curtailing roles; (3) stimulate individual growth of family members which is not based on the family disability created by alcoholism. (1985, p.137)

It should be noted that Dulfano differs from some family therapists who focus on family interactions and place the reduction of drinking in a more subordinate role.

In the first therapy session, the position of each member in the family is assessed. This allows therapists to understand how alcoholism has skewed family relationships and to start planning ways to correct inappropriate interactions. Therapists work with (1) spouses, concentrating on their interactions with each other; (2) the parents, focusing on their roles with the children; and (3) the children, helping them let go of the inappropriate roles they have assumed during the abusive drinking. The children receive assistance in finding compensations in age-related activities and roles.

Therapy focuses on the present. How the family is interacting at the present time is most central to therapy. It may be important to know how the historical material is affecting the present family interaction, but it is only the present interaction that can be changed.

Dulfano says that therapists may need to suggest tasks that will help the family learn new ways to relate to each other. Family therapy is generally much more directive in nature than is individual and group therapy. For example, it may be that the newly sober father will seek to reassert his role in the family by doing "manly" tasks like repairing the house or earning additional money with a second job to make the family's life more pleasant. However, these approaches to reentering the family may not be what is wanted and needed by the children. They may actually want the emotional support and availability of the father rather than material things. Dulfano uses this example to show that if therapists intervene to arrange for the father and children to spend more quality time together, the change can lead to new, more productive ways for them to interact.

The changes in interaction patterns reinforce competency and sobriety in the father. They also allow children to become reinvolved as children and less involved in their parents' problems. This can have an excellent preventive function since it does not lead to the disastrous arresting of developmental patterns seen in some children of alcoholics.

Kaufman's Approach to Family Therapy

Kaufman (1985) is one of the major figures in family therapy and alcoholism. He has combined aspects of several approaches to family therapy for his work with alcoholics (including structural systems and behavioral and psychodynamic approaches). His modification of family therapy offers another way of viewing the disturbance and distortion of family processes in alcoholic families.

Kaufman outlines four different types of families who suffer from alcohol abuse by one of their members. He suggests intervention strategies for each of the four types of families, as follows:

1. The Functional Family System (the Family with an Alcoholic Member). In these systems, family members live in a stable, happy environment. The parents have a loving relationship and the children have good relationships with the parents and each other. The alcoholic member of the family drinks because of sources external to the family or because of neurotic problems. These types of drinking problems exist, but since they do not come to the attention of the treatment centers, they are not often described.

A man observed in therapy some years ago was referred to group therapy sessions by his physician, who had detected his liver problems. The client reported no other major social or family problems. He usually began drinking after ten o'clock at night when his family had gone to bed. He drank until two or three in the morning. It was evident that he had some internal psychological problems, since he had been hospitalized in the past and diagnosed as a paranoid schizophrenic. (He showed none of the symptomatology associated with this diagnosis except for being a bit guarded in the group.) Still, he seemed to have a full and happy family life (and he seemed to want to shield his family from his own problems). He was quite successful at work and left the group when a significant promotion took him to another city.

This type of family avoids psychological intervention and has a minimum amount of visible conflict. Kaufman suggests family education for the functional family. In this way the family may get involved in "educative-cognitive exploration" (p. 386) of the roles each member plays in the family. Family members may also become more aware of observable family interaction. This may lead to an exploration of implicit family rules and the expectations the family has in terms of behavior. These explorations can lead to the development of family contracts and behavioral role practicing. In this type of alcoholic family, intensive exploration of personal and interpersonal family dynamics may not be necessary or may be resisted because the system protects the working homeostatic balance and the adjustments made to maintain that balance.

2. The Neurotic Enmeshed Family System (the Alcoholic Family). Drinking behavior disrupts normal functioning in this family, and the disruption is readily observed by outside helpers. The drinking leads to family conflict and shifts in the roles family members play. In general, the drinking behavior demands that family members adopt new responses. Alcohol use leads to anger in the drinker, despite attempts to deal with this emotion by drinking. There is the possibility of sexual dysfunction and debilitating illnesses in the alcoholic. These changes brought on by drinking in turn produce additional strains on the marriage and cause more role changes for family members.

"Stresses in any single family member immediately affect the entire family. Communication is often not direct but through a third party. Likewise, conflicts are triangulated (projected) onto another family member. . . . Everyone in the family feels guilty and responsible for each other but particularly for the alcoholic and his or her drinking" (p.378).

The couples in these types of alcoholic families are often competitive. Kaufman sees the spouse who has had to give in the most to the other partner as being "de-selfed" (p. 378). This person is at risk for alcohol problems. Once alcoholism occurs, the drinking problem gets entwined in the competition. Each partner tries to gain control over the other; the drinker by drinking, the nondrinking spouse by attempting to block or control the drinking. The nondrinking spouse may control by being blunt, dominating the relationship, or becoming a martyr (suffering). The drinker may attempt to gain control by becoming passive-dependent.

As the drinking continues, there are major role changes in the family. The alcoholic may give up the role of parent a little at a time, first dropping household chores and maintenance functions and finally dropping the role of breadwinner. At this point, assuming the alcoholic member is the husband, the wife may encourage the oldest son to take over the father's responsibilities. Or she may assume the father's role in addition to her own, while the father is relegated to child status. The alcoholic parent, whether mother or father, becomes more isolated and resentful. The alcoholic father verbally abuses the children, and violence and physical and sexual assault may occur. A mother who is alcoholic is more likely to abuse her children by neglect.

Interventions in the neurotic enmeshed family system may include the education and cognitive reeducation suggested for the first group above. However, explicit family psychotherapy is needed in this type of family. Therapy may need to be extended outside the nuclear family because there are several generations and kinship systems that are "interlocked with the nuclear family" (p. 386). Work with just the nuclear family is usually not sufficient. It is necessary to get disengagement by nuclear family members (get them involved with other people and groups outside the nuclear family). Disengagement can be aided by involving the alcoholic and family members in AA and Al-Anon. It is also helpful to get the alcoholic and other family members involved in more significant relationships with the extended family, with new friends, and with community groups.

3. The Disintegrated Family System (the Alcoholic Temporarily Separated from the Alcoholic Family). Kaufman sees this type as a more advanced stage of the enmeshed family. It is also possible for the functional alcoholic family to deteriorate into this phase. In this type of family there has been a history of reasonable family life, but at the point of treatment the family system has broken down completely. Because the family is unlikely to be reunited during the early stages of treatment, therapy is initially directed at the alcoholic. However, exploring the potential ties to spouse, family, kin, and friends is also a part of therapy with this type of alcoholic family. There should be no assumptions that the family and friendship ties can be reconstituted. Only after several months of sobriety and social stability can substantive examination with the nuclear and extended family be undertaken. These sessions focus on reestablishing parental, family, and kinship roles. This is still prior to reuniting the family group. It is important to redefine roles and relationships in the family, whether it is a separated role or a new role in the reconstituted family.

4. The Absent Family System (the Alcoholic Permanently Separated from the Family). In this situation, ties with the family of origin (parents, siblings) have been permanently cut early in the drinking history. These alcoholics have little family contact and few social or vocational ties to people. Their relationships are with social services personnel or with other drinkers. Neither of these relationships offer adequate social support. It is typically impossible for them to be reconciled with their family of procreation (spouse, children), but it is sometimes possible to reestablish contact with their family of origin. If alcoholics in this situation experience successful rehabilitation, they may reestablish new nuclear families. Treatment at this level is directed toward establishing new social networks and new social systems. Many alcoholics who are permanently separated from their families find it difficult to establish new relationships. These individuals will have to live in some type of social support institution. A few of these alcoholics learn over time to participate in new social systems and even to establish new functional families.

THEORETICAL MODELS AND FAMILY TREATMENT

The descriptions of family therapy outlined by Dulfano and Kaufman represent typical approaches used with alcoholic families. There are different theoretical orientations that govern how alcohol treatment is approached by professionals. These theoretical orientations or models are not simply semantic labels. They determine the intervention or treatment philosophy taken by family therapists. The division of family treatment models can be very broad. McCrady's (1989) perspective is followed here. McCrady divides theoretical models of family treatment into three perspectives: (1) the disease model perspective; (2) behavioral perspective; and (3) family systems perspective. Each of these perspectives will be discussed briefly along with its ramifications for treatment.

The Disease Model Perspective

Alcoholism is described as a family disease in the sense that the members of an alcoholic family suffer from a disease just as the alcoholic does. The disease of the alcoholic family has been labeled "co-dependence" (McCrady, 1989, p. 166). Co-dependence is a term that permeates the disease model writings. Briefly, it is the tendency for nonaddicted family members to show many of the traits observed in the alcoholic, for example, anxiety, low self-esteem, denial, depression, and even substance abuse. McCrady cites Cermak's (1986) specific symptoms of co-dependence. These include:

> (1) investing self-esteem in controlling self and others in the face of serious adverse circumstances; (2) assuming responsibility for meeting the needs of others before one's own; (3) experiencing anxiety and distortion of boundaries around issues of intimacy and separation; (4) being enmeshed in relationships with persons with personality disorders or alcohol or drug problems; (5) having at least three from a list of 10 other symptoms, i.e., (*a*) using denial as a primary coping strategy, (*b*) having constricted emotions, (*c*) experiencing depression, (*d*) being hypervigilant, (*e*) displaying compulsive behavior, (*f*) experiencing anxiety, (*g*) being a substance abuser, (*h*) being a victim of physical or sexual abuse, (*i*) having a stress related illness, (*j*) being in a relationship with a substance abuser for two years without seeking help. (McCrady, 1989, p. 166)

Some alcohol treatment programs combine ideas from family systems models. They tend to consider it important to deal with the development of dysfunctional family roles, the development of dysfunctional communications, and the changing family equilibrium in dealing with the alcoholic family member.

In the disease model there is a high probability that the nonalcoholic members of alcoholic families will be treated in separate groups. These groups generally provide education about alcoholism as a disease and how it disrupts family functioning, and offer referrals to other groups. These might include Al-Anon or Adult Children of Alcoholics groups. Many alcohol treatment centers offer inpatient treatment for family members. These programs are typically more abbreviated than those for the alcoholic family member.

Behavioral Perspective

Reciprocal impact in terms of cuing and reinforcing behavior by each partner is emphasized in this model. One member's behavior cues the behavior of the partner, and the partner's response serves as a reinforcer for the first member's behavior. Research within this model suggests that communication is characterized by negative responses and coercive interaction by both husband and wife. There has been a heavy emphasis in this model on couples' behavior. This emphasis has led to a better understanding of the ways couples' behavior changes from sober to drinking states.

In particular, drinking brings about changes in the alcoholic's behavior that can be seen as positive by the alcohol abuser and that may lead to reinforcing behavior changes in the people around the drinker. For example, alcohol use may increase the amount and rate of speech, leading the alcoholic to engage in more assertive and aggressive statements. Thus, drinking may provide the alcoholic with reinforcements. At the same time, the nondrinking spouse may decrease negative responses toward the drinker. The behavioral model focuses on developing ways to replace positive reinforcements gained when drinking with reinforcers that occur in response to sober behaviors. The actions of the nondrinking partner are very important in accomplishing this shift in reinforcement patterns. (See the example of Hunt and Azrin's research in Chapter 7.)

The nondrinking spouse's ineffective coping responses are another focus of the behavioral model. For example, some of the spouse's behavior is seen as a cue or a reinforcer for the alcoholic mate's drinking. Therapists using the behavioral model have shaped nondrinking spouses' behavior to provide reinforcement for therapy-related behaviors, such as taking disulfiram.

Behavioral models view abusive drinking behavior as being maintained by a wide range of reinforcement contingencies, including reinforcements outside the family. Therapy may also include individual behavioral treatment for the alcoholic at the same time marital therapy is underway.

Family Systems Perspective

The family systems perspective borrows from family therapy the concepts that emphasize family organization and the need for balance or homeostasis. In addition, the notion that events are caused by multiple interactions and their feedback within the family unit comes from family therapy. Alcoholism is an organizing principle in alcoholic families; that is, the pattern of interactions, the family structure, and the roles people play in the family are all organized around the abuse of alcohol. Alcoholic families have been found to have very different interaction patterns depending upon whether the drinking member is using alcohol or is in a state where alcohol use is unstable (for example, the alcoholic may go for long periods without drinking and then suddenly go on a binge). Family interactions tend to be more rigid in drinking and unstable families than in those families where abstinence has been established.

From this perspective, therapy focuses on the interactions of the family unit rather than on issues or concerns of the individual family member. The drinking problem is viewed as a problem to be dealt with by the family unit. The contributions of each family member to the drinking problem are examined. The main focus of the intervention is the interactions of family members and the impact of alcohol on these interactions.

Two different examples of how alcohol can distort roles in the family may be useful here. In the first case, a midwestern father had suffered from alcohol problems for many years. While his relationship with his wife had been adversely affected by his drinking, it was still intact. His relationship with his four daughters had been good throughout his drinking career, and at the time he was treated for alcohol problems, the three oldest daughters had either married or moved out of the home to begin their own careers. Both husband and wife saw their daughters as having healthy childhoods and productive adult lives. None of the daughters had any difficulties with school, the legal system, or any other aspect of their lives, and they were very close to their father. He was warm, affectionate (although often intoxicated), and generous. The same history had been true for the youngest daughter until Dad achieved his sobriety. One result of the father's sobering up was an improved relationship with his wife. The couple went everywhere together and did everything together. They went to AA and Al-Anon meetings two nights a week, going to the same location and stopping for coffee on the way home. One night a week they went together to couples therapy. The other two week nights they also spent together, bowling or playing bingo. They were pleased with their new-found togetherness and enjoyed their closeness. The parents were devastated when the youngest daughter, who had never been in trouble, was arrested for shoplifting. Through therapy it became obvious that the major shift in relationships following the father's sobriety had left the youngest daughter alone and isolated. Once the problem was pointed out to the parents, who cared very much for their children, they began to include the daughter in more family-related activities and to provide the attention and affection she had been missing. Since the shoplifting had been done in a desperate attempt to get attention, no other problems were encountered by the family.

The second case did not turn out so positively. As in the previous example, father and mother sought therapy because of their daughter's behavior following the father's sobriety. However, in this case there had been considerable intrafamily conflict. In this family, a teenage daughter had become the referee for fights between the parents, and she was the one who took Dad's side and was supportive of him throughout his drinking career. When he achieved sobriety, the daughter began to isolate herself from the family and to withdraw from all family interactions. Within the first 6 months of the husband's sobriety, the daughter and the parents attended one therapy session together; but it was obvious that the daughter was unwilling to discuss anything in front of them. She denied that she had any problems and simply said that she felt like being alone for a while and that was all there was to the change in her behavior. She was scheduled to see the therapist for an individual session. She failed to return, and the parents called to say that they could not persuade her to participate. Since the parents were being seen in couples therapy elsewhere, no additional contact with this family was possible. One can only speculate about what the origin of the above withdrawal was. The possibility of sexual abuse could be raised. On the other hand, it may have been simply a reaction to a loss of an important and meaningful role with the father.

In both these cases, following sobriety, the parents became very close and did everything together. But in the latter, the father moved aggressively to reestablish his role as father and to "bring the children into line." When these things happen in recovering families, some type of oppositional behavior on the part of teenage children may occur. This may have been the most acceptable way for the daughter to state that she needed attention and care.

These case examples show that sobriety also requires considerable adjustment by families and that some of these adjustments can be quite dramatic. It should be noted that the relationships between husbands and wives in these cases were also dramatic shifts.

In family therapy following a family systems perspective, roles are redefined for family members, alliances between family members are discussed and modified, and attempts are made to change patterns of communication within the family. A central issue in this therapeutic approach is how drinking changes patterns of interaction in the family.

OUTCOME RESEARCH ON THE THREE MODELS/PERSPECTIVES

The research bearing on these three models has been nicely outlined by McCrady (1989). There has been relatively little research on the disease model, even though this is the model that is most widely employed in the United States. The studies undertaken with this model are limited by reliance on self-report measures and a lack of control or comparison groups. The existing studies do not provide information on the impact of treatment on the whole family. They also fail to link treatment with the drinking behavior or adjustment of the alcoholic. The studies do not indicate how the treatment affected the family members' psychological and social functioning in areas other than dealing with the drinking problems. In brief, the studies dealing with outcome research based on the disease model are simply inadequate and limit the evaluation of the impact the treatment approach has on the alcoholic's family and on the alcoholic.

Although behavioral treatment is less frequently used to treat alcoholism in the family, some of the best research studies are in this area. Results obtained in this area suggest some specific ways that applications of behavioral family therapy can be effective (McCrady, 1989).

In particular, there have been promising results from behavioral techniques used in the treatment of couples. Training the nondrinking spouse to be reinforcing toward disulfiram treatment for the alcoholic mate has proven to be effective, at least in short-term follow-up studies. Short-term results for behaviorally based marital therapy with the alcoholic and spouse have been more positive when compared with "interactionally oriented treatment . . . " (McCrady, 1989, p. 174).

Behavioral therapy approaches seem to have their greatest impact in assisting alcoholic couples to deal with the threat of relapse following treatment. This approach may also be useful in helping alcoholics and their spouses work harder toward maintaining long-term abstinence from alcohol. Despite the fact that this approach with alcoholic couples has been one of the most successful and most carefully described in terms of treatment procedures, it has gained little acceptance in alcohol treatment programs. Much of this may be due to the limited training of alcohol workers in learning theory and to theoretical-ideological splits between learning approaches and the prevailing disease model. (See Chapter 7 for a more comprehensive description of the application of the learning model to alcohol treatment.)

The family systems model has been enthusiastically adopted by many therapists who treat alcoholics. Surprisingly, there has been relatively little outcome research on this model. It has established that intensive therapy with couples is workable. There is also some suggestion that this therapy approach with couples may lead to a better treatment outcome than individually oriented treatment. The reason for the lack of research data on this approach is unknown. Perhaps the usual clinical investment in helping alcoholics and their spouses has led to a focus on clinical helping instead of research. Such an outcome would not be surprising since professionals who treat alcoholics are people who care very much about clients and their welfare.

There is one other area of research from the family therapy perspective that is thought provoking. This is the research on factors that contribute to the passage of alcohol problems from one generation to another in an alcoholic family. In particular, Wolin and Bennett's (1984) research recently reviewed by Bennett (1989) illustrates how certain factors in family interaction seem to either buffer succeeding generations or make them more vulnerable. The impact of family alcoholism on children, both as immediate members of a drinking family and as a long-term effect extending into adulthood, is of central concern.

It is possible to view the family as a mini-culture that helps acculturate its members, and particularly its younger members, into appropriate family cultural behavior. This is one way of viewing the premise of Bennett, Wolin, Reiss, and Teitlebaum's research (Bennett, Wolin, Reiss, & Teitlebaum, 1987; Wolin & Bennett, 1984). Bennett (1989) summarizes this group's research findings.

> In the first study of 25 families, those families that kept their most valued family rituals (such as dinner time and holidays) relatively intact and undisrupted dur-

ing the heaviest drinking period of the alcoholic parent evidenced less transmission of the alcoholism to the offspring generation. In the second study of 30 extended families with 68 "offspring couples," those adult married couples from alcoholic backgrounds that deliberately planned and executed their family rituals in a planful way experienced significantly less transmission of the alcoholism into their own family. (p.122)

These studies are seen as ways to determine factors that may influence the transmission of psychopathology through family culture. The Wolin, Bennett, Noonan, and Teitelbaum (1980) research is interesting because it suggests that there may be factors, like family rituals, that can affect the transmission of alcohol family problems from one generation to the next. Isolating these types of factors may help to establish ways of reducing family effects of alcohol abuse.

The intervention and prevention of the immediate and long-term effects of being reared in an alcoholic family is still an unsolved problem. In order to understand how alcohol abuse can affect children, it is necessary to review the literature on children of alcoholics. This topic has both widespread significance and interest at present and deserves to be reviewed in some detail.

Researchers suggest that maintaining family rituals like holidays may reduce the transmission of alcoholism across generations. *(Photograph courtesy of Jim and Pat Cole, Lincoln, Nebraska.)*

CHILDREN OF ALCOHOLICS

Some of the early studies of children of alcoholics focused on personality and social performance issues that placed them at high risk for psychological, social, and substance abuse problems. These high-risk characteristics included low self-esteem, poor school performance, trouble in school, poor peer relations, low frustration tolerance, tantrums, aggressiveness, and adjustment problems in adolescence and early adulthood (Chafetz, Blane, & Hill, 1971; Lund, Landesman-Dwyer, 1979; McKenna & Pickens, 1981; Nardi, 1981). While these high-risk characteristics may describe children of alcoholics who have been seen in child guidance centers and the courts, Black (1979) argues that this group may make up a small minority of the total population of children of alcoholics. She sees most children in alcoholic families as making adjustments to the family that allow survival. These survival adjustments are primarily in the form of the roles that children adopt.

Black suggests the following roles that children may learn to play to help them adapt to the alcoholic family:

1. *The responsible one.* This child is not only responsible for himself or herself at an early age but is also responsible for siblings and even the parents. This child provides stability for members of the family in the often chaotic environment of the alcoholic family. Usually, it is the oldest or only child who fills this role in the family.

2. *The adjuster.* This child follows directions easily but does not feel the tremendous responsibility of the "responsible one." This child simply makes an "adjustment" so that there is the least possible amount of stress from the alcoholic family situation.

3. *The placater.* This child smooths over conflicts. He or she is sociable and much admired for helping others feel comfortable. Black feels that the child takes this role to ease the guilt felt for "causing" the alcohol problem.

Coping strategies have been described by other researchers. It is interesting that while these strategies have been given different names, they are remarkably similar to those described by Black.

Booz-Allen and Hamilton (1974) used volunteer subjects who were more educated and from a higher socioeconomic group in general than were Black's. Many of their subjects were also young adults at the time they were studied. The roles they identified included the following:

1. *Flight.* These researchers reported flight or escape behavior as most common. The escape could be physical, mental or emotional. More specifically, it could involve running away, hiding, spending time away from the house, high academic or work involvement, and early marriage.

2. *Fight.* The child who fights is viewed as aggressive and a behavior problem.

3. *The Perfect Child.* This child never does anything wrong and never bothers anyone. These authors see the child who adopts this role as being presented as a model child, a child who is frequently forgotten and emotionally starved.

4. *The Super-coper.* This is an active child who does everything right but usually for others. This child strives to be better in order to make the family better.

Ford (1980) labels these four patterns as *Get Out, Act Out, Left Out,* and *Help Out,* respectively.

In adulthood, Black (1979) perceives the primary problem facing children of alcoholics as maintenance of intimate relationships. She also sees them as suffering from depression, loneliness, and lack of meaningfulness. A more recent study by Jarmas and Kazak (1992) seems to confirm that paternal alcoholism has a long-term impact on children of alcoholics. Jarmas and Kazak found that children of alcoholic families are more depressed and tend to use more aggressive defenses. It should be noted that Black, Booz-Allen and Hamilton, and others in the field never see these children as competent. They seem to see all children from alcoholic homes as vulnerable. This is a consistent description given by most of the writers in the clinical literature.

One of the reasons that children of alcoholics are seen as vulnerable is that most of the research and clinical writing until recently has focused on clinical populations, that is, those children so severely disturbed by being in an alcoholic family that they have sought help. These types of samples represent only a portion of those people who have been reared in alcoholic families. It is possible (and probable) that children reared in alcoholic homes can have quite different lifetime reactions; some show disruption and pathology, and others show no obvious effects.

West and Prinz raise these issues in a 1987 review of alcohol abuse's impact on psychopathology in children. They note, "Neither all nor a major portion of the children from alcoholic homes are inevitably doomed to psychological disorders. . . . That childhood psychological disorder was not pervasive underscores the need to study individual differences in this population of children and to uncover specific factors that lead to positive outcome" (pp. 214–215).

One of the problems with connecting alcoholism in the family to immediate and long-range outcomes is that there are usually several factors in alcoholic families that would cause risk to children. Alcoholic families have higher divorce rates, more family conflict, more parental psychopathology, the obvious substance abuse, more crime by parents, increased poverty or other economic threats, physical abuse and neglect, and more birth complications (West & Prinz, 1987). Any of these factors may increase the probability that short-term and long-term psychological, social, and physical problems may develop in offspring. Given the multiple risks that children of alcoholic families are exposed to, it would seem probable that, despite West and Prinz's statement, the majority would show psychopathology. However, there have been several studies suggesting it is a minority of children who are affected. At the same time, the possible exposure to multiple stressors may help explain why some children from alcoholic families show psychopathology and others do not. That is, if the child is exposed to divorce, child abuse, poverty, and alcoholism in the family at the same time, that child may be at much higher risk than if only substance abuse is present and there is minimum family instability.

Despite the increased risk, there are indications that some children are "resilient" and show little or no impact from being reared in an alcoholic home. A recent study by Werner (1986) followed forty-nine children from alcoholic homes across several points in their lives (1, 2, 10, and 18 years of age). The subjects were born on the island of Kauai, Hawaii, in 1955 and had alcoholic parents. This research is important because it allows a longitudinal look at the children at various stages of development. These types of studies of children of alcoholics are almost nonexistent.

Werner found that males and the offspring of alcoholic mothers had higher rates of psychosocial problems in childhood and adolescence than did females and children of alcoholic fathers. The majority of Werner's children of alcoholics were reared in poverty (75 percent) and received little emotional support from their families in early and middle childhood (78 percent). For the majority of children, there was little educational stimulation in the home (65 percent). Around two-thirds of the children had contact with the department of social services during their childhood. One of the findings was that the proportion of children of alcoholics who had psychological problems and who used social services in this rural Hawaiian island was "remarkably similar" (Werner, 1986, p.36) to those found in a study of an African-American population in California (Miller & Jang, 1977) and of Caucasian teenagers in Stockholm, Sweden (Rydelius, 1981).

It should be noted that the risk for developing serious learning and behavior problems was considerable for children of alcoholics as opposed to a comparison group from nonalcoholic families. Despite this finding of increased pathology, 59 percent of the children in Werner's study did not show psychosocial problems at age 18. As Werner notes, "As far as we could tell from our interviews with them and from their records in the community, this 'resilient' group managed to do well in school, at work, and in their social life, and had realistic goals and expectations for the future. They 'worked well, played well, loved well, and expected well'" (1986, p.36).

An understanding of how these "resilient" children differ from those children from alcoholic homes who develop psychosocial problems may help bring about a better understanding of how to intervene and to prevent long-term problems in children of alcoholics. Werner found that the difficulties correlated with parents' alcoholism could be lessened if the children had the following:

1. A temperament that leads to positive attention from primary care-takers such as the parents.
2. At least average intelligence and solid communication skills in reading and writing.
3. An achievement-oriented attitude.
4. A responsible, caring attitude toward people.
5. A positive self-concept.
6. An internal locus of control, that is a sense that one is in command of one's life and that one is able to change things.
7. A belief in self-help, that is, a strong belief that one should help oneself, and get things done on one's own initiative.

These seven factors were not simple and direct. The caretaking environment also affected whether or not these resilient children could avoid the negative psychosocial effects of alcohol abuse by their parents. According to Werner,

> ... to the extent that the boys and girls in this study were able to elicit predominantly positive responses from their caregiving environment, they were found to be stress-resistant despite parental alcoholism and chronic poverty. But to the extent that they elicited negative responses from their caregivers (especially if the mother or both parents were problem drinkers, and there were no substitute parents), they were found to be vulnerable. Thus, it was not solely the risk of parental alcoholism, but the balance between that risk factor, the accumulation of stressful life events and protective factors within the child and his caregiving environment that accounted for the range of adaptive outcomes observed among the offspring of alcoholics in this study. (1986, p.39)

These results suggest that it is possible to buffer children of alcoholics against the long-term effects of alcohol abuse. However, for a significant portion of children of alcoholics, there are long-term effects that mar their lives in significant ways. Perhaps the most damaging effect is in interpersonal relationships and the sense of self-worth. Adult children of alcoholics frequently show extreme difficulty in sharing themselves in intimate ways with other people.

Several writers, for example Black (1981) and Wegscheider (1981), suggest that living in an alcoholic family forces children to not feel, to not trust, and to not talk about what goes on in the family. It is almost as if the alcoholic family is walking on egg shells, and the children in particular fear that their actions will set off the unpredictable action of drinking by the alcoholic parent. To avoid such upsets, children try to close down on their own needs and emotions and do not talk about the drinking parent's behavior, either inside or outside the home. Since the family is the context in which children usually learn to express their feelings, to love and express affection, and to trust and to share intimate aspects of their lives, it is understandable that many adult children of alcoholics have significant problems with psychosocial adjustment. Some of these problems lead to bizarre self-perceptions and actions by adult children.

In a therapy group for children of alcoholics, a college female was asked about her dating. The young woman, a college junior, had not had a date since high school and gave as her reason that all the men she dated turned out to be "jerks." Her last boyfriend had been a serious drug addict. However, as the group proceeded, it became apparent that it was the young woman's sense of self-worth and low self-esteem that made her feel she could date only the "dregs of mankind." While this could be seen as an isolated example, it is not. Many females in these groups (even those who have good relationships with males) have doubted their self-worth. Most say something like, "He's only dating me because he feels sorry for me" or "As soon as he finds out who I really am, he'll drop me."

In males, there have been continuing problems with the expression of anger. (It should be noted that expression of anger and other emotions are difficult for both sexes. It is the expression of feelings per se that seems to be generally affected.) One dramatic incident, which occurred in group therapy with adult children of alcoholics, serves as an example. A male undergraduate student suddenly got in touch with the anger he felt toward his father. One minute he was talking casually, the next he was in an enraged posture with loud voice, protruding blood vessels, and an aggressive clenching of his fists. This set the group back on its heels. Unfortunately, despite attempts by the leader to reinforce and support the expression of these feelings, the member was never able to talk emotionally about his anger again. It had simply been too much for him to face and it broke through too suddenly and probably too early for him to deal with it.

In another, more successful case, a young mother began to see the connections between her own marriage to an alcoholic and her own experience as the child of an alcoholic. Her husband physically abused her. With the support of the group, she was able to move out of the home temporarily and to a shelter for abused women and children. She made her return and the continuation of the marriage contingent on the husband dealing with his drinking. She also began a phone call arrangement with her brother who lived in another state, so they could talk about the things that had occurred in their family when they were growing up. Both siblings were amazed, in retrospect, that they had never talked in any way about the things that occurred in the family as a result of their alcoholic parent's drinking episodes.

These two cases indicate the degree to which family alcoholism can have long-term effects on some children of alcoholics. This phenomenon is real and emotionally narrowing for many adult children of alcoholics. However, support and therapy groups for this population can be of considerable help for those people willing to confront their history and their feelings (e.g., Brown, 1992). Unfortunately, some choose to live more emotionally restricted lives because of the threat they feel in dealing with the issues surrounding their psychological past.

On the other hand, the majority of children from alcoholic homes seem to be able to live adaptable, happy, and complete lives. They face the issues of adulthood with the same level of competence as those who have not been reared in alcoholic homes.

Alcohol has a tremendous impact on family functioning. The application of family therapy seems to improve in a small but significant way the long-term outcome of psychotherapy with alcoholics (McCrady, 1989). It may also help reduce the potential long-term effects alcohol abuse has on children, by allowing the family to openly discuss and resolve emotional and social issues surrounding drinking. Certainly, the involvement of the family allows children to change and modify their perceptions of the drinking member so that they do not become unknowing contributors to the initiation of drinking by the affected member. For these reasons, family therapy occupies an important place in the treatment of alcohol problems.

REFERENCES

Bennett, L. A. (1989). Family, alcohol and culture. In M. Galanter (Ed.), *Recent developments in alcoholism: Vol. VII. Treatment Issues* (pp.111–127). New York: Plenum Press.

Bennett, L. A., Wolin, S., Reiss, O., & Teitlebaum, M. A. (1987). Couples at risk for transmission of alcoholism: Protective influences. *Family Process, 26*, 111–129.

Black, C. (1979). Children of alcoholics. *Alcohol, Health and Research World*, Fall, 23–27.

Black, C. (1981). *It will never happen to me.* Denver: M.A.C.

Booz-Allen & Hamilton (1974). *An assessment of the needs of and resources for children of alcoholic parents.* Rockville, MD: National Institute on Alcohol Abuse and Alcoholism.

Brown, S. (1992). *Safe passage: Recovery for adult children of alcoholics.* New York: John Wiley.

Cermak, T. (1986). *Diagnosing and treating co-dependence.* Minneapolis: Johnson Institute Books.

Chafetz, M. E., Blane, H. T., & Hill, M. J. (1971). Children of alcoholics. *Quarterly Journal of Studies on Alcohol, 32*, 687–698.

Dulfano, C. (1985). Family therapy of alcoholism. In S. Zimberg, J. Wallace, & S. B. Blume (Eds.), *Practical approaches to alcoholism psychotherapy* (2nd ed.) (pp. 131–152). New York: Plenum Press.

Ewing, J. A., & Fox, R. E. (1968). Family therapy of alcoholism. In J. H. Masserman (Ed.), *Current psychiatric therapies, Vol. VIII* (pp.86–91). New York: Grune & Stratton.

Ewing, J. A., Long, V., & Wenzil, G. G. (1961). Concurrent group psychotherapy of alcoholics and their wives. *International Journal of Group Psychotherapy, 11,* 329–338.

Ford, W. E. (1980). Unpublished Nebraska Division on Alcoholism grant proposal. Lincoln, NE: Department of Public Institutions.

Gliedman, L. H. (1957). Concurrent and combined group treatment of chronic alcoholics and their wives. *International Journal of Group Psychotherapy, 7,* 414–424.

Gliedman, L. H., Nash, H. T., & Webb, W. L. (1956). Group psychotherapy of male alcoholics and their wives. *Diseases of the Nervous System, 17,* 90–93.

Gliedman, L. H., Rosenthal, D., Frank, J. D., & Nash, H. T. (1956). Group therapy of alcoholics with concurrent group meetings of their wives. *Quarterly Journal of Studies on Alcohol, 17,* 655–670.

Jackson, J. K. (1954). The adjustment of the family to the crisis of alcoholism. *Quarterly Journal of Studies on Alcohol, 15,* 562–586.

Jacob, T. (1987). Alcoholism: A family interaction perspective. In P. C. Rivers (Ed.), *Alcohol and addictive behavior: Vol. 34. Nebraska Symposium on Motivation* (pp. 159–206). Lincoln: University of Nebraska Press.

Jarmas, A. L. & Kazak, A. E. (1992). Young adult children of alcoholic fathers: Depressive experience, coping styles and family systems. *Journal of Consulting and Clinical Psychology, 60,* 244–251.

Kaufman, E. (1985). Family therapy in the treatment of alcoholism. In T. E. Bratter & G. G. Forrest (Eds.), *Alcoholism and substance abuse: Strategies for clinical intervention* (pp. 376–397). New York: Free Press.

Lund, C. A., & Landesman-Dwyer, S. (1979). Predelinquent and disturbed adolescents: The role of parental alcoholism. In M. Galanter (Ed.), *Alcoholism: Biomedical issues and clinical effects of alcoholism.* (pp. 339–348) New York: Grune & Stratton.

McCrady, B. S. (1989). The outcome of family-involved alcoholism treatment. In M. Galanter (Ed.), *Recent developments in alcoholism: Vol. VII. Treatment issues* (pp. 165–181). New York: Plenum Press.

McKenna, T., & Pickens, R. (1981). Alcoholic children of alcoholics. *Journal of Studies on Alcohol, 42,* 1021–1029.

Meeks, D. E., & Kelly, C. (1970). Family therapy with the families of recovering alcoholics. *Quarterly Journal of Studies on Alcohol, 31,* 399–413.

Miller, D., & Jang, M. (1977). Children of alcoholics: A 20-year-long longitudinal study. *Social Work Research Abstracts, 13,* 23–29.

Nardi, P. M. (1981). Children of alcoholics: A role-theoretical perspective. *Journal of Social Psychology, 115,* 237–245.

Rodgerson, M. (1974). Alcoholism and the family. Unpublished manuscript, University of Nebraska, Department of Psychology, Lincoln.

Rydelius, P. A. (1981). Children of alcoholic fathers: Their social adjustments and their health status over 20 years. *Acta Psychiatrica Scandinavica, Supplement No. 286,* 1–89.

Satir, V. M. (1967). *Conjoint family therapy.* Palo Alto, CA: Science and Behavior Books.

Seixas, J. S. & Youcha, G. (1985). *Children of alcoholism: A survivor's manual.* New York: Harper & Row.

Steinglass, P. (1976). Experimenting with family treatment approaches to alcoholism, 1950–1975: A review. *Family Processes, 15,* 97–123.

Steinglass, P. (1977). Family therapy in alcoholism. In B. Kissin & H. Begleiter (Eds.), *The biology of alcoholism Vol. 5. Treatment and rehabilitation of the chronic alcoholic* (pp. 259–299). New York: Plenum Press.

Steinglass, P., Davis, S., & Berenson, O. (1975). In-hospital treatment of alcoholic couples. Paper presented at the American Psychiatric Association Annual Meeting, May.

Wegscheider, S. (1981). *Another chance: Hope and health for the alcoholic family.* Palo Alto, CA: Science and Behavior Books.

Werner, E. (1986). Resilient offspring of alcoholics: A longitudinal study from birth to age 18. *Journal of Studies on Alcohol, 47,* 34–40.

West, M. D., & Prinz, R. J. (1987). Parental alcoholism and childhood psychopathology. *Psychological Bulletin, 102,* 204–218.

Whalen, T. (1953). Wives of alcoholics: Four types observed in a family agency. *Quarterly Journal of Studies on Alcohol, 14,* 632–641.

Wolin, S. & Bennett, L. A., (1984). Family rituals. *Family Process, 23,* 401–420.

Wolin, S., Bennett, L. A., Noonan, D., & Teitlebaum, M. (1980). Disrupted family rituals: A factor in the inter-generational transmission of alcoholism. *Journal of Studies on Alcohol, 41,* 199–214.

Group Therapy

_____ *chapter 11*

Group therapy is a procedure that has been employed with a wide range of clients and problems. In the past, it has often been perceived as simply a way to increase the number of people a therapist could treat at one time. However, as experience with group therapy has accumulated, it has been increasingly recognized as qualitatively different from individual therapy. The differences flow from the additional opportunities and potentially curative forces that operate in a group context. In group therapy each member is exposed to the multiple perceptions and suggestions of all the group members. The potential solutions to a group member's stated problem are limited only by the resources of all the group members. A second advantage of group therapy is that the therapist can observe each member's interaction patterns in the group. Inappropriate and maladaptive patterns of interaction can be challenged by the group leader or other group members. The group also provides the opportunity for group members to model appropriate behaviors and solutions for other members. Finally, the group provides a forum for members to try new ways of handling issues in their lives.

Group solidarity is an important part of the effectiveness of groups. The closeness and cohesiveness of group members encourage both acceptance and honest confrontation. This increases the social facilitation of new ways of dealing with problems and the social prohibition of old, ineffective, and destructive ways of dealing with personal concerns.

There are a large number of approaches and procedures developed for group rehabilitation and group therapy. A general requirement in many group therapy situations is that there be homogeneity, that is, people with a common difficulty or goal. This is especially true for alcoholics. Group homogeneity refers to the sharing of a common problem. Members of alcohol groups are just as heterogeneous as other types of treatment groups in terms of personality, social, and intellectual factors. This is important to remember in group treatment of alcoholics, because often the common problem can overshadow the individual differences that need to be dealt with in the group. It is possible to spend too much time dealing with alcoholism and too little time dealing with the specific problems of the group members, which might involve the inability to relate to people, to deal with emotions, or to solve problems.

The size of the group becomes a critical factor when the group's purpose involves the intense emotional interaction of patients with each other. In these types of groups, most therapists seem to prefer between seven and ten members. Having more than ten members often makes it difficult for all patients to participate. Some authors have noted that the opportunity for equal participation is especially important when working with alcoholics because they often enter the group with deep feelings of rejection, and such feelings should not be reinforced by the treatment process. Larger groups (fifteen to thirty people) can be utilized in didactic groups and in psychodrama, both of which will be discussed later in this chapter.

For the person working with alcohol abusers, a large number of group techniques have potential utility. These approaches reflect different premises and theories. For the purpose of this discussion, it is important to keep in mind several general characteristics present in many alcohol abusers. These include:

1. Denial and Misattribution.   Alcoholics frequently deny that they have a problem with alcohol or that their drinking is causing any difficulty in their lives. They frequently attribute the drinking to other causes, for example, problems at work or home. It is difficult to get alcohol clients to confront their problem. A group format is potentially very powerful in that process.

2. Emotional Constriction.   Alcoholics show a great deal of emotion while drinking, but often they find it difficult to express their feelings when sober. The group allows an opportunity, in a supportive situation with people who have a similar problem, for alcohol abusers to begin to get in touch with their feelings. It is also helpful when others in the group share their feelings and model appropriate ways of dealing with strong emotion.

3. Need to Learn New Skills.   Alcohol abusers have come to rely on alcohol to "solve" many of the problems in their lives. By interacting with others in the group and confronting real problems, alcohol abusers can learn new ways of coping with everyday problems, particularly those that involve social interaction.

4. Social Isolation. One of the things that occurs as a result of obsessive drinking is that persons become isolated and alienated from other people. Group therapy provides experience with personal interaction.

Each group format addresses some of the above problems with which alcohol abusers must learn to cope. Several group modalities are useful with alcohol abusers. Each of these modalities will be summarized in the description of each group procedure, and each of the following, when applicable, will be covered: (1) how the group is set up and how it is conducted; (2) what theoretical thinking underlies the technique being used and how that thinking guides what happens in the group; (3) what opportunities or forces occur or operate in the group procedure; (4) what the characteristics are of the problems and issues focused on in the group modality.

Initially, the discussion of group procedures is arranged in a sequence that reflects increasing emotional and personal involvement by the client. In the first part of the chapter, the following group procedures are reviewed: didactic or teaching groups; the interpersonal transaction group; transactional theory; psychodrama; and experiential therapy. In the latter part of the chapter, Yalom's interactional approach and a group therapy case study based on this model is discussed in more depth. This discussion is followed by Blume's excellent exposition of the importance of group therapy in the treatment of alcoholism. The chapter closes with a review of clinical and empirical research.

DIDACTIC GROUPS

Didactic or teaching groups are a form of educational group therapy whose function is to help patients acquire the knowledge needed to maintain or to improve their physical and mental health. In the case of alcoholics, this often means that they must learn three things: (1) that something is wrong with their way of life; (2) what this something is; and (3) how they can change it. The didactic group can serve a variety of purposes for alcoholics. It can acquaint them with the management of the disorder, including social and vocational problems. It can orient them to community facilities and agencies available for helping them change. Such a group can also orient members to the roles of the patient, the caretaker (therapist), and the treatment process.

An advantage of didactic therapy groups is that they can enroll patients with alcohol-related problems, including spouses and children, as students rather than as patients. In many cases, such an arrangement is significantly less threatening to the individual's self-esteem. Group treatment can be orga-

A typical didactic group in an alcohol treatment center. *(Photograph courtesy of The Independence Center, Lincoln, Nebraska.)*

nized as a lecture course with active student participation in the discussions, the question-and-answer periods, and the determination of what is to be covered in the "course." Various writers have suggested that such a course might include the following topics: the role of personal and social factors in the etiology of alcoholism; how to recognize danger signals of alcoholism and what to do about them; healthy and unhealthy personality development; and concepts about what is "normal." In addition, the purpose, the method, and the rules of various treatment and service agencies can be clarified.

In didactic group therapy, it is important to include ample time for question-and-answer periods that are guided along psychotherapeutic principles. A common method is to have a seminar-type class with a lecture serving as a stimulus and a moderator for the discussion.

Marsh (1935) pioneered work with group programs that are still thought to have useful applications. He suggests a light touch and pleasant atmosphere in didactic groups and considers the development of peer support and control a useful device. He indicates that the group leader might assign each student the task of aiding or befriending a classmate. Some students might have a very serious and acute alcoholic problem and, in helping a fellow student, they might be inspired to make an effort they might not otherwise make.

Marsh recommends certain exercises in the group technique such as group discussions centered around specific topics. Some examples of discussion topics include: "my earliest memories"; "ingredients of my inferiority complex"; "things I am afraid of"; and "my social assets and liabilities." Marsh notes that allowing alcoholics to share the secret recesses of their hearts gives them an opportunity to realize that they are not as sinful, as morbid, or as abnormal as they had imagined. On the contrary, they will probably find that they are quite like everyone else.

In the treatment of alcoholics, it is often forgotten that many techniques have a long history and that many of the principles laid out by Marsh in 1935 are still being used. For example, "my assets and liabilities" is a task still used by one large treatment system in the Midwest. Each patient is asked to write out a list of assets and liabilities, and then other members of the group also make a list for the patient. The patient then must take all of the lists and consolidate them into a list of personal assets and liabilities. It is perhaps not surprising to find that today's patients have the most difficulty accepting the positive sides of themselves. One wonders if Marsh's patients might have had similar problems dealing with the positive parts of their lives.

Other devices used and recommended by Marsh include tap, folk, or social dancing; informal dramatic groups; and homework, such as patients outlining their job history, love-life history, or mood history. The homework device is meant to give the patients a chance to think through just what has happened to them in relatively nonemotionally laden terms. Again, these attempts by Marsh are consistent with many of the social interaction events currently scheduled in alcohol treatment centers. For example, one alcohol treatment program finds the use of volleyball games to be helpful in understanding just how much the patients have grown during treatment. In another program, dances and mixers are held frequently, so that the patients can begin to practice how to be social without the use of alcohol.

Marsh's approach is quite simple and represents a way of dealing with those who are psychologically unsophisticated, as alcoholics from deprived circumstances are likely to be. A program such as this can initiate treatment and, for those students who have an aptitude for more demanding types of psychotherapy, can lead to deeper involvement in personality reconstruction. For many individuals with alcohol-related problems, a course in didactic group therapy along Marsh's lines will provide them with much-needed temporary support. In some cases, this might be sufficient to allow them to regroup their forces and consequently improve.

Other means of stimulating group discussion and self-assessment in didactic groups have been developed since Marsh's day. These include special films dealing with specific problems of alcoholism or with other problems in living. Schilder (1938) has suggested some basic problems for group discussion, such as aggressiveness and submissiveness, which will quickly lead into areas of concern and conflict. He notes that the direction and freedom of discussion will depend on where the group leader wishes to place the emphasis. It is interesting to note that these old reports on group psychotherapy focus on many of the same issues that are the center of focus in current didactic group therapy.

A slightly different type of didactic group has been used in the more recent work done by Pipher and Rivers (1975). They utilized this basic approach in teaching a course on alcohol and the police to police officers. Following each formal lecture, the students were divided into small groups in which they discussed their personal feelings and attitudes about alcohol and its related problems. For example, police were asked to share their feelings when confronted with a belligerent, intoxicated person. These feelings were discussed and possible alternative ways of conceptualizing what was occurring were explored. Police officers became aware that their feelings of anger might play a role in how they might respond to a drunken, belligerent person and that this could lead to escalating the potential for a violent encounter. Interestingly, the police officers were aware that some of them had more violent encounters than others in this situation and were able to pinpoint the cause in their reactions to the situation.

A didactic group can be virtually any size without losing much efficiency. Generally, size is not a major consideration so long as the group is fairly homogeneous. This type of group can be the beginning of an important part of therapy interaction between people; it becomes more of an interaction group if members are encouraged to answer each other's questions. When the group becomes divided on certain issues and when personality issues enter in, the emergence of feeling occurs.

INTERPERSONAL TRANSACTION GROUP
AND ROTATING DYADS

Landfield and Rivers (1975) and Rivers and Landfield (1985) hypothesize that the alcoholic has major difficulties in social interaction. They state that alcoholics feel alienated from others and that their alienation may precede their alcoholism. Furthermore, alcoholism may be viewed as a way of bridging social barriers or a way of avoiding more profound social interaction.

These researchers utilized Kelly's (1955) personal construct theory as the context within which to develop their ideas about the alcoholic. They noted that persons with alcohol problems may find it difficult to understand the thoughts, feelings, and actions of other people, in addition to being uncertain about their own. Landfield and Rivers further observed that alcoholics seem to have particular difficulty in social decision-making. They either find it difficult to make social choices or, if they make social choices, they find it difficult to follow through on them.

With these ideas about the major difficulties faced by the alcoholic as a background, Landfield and Rivers developed and utilized the interpersonal transaction group and rotating dyads group treatment technique with alcoholics. A primary purpose of the interpersonal transaction group was to provide a context within which to study the development of interpersonal understanding among unacquainted persons. A secondary purpose was to provide constructive experiences in which group participants might learn more about themselves, others, and their interrelationships.

Landfield and Rivers conducted their research and treatment program with individuals who were on court probation as a result of driving while intoxicated. The group members interacted in dyads and rotated from one dyad to another until each individual had interacted with all members of the group. The order of dyadic interaction was predetermined, and each interaction lasted from 6 to 8 minutes. At the beginning of each group session, the members were given simple instructions about what was to be "shared" in the dyadic interaction. In each session, the general nature of the conversations was the same for all dyads, and the emphasis throughout was placed on trying to share and understand one another without being critical. Instructions concerning what the members were to talk about were simple (for example, "Share an important value") so members could feel that they were in control of what was shared.

To help elicit the group members' personal constructs of a highly emotional nature (the way they label their world and what experiences mean to them), group members were asked to write on a piece of paper their first names, statements of how they felt at the moment, and statements of how they did not feel at the moment. They were asked to keep the paper taped to their clothing as they circulated among the group. These mood tags were utilized in the treatment process to help clarify their feelings to the individual members and to communicate those feelings to the other group members. A group leader and the researchers, psychologists Landfield and Rivers, served as participant observers in the group and acted as models, sharing their feelings and experiences with the group as well as carefully listening to the experiences and feelings of others.

These researchers noted that within the typical middle-class alcohol treatment group, there is considerable display of defensive behavior, usually involving intellectualization and denial. One way of overcoming the tendency of alcoholics to avoid issues is to confront the alcoholics and overrun their defenses. A major problem with this method is that when defenses become aroused by confrontation, they become more intense, and individuals may well become more rigid in their defenses, a seemingly losing battle. Additionally, much time and effort is needed before meaningful, personalized responses can be made in psychotherapy.

The interpersonal transaction group allows the circumventing of defensive behavior by keeping threat low and by allowing the group members to progress at their own pace in sharing information about themselves with others. The instructions given to the interpersonal transaction group focus on the sharing and the understanding of feelings, ideas, and values. The emphasis to group members is to not confront, criticize, or punish other members, but rather to share and understand. This overall positive focus is aimed at allowing individuals the freedom to control their interactions, to avoid the necessity of becoming defensive, and to be thoughtful about themselves, others, and their relationships. Landfield and Rivers note that the structuring of group sessions seems to reduce the anxiety that is typically associated with the ambiguity of group therapy. It also seems to maximize group interaction and allow members to find new approaches to social interactions.

TRANSACTIONAL GROUPS

Steiner (1969) has developed his ideas about why alcoholics drink and about methods to treat alcoholics in therapy in his transactional theory. He utilizes the language developed by Berne in his books, *Games People Play* (1964) and *Transactional Analysis in Psychotherapy* (1961). Steiner sees the payoff that a drinker receives from his behavior as being strictly interpersonal and nothing else. He conceptualizes drinking behavior to attain interpersonal rewards into three types of games that alcoholics often play.

The first game is called "drunk and proud of it" and is played by loud and abusive problem drinkers. The payoff these types of drinkers get is that the games force others to show their ineffectiveness as they try to make the drinker stop drinking. Steiner feels that if such persons get into therapy, they are likely to try the game with the therapist or the group and may convince the therapist that their drinking problems are over, only to have a relapse shortly thereafter or even between therapy sessions.

The second game described by Steiner is called "lush." This is the game played by drinkers who need attention or "strokes." The individuals feel deprived of "strokes" under normal conditions but find that they can get a lot of attention when somebody tries to save them from alcohol. Thus, this type of alcoholic is much more likely to volunteer for therapy than is the "drunk and proud of it" player. Therapy for the "lush" involves procuring other sources of "strokes" that are not related to drinking problems.

The third game is called "wino" and is similar to but more extreme than "lush." "Winos" are willing to make themselves very, very sick in order to get "strokes" from rescuers, or even jailers. The fact that they must be so far gone before anybody will help them allows them to say and think very bad things about people, thus justifying their hostility. These are the skid row type alcoholics who feel that they have pulled one over on a judge who sentences them to 30 days of food and shelter.

Steiner reports that he has had a great deal of success using transactional concepts in therapy to point out the games to alcoholics. The difficulty with this approach is that no research has been reported that tests the theory. A number of writers have been critical of Steiner's theory on the basis that he conceives of the disease process as a game and that he seemingly disregards scientific evidence. Critics also charge that he has a nineteenth-century conception of man as an autonomous being with a fully conscious free will.

PSYCHODRAMA

Psychodrama, which is sometimes referred to as role playing or sociodrama, is a therapeutic vehicle developed by J. S. Moreno in 1911. It grew out of his interest in the theater and includes a theory and a battery of techniques to facilitate the change and the growth of human resources. Psychodrama is based on psychoanalytic theory and uses improvisational theater as a method for people to act out troublesome, emotional situations and interpersonal conflicts.

In this form of treatment, individuals are asked to play several roles, and the audience is encouraged to participate. Members of the group serve as actors in each person's psychodrama. Players frequently switch roles within each psychodrama as people attempt to increase empathy and intensify the emotional reality of the scene. One or more persons take the role of themselves in the present, themselves at another time, another person, or an inanimate object. These players enact a hypothetical or real situation in roles they have either chosen or been assigned. The method is viewed as a way of exploring ideas and situations with a goal of helping individuals relive basic conflicts and thereby free them to experiment, at least in fantasy, with more fulfilling and constructive responses to their problems.

Some treatment agents have found psychodrama to be very valuable in treating alcoholic patients because it is such a versatile method. The method can be adapted to accommodate any number of problems, personalities, and situations. Psychodrama has been found to help alcoholic individuals see themselves as others see them and acquire ideas about how to change their reactions to others. The method is said to help alcoholics learn to communicate with others by showing them how to present themselves in such a manner that others will understand what they mean.

Advocates of this method see psychodrama as having many therapeutic benefits for alcoholic patients. By being a participant and an observer and by reliving or fantasizing about important aspects of living, alcoholic behavior can be reconditioned, frustration tolerance can be increased, and immediate, temporary help for specific problems and situations can be provided. Psychodrama is viewed as psychotherapy in action, where individuals dramatize their emotional problems, learn to understand current realities, and develop skills and communications. The method encourages immediate emotional involvement, which is often difficult to obtain in alcoholics who are withdrawn, hostile, isolated, and in need of being reconnected with the social world.

The method is adaptable to almost any type of treatment program. A strong point in favor of psychodrama is that it enables patients to become emotionally involved early in the treatment process. The patients (players) do not need to be highly sophisticated in order to participate fully, and the method can be utilized with patients of any intelligence or from any culture.

Psychodrama has been described as the basis for a spontaneous projection of the inner self. Facing the group as players, alcoholics are able to see themselves as they actually are and not as they verbalize or fantasize themselves to be. Often players experience an immediate assessment of their values and attitudes by seeing themselves played by someone else or by playing someone else and finding out what it is like to be in the other person's shoes. Acting out roles and observing psychodrama can help define the part other people play in the alcoholic's problem. For example, a husband can play his wife and vice versa, and both can immediately see how each views the other.

According to psychoanalytic theory, the alcoholic is a person with deep-seated feelings that must be dealt with. These feelings include dependency, isolation, inadequacy, guilt, repressed sexuality, and hostility. (See Chapter 6 for a detailed discussion of psychoanalytic theory and alcohol problems.) Psychodrama helps the individual recognize these feelings and develop a more spontaneous, less rigid attitude toward living.

Some advocates of this treatment method note that, in some ways, psychodrama may be viewed as a substitute for alcohol. Whereas alcohol may permit inhibited alcoholics to express tender feelings and trust, psychodrama may permit them to do the same thing in a real situation. Here alcoholics can develop the actual and significant feelings of trust, and by expressing their feelings, they can receive warmth and love in return.

Psychodrama in its pure form is utilized in only a limited number of treatment programs because extensive training is required to take on the role of the director. However, role playing at a much less complex level is incorporated into numerous therapy situations and is generally felt to be a worthy tool in working with alcoholics.

EXPERIENTIAL GROUPS

According to experiential theory, alcoholics have compelling needs to rationalize, objectify, and intellectualize; in other words, they are overly rational. Therefore, experiential therapists maintain that it is very important to utilize a nonrational approach with patients. Experiential psychotherapy does not establish rules of conduct and methods. Rather it supplies the setting and the direction for alcoholics to see their "trials" more philosophically and examine them more fully with the help of a therapist's nonrational interpretations.

Certain characteristics are considered necessary in this approach to treatment. The group should interact with emotion; the patients should report their dreams and fantasies, and responses to these dreams and fantasies should be immediate rather than arrived at by a series of analytic thoughts. The foundation of experiential treatment is the equality of the patients and the therapist, the mutuality of their interchange, and their existence together. According to the theory on which this therapy method is based, subjective experiences of group members have the same significance as objective experiences. Periods of nonreason are essential if patients are to change in any meaningful way. Success in the therapy group for alcoholic patients is seen as being dependent on a highly emotional climate and the spontaneous interaction of the group members. According to this approach, as patients experience more of themselves and as they become less objective and more subjective, they strengthen their self-esteem.

Proponents of experiential therapy hold that group psychotherapy is potentially the most effective psychological approach to the treatment of many alcoholics. This is not to say that it is the only treatment method, nor that group therapy alone without the support of other treatment modalities can be relied upon completely. The people who advocate experiential therapy believe that the problems generally found in alcoholics make them poor prospects for individual therapy because they lack motivation for treatment and are often unable to perform evolving relationships with others.

The unique contribution of the therapy group, as compared with individual treatment, is that it allows patients to get together in a supportive atmosphere. Here, their common interests in alcoholism, its treatment, and its prevention are initially handled in a minimally threatening, didactic manner. As the group continues to interact, the therapist takes the task of interpreting the group activity. The initial, single preoccupation of the group with intoxication, drunken escapades, and the control of drinking gradually shifts over time so that members consider themselves more fully and tend to develop more trusting relationships with one another.

Those who adhere to the theoretical framework of experiential therapy note that alcohol addicts have a precarious function in society. In order to maintain themselves, they must become more and more selective in choosing their associates. They must find people who will accept or tolerate their behavior, and they must ignore those who disapprove of them or make demands on them. After a while, even their hand-picked friends may no longer tolerate them. Alcoholics usually wind up with one or two drinking buddies who have followed the same course they have. The last contacts alcoholics have had with society have been in the companionship of other alcoholics in situations where there are no expectations. In many cases, even these contacts disappear as individuals become solitary drinkers.

This type of social behavior before treatment further suggests that the group method might serve alcoholics better than individual therapy. Generally, alcoholics have a facade of easy sociability that hides their extreme sense of isolation and not belonging. Treatment agents utilizing experiential therapy state that alcoholics have a limited ability to confide in others but usually are able to tell other alcoholics of their difficulties with drinking. As they confide in others, they identify themselves as alcoholics. When they receive treatment in a group of alcoholic patients, they feel more at home and therefore are much more likely to stay in the group.

This group theory views alcoholics as seeking treatment because they cannot manage their lives by drinking, not because they are troubled human beings. They are seeking a way to better control their lives and to manage their drinking. In treatment, alcoholics initially see the group as a forum in which to expound upon their beliefs about alcoholism and learn the points of view of other alcoholics. The experiential therapist sees the alcoholic's concept of the group, which overemphasizes the fact that everyone in the group is an alcoholic, as a primary illusion that is maintained for some time during treatment. The fact that all members of the group are similarly affected encourages alcoholics to begin to form tentative relationships. This type of homogeneous group supports rather than threatens alcoholics, and members are able to slowly begin to interact with one another.

This brief summary of different approaches to group therapy for alcoholics points out that ideas about what constitutes an appropriate treatment program vary considerably. However, certain components are held in common by a number of them. There is some consensus about alcohol being used by alcoholics as a means to improve social interaction. There is a general concern about the need for resocialization of alcoholics. Although the methods differ, there is much emphasis on minimizing alcoholics' defensiveness by keeping threat at a low level. Learning to relate to others in some meaningful way, especially by interacting with "real" feelings, is also a common focus.

CLINICAL APPLICATION OF GROUP THERAPY WITH ALCOHOLICS: PROCEDURE AND RATIONALE

There are many reasons to use group therapy for all types of human problems. The preceding review of various approaches gives an overview of how group procedures have been used with alcohol problems. Some writers have proposed general and specific reasons for using group therapy with all types of clinical problems and with alcoholics specifically. Yalom (1975) outlines curative factors in group psychotherapy in general, and Blume (1985) looks specifically at what occurs in group therapy for alcoholics. These two approaches provide a view of what factors may operate to help individuals recover using group therapy sessions.

Yalom (the most recent edition of his classic text was published in 1985) is perhaps the most widely quoted current source on the reasons groups are therapeutic. Yalom identifies eleven curative factors in group psychotherapy. These factors (as outlined by Lawson [1984] in terms of alcoholics who might seek group treatment) can be described in terms of the needs of alcoholic clients. The first curative factor is instilling hope. Many chemically dependent people have given up hope for their lives and for recovering from their problems. The group can help reinstill that hope.

Universality, that is, a sense of shared difficulties, is the second curative factor. In group treatment, alcoholics learn that others have many of the same problems they have and have done many of the same things that they feel they are guilty of doing. Finding others with the same or similar problems enables alcoholics to more readily accept and share their problems.

The third factor mentioned by Yalom is the gaining of information. Alcoholics learn a great deal about the problem of alcohol and how to deal with it from group members, that is, from people who have instant credibility because they have the problem themselves.

The fourth curative factor is altruism. Helping another group member is beneficial to the helper. Giving of one's self to help someone builds self-esteem and positive feelings of self-worth. This factor is so powerful that Alcoholics Anonymous earlier incorporated it into their twelfth step.

Yalom's fifth curative factor is a recapitulation of the primary family group. Groups help alcoholics deal with the multiple issues stemming from unresolved problems in families of origin. Many of these problems are due to alcoholics being reared in alcoholic families.

The developing of a socializing technique is the sixth factor. As noted above, many alcoholics and alcohol abusers have failed to learn basic social skills and are lost in their drinking careers. The group allows them the first opportunity for accurate feedback on how they come across interpersonally. In the group, members learn to experience and express accurate empathy with another person. In addition, the group members become more sophisticated in social interaction in general.

Yalom (1975) sees the seventh factor, imitating behavior, as an important therapeutic element. Learning by imitating others, even when the role does not fit, is often very helpful for group members' personal growth.

Interpersonal learning, the eighth factor, refers to learning how to express emotion correctly from the social microcosm of the group. This factor refers to appropriate, socially acceptable ways of expressing emotion to other people.

The ninth factor is group cohesion. Alcoholics' abusive drinking has robbed them of being able to feel as one with a group of people. Group therapy allows a reexperiencing of that oneness.

The tenth factor is catharsis. This is the ability to get in touch with and explore feelings. Alcoholics have frequently lost the ability to ventilate feelings in socially appropriate ways. It is usual for drinkers to either express feelings in explosive and combative ways or fail to express them at all.

The existential factors of group therapy constitute the eleventh curative factor. These could be seen as several additional factors not included in the first ten. Existential factors are summarized by Lawson (1984) as follows:

1. Recognizing that life is at times unfair and unjust.
2. Recognizing that, ultimately, there is no escape from life's pain and from death.
3. Recognizing that no matter how close one gets to other people, one still faces life alone.

4. Facing the basic issues of life and death and thus living life more honestly and being less caught up in trivialities.

5. Learning that one must take ultimate responsibility for the way one lives life, no matter how much guidance and support one gets from others. (p. 130)

An Application of Yalom's Principles to an Alcoholic Group: A Consideration of Some Frequently Occurring Issues and Themes

It is difficult to describe what actually goes on in group psychotherapy in general and particularly in group therapy with alcoholics. However, it is possible to highlight some major themes that seem to occur often in alcohol treatment groups. Vannicelli, Canning, and Griefen (1984), using Yalom's interactional model of group therapy, detail some of these major themes and issues. They also illustrate how these themes and issues relate to group process and group dynamics. The group these authors describe was a long-term outpatient psychotherapy group at McLean Hospital in Boston.

The group was led by two social workers who had experience leading therapy groups but little experience with alcohol groups. Their supervisor was an experienced group therapist who had worked for several years with alcoholics.

There were nine members who composed what Vannicelli et al. called the "core group." These authors' descriptions of group members, in the authors' words, give the reader a feel for both the potential similarities and differences among alcohol treatment group members.

> *Mr. Kidd:* A small town boy transplanted to the city and working as a janitor. . . . Though the least educated and most unsophisticated member of the group, he has a childlike capacity to overlook and even miss the complexity of human relationships, while at the same time sensing the simplest and most essential core.

> *Mrs. Ruby:* A program administrator for [an exclusive] private health-care facility. . . . Her major issue with the group at the conscious level focuses on whether group members and leaders are special enough to be involved with her, but on a deeper level, revolves around her own anxieties about not being worth anything to herself, and her own fears about bringing her vulnerable self to the group.

> *Mr. Wire:* A middle-aged accountant with low tolerance for ambiguity or conflict. . . . Preferring the rigidity and certainty of AA, he is conflicted about group membership, where greater ambiguity and potential for relating to peers in new ways is threatening.

> *Mrs. Givens:* A sensitive, competent young psychiatric nurse recently out of training, who perceives her own needs (as well as the needs of those who

depend on her) as insatiable. Her core struggle [in the group] focuses around her intense wish to give to others to appease their pain and hunger without frustrating her own need to be given to.

Mr. Carbon: A professor of abstract mathematics in a small city college. His relationships are characterized by proper respectful listening in which he pays careful attention to the words that are shared, without grasping the significance. He often misses the point.

Miss Glass: The youngest member of the group. Her relationships with peers (and group members) are always complicated by her conviction that she is "unworthy of love." [While seeking reassurance] . . . there is a pervasive sense that she deserves the worst (which she often brings on herself with her flagrantly self-destructive behavior).

Mr. Binds: A political scientist who specializes in studying economic conflict. A vibrant, energetic man who [is personally and physically attractive, his] struggle centers around his genuine desire and ability to succeed, which conflicts with his need to defeat and thwart the expectations of others. In the group his conflict gets played out around sobriety, his own most critical goal.

Mrs. Coverall: In contrast to other members of the group, who use intellectualization and denial to hold back and to protect themselves, Mrs. Coverall is openly secretive—consciously fearful that what she has to offer is "rotten." She has an opportunity in the group to work on becoming more spontaneous and assertive.

Mr. Lancelot: The voice of rugged individualism. He serves the role model in the group around [the issue of] sobriety. His style in the group is characterized by a concerned, kindly, ever skillful (even charming) avoidance of affect. . . . [He] . . . seems to be acutely aware of interpersonal conflict and painful affect. (pp. 130–132, used with permission)

Inside the group, these members play out a series of themes or issues. They challenge the leaders about their own drinking history. This challenge is viewed by the researchers as a concern about the leaders' motivation and investment in helping the group members with their problems. Some members were afraid that the therapists would be unable to understand and help. Mrs. Ruby's challenge, on the other hand, was based on her anxiety about the leaders being competent enough and "special" enough to help her work through the interpersonal complications that were raised by her tendency to devalue herself. (Another issue not raised by these authors but which may have to be dealt with in alcohol groups is some group members' fears of being looked down on by nonrecovering leaders. This tendency to anticipate the group leaders' rejection is often related to the low self-esteem present in many alcoholics.)

Vannicelli et al. also stress the need for between-session outreach. A member not attending group or making a last minute phone call to cancel may necessitate intervention from the leaders. In this group, Mr. Kidd, after lengthy sobriety and consistent participation, suddenly failed to show up. Group members were anxious about his absence and asked the group leaders to call. When contacted by phone, Mr. Kidd sounded intoxicated, but denied drinking. The leader could do no more than express concern. Her offer to meet with him individually was turned down. However, following the contact, Mr. Kidd sought hospitalization for his drinking problem. The leader's call added weight to his own perception that he needed to seek outside help.

Another issue or theme that often has to be dealt with in alcohol groups is the expectations of those members who belong to other groups, like AA or an educational group. Often group therapy members who belong to outside groups do not expect the intensity and emotionally charged issues that often occur in group therapy. These members see group therapy as unstructured and less "face valid." In the Vannicelli et al. group, Mrs. Ruby was concerned with the "lack of focus compared to AA" (p. 135). She feared group therapy might be worthless and possibly harmful to participants. As she continued to work in the group, the leaders helped her understand that she was using these concerns to avoid increasing involvement with group members and to meet "her wish to return to the safety of a parent/child (teacher/pupil) relationship" (p. 136). She continued in the group and worked through her discomfort.

Mr. Wire was not able to tolerate the group long enough to work through his discomfort. Like Mrs. Ruby, he had come to the group during a long period of abstinence, which he saw as due to his AA involvement. However, he saw himself as needing help with his rigidity and lack of warmth. He was confronted by Mr. Binds (who at the time was struggling to avoid labeling himself as an alcoholic) about being moralistic and self-righteous. Mr. Wire criticized Mr. Binds's failure to abstain and his lack of knowledge about alcoholism. Other group members tried to reduce the conflict by suggesting that one could get some excellent things from both AA and the current group, but it did not satisfy Mr. Wire. He decided to withdraw because the group was in opposition to AA (which of course it was not).

Mrs. Givens belonged to both a family therapy group and the group described here. The family therapy group had a rule that if a member had a slip (used alcohol), that member was immediately dismissed from the group. In the Vannicelli et al. group, there was a rule against drinking; but slips were to be discussed with the group as part of therapy. While abstinence was the group's rule, members allowed the possibility of renegotiation should a slip occur. Thus Mrs. Givens was being given two different messages by the two groups. As the group worked through this difference in expectations, it was pointed out that, in real life, different demands are often placed on individuals by different people. Thus she was capable of adjusting to and living with the differing expectations of the two groups.

Another theme or concern that is special in alcohol groups is the need to maintain confidentiality for the group. Often, because of their involvement in similar activities together outside the group (for example, AA or alumni groups), the members have occasion to be with each other outside of the group. This is not generally typical of other psychotherapy groups. Miss Glass became very close to an AA friend who was also known to members of the group. Things went fine until the friend's husband made sexual advances toward Miss Glass. At first, Miss Glass was reluctant to bring this issue to the group because she wanted to protect her friend. However, she had made a contract to use the group to help her understand why she tended to have problems with close interpersonal relationships. She finally brought the matter to the group. Her ability to trust the group to honor the confidential boundaries was a turning point in her treatment.

Another major issue that must be dealt with, particularly in outpatient groups, is what to do if members drink. Obviously a member who comes to the group drinking should be dismissed for that session. This is the policy for the overwhelming majority of group leaders.

In the Vannicelli et al. group, Mr. Binds drank frequently while he was a member of the group. (Although not explicitly stated, one assumes these drinking events all occurred away from the group.) He rebuffed all attempts by the group to intervene, because he did not want others to control his behavior. The group's attempts at intervention were seen by him as controlling. The group found that he rejected all the things that they had found to be helpful to them in controlling their drinking. He was confronted about this rejection and asked to come up with his own plan for dealing with his drinking, with the group reviewing his plan. This approach helped to bring Mr. Binds's drinking under control and also helped him explore his self-destructive approach toward dealing with authority and control by others.

Mrs. Givens was an example of a patient who agrees with the group rule about abstinence but who continues to fail. The group was at first supportive and sympathetic toward group members who had slips. But gradually, as the group became capable of dealing with conflict between members, Mrs. Givens's statements that she wanted to quit drinking—while she continued to drink—were examined. Mrs. Givens also began to question whether the group might be enabling her to drink through its supportive, gentle attitude. As discussion continued, Mrs. Givens voiced some of her fears about sobriety, particularly, giving up all the caregiving by others that she now obtained by being ill.

With Mrs. Givens, the group moved toward a different level of caring. They established a contract stating that she would be suspended from the group if she drank again. If suspended, she would be allowed to negotiate possible readmission only if she attended thirty AA meetings within 30 days.

Another theme often seen in alcohol groups is members continuing to discuss their drinking problems in order to avoid talking about more conflictual and threatening issues. In the Vannicelli et al. group, an awareness of this issue developed as the group progressed. For example, in Mr. Binds's case, the group said "Let's get your drinking out of the way so we can get on to what we need to talk about" (p. 145).

This description of the Vannicelli et al. group is necessarily incomplete. Many outpatient alcohol treatment groups (and most inpatient group therapy for alcoholics) are much more structured and confrontive than the one described here. Despite the differences in groups, many of the same themes seem to play out as members are asked to confront their drinking and their overall functioning. The Landfield and Rivers Interpersonal Transaction (IT) groups are quite different from the Vannicelli et al. group. But, the themes outlined by Vannicelli et al. were also seen in the IT groups and have been observed in "traditional" alcohol treatment groups.

As a side note, the Vannicelli et al. group would be seen by some alcohol treatment personnel as "soft" and as not showing "tough love." Vannicelli was criticized for her failure to use more severe confrontation in alcohol treatment (see Lawton, 1982). Other therapists believe that "hard" confrontation should be used with extreme care and only with some types of clients (for example, those with strong sociopathic orientations). It should be remembered that getting the alcoholics to confront their drinking and their problems is the real aim of therapy. That is the critical confrontation. People are best able to confront problems when they feel supported and understood—when they get direct, honest, but caring feedback.

The Importance of Group Therapy in Treating Alcoholism—Blume

Blume (1985) specifies why group therapy is seen as important in the treatment of alcohol patients. She points out that regardless of alcoholics' premorbid personalities, through the use of alcohol they have become emotionally isolated. Alcoholics have only superficial or manipulative interpersonal relationships. The therapy group can break through this isolation to encourage emotional closeness and interdependence.

Blume notes that many alcoholics become overly dependent on the therapist. This is less likely to occur in a group setting. Group members may serve as sources to help keep recovering persons from returning to drinking. Blume also feels that experience in group therapy may help recovering alcoholics accept membership in Alcoholics Anonymous. They learn to tell others about themselves and their problems in the group. This skill serves them well when they attend AA.

Another important aspect of group therapy, according to Blume, is that it helps newcomers to therapy accept the label alcoholic. Being an alcoholic is a positive label within the group (nonalcoholics may be labeled "civilians" by group members). Being an alcoholic in the group therapy setting is a positive endorsement. In other settings, it has been a negative label. Through identification in the group, alcoholics are able to form a positive identity.

Group therapy also has the advantage of allowing the therapist to observe the interpersonal behavior of each group member. The therapist can gain some measure of the accuracy of persons' perceptions of their behavior by comparing self-perceptions with actual behavior. Blume's reasons for using group therapy with alcoholics overlap to some extent with Yalom's curative factors and with Lawson's summary. Blume's work stands out in the group therapy field because she presents some concrete ways groups may be helpful to the alcoholic.

Blume outlines general and specific goals for group psychotherapy with alcoholics. The general goals include:

Sobriety. The therapist must take a positive stand towards sobriety. Alcoholics cannot change their attitudes and behavior problems without sobriety. The therapist should be explicit about the need for sobriety and, whenever possible, should weave a discussion of the sobriety issue into group interactions. Asking questions about how persons manage problems when sober and when intoxicated, about how to avoid drinking, and about how to face problems without drinking helps solidify the importance of sobriety.

Overcoming Denial. Blume suggests two types or levels of denial in alcoholics. First, alcoholics deny that there is a drinking problem or they deny the degree of the problem. This type of denial frequently keeps them out of treatment, and it may continue even after entering treatment. The second level of denial is that, while admitting they have a drinking problem, alcoholics deny having problems in any other area of their lives.

Blume sees the two denial levels as something that can be handled in the group. However, the way denial is confronted can vary widely. She specifies direct and indirect confrontation. She states that confrontation is effective "only if the group member is well-integrated into the therapy group and has made a strong and emotional investment in the group process" (1985, p. 79). Even when the emotional commitment has been made, Blume suggests that confrontation not include direct statements such as "You're a liar" or "You're lying." Instead, using the patient's own words from the past, contrasted with what is said at the present, seems to be an effective confrontational style to be utilized by the group leader. Of course, patient members of the group may confront more directly. The group leader must be alert for occasional scapegoating of a group member since direct confrontation by other members can have a long-lasting impact on the person's participation. The danger of a long-lasting impact is a particular risk when the member is new to the group and has not made an emotional commitment.

Using the indirect approach to confrontation takes into consideration the fact that denial is mostly an unconscious defense mechanism to perceived threat. Indirect confrontation allows the therapist to try to understand the reason for the defensiveness and to tailor the therapeutic intervention so that the denial can be dealt with. For example, Blume sees the denial of sexual problems in males as being based in the blow to self-esteem that would occur if they admitted they were impotent. Having other patients who have faced problems with impotence discuss how they dealt with it may help reduce a defensive group member's level of denial about his own impotence. Thus, Blume sees the ability to identify with other group members as the most effective way to deal with denial.

Motivation. Alcoholics come to treatment because they have been pressured to do so. The ideal goal of treatment is to instill self-motivation to live a life without alcohol. Therefore, it is very important for alcoholics to identify with other recovering alcoholics and to link sobriety to high self-esteem. This internal motivation is closely linked to an individual's general emotional state and may go up and down over the span of treatment. When a group member's motivational level seems to be dropping, the group leader needs to be alert for increased depression or other psychological stress. The leader should continue to monitor group members' motivation levels by periodically asking them these questions: "Do you want to stop drinking?" and "Why?" Ideally, motivation should increase throughout members' tenure in the group, and the commitment and desire to stay sober should be the highest when they leave the group.

Recognition and Identification of Feelings. Blume notes, as have others, that feeling states can play a powerful role in initiating and maintaining drinking. Since alcohol and emotional states have so frequently been paired in many alcoholics' histories, the arousal of feelings is often associated with needing a drink. Both negative and positive feelings may lead to this arousal. Negative emotional states bring pain and discomfort. Alcohol is an immediate, although short-term reducer of these feelings. Therefore it is important for alcoholics to become aware of and label their negative feelings. This process helps them learn to discriminate negative feelings from cravings associated with the use of alcohol.

A similar problem exists in regard to positive feelings. Alcoholics have frequently associated positive feelings with the need to celebrate (a drink is always required) or with the drug-induced euphoria that can accompany drinking. Since positive feelings are the result of building increased self-esteem, alcoholics need to learn new discriminations about feelings. The working group is a constant attempt to make them more aware of and more adept at labeling feelings, so they can make more specific discriminations between feeling and shades of feeling. These discriminations are extremely useful in allowing alcoholics to know that feelings need not be associated with craving. This is particularly true for positive feelings.

Recognition and Identification of Behavior Patterns. Alcoholics frequently drink to manipulate their environment and people around them. Alcohol can be used to avoid responsibility for words or actions, to make other people around them angry, or to "even the score" with someone.

These actions can be seen as "alcoholic games" (Steiner, 1969) and must be pointed out and recognized by alcoholics in order for them to develop more appropriate and more adequate behavior. The group can help by pointing out recurring patterns and by asking the person to examine the history of the behavior. In many cases, other more appropriate behaviors may be recommended by the group members or the group leader.

New Ways to Handle Old Problems. Alcohol has become the solution to many of life's problems for alcohol-abusing members. It is vital that they develop new responses to those situations that in the past might have led to drinking. It may be useful for group members to develop slogans (like the "easy does it" and "one day at a time" phrases used by AA members) to help deal with periodic stress.

Development of an Emergency Plan. The group meeting can be a place to develop an emergency plan for persons either anticipating leaving treatment or who simply may be put into tempting situations. What is needed is a plan for just what to do when overwhelming emotional turmoil occurs. This plan can and should be concrete, written down on a card with a list of phone numbers of people who can be called for help.

Enjoying Life without Alcohol. A general goal of all alcohol treatment is to help recovering individuals develop a rich and enjoyable sober life. Group members learn much about how to do this from other members in the group. When pleasures are enumerated by a group member, it is frequently helpful to ask how alcohol would or would not have enhanced the experience described.

Specific Goals and Advantages of Group Therapy

Blume lists several specific goals of group therapy. These include dealing with specific problems and issues that alcoholics may face.

Problems with Responsibility. Although alcoholics frequently behave in a highly irresponsible manner when drinking, when sober they assume a great deal of responsibility for others and for things that go on around them. In fact, they hold themselves responsible for things for which they are not responsible. The group can be very useful to some alcoholics in establishing and reinforcing a clear demarcation of responsibility. Other alcoholics who have been self-centered and selfish may be encouraged to take on more responsibility for others. One of the indirect ways that responsibility is assumed by group members is by being present for every meeting. Attendance in the group is important because each member contributes to the functioning of the group. When a member is absent, the group is less than it can be. Blume emphasizes helping members recognize the limits of their responsibility and also how they may be helpful to others, even when they are unaware of it. Group members can become aware of their helpful behaviors when those behaviors are pointed out and labeled.

Guilt.   Alcoholics often have unrealistic amounts of self-blame. The group can confront unrealistic self-blame (Blume notes that group members may label it "self-pity"). Through examining guilty feelings, the group can help alcoholics differentiate between realistic and unrealistic guilt. When the guilt is perceived as legitimate (that is, based on something the person has done to others), it is generally dealt with by the identification of that person with others in the group. That is, a person who is perceived as having genuine guilt for a past action is usually reassured by the other group members who can relate similar stories of actions they regret. The group leader can then focus on how people have made amends for their actions. This is usually followed by a group discussion about how to deal with amends. These actions by the group and the leader usually reduce guilt and lead to relief in the group member.

Anger.   Anger is a frequent issue and problem for alcoholics. Many alcoholics have difficulty discussing anger. They appear to store it up for an explosive expression while drinking. Some of the tendency to inhibit expression of anger may be based in childhood training that forbade the expression of hostility. The group can help individuals become aware of and attach labels to their anger. A useful technique is to wait until persons feel real anger in the group and then challenge them about that anger. Frequently, this challenge will raise anger levels to a point where it is clear to everyone in the group that the individual is angry. At the same time, the anger will be well beyond what would be expected for that particular occasion. Once the anger is expressed, the member who provoked the anger can apologize. The outcome is a positive response for the targeted person. Also, the expression of anger is applauded and rewarded by the group. After some practice getting angry in the group, individuals can go through periods when they get angry at a number of people outside the group. This reaction usually quickly corrects itself as they learn how to be appropriately angry.

Some people are passive-aggressive in handling their anger. In these situations, they should be encouraged to realize that they have a right to be angry and that they do not have to be liked by everyone else. At the other extreme are those people who have always had trouble controlling their anger. An example is the case of an individual who, while drinking, would seek out people larger than himself and pick a fight. He was rather short and not a powerfully built person, so he almost invariably lost these fights. When he was sober, he was angry but had difficulty expressing it. In therapy, this individual seemed to be helped by encouragement to express anger openly in the group. Assertiveness training also appeared to be a helpful adjunct to therapy for him.

Blume suggests that tracing anger to its original source is a constructive approach. For example, anger toward a significant person in the individual's past (mother, father, wife, husband), which has been held inside, can be expressed and dealt with through role playing. Group members must learn to unload feelings of anger by talking to sympathetic others. Most people use this technique as a matter of course. Alcoholics must learn to refocus their anger on the appropriate person. They must understand that anger felt toward a significant other in their past has been inappropriately directed toward another person.

Depression. Depressed group members will frequently show depression in the group setting by remaining quiet. Here, the therapist must work to draw the persons out so that feelings, including crying and mourning, can be expressed. The therapist can then use the group and its support to help depressed members begin to feel a degree of mastery over their lives. Once depression starts to lift, the therapist encourages depressed members to accept the fact that they have a right to be happy. Often, this approach speeds recovery.

Fear. Drinking for many alcoholics can be a response to fear or to anxiety. The ideal way of learning to deal with fear without using alcohol is by beginning to deal with the fear in small, controlled doses. Discussions and the role playing of feared situations by the group can help. Or another group member might accompany the fearful person to a particularly frightening and threatening situation (for example, an appearance in court). In group, fears are discussed so that those based on false premises can be eliminated. In situations where the source of fear is another person, having the fearful group member reverse roles with the person feared in a role-play situation can be very helpful, according to Blume.

Blume outlines four generalized fears that are often encountered in treating alcoholism. These are fear of closeness, fear of rejection, fear of failure, and fear of success. The group leader should encourage members to openly discuss these fears and help them learn ways to overcome such fears within the group. Learning how to overcome these fears within the group context is useful in developing ways to deal with fears in real life outside of the group.

CLINICAL AND EMPIRICAL RESEARCH ON GROUP PSYCHOTHERAPY

In general, the existing literature supports the use of group psychotherapy with alcoholics. Although much of the literature is anecdotal, it is not uncommon to read statements such as 60 percent to 70 percent of patients treated in group therapy improve while only 20 percent to 40 percent of patients receiving individual treatment improve. In general, group therapy has been lauded as the treatment of choice in most of these anecdotal reports (Kanas, 1982).

There have been several controlled studies on the effectiveness of group psychotherapy with alcoholics. These research-based studies allow comparisons of the effectiveness of group treatment with individual treatment and group therapy in combination with other forms of treatment, such as disulfiram use or occupational therapy. According to Kanas, Ends and Page (1957, 1959) conducted one of the best-controlled studies in this area. These researchers looked at attitude change in hospitalized, alcoholic group members. Patients were given attitude questionnaires before and after entering either group therapy, an occupational therapy group, or a no-group (control) condition. Measures of motivation and attitude toward alcoholism showed significant improvement in the group therapy patients compared with the other two groups.

In another study, McGinnis (1963) added group therapy to some patients' treatment in an AA-oriented inpatient program. Patients assigned to group psychotherapy experienced significant improvement on the Barron Ego Strength Scale when compared with control patients who did not receive group psychotherapy.

Yalom, one of the leading exponents of group psychotherapy, developed a kind of group psychotherapy that emphasizes insight and interactions between patients, focused on the here and now. In one study, Yalom, Bloch, Bond, Zimmerman, and Qualls (1978) compared the effects of this type of group psychotherapy with twenty alcoholic and seventeen neurotic patients who met on a weekly basis. Outcome measures included nine-point rating scales, which evaluated symptom improvement and attainment of therapeutic goals. Yalom and his colleagues found significant improvement in both populations after 8 and 12 months of therapy. However, there were no significant differences in improvement between the alcoholic and neurotic groups.

Yalom utilized eleven curative factors to evaluate the effectiveness of group psychotherapy (see the description given earlier in this chapter for an elaboration of these factors). In one study (1975), he developed five statements to describe each of the eleven curative factors (one curative factor, interpersonal learning, is broken down into input and output categories on this scale, producing twelve categories). These sixty statements were given to twenty psychiatric patients who had completed an average of 16 months of outpatient group therapy. The patients sorted the statements according to how helpful each one was for their group psychotherapy experience. This procedure, of having subjects sort statements into piles according to how much the statements are true for a specific person, is called a Q-Sort. Yalom developed a rank order of curative factors based on the Q-Sorts. This rank

TABLE 11–1 Group Psychotherapy Curative Factors Compared*

Yalom	Rank Order	Feeney and Dranger
Interpersonal input	1	Catharsis
Catharsis	2	Insight
Group Cohesiveness	3	Interpersonal input
Insight	4	Group Cohesiveness
Interpersonal output	5	Installation of Hope
Existential Factors	6	Existential Factors
Universality	7	Interpersonal output
Installation of Hope	8	Universality
Altruism	9	Altruism
Family Reenactment	10	Family Reenactment
Guidance	11	Guidance
Identification	12	Identification

*Yalom's study used twenty psychiatric outpatients measured after approximately sixty-four hourly sessions (once a week for an average of 16 months). Feeney and Dranger's 1976 study used twenty alcoholic inpatients after thirty-four hourly sessions (five a week for an average of forty-nine days).

(Table taken from Kanas, 1982, p. 1015, and used with permission.)

order is presented in Table 11–1. Interpersonal input (feedback from group members or therapists about how individual patients interacted with other group members), catharsis, group cohesiveness (the feeling of being accepted by group members), and insight were ranked as the four most important curative factors.

Feeney and Dranger (1976) gave Yalom's Q-sort to twenty alcoholic patients who participated in a 90-day rehabilitation program. These researchers' findings were similar to those in Yalom's study of psychiatric patients described previously. In both studies, the patients judged the factor of identification with other patients or with the therapist to be least important. Recently, Vannicelli and her colleagues reported clinical case studies at McLean Hospital in Boston. In one case study (Smith & Vannicelli, 1985), the reactions of an alcohol treatment group to the impending termination of a co-leader are described with details of several defensive maneuvers that occurred in the group. At first, the group tried to flee from the upcoming loss of the co-leader. Pseudomature responses and veiled hostility were displayed by group members. These responses were followed by expressions of abandonment and loss. The authors' describe the group leader as initially going along with the group's tendency to deny the loss they were feeling. However, the leader was later able to help facilitate the group working through the loss of the co-leader.

Rugel and Barry (1990) conducted an empirical study with another type of group by using Yalom's model of group therapy combined with Rogerian theory, based on the work of Carl Rogers. The groups were highly structured, "task oriented support groups" (p. 48). A total of twenty-eight participants divided into four outpatient groups were studied. The participants were early- and middle-stage alcoholics who had been arrested for driving while intoxicated. The focus of the research was the delineation of factors that help such clients overcome denial.

The authors note that "in an effort to protect themselves from the loss of self-esteem that would occur with the admission of drinking problems, alcoholics employ denial to split off from awareness anything within themselves that suggests an alcohol problem. The result is that they are unable to confront their drinking difficulties" (p. 46).

Group members were administered a specially constructed Problem Drinking Scale (PDS), which measured drinking behavior prior to their arrest and group involvement. Measures of psychopathology and self-esteem were also obtained. Increasingly higher scores on the PDS (that is, indications of a more severe drinking pattern or a more severe impact on relationships, work, or finances) were viewed as evidence of reduced denial. In addition, following each group meeting, members rated how much they thought the group accepted them and how much they accepted themselves. At the termination of the group, members completed a modified version of Yalom's curative factors scale. Each Yalom item was rated on a five-point scale based on the value of the item for the group member responding.

The researchers found that the scores on the PDS for the group as a whole increased significantly from pretest to posttest. They interpreted this change in scores as reflecting an increased admission of drinking problems and reduced denial. Group acceptance was related to self-acceptance (the more alcoholics accepted themselves the more accepting they saw the group). Increased self-acceptance was related to higher PDS scores, that is, decreased denial of alcohol problems.

Following the group experience, there was also a significant decrease in scores on the scale designed to measure psychopathology. This indicated less pathology. Three of the Yalom categories (process awareness, identification, and input) were positively related to PDS change, that is, when the members' PDS scores were higher, their scores on these Yalom categories were also higher.

Overall, available evidence points to group psychotherapy as a potentially useful therapeutic tool in the treatment of alcohol problems. At this time, the literature contains a limited number of well-controlled studies. One reason for the lack of research in this area is that it is difficult to carry out. Most clinicians are not researchers and clinicians are generally not given support for research. There is a need for clinicians and researchers to design research together to answer questions about how to best use this important treatment modality.

This review should help the reader understand some of the many ways group therapy has been used in the treatment of alcohol problems. This chapter, of course, is not intended to make the reader a master of group therapy techniques. It is presented to give an overview of some of the clinical understandings and interactions that occur in a group setting. It also outlines the reasons why group therapy has some rather powerful dimensions that are not found in individual therapy.

While group therapy may have started as a way to use fewer therapists to treat more patients, it has developed into a powerful treatment technique, particularly in the alcohol field. The group allows multiple viewpoints and solutions to be brought to bear on alcohol problems. Confronting alcoholics' denial systems is more readily accomplished through group treatment. Alcoholics' frequent social isolation can be dealt with by making them feel part of a socially cohesive group. Sharing with people who have similar problems with alcohol abuse allows group members to gain support and acceptance from others while being challenged to face their problem honestly and realistically. Group treatment is so much a part of the alcohol treatment scene in the United States that it would be difficult to find programs that do not employ this important treatment technique.

REFERENCES

Berne, E. (1961). *Transactional analysis in psychotherapy.* New York: Grove Press.

Berne, E. (1964). *Games people play.* New York: Grove Press.

Blume, S. B. (1985). Group psychotherapy in the treatment of alcoholism. In S. Zimberg, J. Wallace, & S. B. Blume (Eds.), *Practical approaches to alcoholism psychotherapy,* (2nd ed.) (pp. 73–86). New York: Plenum Press.

Ends, E. J., & Page, C. W. (1957). A study of three types of group psychotherapy with hospitalized male inebriates. *Quarterly Journal of Studies on Alcohol, 18,* 267–277.

Ends, E. J., & Page, C. W. (1959). Group psychotherapy and concomitant psychological changes. *Psychological Monographs, 73*(10), 1–31.

Feeney, D. J., & Dranger, P. (1976). Alcoholics view group therapy: Process and goals. *Journal of Studies on Alcohol, 38*(5), 611–618.

Kanas, N. (1982). Alcoholism and group psychotherapy. In E. M. Pattison & E. Kaufman (Eds.), *Encyclopedic handbook of alcoholism* (pp. 1011–1021). New York: Gardner Press.

Kelly, G. A. (1955). *The psychology of personal constructs* (Vols. 1–2). New York: Norton.

Landfield, A. W., & Rivers, P. C. (1975). An introduction to interpersonal transaction and rotating dyads. *Psychotherapy: Theory, Research and Practice, 12,* 366–374.

Lawson, G. (1984). Group counseling in the treatment of chemical dependence. In G. Lawson, D. Ellis, & P. C. Rivers, *Essentials of chemical dependency counseling* (pp. 121–146). Rockville, MD: Aspen Systems.

Lawton, M. J. (1982). Group psychotherapy with alcoholics: Special techniques. *Journal of Studies on Alcohol, 43,* 1276–1278.

Marsh, L. C. (1935). Group psychotherapy and the psychiatric clinic. *Journal of Nervous and Mental Disorders, 82,* 381–393.

McGinnis, C. A. (1963). The effect of group psychotherapy on the ego strength scale scores of alcoholic patients. *Journal of Clinical Psychology, 19,* 346–347.

Pipher, J., & Rivers, P. C. (1975). A course on alcohol abuse and alcoholism for police: A descriptive summary. *Journal of Alcohol and Drug Education, 20,* 18–26.

Rivers, P. C., & Landfield, A. W. (1985). Personal construct theory and alcohol dependence. In E. Button (Ed.), *Personal construct theory and mental health* (pp. 169–181). London: Croom Helm.

Rugel, R. P., & Barry, D. (1990). Overcoming denial through the group: A test of acceptance theory. *Small Group Research, 21,* 45–58.

Schilder, P. (1938). *Psychotherapy.* New York: Norton.

Smith, L., & Vannicelli, M. (1985). Co-leader termination in an outpatient alcohol treatment group. *Group, 9,* 49–56.

Steiner, C. M. (1969). The alcoholic game. *Quarterly Journal of Studies on Alcohol, 30,* 920–938.

Vannicelli, M., Canning, D., & Griefen, M. (1984). Group therapy with alcoholics: A group case study. *International Journal of Group Psychotherapy, 34,* 127–147.

Yalom, I. D. (1975). *The theory and practice of group psychotherapy* (2nd ed.). New York: Basic Books.

Yalom, I. D. (1985). *The theory and practice of group psychotherapy* (3rd ed.). New York: Basic Books.

Yalom, I. D., Bloch, S., Bond, G., Zimmerman, E., & Qualls, B. (1978). Alcoholics in interactional group therapy: An outcome study. *Archives of General Psychiatry, 35,* 419–425.

Alcoholics Anonymous

_____ *chapter* 12

The previous chapters on individual, family, and group treatment deal with professionally trained staff offering care to the alcoholic individual. The focus of this chapter is a grass-roots organization in which members use their own recovery from alcoholism to help others deal with their problems. This grass-roots organization's approach is one of the most effective in helping the alcoholic on the road to recovery. Alcoholics Anonymous (or AA) is perhaps the best-known aid in recovery for alcoholics. This group's effectiveness in helping alcoholics to achieve and maintain sobriety has been lauded by many, especially those individuals who are or have been members of the group and who are no longer drinking alcoholic beverages. Some have looked on the group with skepticism or even disdain, but its performance as well as its current activities in large cities, small towns, penal institutions, mental hospitals, and numerous other places commands respect from any individual who has attempted to deal with an alcoholic.

Alcoholics Anonymous is a fellowship of men and women whose primary aim is to help others in their recovery from alcoholism. This organization was founded in 1935 by a physician, Dr. Bob, and a stockbroker, Bill W., both of whom were alcoholics. Both had previous contacts with the Oxford Group Movement, a group dedicated to the redemption of mankind by striving for absolute good, such as purity, love, unselfishness, and honesty.

In his history of AA, Kurtz (1979) describes four founding moments of the organization.

1. The encounter of a wealthy American alcoholic patient named Rowland H. with Carl Jung. After spending a year in treatment with Jung in Zurich, Rowland returned to the United States, only to begin drinking again. When Rowland returned to Zurich for help, Jung suggested that medicine and psychiatry had nothing else to offer him and that he should seek help through a religious conversion experience. Jung thought that this conversion experience might produce a recovery from alcoholism. Rowland joined the Oxford Group Movement, a nondenominational group that attempted to capture the central features of first-century Christianity. *Jung's influence on Rowland to seek a religious conversion experience was the first founding moment.* Rowland had a conversion experience which led him to influence a close friend, nicknamed Ebby, to use the Oxford Group Movement to achieve sobriety, at least temporarily.

2. Ebby called on his friend Bill Wilson in 1934. *Kurtz calls this conversation between Ebby and one of the two founders of AA the second founding moment.* Bill Wilson, later to be called Bill W., was a stockbroker who suffered from alcoholism. At the time of this meeting, Bill W. was drinking at his home in New York City. After being offered a drink, Ebby indicated he did not need a drink because he had religion. (Ironically, Ebby was soon drinking again and several decades later died of his alcoholism, while Bill W. finished his last binge and went on to develop the program and fellowship of AA [Nace, 1987].)

3. Bill W., despite being originally contemptuous of Ebby's sobriety and religion, decided to investigate this possibility to change further. He was admitted to a hospital in New York under the care of Dr. William Silkworth who had treated him previously during his other admissions. During the stay, Bill W. experienced a deepening depression, followed by an ecstatic spiritual experience. After being reassured by Dr. Silkworth that his spiritual experience was not from brain damage, he accepted this as a truly conversionlike experience.

The future cofounder of AA tried to understand this conversion experience and turned to reading William James's *The Varieties of Religious Experience.* This book by James helped him to better understand what had happened to him. He began to see that one alcoholic could carry the message to another, and then the next drinker who became sober could pass it on to another alcoholic, and so on. *The third founding moment was Wilson's conversion experience and his discovery of William James's writing during the fall of 1934.* Wilson's reading of James's book helped him crystallize the spiritual aspects of his own sobriety. His spiritual experience became one of the reasons why AA relies so heavily on spirituality (Chafetz & Demone, 1962).

4. The fourth and final founding moment came in May of 1935. While in Akron, Ohio, on a business trip, Bill W. began to have an urge to drink.

After several telephone calls to members of the Oxford Group Movement asking to talk to another alcoholic (he knew talking to another alcoholic was necessary to keep him sober), Bill W. was introduced to Dr. Bob Smith. Dr. Bob, as he would later be called, was both an alcoholic and a drug addict. Bill W. and Dr. Bob met later. Following that meeting, Dr. Bob attended a medical convention in Atlantic City, New Jersey, where he had his last alcoholic binge. *The date of Dr. Bob's last drink, June 10, 1935, is given by Wilson as the founding date of Alcoholics Anonymous* (Nace, 1987; Trice and Staudenmeier, 1989).

Originally Bill W. relied on his own conversion experience and tried to convince others to seek such an experience. This did not prove to be effective in getting others to choose this approach to maintaining sobriety. It was when Bill W. began to use the "sickness approach" and indicated that physicians saw alcoholism as more life-threatening than cancer that he became more effective in convincing others to try the AA way. Thus it was the shift from "sin to sickness" that enabled him and others to convince alcoholics to consider abandoning alcohol use and seeking sobriety. (Trice and Staudenmeier, 1989).

While this change in approach was useful and effective, the ability of Bill W. to convince others of the success of this approach also played an important role. Trice and Staudenmeier suggest that Bill W. was a charismatic leader and possessed the characteristics appropriate to this role.

At first the movement grew slowly. For example, in 1939, at the time the classic (Big Book) *Alcoholics Anonymous* was first published, there was an estimated 100 members. Several articles on the organization (such as those written for the *Saturday Evening Post*) appeared in the popular press and helped spread the word about Alcoholics Anonymous. These articles attracted public attention and were the beginning of rapid growth of the organization. In 1941, there was an estimated 8,000 members. In 1968, the membership in the United States and Canada was 170,000. In a recent count made in the 1980s, there were 653,000 members in these two North American countries. This growth testifies to the ability of Alcoholics Anonymous to meet the needs of alcohol-addicted men and women (Nace, 1987).

THE BASIC TENETS AND FUNCTIONS OF AA

The organization has been praised for its ability to help people recover from alcoholism. But how does Alcoholics Anonymous work? What is its structure and how does it function? Alcoholics Anonymous is based upon Twelve Steps and Twelve Traditions. These are outlined in Boxes 12–1 and 12–2, respectively. Although there is no official definition of Alcoholics Anonymous, Nace utilizes the AA preamble as at least a partial definition. The preamble has also been endorsed by Bill W. as perhaps the best definition of Alcoholics

Anonymous that exists. This preamble, taken from the *Grapevine,* (the *AA Grapevine,* Inc., New York, NY 10017) is as follows:

> Alcoholics Anonymous is a fellowship of men and women who share their experience, strength, and hope with each other that they may solve their common problem and help others to recover from alcoholism.
>
> The only requirement for membership is the desire to stop drinking. There are no dues or fees to AA membership; we are self-supporting through our own contributions. AA is not allied with any sect, denomination, politics, organization or institution; does not wish to engage in any controversy, neither endorses or opposes any causes. Our primary purpose is to stay sober and help other alcoholics to achieve sobriety (taken from Nace, 1987, p. 237).

The Twelve Steps are used by AA members to achieve recovery. Silcott (1971, cited in Alibrandi, 1982) surveyed AA members to identify what they felt were the most important aspects of the recovery program. A major emphasis was placed on helping others. Also stressed was the importance of the continuous availability of meetings, a high level of AA activity, and being of service. Each of these factors is related to working with people. Surrender, ego deflation, self deflation, identification with other alcoholics, dealing with anger and resentment, and a need to work on impatience, intolerance, resentfulness, and self-pity were also stressed by the survey respondents. All of these factors illustrate the wide range of needs that Alcoholics Anonymous meets for its members (Alibrandi, 1982).

BOX 12–1
The Twelve Steps of Alcoholics Anonymous*

1. We admitted we were powerless over alcohol—that our lives had become unmanageable.
2. Came to believe that a Power greater than ourselves could restore us to sanity.
3. Made a decision to turn our will and our lives over to the care of God *as we understood Him.*
4. Made a searching and fearless moral inventory of ourselves.
5. Admitted to God, to ourselves, and to another human being the exact nature of our wrongs.
6. Were entirely ready to have God remove all these defects of character.
7. Humbly asked Him to remove our shortcomings.

8. Made a list of all persons we had harmed, and became willing to make amends to them all.

9. Made direct amends to such people wherever possible, except when to do so would injure them or others.

10. Continued to take personal inventory and when we were wrong promptly admitted it.

11. Sought through prayer and meditation to improve our conscious contact with God *as we understood Him*, praying only for knowledge of His will for us and the power to carry that out.

12. Having had a spiritual awakening as the result of these steps, we tried to carry this message to alcoholics, and to practice these principles in all our affairs.

BOX 12–2

The Twelve Traditions of Alcoholics Anonymous*

1. Our common welfare should come first; personal recovery depends upon AA unity.

2. For our group purpose there is but one ultimate authority—a loving God as He may express Himself in our group conscience. Our leaders are but trusted servants; they do not govern.

3. The only requirement for AA membership is a desire to stop drinking.

4. Each group should be autonomous except in matters affecting other groups or AA as a whole.

5. Each group has but one primary purpose—to carry its message to the alcoholic who still suffers.

6. An AA group ought never endorse, finance, or lend the AA name to any related facility or outside enterprise, lest problems of money, property, and prestige divert us from our primary purpose.

7. Every AA group ought to be fully self-supporting, declining outside contributions.

8. Alcoholics Anonymous should remain forever nonprofessional, but our service centers may employ special workers.

9. AA, as such, ought never be organized; but we may create service boards or committees directly responsible to those they serve.

10. Alcoholics Anonymous has no opinion on outside issues; hence the AA name ought never be drawn into public controversy.

11. Our public relations policy is based on attraction rather than promotion; we need always maintain personal anonymity at the level of press, radio, and films.

12. Anonymity is the spiritual foundation of all our traditions, ever reminding us to place principles before personalities.

Rudy (1986) has described affiliation with AA in terms of religious conversion. First, there is intense stress (the "hitting bottom" of AA), which finally drives the person to make contact with an AA representative or group. When contact is made, the drinker is warmly welcomed and, at the same time, is implicitly encouraged to accept the label alcoholic ("first stepping"). While the acceptance of the alcoholic label is coercive in treatment programs, the pressure to accept the alcoholic label is more likely to be covert in AA meetings. Once the initial acceptance of being an alcoholic is established, the group exerts pressure on the new member to become ideologically, socially, and behaviorally allied with Alcoholics Anonymous ("making the commitment"). Once committed, the person soon experiences "mortification," which results in the individual becoming subordinate to the group and adopting the ideological tenants of AA ("accepting one's problem"). Some time later, the new member tells the story of how bad things were before joining the group and how good life is now in AA ("telling one's story"). This is a public acknowledgment of one's alcoholic identity. Further identification with the group is accomplished by the individual spreading the message of AA and by working to strengthen the group and its function ("doing twelfth step work") (taken from Emrick, 1989a, p. 6).

Concrete descriptions of what happens at AA meetings have been presented by several writers, including Rodin (1985) and Nace (1987). Essentially, there are two types of meetings. One type of meeting is "open" and may be attended by anyone. The second type of meeting is the "closed" one, which is attended only by recovering alcoholics or by those who have a desire to stop drinking. It should be noted here that because people who are still attempting to quit drinking are in the audience, there can be drinking participants at closed meetings. Open meetings can be quite large, but usually average about forty participants. However, there is a tremendous range. One held in conjunction with an "alcohol school" had over 200 participants. The closed meetings are usually smaller than the open meetings. Either type of meeting can take one of three formats. There is a discussion meeting, which focuses on a particular topic. In some locales, the discussion meeting is the most frequent type of meeting. A step meeting focuses on the meaning and implications of a given step. The third is the speaker's meeting (another frequently occurring format). After the reading of the preamble, there is a 20- to 30-minute talk by a member who relates a personal struggle with alcohol. Following the presentation, comments are invited from the audience. These can take the form of the listeners telling what the presentation has meant to them in terms of dealing with their own personal alcohol problems.

One part of the AA meeting that may have been underplayed in the past is the informal conversations before and after the meeting. A recent study by Waldersee (1987) found that a sample of AA members rated this as one of the most important and helpful parts of the meetings. It affords an opportunity for members to meet other members, to develop and personalize relationships, and to increase their sense of belonging. (For an AA member's description, see Box 12–3.)

BOX 12–3

An AA Member's Perspective

Hi, my name is Lee, and I am an alcoholic and a member of Alcoholics Anonymous. I need to state that the views that I express here are entirely my own and I am not a spokesperson for Alcoholics Anonymous. I hope to share with you my experience, strength, and hope as a member of AA—nothing more, nothing less.

I have been a sober member of AA for over eight years now, and I must say that it has been an exciting adventure the entire time. It has been eight years of joy and fear, of excitement and dread, and—in the past several years—of peace and contentment.

While the only requirement to be a member of Alcoholics Anonymous is the desire to stop drinking, there are, in my opinion, at least twelve requirements one must meet, and continue to meet, to maintain that membership. These are the Twelve Steps of AA. It has been my experience that if I do not attempt to place into practice the principles of Alcoholics Anonymous on a daily basis, my life will almost certainly take a turn for the worse. Ultimately it may lead to the resumption of my drinking and therefore a return to a way of life that I no longer desire.

My drinking was of the daily sort, especially in the last two years of my drinking career. I have experienced blackouts, the shakes, and the desperation the alcoholic feels when he realizes that he can no longer face life with or without alcohol. The latter was the most disturbing aspect of my drinking; it is a terrible dilemma that in some ways can only be appreciated by another alcoholic. This common experience is what binds us together in AA and forms our basis of recovery—one alcoholic working with another.

Within AA I have found it necessary to engage in some actions that many nonalcoholics may find peculiar. I have found I must surrender to the idea that I myself cannot hope to be a sober member of Alcoholics Anonymous without the help of other members. It is a paradox that by surrendering I have actually gained the ability to meet and handle situations that I would have avoided or even run from while I was drinking. It is my understanding that AA is not really about not drinking. If it were, then all I would have had to do was stop drinking and everything would have been all right. I tried that and it did not work! AA helps me to meet life on life's terms. AA is about finding solutions to problems that used to render me useless.

There are many things that I do to meet life on life's terms, all of which I learned in Alcoholics Anonymous. First, I attend AA meetings. In fact, I attend three or four meetings a week. Someone once asked me if I still go to those meetings, and I replied, "Yes, I do." I was sober about four years at that time and my friend wanted to know why I still went if I didn't drink anymore. I told him that was why—I didn't drink anymore and I didn't want to drink again. If I continue to go to meetings and continue to meet life on life's terms then I probably won't drink. Second, I have a sponsor. A sponsor is a member of Alcoholics Anonymous who is sober longer than you and helps you to work through the Twelve Steps of Alcoholics Anonymous. He also suggests ways to meet life on life's terms. I also sponsor several men in AA. That's another paradox of the program—I must give it away to keep it. Third, I try to carry the message of AA, especially to newcomers. I need to work with newcomers since they are closer to their last drink than I am. I can intellectually remember my last drink but I don't really remember it emotionally. By working with newcomers, I can share in the desperation and pain of their last drink and it serves as a powerful

reminder of what it was like before I got to AA. Fourth, I have a relationship with God of my understanding that helps me to remain sober. At
times, this relationship was the only defense I had against that first drink
early in sobriety. That relationship has evolved into one that helps me
meet the problems of today and to be of service to my fellows. Finally,
there are the books and other literature published by AA that I read. It is
funny, because even after eight years of sobriety I still find sentences
and phrases that I never knew were in the "Big Book" of Alcoholics
Anonymous. This only reinforces the belief that I have much more to
learn and do in Alcoholics Anonymous.

   I would not (want) one to be left with the impression that participating in AA is all that I do. Although AA is a way of life for me, I do not
spend every waking hour at meetings or working with newcomers or
any of the other things I have mentioned. My consistent participation in
AA is the first priority in my life. However, because this is the case, I am
also able to fully participate in all other areas of my life. I am able to be
a good father and husband, a productive citizen of my community, a
good son and son-in-law, and to be of service to others. It is because of
my commitment to the way of life I have learned in AA that I am able to
be all these things. None of this was possible before I got to AA and I
am convinced that AA is responsible for these things. For that I am forever grateful and have the responsibility of ensuring that the hand of AA
is there when anyone, anywhere reaches out for it.

These meetings and discussions can sometimes appear to be quite
mundane to the casual observer. For one thing, there is a considerable repetition of stock phrases that seem to have a special and important meaning for
recovering alcoholics. "Let go and let God" and "one day at a time" are
examples of these phrases. "Drinkalogues," the anecdotal stories told by
recovering alcoholics which describe their history with alcohol, are frequently told over and over in groups in detail. Despite their frequent retelling,
they seem to be very important to recovering alcoholics and seem to play a
central role in their continued sobriety. These stories also seem to inspire
new thoughts in listening alcoholics, so that despite the repetition, group
members pay considerable attention to these oft-repeated stories, even
though they have heard them several times.

   The reasons that Alcoholics Anonymous is effective have been frequently debated. One of the earlier professional accounts concerning why
AA was successful was given by Chafetz and Demone (1962). These writers
interpret AA ideology from a psychoanalytic perspective. They feel that
AA's effectiveness is due to several social and psychological mechanisms
including:

1. Alcoholics Anonymous groups focus on the symptom rather than the underlying cause of alcoholism (that is, there is no deep personality analysis, just a focus on the concrete problems that face the alcoholic). There is a rewarding maternal reunion symbol produced by doing for other alcoholics (that is, help other alcoholics get and stay sober) and by emphasizing spiritual conversion. This symbol is much like that formerly played by alcohol in the alcoholic's life.

2. AA groups also focus on the mechanism of compulsion. These writers see AA members as having a compulsive attachment to the group's way of life. They attend meetings several times a week and are fervent advocates of the AA way to recover from alcohol abuse. Chafetz and Demone see AA as utilizing the compulsive behavior formerly used in drinking to help maintain sobriety.

3. AA shows the way back to middle-class life. Chafetz and Demone see the essence of AA as being derived from the "Protestant ethic": emotion control, cleanliness, strength, and godliness. Drinking violates this ethic since it symbolizes failure and a basic weakness in alcohol abusers. Alcoholics must continue to drink to avoid confronting the culturally defined puritan image. However, Alcoholics Anonymous offers redemption by allowing drinkers to admit their feelings and turn their lives over to God for His higher power.

4. There is a sect or cultlike aspect to AA. Chafetz and Demone see cult or sect aspects present in AA in terms of history, structure, and even the charisma of the leader, Bill W. The Big Book (*Alcoholics Anonymous*) can be seen as a bible for this group (and it is sometimes referred to as that by AA members). Chafetz and Demone go on to draw several other parallels with Judeo-Christian religion. The New Testament is the Twelve Steps and the Twelve Traditions, and Bill W. is the group's Jehovah. While voicing hesitations about dealing with a theological perspective, these writers do see the spiritual aspects as a central theme of the organization. They see AA as using a combination of the sociological, the psychological, and the spiritual to deal with a psychological problem. The God of AA is a personal one who will give help. There is a very emotional relationship with the "Higher Power" of AA, and this seems to meet the needs of the group's members (Chafetz & Demone, 1962).

Other writers have pointed to similar and additional reasons that AA is so effective with its members. Most of these writers note the program's implicit psychological factors that are helpful to its members. Alibrandi (1985) characterizes this group of factors as "the folk psychotherapy of Alcoholics Anonymous," for example. She emphasizes the role of sponsors, who are members who have been sober for a period of time and who become advocates for new arrivals. To be a sponsor, the person must have been sober for some time and have done Twelve-Step work. Making a Twelve-Step call to explain the program of AA can be considered the beginning of becoming a sponsor. They explain the program as they understand it and tell of their own experiences with alcohol. Sponsors then try to help newcomers over the rough spots by answering questions, helping them get to meetings, and introducing them to the other group members. While sponsors take an interest in the progress of new members, they are not supposed to take responsibility for the newcomers. The responsibility for recovery is placed on the new member, which frees sponsors to enjoy and observe the new sobriety of the protégé and to be reminded of their own recoveries (Alibrandi, 1985).

Sponsors develop close ties with their new member. This can last for a brief time or for a lifetime, according to the dependency needs of the new members. The central role of sponsors is to teach newly recovering persons how to stay sober and how to rely on themselves to maintain sobriety. While sponsors may not know the details of how to stay sober, they do know what should be avoided—alcohol.

It is important for newcomers to become actively involved in the recovery process. They must take ultimate responsibility for their own recovery; AA is only a tool to be used in helping maintain that sobriety. They learn that they have been invited to share not only in their own recovery but in that of others as well, and they find that it is difficult to "con" their fellow alcoholics in their discussions of and commitment to sobriety (Alibrandi, 1985).

Alibrandi conducted an empirical study of the advice given by sponsors as "tools" to maintain sobriety in newcomers. These tools for recovery give some insight into how sponsors see the important issues for recovery. They also help provide a better understanding of what specifically occurs in an AA group. Alibrandi breaks these tools down into several stages, with each stage composed of a sobriety tool, a program tool, and a self-change tool. Examples of sobriety tools include staying away from the first drink, avoiding getting hungry, getting to AA meetings, and using the 24-hour plan (one day at a time). Program tools include things like finding a sponsor, turning one's life over to a Higher Power, sharing pain with others, using the serenity prayer, and coming to believe in a Power greater than oneself. Self-change tools would include changing old routines, watching out for elation, letting go of old ideas, and accepting life as it comes. These various types of tools may be one way to understand how AA functions and what it is trying to accomplish in maintaining the sobriety of its members. It should be noted that as persons spend more time in the AA program, fewer sobriety tools are suggested, and the program and self-change tools become more numerous. Various tools are moved around under the various headings, depending upon the length of time individuals have been in the program. The most numerous self-change tools occur in the final stage after individuals have had at least a year's sobriety. The self-change tools may be useful for a period of time following that. The steps of AA are implicitly and explicitly woven into the recovery tools in Alibrandi's work.

Alibrandi believes that an understanding of the tools that govern how AA functions can lead to a new understanding of the AA process. Outlining these recovery tools helps make explicit the intuitive, implicit understanding of the AA sponsor. The outline also makes the process of recovery for the alcoholic using the AA approach more visible and understandable.

As noted above, the advice given to the recovering persons by sponsors is different at different times in the recovery process. Most important to the newcomer is surrender, participation in the fellowship, and some very specific instructions on how to maintain sobriety. In the beginning of the sobriety process, emphasis is placed on specific advice concerning sobriety and attempts to boost the morale. As the amount of time a person has been sober increases, there is a move toward advice on self-change, toward spirituality, and toward the steps that involve action by the recovering persons.

Most of the alcohol treatment programs in the United States are based on AA's philosophy (see Tournier, 1983). Some of the possible negative and positive consequences of this fact are discussed later. Alibrandi (1985) describes some of the ways that the AA philosophy affects the formats of most current treatment programs.

One of the factors Alibrandi explicitly leaves out of her description of AA functions is the education aspect of AA. A good deal of the information that newcomers are trying to process revolves around the new way of understanding what has happened to them.

Wallace (1982) outlines the phenomenological confusion that so many alcoholics experience. The confusion, chaos, and sense of being overwhelmed that the newcomers to AA implicitly experience are dealt with by educating them about the disease of alcoholism. Each person's story reinforces the idea that here is an explanation for what has happened to me. In addition, the specific instructions at the beginning of sobriety provide the structure that newcomers need. They are psychologically ready (and neurologically ready) to deal with concrete steps. At this point, they may be better able to deal with the concrete than with the abstract ideas. It is for this same reason that most alcohol treatment programs are highly structured throughout and usually spend time, particularly at the beginning, explaining alcoholism. The use of recovering alcoholic counselors in treatment programs is akin to what happens in AA meetings. The fact that the counselors are recovering allows patients to identify with and trust them. In addition, the enthusiasm and personalized approach that recovering counselors have toward their own sobriety makes the possibility of recovery more believable and obtainable to the newly recovering patient.

It is also true that most alcohol treatment programs use the disease of alcoholism to explain why individuals have been overwhelmed by drinking. The disease concept offers a simple solution to their immediate problems— stop drinking and many of your problems can be dealt with. As Wallace (1985) says, it is not really true that quitting drinking will solve all of the recovering person's problems, but it does present an immediate, positive, and achievable goal. Patients only have to look at a recovering counselor to see someone who has managed to achieve sobriety.

PSYCHOLOGICAL/THEORETICAL PERSPECTIVES OF AA

Psychological and psychiatric explanations for Alcoholics Anonymous have been made by several writers. A frequent analysis in the literature is to translate AA processes into psychological group processes. For example, Gellman (1964) bases his analysis of AA on Jerome Frank's five basic functions of a group in the therapeutic process: permissiveness, support, stimulation, verbalization, and reality testing.

Permissiveness allows alcoholics to feel accepted into the AA fellowship. Gradually, the guilt and anxiety typical of new members change into confidence in both themselves and AA. Dignity replaces the sense of degradation that the alcoholic suffered while drinking. While the new acceptance is frequently limited to those in AA (those outside still see them as the occasionally drunk person), it is still a powerful support system because it comes from those who truly understand and respect them.

The second therapeutic function, support, is offered to alcoholics in AA in several ways. First, there is no judgment as to who they have been, but rather an empathy and understanding of what they can become. The group allows members to see the possibility of change for themselves; they do not always have to remain who they are, persons overwhelmed by alcohol. In addition, new members, even after a few days, have the opportunity to help someone else who is worse off than they are. This significantly increases their self-confidence.

Stimulation and verbalization are ongoing parts of the AA process. These occur as the group encourages self-acceptance by having newcomers identify with the problems of others. Talking about their own problems is made easier, and newcomers are stimulated to discuss their problems by hearing others discuss theirs. Verbalization allows them to put feelings into words, and this allows both labeling and clarification of feelings. Once feelings have been verbalized, clarified, and identified as being similar to those experienced by others, the feelings can often be changed.

The last of Frank's group functions, reality testing, is a central characteristic of the AA process. Only (1974) essentially agrees with what Chafetz and Demone (1962) say about how Alcoholics Anonymous works, that is, the tendency to focus on symptoms and not underlying dynamics or causes of the drinking. The alcoholic must deal with the reality of finding out how to gain and maintain sobriety. Achieving sobriety is the main goal, and avoiding the first drink is the main thing to watch out for. Therapy is focused on these goals and not on discovering motivation or causes of drinking behavior.

Nace (1987) and others have pointed out that AA fellowship can be understood from the standpoint of Yalom's (1975) elements of group psychotherapy. (These elements are discussed in more detail in Chapter 11.) Hope is provided by recovering alcoholics who model sobriety. New members see that recovery and a normal life are possible for them also. Universality can be found in the sharing of experiences by AA members. This sharing reduces the isolation of those who have felt socially isolated. Information is provided through the organization's pamphlets and books and in informal talks among members. Watching other recovering alcoholics manage their lives allows newcomers to use imitation as a recovery tool; thus the learning of the new social skills can be accomplished. The structure of AA meetings, either in the speaker or discussion format, allows alcoholics to have the opportunity for catharsis. In the process of sharing a common problem and dealing with similar problems that others do not understand as they do, cohesiveness is reinforced. Nace also speculates that the deflation of pathological narcissism (the term *the Big I* is used by some alcoholics to describe this phenomenon) may be another psychotherapeutic reason that AA works.

Maxwell (1983) offers a more social-descriptive analysis of what occurs in AA. He notes that for change to occur in alcoholics, they must first admit their lack of control and have the conviction that any idea of controlled, safe drinking is impossible for them. Maxwell conducted a study which indicated that alcoholics must be aware that they are uncontrolled drinkers. This awareness is disillusioning, but it is necessary for change to begin. Maxwell lists examples of comments made by alcoholics in his study. These include: (1) "Complete feeling of being licked"; (2) "The feeling [that] I was just in a sort of whirlpool which was slowly taking me beyond hope"; (3) "A beaten, hopeless person, my back to the wall"; (4) "At the end of the rope" (p. 289).

In the face of this sense of being overwhelmed, it is very convincing for newcomers to hear that AA works from a "flesh and blood example" (p. 289) for whom the program has been effective.

> Thus the first three steps in the AA program are seen to consist of the necessary admission of powerlessness over alcohol and a hopeful willingness to let more productive forces in the individual and his situation prevail. To the degree that the three prerequisites are met, the formerly impossible begins to happen. The log jam is broken. The emotional constriction is relaxed. The release of potential resources begins. Satisfying interaction with other persons again becomes possible. In short, the movement toward help begins. (p. 291)

Maxwell summarizes the Twelve Steps of AA by saying, "You admit you're licked; you get honest with yourself; you talk it out with somebody else; you make restitution to the people you have harmed; you try to give of yourself with no demands for rewards; and you pray to whatever God you think there is, even as an experiment, to help you to do these things" (p. 291).

The personality changes in members of AA supported by his research are outlined by Maxwell. He says,

> ... summarized, the list of reported changes was led on the one hand by the reduction of interpersonal anxieties, ego inflation, hostility, and intolerance, and in a listing of values gained, by an increase in the ability to interact more satisfyingly with other persons. Reportedly gained was the greater enjoyment and appreciation not only of other persons but also of other facets of life; a greater ability to face and accept reality; . . . an increase in the sense of security, adequacy, confidence, worth, and accomplishment; physical and emotional relaxation; and finally—and frequently listed—"peace of mind." (p. 292)

Maxwell also sees the actions of joining a new group and learning that new group's culture as partially responsible for the alcoholics' recoveries. The AA subculture is a more realistic way of life, allowing new members to get closer to people. This closeness to people provides them with emotional security and helps develop more productive lives. The AA group can be seen as a very influential primary group because it is intimate and its members are totally involved with each other. Maxwell spent a summer as a participant observer in an AA group and was impressed with the mutual acceptance, intimacy, and identification among group members.

Maxwell describes the AA subculture as providing its members with objective knowledge about alcohol, and particularly about alcoholism; alcoholism is a disease, not a normal failing. This is a redefinition for alcoholics. Alcoholics Anonymous also demands that alcoholics face the connection between stress and drinking and assists them to do so. Alcoholics begin to recognize that drinking is an obsession, and myths and rationalizations are refuted.

The anxiety about drinking is reinforced, and the idea that one drink will lead to drunkenness for alcoholics is repeated over and over. While alcoholics can deal with their problem by not drinking, they cannot ever return to alcohol use. This knowledge is restated each time recovering persons introduce themselves at AA as "an alcoholic." The one-day-at-a-time concept allows them to reduce their anxieties about alcohol. They do not have to worry about next week, next month, or next year, just today. Twelfth-Step work also allows alcoholics to further identify with the philosophy of AA by teaching it to others by example.

Maxwell also perceives the talking-out process and the structuring of freedom, accomplished in informal conversations before and after AA meetings, as very important. The AA approach allows alcoholics to learn new ways to seek relief from life's stresses and anxieties. This process tends to lower the stress below the level that existed prior to pathological drinking.

Finally Maxwell points out that it would be idealistic to believe that AA groups are always ideal learning environments. Even in the same groups, some people get more out of the group than do others. He notes Trice's

(1957, 1959) work, which indicates that the responsibilities of sponsorship are not carried out evenly in AA groups. Some new members are not provided with sponsors at all. Maxwell's observations support Trice's in finding variability in the ways groups reach out to new members and in the ways they provide sponsors and deal with new members as peers. These observations are consistent with others' observations. Groups show considerable variability and goodness of fit. This sometimes means that it is necessary for newcomers to shop around in order to find a group with whom they are comfortable.

CRITICISMS OF AA

Discussion of these negative performance issues leads to a review of the literature that evaluates AA. Several criticisms have been raised in the professional literature. Following this discussion, some specific characteristics of members and groups that may affect AA functioning will be outlined.

Leach and Norris (1977), Ogborne and Glaser (1985), and Ogborne (1989) summarize some of the typical criticisms of AA.

1. The opposition by some members to medication, even the use of disulfiram, which is not a psychoactive drug.

2. Failure to maintain adequate drug therapy for psychotic, dual-diagnosis patients and so deprive those patients of the best available care. In defense of AA, it should be pointed out that AA has noted in its Big Book, *Alcoholics Anonymous*, that the use of psychiatrists (and by implication, their prescribed medication) is important in the alcoholic's treatment: " . . . we should never belittle a good doctor or psychiatrist. Their services are often indispensable in treating a newcomer and in following the case afterward" (p. 133).

3. AA has been described as repressive towards hostility while promoting a passive and placid approach to life.

4. Cain (1964) criticizes AA members for being cultish, antiprofessional, ritualistic, and not always truthful. Chafetz and Demone (1962) also comment on the cult status of AA.

5. Elkins (1966) criticizes AA group members for being ignorant, fearful, omnipotent, angry, dishonest, idolatrous, and indolent.

6. There have been many criticisms about the nonprofessionalism of AA, and there has also been a belittling of the special empathy that AA members have for one another. In point of fact, AA might consider this criticism as a compliment. Its tenets hold that alcoholics should forever remain nonprofessional and should not engage in professional treatment, defined as treating alcoholics for a fee.

7. AA has been accused of perpetuating the "sick role" and preventing

alcoholics from separating themselves from the stigma of alcoholism.

8. Pittman and Snyder (1962) are critical of the outreach work of AA groups to new members. They see some members as being intolerant of recovering people who have slipped. They feel that some alcoholics are not reached by AA and that some members do not achieve relative autonomy from external therapy support.

9. More recently, the group's anonymity has been attacked. By remaining anonymous, some critics argue, the groups perpetuate the stigma of alcoholism. While anonymity may have been originally used to deal with stigma, it is now frequently explained as an attempt to subjugate individuals to the broader goals of the group, that is, to deal with the egocentrism frequently found in alcoholics.

10. AA's labeling of alcoholism as a "disease" has been criticized since it does not meet the standards for a physiological impairment of an organ system, used by some people to define disease. However, Leach and Norris (1977) note they are not sure that this is a central concern for the day-to-day function of AA groups. As noted above, the disease concept has been useful in the history of Alcoholics Anonymous and still plays a major role in explaining the disorder to new members.

11. The Twelve Steps have been viewed as containing exhibitionism, dependence, and rebellion against authority.

12. Trice (1983) points out that while there are many AA successes, there are also factors operating against persons affiliating with AA. He notes that AA's therapeutic impact may be limited to those who can adjust to its intense group-life program. He sees many alcoholics as being untreatable using this approach.

13. Tournier (1983) raises the issue of AA's limitation. He sees the AA model as dominating treatment systems in the United States. He feels that the AA approach is capable of reaching only a portion of alcoholics and is limited in its application to the total group of people suffering from alcohol abuse.

14. Finally, Ogborne (1989) points out that AA's emphasis on drinking as the principal cause of the member's problems may ignore conditions that precede and follow the active drinking career of the alcoholic. For example, many problem drinkers have difficulties with anxiety, depression, and phobias that precede and follow alcoholic drinking. AA's focus on drinking as the central problem and its emphasis on upbeat stories of how nondrinking has changed the members' lives may discount the need for treatment in the other problem areas. The overemphasis on drinking as the major or only problem area is inconsistent with the current trend to diagnose and

treat individuals who suffer from both psychiatric and substance abuse problems. As noted earlier, these dual-diagnosis individuals have become an increasing issue in the alcohol treatment area. AA might counter this criticism with the idea that it tries to help the alcoholic with alcohol problems and is doing what it does best. AA would suggest that the alcoholic needs to seek treatment from others (psychiatrists, psychologists, and social workers) for mental health problems.

CHARACTERISTICS OF PEOPLE WHO JOIN AA

Ogborne and Glaser (1985) analyzed AA's literature. They conducted an extensive review, which sought to present ideas and evidence about the types of people for whom AA might be most appropriate. Ogborne and Glaser's findings illustrate at least one attempt to use the existing literature to point out various factors that may affect affiliation with Alcoholics Anonymous. These researchers assert that some important research has been done and that the resulting data can be used to determine who would be most appropriate as AA members. According to Ogborne and Glaser, certain characteristics are associated with AA affiliation.

Personality. Authoritarianism is a characteristic associated with affiliation with AA. Trice and Roman's (1970) research suggests that high affiliative and group dependency needs, personal guilt, and exposure to social processes that have labeled the potential member as deviant are associated with members joining AA. Other research suggests that tendencies to identify with one's mother, to rationalize, to lack social inhibition, to use the defense mechanisms of reaction formation, to be obsessive-compulsive, or to be overcontrolled may be characteristics of AA members. However, these personality characteristics were established with projective techniques, which are not highly reliable. Thus they should be accepted cautiously. These findings do suggest that personality factors may play some role in AA affiliation.

Perceptual Style. This is typically measured with a Rod and Frame Test or the Imbedded Figures Test. These instruments measure the tendency of persons to use internal cues (be field independent) or external cues (be field dependent) to locate themselves physically in their environment. Field dependent subjects are more likely to affiliate with AA. However, some studies have found that AA members are less field dependent than are other alcoholics. Some researchers suggest it is the cognitive process (simplistic versus complex thinking) that is the crucial variable in affiliation with simpler cognitive processes being characteristic of AA members.

Social Characteristics and Social Functioning. AA members have, in the past, tended to be middle-aged and male (this is currently changing as more and more younger people and females deal with their alcoholism earlier). There are several studies which suggest that this organization appeals more to socially stable alcoholics (for example, those employed and living with family) than to socially unstable alcoholics. AA is also seen as more attractive to middle- and upper-class alcoholics than to lower-class abusers. It also seems that those whose lives have been less destroyed by drinking can use AA more effectively. People who can function well and who are in other types of groups seem to work well in AA.

Drinking History and Drinking Problems. Persons who have longer and more adverse interactions with alcohol in their lives are more likely to use AA successfully. This is consistent with the AA notion of "hitting bottom." (But some resources must still exist for the alcoholic or else it is very difficult to recover; see above.) The presence of physical dependence and loss of control is also associated with gamma alcoholism, as defined by Jellinek. Jellinek's research suggests that gamma alcoholics are more likely to be attracted to AA. Ogborne and Glaser (1985) report that AA attenders score higher on loss of control than do nonattenders. They go on to say that drinkers with relatively long histories of abusive and binge drinking, who have physical dependence on alcohol, can be very suitable candidates for Alcoholics Anonymous.

Value, Attitudes, and Beliefs. Ogborne and Glaser, after reviewing the research literature, conclude that AA's Twelve Steps carry with them a religious flavor gained from its beginnings with the Oxford Group. The question can be raised, does AA appeal to people who have a basic sympathy to religion? Whether or not it does is not known since such a factor has not been reported in research. Among the values stressed by AA speakers are friendship, honesty, humility, faith, courage, helping others, spirituality, and personal responsibility. Ogborne and Glaser feel that people with ties to organized religion are more likely candidates for the group. Also, a sense of powerlessness, external locus of control, and existential concerns would be characteristic of good candidates for the group.

Group Processes and Affiliation. Some people have suggested that AA members are supreme conformists, that is, they have less ego strength, lower impulse control, less tolerance for ambiguity, less self-insight, less spontaneity and originality, and less acceptance of responsibility. Members have also been seen as having greater prejudicial attitudes and as placing a greater emphasis on external, socially approved values. Alcoholics Anonymous, like other social groups, offers members a frame of reference for self-definition and provides friendships, social approval, support, and prestige. Meeting these needs in AA groups reinforces group affiliation.

These characteristics of who will and who will not join AA should be regarded with great caution. A more recent review of the literature by Emrick (1989b) led him to draw more limited conclusions about the association of personal characteristics to affiliation with AA. He concluded that it does seem that those alcoholics with more severe alcohol problems are more likely to join. However, once a person has joined, it is not possible to predict from existing research who will do well and who will do poorly. He draws the following conclusions regarding the effectiveness of AA in terms of the characteristics of those who join:

> ... individuals who volunteer to go to AA before, during, or after receiving other forms of treatment do as well as, if not better than, those who do not volunteer, that is, except those who reduce drinking. Among reduced drinkers, AAs probably do worse than non-AAs. Furthermore, AA participation is associated with relatively high abstinence rates but with only average percentages of total improvement in drinking behavior. Importantly, AA has *not* been proven to be more effective than no treatment or comparison treatments when evaluated in randomized clinical trials for court-mandated patients. If anything, AA exposure has resulted in worse outcomes for this "type" of alcohol dependent individual (i.e., a person who has been told to go to treatment as a condition of probation or to keep an automobile operator's license). Finally, those who achieve abstinence appear to participate more than those who become reduced drinkers or remain unremitted. (p. 49)

Emrick draws strong conclusions from his literature review, and these conclusions may be softened as we become more aware of who can and who cannot benefit from AA. However, at present he argues that it is unethical as a therapist to expose "every patient to large 'doses' of AA." (p. 49) While this may seem almost heretical to those who have used AA and to those who routinely refer patients to the organization, one must remember that Emrick's conclusions are based on AA's effectiveness. As already noted, new data may provide information on how to better match AA with the people who can use it most effectively. At present, the conservative approach of exposing to the organization's message all alcoholics who will listen seems to be the most prudent approach. On the other hand, allowing a choice once the prospective member knows about the organization also seems both appropriate and realistic.

As can be seen here, a number of specific and nonflattering comments have been made about AA and about the people who affiliate with it. It has also been criticized because it is not scientific enough in its approach to achieving sobriety. This argument is probably inappropriate. AA bases much of its functions on nonscientific approaches and includes such things as an emphasis on spirituality, which is inconsistent with most scientific approaches. A number of researchers have made the point that to disregard AA because its practice does not follow accepted scientific procedures would be a shortsighted waste of clinical materials.

Some have felt that the concept of alcoholics "hitting bottom" before they can be helped is a meaningful one, while others have been very critical of this requirement. The critics indicate that by the time individuals reach this "bottom" in their drinking habits their entire social environment has deteriorated to the point that recovery is much more difficult than it would be if they had sought treatment while some of their social world was still intact, that is, before they lost their jobs, money, families, or health.

Blum and Blum (1969) state that there is no doubt that AA fellowships offer lonely, humiliated, oftentimes socially inept, and defeated persons opportunities to find sources of hope and new ways of learning to get along with each other and with society. The technique of public confessions relieves guilt and removes at least one source of low self-esteem. Since alcoholics are often viewed as moral weaklings and are shunned by both society and professional groups, perhaps membership in a large organization that welcomes rather than looks down on them is one of AA's major attractions.

One of AA's outstanding qualities is its availability. It can be found throughout the United States and is close to almost every city and small village in this country. Therefore, it can be readily used by all people who seek its help throughout the United States. It is also available without cost. Its availability and affordability make it one of the most widely used treatment programs in the country. Another point is that those people who do join AA have a higher probability of obtaining and maintaining sobriety than those who do not join AA. In other words, the success rate seems to be much higher for those who seek therapy and also join AA than for those who seek therapy alone.

Trice and Staudenmeier (1989) comment on AA's growth and current status.

> In essence, AA had by the 1970s come of age in the sense that it had finally experienced the bitter taste of denunciation and unkind—often unfair—criticisms *at the same time the organization was being widely imitated.* Their earlier world of near universal acclaim and admiration had come to an end. Not only had they experienced the detached, objective, cold-blooded scrutiny of professional researchers who usually held them in respect, but they had now encountered an emotionalized bitterness from sophisticated observers who obviously held them in considerable contempt. [an undercurrent of negative reaction occurred] . . . at the same time, it seems to have been a minor theme in AA's history, one that a highly admired and publicly acclaimed movement could scarcely avoid. The amazing feat is that AA managed to avoid well-publicized negative reactions for almost 30 years and, in doing so, appears to have continued its highly favorable image over four generations. (p. 31)

The greatest contributions of AA have been the following: the part it has played in arousing public interest in changing an attitude of hopeless-ness to one of hope; its widespread system of chapters that offer a potential resource to every alcoholic; the simplicity and concrete structure of its pro-gram, which can be understood by nonpsychologically oriented people and which offers an observable and immediate indication of progress ("one day at a time"); its acceptance of relapses and the need for continuing, even life-long "treatment"; its missionary system of using the patient as the next man's therapist; and the recognition that therapists change as they bring about changes in others. These are all important components of AA's effectiveness. Additionally, AA has served as a model for other recovery organizations. One of the earliest was Al-Anon (see Box 12–4). There are several others that emulate the procedures of AA to help people recover from overeating, nar-cotic addiction, and other problems.

BOX 12–4
Al-Anon

Cermak (1989) has outlined the history and function of Al-Anon. Simply stated, Al-Anon serves the same function for family members and signifi-cant others who are associated with an alcoholic individual as AA does for the alcoholic. These groups provide support and encouragement to those who are living in an alcoholic relationship. The members do not have to be associated with a recovering alcoholic and many are involved with someone who is still drinking.

Al-Anon is a contraction of the words Alcoholics Anonymous, showing the close relationship to that organization historically and in terms of tenets. It developed out of the need for families of alcoholics to deal with their specific problems. While informally established earlier (Bill W.'s wife was involved in getting some of the early groups started), in 1951 wives of alcoholics began their own clearinghouse to coordi-nate family groups already functioning (about ninety in number at that time). Cermak indicates that today there are currently 28,000 weekly Al-Anon groups; Alateen groups are for teenagers who are children of alco-holics or who are in some way associated with an alcoholic. There are about twelve to fifteen members in the average group.

Cermak summarizes a 1984 survey by Al-Anon. These results should be interpreted with caution since administration of the question-naire was uncontrolled. It is possible that the results reflect responses of members who are strongly committed to the organization. The survey found 88 percent of Al-Anon responders were women, but Alateen members were only 57 percent female. The mean age of Al-Anon members was 43.6, with the majority falling between the ages of 36 and 53. About half (49 percent) had some college education. Only 19 percent were primarily homemakers and 96 percent were white. Another finding was that responders were frequently in contact with more than one alcoholic (for example, a spouse and a parent or child).

Al-Anon focuses members' attention on their own behavior. According to Cermak,

> . . . Al-Anon is designed to focus its members' attention on their own behavior and personality. Al-Anon members are striving to recover from a self-acknowledged dysfunctional state of being, which is characterized as destructively other directed, overcontrolling, suffused with denial, isolated, and often without a substantial sense of identity. Although their words are purposively nonpsychological, they describe a state of attrition of the true self through excessive reliance on the facade of a false self. (p. 93)

One of the issues that Al-Anon obviously deals with is co-dependence. Cermak sees co-dependence as the family member(s) having the same symptoms as the alcoholic. Co-dependence can be dealt with through the Al-Anon Twelve Steps (which are the same as the AA Twelve Steps—see Box 12–1). Step one acknowledges one's powerlessness over alcohol and that one's life has become unmanageable. In general, this means that the Al-Anon members must accept that they are powerless to control the alcoholic's drinking. Their lives have become unmanageable, but the first step confronts their attempts to be superhuman and to try to control events no human can control. The co-dependents' ideas that they exist only because they are needed by the drinker creates anxiety.

The second and third steps suggest that people do not have to stand alone to solve their problems and encourages belonging. Step four is an exercise in self-honesty, but the inventory can be completed only by completing the fifth step, sharing it with someone else. "Rigid honesty" is required by these two steps, according to Cermak. The sixth step suggests that the member should let God remove defects of character (these are the same steps used by AA members with only a slight modification of emphasis). While letting God remove defects of character is a leap of faith by group members, they do not have to handle it alone. They can rely on their Higher Power for help. The next three steps reinforce the total honesty of the individuals by turning honesty into a way of life. Once one deals with the past, the tenth step is a commitment to remaining honest on a daily basis. According to Cermak, the tenth step also gives Al-Anon members a solid, internal base for self-esteem. Dealing honestly with themselves and all their shortcomings allows them to live for themselves and not for the opinions of others. The valuing of personal integrity and living for oneself is opposite that of an actively co-dependent person. The final two steps bring a stronger sense of identity, which allows people to feel they belong instead of seeking identity from their partners. They do not feel as isolated as they do when they are acting in a co-dependent role.

Cermak suggests that by using the Twelve Steps people who attend Al-Anon groups begin to recognize denial and how to deal with it and they learn how to take chances in life. The ability to deal with the fear of risk-taking begins with the support received in Al-Anon groups and with the use of the Twelve Steps. It can be profitably utilized for any additional treatment that may be undertaken in addition to Al-Anon.

For those who are interested in learning more about AA from its own literature, the following books are suggested:

Alcoholics Anonymous Comes of Age: A Brief History of AA (1957). New York: AA World Services, Inc.

Dr. Bob and the Good Oldtimers (1980). New York: AA World Services, Inc.

Pass It On: The Story of Bill Wilson and How the AA Message Reached the World (1984). New York: AA World Services, Inc.

Alcoholics Anonymous, 4th edition (1976). New York: AA World Services, Inc.

The Twelve Steps and Twelve Traditions (1952). New York: AA World Services, Inc.

REFERENCES

Alcoholics Anonymous, 4th edition (1976). New York: AA World Services, Inc.

Alibrandi, L. A. (1982). The fellowship of Alcoholics Anonymous. In E. M. Pattison & E. Kaufman (Eds.), *Encyclopedic handbook of alcoholism* (pp. 979–986). New York: Gardner Press.

Alibrandi, L. A. (1985). The folk psychotherapy of Alcoholics Anonymous. In S. Zimberg, J. Wallace, & S. B. Blume (Eds.), *Practical approaches to alcoholism psychotherapy* (2nd ed.) (pp. 239–256). New York: Plenum Press.

Blum, E. M., & Blum, R. H. (1969). *Alcoholism: Modern psychological approaches to treatment.* San Francisco: Jossey-Bass.

Cain, A. (1964). *The cured alcoholic.* New York: John Day.

Cermak, T. L. (1989). Al-Anon and recovery. In M. Galanter (Ed.), *Recent developments in alcoholism: Vol. VII. Treatment Issues* (pp. 91–104). New York: Plenum Press.

Chafetz, M., & Demone, H. (1962). *Alcoholism and society.* New York: Oxford University Press.

Elkins, H. K. (1966). Our mutual sins. *AA Grapevine, 22,* 28.

Emrick, C. D. (1989a). Overview. In M. Galanter (Ed.), *Recent developments in alcoholism: Vol. VII. Treatment issues* (pp. 3–10). New York: Plenum Press.

Emrick, C. D. (1989b). Alcoholics Anonymous: Membership characteristics and effectiveness of treatment. In M. Galanter (Ed.), *Recent developments in alcoholism: Vol. VII. Treatment issues* (pp. 37–53). New York: Plenum Press.

Gellman, I. P. (1964). *The sober alcoholic: An organizational analysis of Alcoholics Anonymous.* New Haven, CT: College and University Press.

James, W. (1958). *The varieties of religious experience.* New York: Mentor Books. (Original work published in 1902.)

Kurtz, E. (1979). *Not-God: A history of Alcoholics Anonymous.* Center City, MN: Hazelden.

Leach, B., & Norris, J. L. (1977). Factors in the development of Alcoholics Anonymous. In B. Kissin & H. Begleiter (Eds.), *The biology of alcoholism: Vol. 5. Treatment and rehabilitation of the chronic alcoholic* (pp. 441–543). New York: Plenum Press.

Maxwell, M. A. (1983). Alcoholics Anonymous: An interpretation. In M. E. Kelleher, B. K. MacMurray, & T. M. Shapiro (Eds.), *Drugs and society: A critical reader* (pp. 288–295). Dubuque, IA: Kendall/Hunt.

Nace, E. P. (1987). *The treatment of alcoholism.* New York: Brunner/Mazel.

Ogborne, A. C. (1989). Some limitations of Alcoholics Anonymous. In M. Galanter (Ed.), *Recent developments in alcoholism: Vol. VII. Treatment issues* (pp. 55–66). New York: Plenum Press.

Ogborne, A. C., & Glaser, F. B. (1985). Evaluating Alcoholics Anonymous. In T. E. Bratter & G. G. Forrest (Eds.), *Alcoholism and substance abuse* (pp. 176–192). New York: Free Press.

Only, M. (1974). *A farewell to the pain of alcoholism.* Englewood Cliffs, NJ: Prentice Hall.

Pittman, D. J., & Snyder, C. R. (1962). Responsive movements and systems of control. In D. J. Pittman & C. R. Snyder (Eds.), *Society and culture and drinking patterns* (pp. 547–552). New York: John Wiley.

Rodin, M. B. (1985). Getting on the program: A biocultural analysis of Alcoholics Anonymous. In L. A. Bennett & G. M. Ames (Eds.), *The American experience with alcohol: Contrasting cultural perspectives* (pp. 41–58). New York: Plenum Press.

Rudy, D. R. (1986). *Becoming alcoholic: Alcoholics Anonymous and the reality of alcoholism.* Carbondale: Southern Illinois University Press.

Silcott, E. J. (1971). *The correspondence between Alcoholics Anonymous and the adaptive capacities of its members.* Ann Arbor, MI: University Microfilms.

Tournier, R. E. (1983). Alcoholics Anonymous as treatment and ideology. In D. A.

Ward (Ed.), *Alcoholism: Introduction to theory and treatment* (2nd ed.) (pp. 363–369). Dubuque, IA: Kendall/Hunt.

Trice, H. M. (1957). A study of the process of identification with Alcoholics Anonymous. *Quarterly Journal of Studies on Alcohol, 18,* 39–43.

Trice, H. M. (1959). The affiliation motive and readiness to join Alcoholics Anonymous. *Quarterly Journal of Studies on Alcohol, 20,* 313–320.

Trice, H. M. (1983). Alcoholics Anonymous. In D. A. Ward (Ed.), *Alcoholism: Introduction to theory and treatment* (2nd ed.). Dubuque, IA: Kendall/Hunt.

Trice, H. M., & Roman, P. M. (1970). Sociopsychological predictors of affiliation with Alcoholics Anonymous: A longitudinal study of "treatment success." *Social Psychiatry, 5,* 51–59.

Trice, H. M., & Staudenmeier, W. J., Jr. (1989). A sociocultural history of Alcoholics Anonymous. In M. Galanter (Ed.), *Recent developments in alcoholism: Vol VII. Treatment issues* (pp. 11–35). New York: Plenum Press.

Waldersee, R. (1987). Needs of recovering alcoholics met by Alcoholics Anonymous. Unpublished manuscript, University of Nebraska, Department of Psychology, Lincoln.

Wallace, J. (1982). Alcoholism from the inside out: A phenomenological analysis. In N. J. Estes & M. E. Heinemann (Eds.), *Alcoholism: Development, consequences, and intervention* (2nd ed.) (pp. 1–15). St. Louis: C. V. Mosby.

Wallace, J. (1985). Critical issues in alcoholism therapy. In S. Zimberg, J. Wallace, & S. B. Blume (Eds.), *Practical approaches to alcoholism psychotherapy* (2nd ed.) (pp. 37–49). New York: Plenum Press.

Yalom, I. D. (1975). *The theory and practice of group psychotherapy* (2nd ed.). New York: Basic Books.

Prevention and Intervention

_____ *chapter 13*

One of the basic assumptions behind the concept of prevention is the need to reduce or eliminate the occurrence of new cases or alcoholism. The goal in the alcohol field is to reduce abusive and alcoholic drinking problems by eliminating or reducing the number of new cases. A parable illustrates the general goals of prevention. Imagine that people keep falling off a cliff and injuring or killing themselves. People who wish to intervene may either stand at the bottom of the cliff and deal with the casualties, or they may go to the top of the cliff and find a way to keep people from falling. This clearly illustrates the difference between treatment (treating the people who fall off the cliff) and prevention (finding a way to prevent people from falling off).

Neither prevention nor treatment is a simple concept. Prevention is a complex and still debated topic. Prevention approaches and philosophies vary considerably and are not independent of sociocultural and political or economic considerations. The question of whether it is better to educate the public about the dangers of alcohol or to pass strict laws regarding the use and abuse of alcohol can be tied to prevailing sociocultural or political and economic considerations. The prohibition amendment was one attempt to reduce the number of new alcohol problems. That amendment was passed in a particular political and sociocultural context. The prevailing philosophy of prevention may vary across time as a society's perception of alcohol and its control changes.

DEFINING THE BASIC LEVELS OF PREVENTION

It is important to first define some basic terms in order to better understand prevention. Generally, prevention efforts are seen as operating at three levels, which were developed in the public health area.

> Tertiary prevention refers in a general way to treatment, secondary prevention refers to early identification of at-risk populations and appropriate interventions, while primary prevention involves altering the individual or the environment (e.g., aid the individual or the environment in developing conditions by which alcohol abuse and alcoholism problems are reduced) so that the injurious social, emotional, and physical effects of alcohol are no longer destructive. . . . (Wright & Watts, 1985, p. xi)

Another way of describing primary prevention is that it is the prevention or reduction of new cases of a disorder. In terms of alcohol problems it might be providing education, controlling how alcohol is dispensed, or changing the living conditions of people in society so that alcohol would no longer be needed as a tranquilizer.

PERSPECTIVES ON PREVENTION STRATEGIES

In the past, people have taken differing perspectives on alcohol problems and their prevention. Robinson (1982) outlines the implications some of these different perspectives have for prevention strategies. He divides the perspectives on the source of alcohol problems into three categories: (1) "The problem is alcoholics"; (2) "The problem is society"; and (3) "The problem is alcohol." Robinson advocates an approach to prevention that utilizes strategies derived from all three of these viewpoints on causality.

The Problem Is Alcoholics

The assumption that alcohol abuse is limited to alcoholics has several implications for ways to approach prevention. You can focus on ways to prevent the problem or treat the people in the population who are at risk or both. The later temperance movement was aimed at reducing the number of alcoholics. Robinson notes that during the nineteenth century addiction was assumed to be inherent to using alcohol. Thus all drinkers were potentially alcoholic. For those who held this point of view, prohibition was the obvious solution. (It should be noted that the temperance movement originally had the goal of "tempering" not abolishing alcohol use. See Chapter 1 for more information.)

In post-prohibition America, the notion of alcohol addiction has survived, but with an important change in focus. Addiction is now seen as something inherent in the alcoholic, not in the alcohol itself. According to this view, some people, for reasons unknown, are simply susceptible to becoming addicted to alcohol should they use it. For a small percentage of alcohol users (Robinson suggests 2 to 3 percent), alcohol consumption causes a series of problems over which the users have no control. These individuals have the disease of alcoholism. The only way they can manage to deal with alcohol problems is to abstain. This philosophy is the foundation of Alcoholics Anonymous groups. It is also the popular conception of alcoholics held by the average person in this country.

According to this viewpoint, there are two types of drinkers: normal drinkers and alcoholics. Alcoholics cannot control their drinking and can be expected to suffer physical, mental, and social damage. Those who drink normally can control their consumption and thus do not experience difficulties because of their drinking.

Separating drinkers into two types has a number of positive results. It makes common sense and is a comfort to "normal drinkers." It neatly defines the target population for government departments and treatment facilities. It also does not threaten the sellers of alcoholic beverages. This "two population" approach has led to an alcohol prevention, intervention, and treatment system that is devoted to dealing with the sick minority of drinkers—the alcohol addicts.

According to Robinson, the corollary to this approach is that the main prevention effort has been secondary prevention. In secondary prevention, efforts are focused on devising ways to get people to recognize the early signs of alcoholism in themselves and others. The major method for meeting the goal of early recognition is to have people ask themselves questions about their drinking and its effects. Checklists at various levels of complexity are published in newspapers and magazines. These lists usually have a specific agency's address and phone number for the reader to contact. The number of contacts made by readers provides a measure of impact. Follow-up by alcohol agencies and personal reports to professionals indicates that a good number of people have used such lists to confront alcohol problems in their families.

Secondary prevention strategies also target professionals. Psychologists, physicians, clergy, and others are asked to look for alcohol problems in the people they serve and to refer them for treatment. Robinson notes that there has been a recent increase in education for nursing, medical, and social work professionals, and specific guidelines have been devised to help identify alcohol-related problems. For example, such professionals are told that alcohol problems are correlated with child and spouse abuse, so they should look closely for signs of alcohol problems when clients report to treatment with these problems.

High-risk groups have also been the target of the secondary prevention strategy. Children of alcoholics are an example of a group who are at high risk for developing alcoholic drinking patterns. Some other examples of high-risk groups include delinquents, drinking drivers, and people who suffer recurrent accidents.

Individuals and groups who believe that alcoholics are the real problem are likely to see placing limitations on overall alcohol consumption as irrelevant. Such limitations would not prevent alcoholism in the alcoholics and would inconvenience the overall majority.

Robinson views the "alcoholics are the problem" perspective as being limited in terms of prevention. He points out that when research is focused on the general population, rather than those people seen in alcohol treatment centers, almost all of the problems alcoholics have with alcohol are shared by people in the community at large. He argues that, in reality, there are many major alcohol problems and many different populations that overlap only to a certain extent. Robinson states that developing a treatment system that can deal with alcohol problems is both a humane and necessary thing to do. However, the treatment system should not be developed at the expense of a coordinated approach to the much greater number of different alcohol problems that affect the wider community. A prevention approach based on the idea that there are only "two populations" (the alcoholics and the normal drinkers) is unsatisfactory, to say the least.

The Problem Is Society

Many people think that society is to blame for alcohol problems. Society's attitudes toward drinking and the resulting unhealthy drinking patterns are the root of alcohol problems. Unhealthy drinking includes drinking to be tough, to help solve problems, or to help deal with unbearable social or psychological situations.

This perception of the problem leads to prevention focused on a healthy use of alcohol in everyday life. This sociocultural approach to alcohol problems has developed out of studies of different cultures and ethnic groups and their different rates of alcohol problems. Robinson cites Blacker (1966) to summarize these studies' conclusions as to what is needed to prevent alcohol problems in a society.

> In any group or society in which drinking customs, values, and sanctions ... are well established, known, and agreed upon by all, consistent with the rest of the culture, and are characterized by prescriptions for moderate drinking and proscriptions against excessive drinking, the rate of alcoholism will be low. (cited in Robinson, 1982, p. 462)

Overall, Blacker suggests that a national set of drinking norms be established to govern how people should drink. Such norms would replace the society's fragmented and often contradictory notions about drinking with more consistent and universally agreed upon guides for alcohol use. The main tool of prevention, using this approach, is to advocate positive health education on how to use alcohol in a moderate and healthy way. This would point out the dangers of the destructive use of alcohol and suggest ways to use alcohol in a constructive fashion. Robinson gives some examples of this approach taken from the Second Special Report to the United States Congress. The advice given in the report includes the following:

1. Alcohol should improve relationships rather than impair or destroy them.
2. Make sure the use of alcohol is an adjunct to activity rather than being the primary focus of action.
3. Make sure alcohol is used carefully in connection with other drugs.
4. Make sure human dignity is served by the use of alcohol.
5. Respect the person who chooses to abstain.
6. Respect the person who chooses to drink in moderation; do not be insistent about "refreshing" drinks or refilling glasses.
7. Provide food with alcohol at all times; especially protein such as dairy products, fish, and meat.
8. Provide transportation or overnight accommodations for those unable to drive safely, recognizing that the host is just as responsible for preventing driving while intoxicated as are the guests. (DHHS, 1974)

Robinson (1982) states that those who believe society is the source of alcohol problems also believe that drinking problems can be reduced by encouraging people to develop healthy drinking practices. Healthy drinking practices include such practices as drinking wine with meals and integrating alcoholic beverages into all types of social situations, such as sporting events. A goal is to use alcohol in social contexts where it would be only incidental to the event, not the major focus.

If alcohol would be integrated into total lifestyles, restrictions on the sale of beverages (age, time, and place of sale, etc.) would have to be relaxed. A relaxation of the present rules surrounding the sale of alcohol would increase the probability of it being integrated into people's total life situations.

Research shows that young children learn about alcohol early in life (e.g., Zucker, 1987) and know its effects on adults' behavior. These findings are consistent with the notion that children should be taught about alcohol. Some authorities have argued that alcohol should be given in small amounts to children throughout their early years. The argument is that early introduction of alcohol will increase the probability that children will not have difficulty with alcohol as adults.

However, Robinson (1982) notes that most parents have ambivalent attitudes toward alcohol use, and often that ambivalence is communicated to their children. Early introduction of alcohol from parents with ambivalent attitudes toward use of the beverage may be even more negative than later introduction.

The Problem Is Alcohol

As noted previously, in the nineteenth century, alcohol was seen as the problem in the sense that it was thought everyone could become addicted to it. The answer, then, was the total prohibition of alcohol. "Alcohol is the problem" has again moved into central focus in terms of prevention of alcohol problems, but this new emphasis does not necessarily lead to advocating total prohibition.

From looking at the distribution of consumption within certain populations, the argument has been made that the number of heavy drinkers in a given population or country is directly related to the average per capita consumption in that population or country. Therefore, in countries where consumption rates per capita are higher, there are also more heavy drinkers and problem drinkers.

Parallel to the establishment of the distribution of consumption model, it was found that any relaxation of drinking controls led to a greater consumption of alcohol. It was also established that any increase in consumption led to more alcohol-related problems of all kinds in a given community. The conclusion that seems to follow is that any realistic policy to prevent alcohol problems must control the availability of alcohol.

There are several ways to control the availability of alcohol. Attempts can be made to control drinkers, to control settings in which they drink, or to control the alcohol itself. The principle regulation efforts that have been proposed attempt to control the number of places where people can buy alcohol, the type and location of outlets, the age at which people buy and consume alcohol, the daily hours for sale, the amount of alcohol in the drink, and differences in tax and price of the beverage. Robinson states that the most frequently heard proposal deals with the price of alcohol.

Attempts to control the availability of alcohol must include careful attention to some possible negative outcomes. If the alcohol restrictions become too severe, illicit liquor can be profitably produced. New controls were placed on alcohol availability in the former Soviet Union. As a result, sugar—a major ingredient of "home brew" and other "homemade" alcoholic beverages—became scarce. Resentment towards taxes and prices often leads to difficulty enforcing restrictions on alcoholic beverages. For example, as a result of the sugar shortages and the general outcry about the severity of alcohol restrictions, Soviet authorities had to make more alcoholic beverages available at more reasonable prices. They also publicly announced a change in policy regarding the price and availability of alcoholic beverages.

When alcohol is produced outside of government regulation, tax-generated revenue and control over distribution is lost. Despite the risks when alcohol availability is controlled, many argue that judiciously following this approach to alcohol prevention, in combination with community education, can reduce consumption levels and also the related drinking problems.

Robinson suggests that parts of all of these approaches need to be combined. Careful attention must be given to areas where implementation of one perspective would interfere with another approach (for example, using the "alcohol is the problem" approach would be inconsistent with teaching people to use alcohol in moderation). Following Robinson's wise advice would not be simple. One of the more obvious problems is that a wide range of government bureaucracies, which have very different goals, would be involved in such efforts. Whether this country or any other country has the ability to develop and follow through on Robinson's suggestion is an unanswered question.

MODELS OF PREVENTION

Three major models have been employed in discussing the prevention of alcohol problems. These are usually referred to as: the public health model; the sociocultural model; and the distribution of consumption model. These three dominant models will be discussed in some detail in order to present both the strengths and the weaknesses of each. It is also important to consider, at some length, the underlying assumptions for each model and how those assumptions might be operationalized.

Public Health Model

The "oldest model" (oldest, according to some writers) has been borrowed from the public health sector. Blane (1976) and McNeil (1985) have outlined the basic premises of the public health model. Blane has done an excellent review of the prevention area. He notes that the classic public health model details and analyzes the relationship of a disorder to agent, host, and environment. By mapping this relationship over time and space, it is possible to propose ways to control and/or prevent the disorder. The public health model has been very effective in finding, controlling, and in many cases, preventing infectious diseases. This effectiveness makes it a natural to extend to chronic diseases and to problem social behavior, which "could be defined as disease entities" (p. 592). In the 1950s and 1960s, the application of the public health model to mental health, juvenile delinquency, suicidal behaviors, drug behaviors, and alcoholism was strongly pursued.

The levels of prevention introduced earlier were frequently discussed during the 1960s. These levels included primary, secondary, and tertiary prevention. Blane defines primary prevention as removing or preventing the causes of a problem or of increasing the numbers of a population who are immune to a particular disorder. Secondary prevention is the arresting of a disorder by early treatment prior to its becoming a full-blown problem. Tertiary prevention is treatment of a disorder after it has reached its full potential. The goal of tertiary prevention is to prevent the disorder from becoming chronic.

Levels of prevention have been criticized in the literature from both conceptual and pragmatic points of view. For example, Blane and others have pointed out that it makes little sense to identify tertiary prevention with treatment since these are two separate domains. Treatment has never adequately controlled any disease in a population because it has never prevented the problem. Also, tertiary prevention does not reduce the incidence of new cases, which is the main thrust of prevention.

Some researchers (e.g., McGavran, 1963) argue that secondary prevention, with its focus on early diagnosis and treatment of a disease, has not been established as an effective prevention technique. Blane (1976) suggests that secondary prevention has been at least partially successful in the areas of reducing communicable diseases like syphilis. However, he notes that the prevention of physical diseases may not be consistent with how secondary prevention may work with social problems.

Primary prevention has been attacked on the basis of difficulties with implementation. Because too little is known about how to mount an effective primary prevention program, some writers (e.g., Cross, 1967) suggest that it is appropriate to place the major effort at a secondary prevention level. Blane (1976), however, indicates that some specific primary prevention programs have been implemented since Cross, and others have written about the issue. Blane questions whether secondary prevention has been well established as an effective prevention level.

Sociocultural Model

Blane notes that various models of prevention have not always been labeled in a consistent manner. He refers to the sociocultural model as the "social science model." More recent writers (e.g., McNeil, 1985) label the model "sociocultural." Blane's description may be broader than those of other writers who have used the sociocultural label.

According to McNeil, the sociocultural model of prevention is the oldest of the three prevention models in the alcohol field. It focuses on the correlation between alcohol problems and the norms in a population that specify how alcohol should be used. Particular attention is paid to the context in which drinking occurs. Both the structure and the content of these social norms are a major concern. In particular, the quality and content of social norms are the prescriptions for responsible drinking and proscriptions against excessive drinking. (See Chapter 8 for additional discussion of prescriptive and proscriptive norms.)

Frankel and Whitehead (1981) suggest that there are four types of normative conditions that are related to alcohol abuse in a population.

1. When alcohol use is forbidden (proscribed) and there are no prescriptive norms for how one should use alcohol, alcohol-related damage appears high. (This is a proscriptive environment for drinking.)

2. When prescriptive norms are prominent in a society (and drinking is highly integrated into the culture, that is, the members drink in a wide variety of social situations) and there is an absence of proscriptive norms, then the prevalence of alcohol-related problems is high. (This is a prescriptive environment.)

3. When the social norms for alcohol use are ambivalent (and the drinking practices are not integrated in the social situations of a population), alcohol-related damage is high. Norms in the United States and Canada fall under this category. (This is an ambivalent environment.)

4. In populations where there are clear prescriptions for moderate drinking (and proscriptions against abusive drinking) and drinking practices are well-integrated into the society, alcohol-related damage is low. (This is an unambivalent environment.)

This model clearly emphasizes social and cultural components. Empirical support for this model comes from the work of sociologists, anthropologists, and epidemiologists who are all scholars in the social and behavioral sciences. The research on which the model is based provides the reason for Blane (1976) labeling it the social science model.

In this model, drinking would be expected to vary along cultural, national, and religious lines. The use of alcohol in diverse populations would vary according to the values, mores, beliefs, and prescriptions and proscriptions about alcohol use and abuse.

Prevention within this model focuses on changing the quality and structure of societal norms to help reduce the damaging effects of alcohol. In order for this to occur, some type of national consensus about prescriptive and proscriptive drinking norms would be necessary. Wilkinson (1979) suggests that changes in drinking norms should lead to the following behaviors:

1. Drinking should occur in the context of other activities without special significance being attributed to drinking.

2. Children should be taught the customs that govern drinking behavior in a controlled and unemotional way.

3. Restrictions on the availability of alcoholic beverages should be removed to eliminate the mystery surrounding them. (cited in McNeil, 1985)

Changing an entire society's quality and structure of norms toward drinking is a difficult task. There are some indications that at least some of the norms held by a society can be modified by intensive grass-roots educational and legal efforts. The attitude towards drinking and driving is a prime example. Due to a heavy emphasis in the media, schools, and elsewhere on the dangers of drinking and driving, attitudes have changed considerably in the past decade. Although public surveys on the topic may be unavailable or unreliable, there is no doubt that the norms for drinking and driving have changed. In the mid-1970s some residents of a midwestern city viewed the arresting of intoxicated drivers by Alcohol Safety Action Project police officers as harassment. Some 15 years later, the community was supporting police arrests of drinking drivers and the potential removal of their driving privileges. Much of the increased awareness of the dangers of drinking and driving has come about through grass-roots groups such as Mothers Against Drunk Driving (MADD). This group, and others like it, have lobbied for legislation that will help remove drinking drivers from the road.

Laws have been changed in most states to set the minimum legal age for drinking alcoholic beverages at 21 years. A major reason for raising the minimum drinking age was to reduce deaths resulting from drinking and driving by young people. Some states report lower incidences of highway deaths related to drinking and driving following the higher age requirement for legal drinking. However, it is still too soon to know the long-term effects for society.

These changes in law occurred in the context of much discussion in the press about alcohol's social, psychological, and physical effects on people. These discussions have led to increased awareness of the effects of alcohol use on health. Health information combined with the emphasis on maintaining a healthy lifestyle has led to a significant decrease in the sales of hard liquor. Drinking habits are changing; hard liquor is being replaced by beers, wine coolers, and nonalcoholic beverages at parties. This illustrates how when norms in one area of society are changed—for example, drinking and driving—the change can have a ripple effect on alcohol use throughout society. The societal context into which the new way of viewing alcohol is introduced is very important. With the new interest in healthy lifestyles and alcohol's association with various health problems, it becomes easier to begin to discuss the reduction or elimination of alcohol use. (McNeil, 1985)

The Distribution of Consumption Model

The sociocultural model assumes the need for considerable effort to change people's attitudes so that they view alcohol differently and behave in different ways toward its use. Compliance is voluntary. The distribution of consumption model does not rely on voluntary compliance. Rather, it suggests that the availability of alcohol is crucial to reducing its use. The model also indicates a need for governmental control. According to the distribution of consumption model, the amount of alcohol available per person in a society is directly related to the degree of problematic drinking in that society.

The greater the amount of alcohol consumed per capita, the greater the alcohol problems in that society. Thus, in this model, prevention of alcohol abuse focuses heavily on reducing the amount of alcohol consumed by the total society (not just the problem drinkers). Prevention is accomplished by using a variety of governmental strategies such as pricing policies, legal drinking ages, legal drinking hours in public places, and alcohol content in alcoholic beverages. It should be noted that changes in these areas are brought about by governmental control. There are not necessarily any changes in attitudes toward alcohol use in the population at large. Proponents of this model argue that restraints in the use of alcoholic beverages cannot be left to personal choice. The dimensions of irresponsible behavior are too great.

In recent years, several writers have reported research in support of this strategy. However, Parker and Harman (1980) criticize the distribution of consumption model and suggest that it is based upon the following six flawed propositions:

1. *There Is a Direct Relationship between Heavy Drinking and Premature Death.* While clinical and nonclinical samples indicate that alcohol abuse is related to premature death, a closer look at the research findings indicates that mortality rates vary depending upon the method of identifying users.

2. *There Is a Direct Relationship between Abusive Drinking and Physical Illness.* A close look at the research data indicates that heavy smoking, poor nutrition, and emotional distress have a causal role in illnesses often attributed to abusive drinking.

3. *The Distribution of Drinking Is Unequal in the Population.* This assumption suggests that a relatively small group of drinkers are responsible for a large percentage of the total amount of alcohol consumed. This is consistent with general observations since many people are abstainers, many are moderate drinkers, and only a few are heavy users of alcohol. It is suggested that 10 percent of the population consumes 50 percent of the alcohol sold in the United States. So this assumption is supported by research.

4. *There Is a Constant Relationship between per Capita or Average Consumption Levels and the Prevalence of Heavy Alcohol Use.* The criticism of this is that knowledge of per capita consumption is not sufficient to predict the prevalence of heavy alcohol use.

5. Physical Health Problems Can Be Reduced by Lowering per Capita Consumption. This supposition does not adequately recognize the many intervening variables that may affect physical health rates.

6. Per Capita Consumption of Alcohol Can Be Lowered by Raising the Price of Alcoholic Beverages. It has not been established that raising prices reduces to any great degree the consumption of alcoholic beverages. This failure in reducing consumption is especially lacking in the targeted groups, those which consume the most alcohol.

The first three propositions seem to support the distribution of consumption model's rationale. However, the last three propositions raise serious questions about the model's credibility. Parker and Harman conclude that the model has serious limitations. They view empirical support as limited, inconclusive, or even negative.

McNeil (1985) suggests an alternative to Parker and Harman's way of looking at the distribution of consumption model. Following Smart (1980), McNeil points out that there are several ways to view availability. There is, for example, Smart's notion of subjective and social availability of alcoholic beverages. Subjective availability refers to the amount of energy or resources one is willing to expend to obtain alcoholic beverages. Empirical research suggests that an individual's actions are influenced more by subjective estimates of cost and risks than they are by real costs and risks. Social availability refers to the influence exerted on an individual's drinking patterns by small and informal groups such as family, friends, and peers. In a study of fifty states, Smart found a significant relationship between consumption and availability. However, he found an even higher correlation between consumption and income. The distribution model raises considerable questions and has some serious conceptual and methodological limitations. Despite its limitations, the model has served to stimulate policy makers to consider the role of government policy in reducing alcohol problems.

The public health, sociocultural, and distribution of consumption models provide the major frameworks for prevention of alcohol problems. Models offer ideas about how to prevent alcohol problems. However, the specific procedures for carrying out the models' aims are implemented through specific techniques or strategies. These prevention techniques and strategies will be examined at this point.

TECHNIQUES AND STRATEGIES OF PREVENTION

A number of techniques and strategies for implementing prevention in the alcohol field have been suggested and used. Through the years, various writers have outlined the major techniques. The major approaches have not changed a great deal in the past 10 to 20 years. Blane's (1976) writing in the area remains one of the most comprehensive overviews of prevention techniques.

Blane states that there are techniques of prevention, which include

> education through the school system, information and education for the public at large, including advertising, manipulation of substance, person, and environmental factors affecting consumption patterns, and singling out for special attention subpopulations which have characteristics that make them especially suitable targets for preventive work. These techniques are simply tools of social control available to makers of public policy and say nothing about the philosophy, aims, and directions of any particular prevention policy. . . . (pp. 535–536)

Public information and education is an explicit component of most prevention programs. When it is possible to control the media, as is true in some Western European countries, a united front can be presented. Media are not controlled in the United States, so information about alcohol and abuse can come from several sources. The information presented need not always be consistent (and frequently, it is not). For example, in any large city there can be agencies promoting strict abstinence coexisting with others promoting moderate drinking.

Blane notes the split between formal government agencies like the National Institute on Alcohol Abuse and Alcoholism (NIAAA) and the National Highway Traffic Safety Administration (NHTSA). These agencies present different points of view on how to deal with the alcohol problem. Both agencies place heavy emphasis on media presentations. However, the goals of media use vary according to the prevention philosophy each agency follows. For example, the NIAAA initially followed a multimedia campaign policy that emphasized moderate drinking and the use of alcoholic beverages with lower alcohol content. Acceptance of nondrinkers and of parties where both alcoholic and nonalcoholic beverages are available was accented. The idea that food should be served with alcoholic beverages was highlighted in media messages. This is consistent with reducing blood alcohol levels, which was one of the goals of the NIAAA approach. While this NIAAA approach has been less intensely promoted in recent years, at least one of its goals seems to have been achieved. There has been an increase in the sale of low-alcoholic-content beverages and a decrease in the sale of hard liquor. It may be that the advertising campaign was an important factor in achieving this goal (it could also be attributed to other nonrelated factors). Outcome evaluation from prevention efforts is always delayed to some extent. One side effect of the delay is that prevention is difficult to "sell" to legislators.

The main thrust of the public information approach is to utilize all available avenues to disseminate information about the use and abuse of alcohol. Often, existing networks like the public schools, parent-teacher organizations, or church groups can be used to disseminate information. The NIAAA used the Junior Chamber of Commerce to help establish a nationwide educational program in the 1970s. The prevailing philosophy of this earlier NIAAA program was to educate the public to use alcohol in a moderate fashion.

A different strategy is espoused by groups who adhere to the distribution of consumption model. While they would also like to reduce the total amount of alcohol consumed, they approach this task by focusing on the cost and availability of the beverage. They use the media to help gain public support for increased prices. The goal is to convince the public that alcohol is doing considerable damage to society so that there will be less resistance to increasing the cost of alcoholic beverages.

In 1976 Blane concluded that public information and education programs had not had a demonstrated effect on drinking rates. At that time, in some countries with advocacy for temperance or abstinence, there had actually been an increase in drinking. Blane speculated that these types of campaigns might be self-defeating.

Blane suggested that the drinking-and-driving educational campaign in the United States during the 1950s and 1960s had been unsuccessful. The efforts of the campaign were generally thought to have had little effect on drinking and driving and its consequences—accidents.

Prevention efforts must be seen as part of the larger societal picture. Changes in social and political thought have led to dramatic changes in how drinking and driving is perceived in this country. During the 1970s, there were attempts to deal with drinking and driving through public education and Alcohol Safety Action Projects. These attempts were interpreted by some people as a sign that Big Brother was watching, and they reacted to police stopping drivers for breath-analyzer checks as interfering with individual freedoms. In at least one city, even highly placed public officials were arrested for drinking and driving. Following these arrests, there was a public outcry to reduce the number of police patrols in the city because the police were harassing important citizens. Today it is unlikely that these types of public reactions would occur.

Now the majority of citizens view drinking and driving as a serious offense and as a socially irresponsible thing to do. Society's views of drinking and driving have changed, but it is difficult to know exactly why these changes have occurred. Perhaps it is due in part to the effective grass-roots work (and political influence) of MADD. Individuals who make up this group have been scarred by automobile deaths in their own families due to drinking drivers. They have persuaded the general public and state legislators that every possible means should be used to reduce drinking and driving. The MADD organization has been in the forefront of getting laws changed to the extent that, in many cases, drivers go to jail for the first driving while intoxicated (DWI) offense. In other cases, drivers must accept education and/or treatment in order to continue operating a motor vehicle.

Was it the work in the early 1950s and 1960s that finally led the U.S. public to take drinking and driving more seriously? Will the effects of the new laws and social awareness reduce the number of alcohol-related car accidents? These questions are difficult to answer. While there are some suggestions that alcohol-related accidents for young people may have decreased in the past few years, it is still too early to tell whether these figures are an anomaly or the beginning of a trend. That is the problem with alcohol prevention efforts in general. They may or may not work, but it probably will not be known until several years later just what their effectiveness has been. The effectiveness of prevention programs in the alcohol field will be discussed at the end of this chapter. The evaluation of prevention programs is critical not only for improving effectiveness, but also for maintaining funding from legislative sources.

Blane outlines one of the major difficulties in assessing prevention programs in the United States. In this country, several different organizations may undertake prevention efforts with widely different aims, objectives, and practices. This results in the public being exposed to a multimedia campaign that presents conflicting messages. It is extremely difficult to know or understand just what effects multiple messages have on the public.

Blane hypothesizes that multiple messages tend to reinforce multiple values and behaviors toward alcohol. Thus it is possible that prevention approaches aimed at building a nationwide, normative consensus toward alcohol are often subverted by contradictory messages from other sources and interest groups. Blane suggests that an alcohol policy is needed that takes into account all interest groups and allows coordination in media campaigns among groups. Establishing such a policy would be very difficult since various groups hold such widely divergent beliefs about alcohol.

Despite the problems that make public information and education campaigns a complex matter, these strategies are a very necessary part of prevention approaches to alcohol use and abuse. Such campaigns raise and maintain public consciousness about alcohol problems, even if they do not always achieve their stated goals. Blane suggests that information and education programs should be thoroughly and rigorously pretested before mass distribution. Programs in their final forms should also be carefully monitored. Blane states that since populationwide attempts to change health behaviors through information and education have been relatively unsuccessful, it might be more effective to direct resources toward more limited programs with defined target populations and goals specific to those populations. The issue of targeting prevention will be examined under strategies for implementing prevention programs.

MANIPULATION OF SUBSTANCE, PERSON, AND ENVIRONMENT FACTORS

The classic public health model consists of manipulating each of these components—substance, person, and environment—to reduce alcohol intake. These three are the key elements in primary prevention and can be used to lower overall consumption, as in the distribution model, or to adjust consumption patterns that result in problems, as in the sociocultural model.

Substance Factors.   Blane suggests that attempts to alter the substance, alcohol, have not been very successful. On a theoretical level, modifying alcohol to reduce its addictive properties would be an ideal primary prevention effort. An example would be to add another substance to alcohol so that a drinker's blood alcohol level would be kept lower. The problem is that most substances that can modify the metabolism of alcohol have side effects that are medically dangerous. This is true, for example, of disulfiram (see Chapter 4), which is contraindicated for people with heart conditions. Another less dramatic approach to modifying the substance is to lower the alcohol content in beverages or promote the use of weaker alcoholic beverages rather than stronger ones. However, some AA members have said that such beverages lure people into using alcohol because the drink is not seen as harmful and later those people may turn to beverages with higher alcohol content and may become addicted.

Person Factors.   Strictly speaking, age, gender, and prior drinking habits cannot be manipulated or changed by the researcher. It is the rules or laws concerning age, gender, and prior drinking habits that are manipulated to control the drinking of alcoholic beverages. In this country, there are many rules regarding alcohol use that are related to age. There are fewer rules related to gender. Other countries have different rules regarding alcohol use. For example, in some Scandinavian countries, persons officially identified as having alcohol problems can be restricted in terms of purchasing alcohol (Blane, 1976). Some writers (e.g., Plaut, 1967; Wilkinson, 1970) recommend removing all age restrictions for the purchase of alcohol. The rationale for removing or lowering age restrictions is to remove the "forbidden fruit" image of alcohol. Many people believe that since most people below the legal age use alcohol despite rules against such use, age restrictions make no sense. For a period of time, age limits for purchasing and using alcohol were lowered in this country. Most states have reversed their lower age limits so that alcoholic beverages are not legally available to anyone under 21 years of age. The change back to higher age requirements came in response to research that suggested that raising drinking ages reduces automobile accidents and deaths among young people.

Environment Factors. According to Blane (1976), manipulation of environmental factors is the area most often proposed as a prevention strategy. Blane presents an extensive list of proposed actions including

1. providing safe drinking facilities on college campuses
2. revising tax scales to increase the financial attractiveness of purchasing low-strength beverages
3. revising tax scales to make every beverage equally expensive per unit of absolute alcohol
4. eliminating restrictions on decor and interior of on-premise drinking locations
5. developing model neighborhood taverns
6. removing prohibitions against Sunday drinking
7. integrating drinking with varied leisure activities
8. permitting grocery stores to sell alcoholic beverages and liquor stores to sell food
9. providing retailers with training in alcohol control, drinking, and alcohol problems
10. establishing penalties for selling alcohol or extending credit to intoxicated persons
11. coordinating the alcohol control and health promotion functions of government agencies
12. controlling hours of sale
13. manipulating numbers and types of outlets
14. planning for the presence of nondrinking drivers at social and recreational activities where alcohol is served
15. promoting activities which are functionally equivalent or preferable to the use of alcohol
16. abolishing liquor advertisements
17. displaying natural drinking situations in advertising
18. removing information on labels which indicate amount of alcohol content (p. 542)

Blane notes that this list is often contradictory. It is also surrounded by the emotionalism that is typical of the alcohol field. The question remains as to how effective the factors listed would be in preventing alcohol problems. The research in this area is weak, but some conclusions can be drawn. Strict systems of legal and organizational control appear to be related to a low per capita consumption but to a high rate of visible behavior problems, according to Blane. During the prohibition era, alcohol consumption was reduced. Cirrhosis mortality rates were also significantly reduced. However, prohibiting alcohol led to other serious societal problems.

Blane points out that the consumption levels of alcoholic beverages (wine, beer, distilled spirits) can be readily influenced by differential pricing policies. Differential pricing has been successful in Denmark, Norway, Sweden, and Switzerland. When this finding is combined with the known effectiveness of commercial advertising on influencing people to select products, it suggests that getting people to buy beverages with low alcohol content might be effective. Unfortunately, using factors such as numbers, type, and location of drinking places; on- and off-premises drinking; hours of sale; and private licenses or state monopoly has not been demonstrated to have specific prevention effects.

Blane states that the research in the prevention area has not been of high quality. But despite the poor quality of the research, prevention effects described earlier have been well-established. Blane also notes that while the interventions listed here do affect drinking behavior, some of the effects on alcohol problems are not evident. In spite of multiple attempts to reduce alcohol problems, drinking problems are on the rise in industrialized countries.

SECONDARY PREVENTION

Secondary prevention is another aspect of the prevention model generally and the public health model specifically. This approach is recommended by several writers. Blane suggests that there are few programs that meet the definition of secondary prevention. Secondary prevention is most commonly recommended for early problem drinkers and for groups at high risk for becoming problem drinkers. Recent research (West & Prinz, 1987) suggests that some children of alcoholics are at higher risk for alcohol problems than are children in general. It is appropriate to focus prevention efforts on this population. Other high-risk groups include delinquents, recurrent absentees from school, drinking drivers, and collegians who suffer accidents and injuries. The factors that will lead to a reduction of risk in these groups are still under debate. Treatment, special education programs, disciplinary action, and imposition of legal controls have been suggested and implemented in several programs.

Most secondary programs that have been implemented target drinking and driving. Although many individuals who are arrested for DWI are in the late stages of alcohol problems, the majority are considered to be in the early stages. Secondary prevention for DWI offenders usually involves treatment, education, and/or the imposition of legal sanctions. Automatic sentencing to jail for a limited period of time has recently been discussed or implemented in some states. As of yet, the specific interventions that are most effective are unknown.

In the 1980s, lobbying groups advocating tougher drinking driver laws increased dramatically. The numbers of new antidrunk driving chapters in the United States, for example, MADD and RID (Remove Intoxicated Drivers), increased from 2 in 1978 to 117 in 1983 (Hingson, Howland, Morelock, & Heeren, 1988). Many of the DWI programs that have been implemented are effective in their early stages but show a return to increasing rates of alcohol-related traffic accidents and deaths when public awareness decreases. For example, Hingson et al. cite the state of Maine, where media attention, community organization, and legislative activity, combined with a law change, led to an initial reduction of accidents from 1980 to 1985. But, there was an increase in accident rates in 1986.

Hingson et al. state that it is difficult to ascertain the effects of changes in drinking and driving laws because there have been so many changes in the past decade. However, there are some common threads that can be drawn from a review of DWI studies.

Increases in drinking age appear to reduce, but clearly do not eliminate, drunken driving and fatal crashes among teenagers. In the relatively few areas where enforcement of drinking age laws have been studied, enforcement appears to be minimal. Teenagers who want to drink get older friends to purchase alcohol for them. According to Hingson et al., traffic fatalities in the United States are beginning to rise again. This leads to the suggestion that alternative strategies will be needed to deal with these problems. There have been several studies (e.g., Voas & Hause, 1987) which suggest that increased drinking-and-driving arrest programs can reduce traffic fatality rates.

Secondary prevention can also be focused on populations such as juvenile delinquents (Blane, 1976). Blane planned and implemented a program that targeted delinquents. He found no overall differences between a treated experimental group and a nontreated group, although there were improvements in individual cases. This is a frequent finding in educational and treatment interventions with groups having difficulty with alcohol problems.

EDUCATION IN THE SCHOOL SYSTEM

It has been generally assumed that health education, in general, and alcohol education, in particular, may be effectively implemented in the school system (Blane, 1976). However, research in the alcohol field suggests that the school setting may not be the critical place for learning drinking attitudes and behavior. Instead, the family may be the key educator for attitudes and actions toward alcohol. Blane questions whether teachers are effective and viewed as believable by their students when they act as alcohol educators.

Even when alcohol education programs in the schools are clearly targeted, well-executed, and evaluated, the effects and the evaluation of effects can be misinterpreted. Pipher and Rivers (1982) report research with junior high school students in a health course. The students were encouraged to move in the direction of accepting moderate drinking as an ideal goal. The initial data analyses comparing attitudes before and after training suggested there were no changes in class attitudes and behaviors. A more careful appraisal of change showed that some students did, in fact, show slight change. However, a significant proportion of the students changed in the directions of either accepting positive drinking as a goal or of accepting more abusive drinking as the most desirable pattern to follow.

The effect of the alcohol education information was to move students either in the direction of the proposed goal of moderate drinking or toward the undesirable goal of abusive drinking. Students who indicated that their parents would punish them severely if they came home intoxicated were most likely to change towards the desired moderate drinking goal. Students who indicated their parents would not do very much to them should they become intoxicated were more likely to move in the direction of endorsing items associated with less control and less moderate drinking. While this is only one study, it could be asked, Do many well-executed alcohol education programs have these types of divergent effects, which cancel each other out so that there appear to be no differences between trained and untrained students?

STRATEGIES AND PREVENTION

Bloom (1970) identified three strategies that are frequently used in prevention programs: the milestone strategy; the high-risk strategy; and community-wide strategy.

Milestone strategy targets a specific period in persons' lives when they are exposed to the prevention program. Prior to the time of exposure, they have no protection. An example in the public health field is the requirement that children receive certain inoculations before entering grade school. There are also psychological programs that have a similar function. Two examples are providing extra support for students in their first semester of college and helping children adjust to the birth of a sibling. In general, alcohol education programs are milestone programs.

There are some potential advantages and disadvantages to milestone programs. If wise choices are made in terms of the developmental point at which programs are initiated, considerable impact might be obtained at relatively low cost. In the alcohol area, it is difficult to know just when to implement alcohol programs. In the Pipher and Rivers (1982) study noted earlier, some of the students had begun drinking. This made the material on making

A rock band and participants at "Moonburn '89," Lincoln, Nebraska. This yearly school-closing party for all the city's high school students could be seen as a "milestone" type of prevention effort. The Lincoln Council on Alcohol and Drugs, which sponsors the event, indicates it is designed "to prevent teen deaths resulting from alcohol-related incidents such as car crashes, boating accidents, suicides, etc. . . . It is also intended to reduce/eliminate involvement in legal issues as a result of alcohol use, i.e., MIP's [minors in possession], DWI's [driving while intoxicated]." *(Quoted material from handout promotional material from the sponsoring agency, 1992. Photograph courtesy of the Lincoln Journal Star Press Company and used with permission.)*

decisions about whether or not to use alcohol irrelevant from their points of view. Students who had not yet started to use alcohol found discussions about drinking equally irrelevant; the information had no personal meaning to them. Thus, the section of the course that dealt with making decisions about alcohol use ended up being, perhaps, irrelevant to a majority of the targeted population.

The success of a milestone program is tied to finding the appropriate developmental point and, of course, having a well-designed intervention. For example, a milestone approach for a program on drinking among college students would begin early in the first term of the freshman year. This would help students develop a more healthy perspective on alcohol before other negative alcohol attitudes and behaviors become well established.

The high-risk strategy has perhaps the highest probability of effectiveness. This strategy focuses on vulnerable populations. Groups who are viewed as vulnerable to certain disorders are identified and given special programs.

In the alcohol field, children of alcoholics make up a population considered to be at high risk for developing alcohol problems. All high-risk programs can be seen as secondary prevention programs, since the subjects have already been exposed to risk of the disorder.

High-risk programs have the highest probability of success in affecting the people most at risk. Thus the approach yields the most impact per dollar spent. However, the problems associated with implementing this strategy are potentially more serious than the milestone strategy and the communitywide strategy which is discussed later in this chapter.

Overprediction is the most serious problem with high-risk programs. Identifying persons as prealcoholic may have social, economic, and psychological effects on them. For example, labeling groups of children of alcoholics as prealcoholic might be ethically irresponsible, since not all of them will become alcoholics themselves.

A relevant question to be asked in the high-risk strategy is, if people are labeled early in their lives as having a potential alcohol problem, might this lead them to expect (and in many cases, develop) the problem? One possible effect of such labeling is that significant others may react to them differently than they would if they were not labeled. Rosenthal and Jacobson's (1968) classic study of labeling school children is an example of the potential effects of the labeling process. Rosenthal and Jacobson randomly labeled children as either improving or declining in classroom performance. The children's teachers tended to give higher or lower grades to the students depending on the label they were randomly given by the researcher. It is just as important in alcohol programming and research as it is in classrooms to avoid creating self-fulfilling prophecies by labeling.

Bloom's (1970) third prevention strategy is the communitywide program. Here, all residents of the community are potential recipients of the program. Examples from the public health field are swamp drainage and rating of restaurants. The main problem with this strategy is that a lot of money is spent implementing the community program, often with little impact on the people most important to reach. An example of this is the children's television program "Sesame Street." The program was designed for educationally disadvantaged children, but the people most likely to use the program are middle-class families who do not have any major educational deficiencies.

Using this strategy in the alcohol field as an attempt to reach people at risk for alcohol problems may lead those persons who most need the program to discount or ignore the message. Thus, the very people at which the program is aimed "fail to hear" or downplay the message given them. Despite these limitations, there are some advantages to using communitywide alcohol programs. With such programs, no one is labeled prealcoholic. In addition, the programs may reach people in the community who would not be affected by other programs.

Great care needs to be taken in the ways that prevention programs are implemented when they are based on an earlier identification of problem cases (such as children of alcoholics in the high-risk group). As noted earlier, labeling persons as having a problem or as potentially having a problem can lead to negative circumstances for them. Heller and Monohan (1977) suggest that early identification programs should pass through four evaluation stages.

1. What is to be accomplished with the prevention program should be defined precisely. What is to be predicted must be defined. If the ultimate goal of prevention efforts cannot be defined, it cannot be predicted.
2. "Prealcoholics" should be able to be reliably identified, and it should be shown that being a "prealcoholic" has a risk for the person's life.
3. Once "prealcoholics" have been identified, it must be clear that an effective intervention program is available. For "prealcoholics," the intervention should significantly reduce the probability that individuals who receive the intervention program will develop alcohol problems when compared with people who do not participate in the program.
4. The effects (particularly the negative effects) of the prevention program on people who have been incorrectly identified as future problem cases should be carefully evaluated.

Heller and Monohan state that a secondary prevention program should be undertaken only when these four factors have been carefully weighed.

Room (1974) discusses the "governing images" or philosophies that dominate thinking about prevention of alcohol abuse and alcoholism. He outlines three primary images.

The first governing image is that of alcohol as an irresistibly attractive but highly dangerous substance. The substance is viewed as powerful and the potential users are seen as being weak. Since the people who use the substance are weak (and the substance is powerful), it is the state's duty to save people from themselves. The public health model can be seen as adhering to this philosophy.

Room's second governing image is that alcohol problems come out of ambivalence toward drinking. This ambivalence is characteristic of the American culture. Psychologists and sociologists frequently view alcohol problems in this light. Doing so brings critical alcohol issues into their areas of competence. Prevention following this image focuses on education of people in general. It aims at influencing the norms and attitudes on drinking. An example in the alcohol field is teaching "responsible drinking" (that is, drinking in moderate amounts and avoiding intoxication).

The third governing image presented by Room is that the problems of alcoholism are a manifestation of a specific disease known as alcoholism. Alcoholism's physiological or developmental causal links are still unknown. Those links predate the drinking rather than being a result of it. This is the disease concept of alcoholism. Prevention efforts following this philosophy revolve primarily around finding cases of "hidden alcoholics" in the general population. The goal is to insure that those persons get treatment. According to this view, alcoholism is defined by affected individuals' complete inability to control their drinking. From this point of view, other prevention efforts are completely irrelevant.

Room notes that each of these philosophies converge, even though they view alcoholism from different perspectives, that is, one draws upon epidemic concepts, one draws upon social pathology and psychopathology, and the last draws upon physiological differences or dependence. Each of these images presupposes some inadequacy in the individual. In the first image, the person is weak; in the second, the person is confused; and in the third, the person is susceptible to a disease. Room suggests that it is possible to subsume each of the three approaches under a disease conceptualization of alcoholism. Since the disease concept is invoked in Room's three images, prevention for each image would focus on secondary prevention. The ultimate aim of prevention would be to find unlabeled cases and get them into treatment.

The alcohol scene in the United States is dominated by the disease model. Primary prevention is a poor fit in this conception of alcohol abuse. Nathan (1987) is one of the persons in the alcohol field who has been most critical of the overall approach to prevention in the United States. According to Nathan, alcohol prevention efforts in the 1980s have been alcohol education programs directed at groups of high-risk individuals including women, adolescents, minorities, and the elderly. The programs have the dual role of educating people on the effects of alcohol in terms of "behavioral, psychological, and psychiatric effects of alcohol, the range and variability of both normal and abusive drinking in the United States, and alcohol's short and longer term effects on both social drinkers and abusive drinkers; and to make attitudes toward consumption, especially negative consumption, more negative—or at least more wary" (Nathan, 1987, p. 19). The goal of these efforts is to reduce consumption in general, as well as reduce the specific problems of alcohol abuse and alcoholism.

Nathan compares progress in the alcohol field in 1935 with today's efforts. He concludes:

> The net results of current efforts to prevent alcoholism have been disappointing in the extreme. These efforts which generally differ little in methods, goals, or achievements from those of 1935, have consistently yielded reports of increased public awareness of the hazards of alcohol use and of desirable

changes in attitudes toward drunkenness and alcoholism. But there are few documented instances of change in level or pattern of alcohol consumption by the groups to which alcohol education has been directed. (p. 20)

Nathan does point out that there have been gains in reducing drinking and driving and the fetal alcohol syndrome. There has also been an increase in arrests for drunken driving.

It is probable that measurable progress in changing how alcohol is used and the rates at which it is abused will come only gradually in this country. Westermeyer (1992), in predicting the reactions to substance use disorders in the 1990s, notes, "Federal, state, and local governments are unlikely to commit the resources or to undertake the sociocultural changes that would effectively reduce the prevalence of substance use disorders in the 1990s. . . . " (pp. 9–10). Some specific progress has been made in some areas, for example, drinking and driving reduction. It is clear, however, that a major shift in how alcohol is viewed and the role it plays in society is necessary before long-term reduction in alcohol abuse can be achieved.

REFERENCES

Blacker, E. (1966). Sociocultural factors in alcoholism. *International Psychiatry Clinics, 3*, 51–80.

Blane, H. (1976). Education and the prevention of alcoholism. In B. Kissin & H. Begleiter (Eds.), *The biology of alcoholism: Vol. 4. Social aspects of alcoholism* (pp. 519–578). New York: Plenum Press.

Bloom, I. L. (1970). The evaluation of primary prevention programs. In L. M. Roberts, N. S. Greenfield, & M. Miller (Eds.), *Comprehensive mental health: The challenge of evaluation* (pp. 117–135). Madison: University of Wisconsin Press.

Cross, J. N. (1967). Epidemiologic studies and control programs in alcoholism. I. Public health approach to alcoholism control. *American Journal of Public Health, 57*, 955–966.

Frankel, G., & Whitehead, P. C. (1981). *Drinking and damage: Theoretical advances and implications for prevention.* New Brunswick, NJ: Rutgers University Center for Alcohol Studies.

Heller, K., & Monohan, J. (1977). *Psychology and community change.* Homewood, IL: Dorsey Press.

Hingson, R., Howland, J., Morelock, S., & Heeren, T. (1988). Legal intervention to reduce drinking, driving and related fatalities among youthful drivers. *Alcohol, Drugs and Driving, 4*, 87–98.

McGavran, E. G. (1963). Facing reality in public health. In *Key issues in the prevention of alcoholism* (pp. 55–62). Harrisburg, PA: Department of Health.

McNeil, J. S. (1985). An analysis of models of alcoholism and prevention of and their applicability to American blacks. In R. Wright, Jr., & T. D. Watts (Eds.),

Prevention of black alcoholism: Issues and strategies (pp. 51–64). Springfield, IL: Charles C. Thomas.

Nathan, P. E. (1987). What do behavioral scientists know and what can they do about alcoholism? In P. C. Rivers (Ed.), *Alcohol and addictive behavior: Vol. 34. Nebraska Symposium on Motivation* (pp. 1–25). Lincoln: University of Nebraska Press.

Parker, D. A., & Harman, M. S. (1980). A critique of the distribution of consumption model of prevention. In T. C. Harford, D. A. Parker, & L. Light (Eds.), *Normative approaches to the prevention of alcohol abuse and alcoholism* (pp. 67–88) (NIAAA Research Monograph No. 3) (DHEW Publication No. ADM 79–847). Washington, DC: U.S. Government Printing Office.

Pipher, J. S., & Rivers, P. C. (1982). The differential effects of alcohol education on junior high school students. *Journal of Alcohol and Drug Education, 27,* 73–88.

Plaut, T. F. A. (1967). *Alcohol problems: A report to the nation by the Cooperative Commission on the Study of Alcoholism.* New York: Oxford University Press.

Robinson, D. (1982). Alcoholism: Perspectives on prevention strategies. In E. M. Pattison & E. Kaufman (Eds.), *Encyclopedic handbook of alcoholism* (pp. 458–467). New York: Gardner Press.

Room, R. (1974). Governing images and the prevention of alcohol problems. *Preventive Medicine, 3,* 11–23.

Rosenthal, R., & Jacobson, L. (1968). *Pygmalion in the classroom.* New York: Holt, Rinehart & Winston.

Smart, R.G. (1980). Availability and the prevention of alcohol-related problems. In T. C. Harford, D. A. Parker, & L. Light (Eds.), *Normative approaches to the prevention of alcohol abuse and alcoholism* (pp. 123–146) (NIAAA Research Monograph No. 3) (DHEW Publication No. ADM 79–847). Washington, DC: U.S. Government Printing Office.

U.S. Department of Health and Human Services, Second Special Report to Congress on Alcohol and Health (1974). (DHHS Publication No. (ADM) 75–212) Washington, DC: U.S. Government Printing Office.

Voas, R., & Hause, J. (1987). Deterring the drinking driver: The Stockton experience. *Accident Analysis and Prevention, 19,* 81–90.

West, M. D., & Prinz, R. (1987). Parental alcoholism and childhood psychopathology. *Psychological Bulletin, 102,* 204–218.

Westermeyer, J. (1992). Substance use disorders: Predictions for the 1990s. *American Journal of Drug and Alcohol Abuse, 18,* 1–11.

Wilkinson, R. (1970). *The prevention of drinking problems: Alcohol control and cultural influence.* New York: Oxford University Press.

Wright, R., Jr., & Watts, T. D. (Eds.) (1985). *Prevention of black alcoholism: Issues and strategies.* Springfield, IL: Charles C. Thomas.

Zucker, R. A. (1987). The four alcoholisms: A developmental account of the etiologic process. In P. C. Rivers (Ed.), *Alcohol and addictive behavior: Vol. 34. Nebraska Symposium on Motivation* (pp. 27–83). Lincoln: University of Nebraska Press.

Index